Credit and Debt in Eighteenth-Century England

Throughout the eighteenth century hundreds of thousands of men and women were cast into prison for failing to pay their debts. This apparently illogical system where debtors were kept away from their places of work remained popular with creditors into the nineteenth century even as Britain witnessed industrialisation, market growth, and the increasing sophistication of commerce, as the debtors' prisons proved surprisingly effective.

Due to insufficient early modern currency, almost every exchange was reliant upon the use of credit based upon personal reputation rather than defined collateral, making the lives of traders inherently precarious as they struggled to extract payments based on little more than promises. This book shows how traders turned to debtors' prisons to give those promises defined consequences, the system functioning as a tool of coercive contract enforcement rather than oppression of the poor. *Credit and Debt* demonstrates for the first time the fundamental contribution of debt imprisonment to the early modern economy and reveals how traders made use of existing institutions to alleviate the instabilities of commerce in the context of unprecedented market growth.

This book will be of interest to scholars and researchers in economic history and early modern British history.

Alexander Wakelam is an Affiliated Researcher of the Cambridge Group for the History of Population and Social Structure. His research focusses on the economic and social history of Britain in the long eighteenth century and examines practices of exchange, work, and the experiences of economically active women.

Perspectives in Economic and Social History

Series Editors: Andrew August and Jari Eloranta

54 **Small and Medium Powers in Global History**
Trade, Conflicts, and Neutrality from the 18th to the 20th Centuries
Edited by Jari Eloranta, Eric Golson, Peter Hedburg, and Maria Cristina Moreira

55 **Labor Before the Industrial Revolution**
Work, Technology and their Ecologies in an Age of Early Capitalism
Edited by Thomas Max Safley

56 **Workers, Unions and Payment in Kind**
The Fight for Real Wages in Britain, 1820–1986
Christopher Frank

57 **A History of States and Economic Policies in Early Modern Europe**
Silvia A. Conca Messina

58 **Fiscal Policy in Early Modern Europe**
Portugal in Comparative Context
Rodrigo da Costa Dominguez

59 **Workers, Unions and Truck Wages in British Society**
The Fight for Real Wages, 1820–1986
Christopher Frank

60 **Early Modern Overseas Trade and Entrepreneurship**
Nordic Trading Companies in the Seventeenth Century
Kaarle Wirta

61 **Credit and Debt in Eighteenth-Century England**
An Economic History of Debtors' Prisons
Alexander Wakelam

For more information about this series, please visit www.routledge.com/series/PESH

Credit and Debt in Eighteenth-Century England

An Economic History of Debtors' Prisons

Alexander Wakelam

Routledge
Taylor & Francis Group

LONDON AND NEW YORK

First published 2021
by Routledge
2 Park Square, Milton Park, Abingdon, Oxon OX14 4RN

and by Routledge
605 Third Avenue, New York, NY 10017

First issued in paperback 2022

Routledge is an imprint of the Taylor & Francis Group, an informa business

Publisher's Note
The publisher has gone to great lengths to ensure the quality of this
reprint but points out that some imperfections in the original copies
may be apparent.

British Library Cataloguing-in-Publication Data
A catalogue record for this book is available from the British Library

Library of Congress Cataloging-in-Publication Data
A catalog record has been requested for this book

ISBN: 978-0-367-51429-7 (pbk)
ISBN: 978-0-367-13711-3 (hbk)
ISBN: 978-0-429-02821-2 (ebk)

DOI: 10.4324/9780429028212

Typeset in Bembo
by codeMantra

For my father, Prof Michael Wakelam (1955–2020)

Contents

List of illustrations   *viii*
Acknowledgements   *ix*

Introduction   1

1   Indebtedness and insolvency in eighteenth-century England   18

2   Enlightened capitalism: use and structure of debtors' prisons   51

3   Coercive contract enforcement: debtors' prisons as economic institutions   85

4   The debtor economy: obtaining release from debtors' prisons   115

5   The Insolvency Acts: when debtors' prisons failed   139

6   Private enterprise: operating a debtors' prison   160

7   Reform and the unmaking of debtors' prisons   186

Conclusion   211

Bibliography   *221*
Index   *249*

Illustrations

Figures

2.1 Annual Commitment Rate 1725–1815 at Wood Street
Compter, Fleet Prison, and Lancaster Castle 62
2.2 Calculated Monthly Population of the Fleet, Wood Street
Compter, and Lancaster County Gaol, 1733–1815 66
3.1 Share of Prisoners for Debt Held for a Minimum Number of
days (1735–1815) 95
3.2 Percentage of those Released to the Nearest Hundred Days
Who Were Discharged 97
3.3 Annual Death Rates at the Fleet Prison and Wood
Street Compter 101
4.1 £5 Moving Average of Commitment Length by Debt
Owed at the Fleet Prison, Wood Street Compter, and
Lancaster Castle Gaol (1730–1815) 118
6.1 Estimated Income from Commitment Fess, Release Fees,
and Rents at the Fleet, Wood Street Compter, and Lancaster
Castle 1730–1815 169
6.2 Ludgate Profits and Income from Various Sources, 1756–1763 174

Tables

2.1 Debts Owed at the Fleet Prison, Wood Street Compter
(Without Court of Request Debtors), and Lancaster Castle
Gaol, 1735–1815 71
2.2 Occupations of Insolvency Act Applicants (1725–1797) 73
3.1 Distribution of Commitment Lengths at the Fleet Prison,
Wood Street Compter, and Lancaster Castle Gaol, 1735–1815 89
3.2 Categories of Release at the Fleet, Wood Street Compter,
and Lancaster Castle, 1733–1815 93
6.1 Declarations of Rent Paid by Accommodation Type during
Old Bailey Trails in London, 1740–1800 168

Acknowledgements

This has been a long project occupying over four years of my life, encompassing both doctoral study and precarious early career employment; I have found myself confined within the debtors' prison for longer than 98% of the individuals I have studied. While they were busy clearing their debts, I have done nothing but acquire them.

This study of debt imprisonment began life as a PhD thesis on female financial accountability completed in 2018 at the University of Cambridge upon the first two chapters of which this book is founded. I am eternally grateful to my supervisor and continued mentor Dr Amy Erickson. She not only encouraged the tangent into imprisonment my research took but challenged me to continue diversifying the archival basis of my analysis. Her intellect, perseverance, and most importantly her warmth are an inspiration. The Cambridge Group for the History of Population and Social Structure provided me with a home for much of my doctoral studies and it would not be an overstatement to say that the most important moments in the development of my research occurred during the daily refuge of group coffee. I continue to rely on and am grateful to many members of the group (past and present) though wish to thank in particular Dr Leigh Shaw-Taylor, Dr Xuesheng You, Dr Oliver Dunn, and Dr Spike Gibbs. Additionally, while it is now many years since my undergraduate studies at the University of York, it was there that my life-long keen interest in history was honed into a fascination with eighteenth-century commerce. Dr Natasha Glaisyer particularly shaped this development as did Prof James Sharpe who first encouraged me to consider doctoral study. The University of Cambridge provided funding for my doctoral research as did the Economic History Society, I am similarly grateful to those who have employed me during the writing of this book to ensure that precarity did not prevent its completion.

Numerous people have provided vital thoughts during the progress of this research (from its inception to its completion) including Dr Judy Stephenson, Prof Jeremy Boulton, and Prof Craig Muldrew, my internal examiner who separate to his titanic research on credit is an unending source of anecdotes on the early modern debtor. I am enormously grateful to Dr Tawny Paul who as well as being my external examiner has proved my tireless advocate and supporter. She has, more than anyone else, challenged that way I think about debt in the early modern period (both in person and in her writing), and this book would be considerably lesser without her. I would like to thank John Levin for sharing his own estimations of application rates to the *London Gazette* before their publication as well as for his efforts to make eighteenth-century legislation available to a wide audience. Separately, I am thankful to Dr Richard Bell and Kiran Mehta, the organisers of the "Towards New Histories of Imprisonment in England, 1500–1850" conference in Oxford of July 2019. I was fortunate enough to be invited to present the data which became the first third of this book, the comments of those in attendance providing a wealth of insights which significantly improved the subsequent monograph. Additionally, the papers of all in attendance but particularly those of Prof Joanna Innes and Prof Rachel Weil have informed my analysis – the work on display at this conference suggests that the future of the study of early modern imprisonment is likely to be bountiful. Elements of this research were also presented to the Cambridge Economic and Social History Workshop, the Economic History Society Conference in Keele, the *Ordering the Margins* Workshop at the Institute of Historical Research, and the *Prison/Exile: Controlled Spaces in Early Modern Europe* Conference in Oxford, which all provided useful thoughts and suggestions on its development. I am also grateful to the variety of helpful and cheerful archival staff who assisted in this research particularly at the London Metropolitan Archives. Similarly, I am indebted to the National Archives who brought the Lancaster Commitment Register out of storage specially for me, a gesture which significantly altered the scope of the book. I would like to thank the editorial staff at Routledge who *made* this book happen, its invisible co-authors. Natalie Tomlinson took a chance on the emerging research of a doctoral student and guided me through the process of formulating a book proposal, while Lisa Lavelle has patiently dealt with my *many* questions and queries with unrivalled clarity and patience. My unending thanks go to both of them.

Beyond my scholarly debts, I'm thankful for all those who have supported me in any way during the difficult process of writing this book including the residents of Burntwood Lane and my brother Patrick Wakelam though one of my most regular debts is owed to James Claughton and Katy Reinhardt whose companionship has been most cherished and valued. I am blessed to rely upon the support of Rachel Walter. She has gone above and beyond in standing by me, frequently physically as I forced her to stand where a debtors' prison used to be 200 years ago but more often emotionally for which words cannot express my thanks. Without her I would certainly have never managed to complete this work. Finally, I would be nowhere without my parents, Michael and Jane, who have supported my historical endeavours from a young age. I know this has not always been easy, but they have made it appear the most natural thing in the world and provided material, emotional, and intellectual support from cradle to publication. I owe them more than I can possibly say. Tragically, we unexpectedly lost my much-loved father while this book was about to enter press. He was an academic titan and an intellectual inspiration but he was also a sweet and humble man taken too soon. I will always regret he did not get to read this book, but I know that my writing of it made him proud. His was a shining example of what it meant to be a human being which will remain with all who knew him.

Introduction

Two hundred years after his death in 1718, Richard Hogarth, author, school-master, and businessowner, remains forever tainted by his imprisonment for debt. Born shortly after the Restoration in a Westmoreland shepherding community as his parents' third son, Richard received little more than a basic grammar school education upon which he was forced to rely when his eldest brother inherited the small family freehold. Like many other ambitious young men and women born into this new age, Richard was not satisfied with accepting the status quo of his birth. In his early twenties he bid farewell to the home of his ancestors and embarked upon the almost 300-mile jour-ney south to London. Arriving without recommendations, contacts, or the reputation conferred by a university education, Richard managed through his own guile to carve out a place for himself in the city as a scholar. In his first decade in London he worked as a schoolmaster, married advantageously, and published his ingenious *Thesaurarium Trilingue Publicum* (1689) – a work designed to teach Latin and Greek to those outside of the academic elite – as well as abridging works on Classics for the popular market. It was as an 'au-thor' rather than a schoolmaster that the artist William Hogarth would even-tually memorialise his father. Additionally, Richard furthered his income by waiting upon the dowager Countess of Carlisle, gaining important social and commercial contacts who advocated for his appointment to venerable schools. At the start of the new century, having established himself in the city and with a swelling young family, Richard poured his hard-earned credit and capital reserves into London's Consumer Revolution. In 1704, 'Hogarth's Coffeehouse' opened within the striking St John's Gate in Clerkenwell, dis-tinguishing itself from the hundreds of similar nearby venues by advertising to the public that there 'daily some Learned Gentlemen ... speak Latin read-ily, ... any Gentleman that is either skilled in that Language, or desirous to perfect himself in speaking thereof, will be welcome'.[1]

Though Richard was initially in sufficient prosperity to embark upon this business venture, within a few years his finances had apparently declined significantly as he was eventually arrested and confined within London's infamous Fleet debtors' prison. This moment of fiscal collapse has forever marked the father of the famous artist and much of the limited discussion of

Richard has consequentially been fatalistic; his life portrayed as somehow being upon an inevitable path from the sheep dotted hills of Westmoreland to the cold despair of the Fleet. In histories of William, Richard is depicted as an 'outsider' whose ventures always 'came to nothing' and his writings are unfairly described as 'hack' publications. William's own failure to mention his father's imprisonment is frequently emphasised, as is probably the only visual depiction of Richard, the shabby debtor in plate VII of his son's *A Rake's Progress*, set in the Fleet. The core of condemnation, however, focusses upon his apparent foolishness in the opening and administration of his coffee-house. His efforts are described as 'idealistic' rather than entrepreneurial and it is popularly erroneously claimed that 'only Latin could be spoke' within "Hogarth's". Richard therefore usually appears as a joke, as a sign of the ignominy from which his more famous son arose, or of the perpetual cruelty of the debtors' prison which haunted the unfortunate and economically untalented.[2]

This degradation arises from the very fact of Richard Hogarth's imprisonment – it appears as conclusive evidence of his existence as a "failure" who was cast into hell with no chance of escape. Surely, Richard must have committed extravagances and conducted business poorly so as to have become utterly destitute and force his creditors into feeling they had no option but to banish him from society. However, while Hogarth was not a man of unrivalled and constant success, neither was he a penniless failure. After his release from debtors' prison in September 1712, from which he had continued to publish, he produced an array of scholarly material and by 1715 had taken over the management of a notable Grammar School which he relocated to Cheapside, the commercial hub of the city.[3] Nor was his business strategy at "Hogarth's" as naïve as has been assumed; while he did cater to the scholarly elite, he also hosted more plebeian entertainment such as 'Comical Dances' and impressionists, the coffeehouse also being a meeting place for 'a Society of Trades'.[4] Furthermore, Richard's experience of confinement, while not brief, was shorter than usually suggested. Most accounts assume that Richard must have been imprisoned c.1707–1708 when the last adverts for the coffeehouse survive, but he does not appear in the commitment registers of the Fleet until 13th May 1709, spending three years and four months in gaol rather than the four or five years usually posited.[5]

What is perhaps most unjust though, is that there is no particular evidence that 'Hogarth's Coffeehouse' *failed* despite the fact that this business was almost certainly what led him to debtors' prison. In 1712, Richard produced a schedule of all the debts which were both owed *to* and *by* him revealing that, like almost all commercial people in the eighteenth century, Hogarth was both a debtor and a creditor. While he owed £190 19s 6d to twenty-six creditors including £25 to his own brother, he was himself owed £167 7s 6d by twenty-seven different debtors.[6] Almost all his wealth was therefore tied up in the commercial lives of his customers whom he had been unwilling to forcibly pursue, viewing a £23 difference in his accounts as unthreatening and his business healthy. Hogarth was presumably unalarmed when an impatient creditor first hurried him to gaol, his only failure at this point being yet to pay rather than being unable to do so. It was only after his confinement continued to drag on and he found it impossible to recover his wealth from his debtors that it became clear he had trusted unwisely, his generosity of credit rather than his overencumberance of debt or his management style ultimately ruining his coffeehouse which closed due to the absence of its master.

★★

Richard Hogarth's experience sits uncomfortably with what we assume to be true about debt imprisonment. It seems obvious that those unlucky enough to be carried to a debtors' prison only escaped the gaol in a casket as imprisonment 'would only increase the unlikelihood of repayment'.[7] Even if debtors were not entirely destitute, there appears little logical about confining those who owe you money away from their place of work. If the purpose of prisons was not financial then, it is suggested, they must have been punitive. This has drawn the ire of scholars from across the ideological spectrum including both Smithian economic rationalists and Marxists, the latter portraying debt imprisonment as a tool of social control conducted by the wealthy against the penniless. The anarchist anthropologist David Graeber declared in 2011 that 'the criminalisation of debt ... was the criminalisation of the very basis of human society'.[8] Nor is this merely an accusation dependent upon modern economic language.[9] Writers from across the period agreed that the practice was both cruel and generally unproductive. In 1706 Charles Gildon damned debt imprisonment as 'foolish and Preposterous ... as well as Barbarous, for instead of the Creditor's getting the Debt, it only makes sure that he shall never have it' while in 1788 F.A.S. Murray denounced it as 'so extremely incongruous to Common Sense'.[10] The heroine of Charles Dickens's *Little Dorrit*, a novel which has done much to shape impressions of debt imprisonment in both the scholarly and popular imagination, expressed a similar sentiment in damning the injustice and fatal consequences of confinement on the debtor in 1857: 'It seems to me hard that he should pay in life and money both'.[11] Antiquated and incongruous with the modern economic system Britain was forging, the debtors' prison was, we assume, merely another medieval institution which declined into non-existence, inevitably brushed aside by the development of commercial rationality and enlightened ideas which rejected the punishment of the impoverished.

And yet, debt imprisonment lingers. The American debtors' prison disappeared in the early nineteenth century, the institution taking successive blows at the state and finally federal level. The young republic was largely ahead of European nations in enacting abolition. As late as 1905, the State Department were stunned to discover the practice persisted in parts of the old continent and hurried to secure 'antidebt-imprisonment provisions' for its citizens travelling abroad in treaties with the Netherlands.[12] However, just over a century later, in the early years of the global financial crisis and the tightening of administrative budgets, a number of stories began to emerge of 'the new debtors' prisons'. A few concerned voices highlighted the practice of local governments confining those unable to pay traffic fines, essentially 'throwing them in jail for being poor', behaviour which reporters asserted in major national newspapers 'comes straight from the pages of *Little Dorrit*'.[13] Despite having committed minor infractions, victims (generally from poor minority neighbourhoods) can be trapped for unlimited periods, the courts holding them hostage until terrified families and friends turn over the money on their behalf.[14] Though few nations continue to explicitly breach the UN treaty on debt imprisonment, when in December 2017 then Attorney General Jefferson Sessions retracted an Obama-era memo asserting the illegality of the practice, an implied acceptance of imprisoning debtors was restored to the twenty-first-century United States of America.[15]

This modern incarnation of the debtors' prison through which municipalities illicitly squeeze extra funding from the "guilty" is a far cry from the eighteenth-century practice of private individuals arresting customers and business contacts. However, their shared characteristics – the attempted coercion of payment through indefinite confinement, treating the debtor as a hostage – suggest that in economies separated by time and sophistication, people have seen a value in debt imprisonment. While modern enablers of this system have to be dragged into the light – denying vociferously the injustice of their actions – eighteenth-century debt imprisonment was conducted without secrecy or shame. Far from being a shunned medieval hangover, arrest for debt was a public and accepted feature of commercial life conducted in broad daylight (except on Sundays). The prisons were pervasive, seeping into all corners of eighteenth-century society and regions of the Kingdom, being experienced on an everyday basis in a fashion matched by few secular institutions. Hundreds of thousands of women and men were imprisoned in the long eighteenth century, impacting not only their lives but those of their families and friends. Thousands more found employment through the operation of debtors' prisons, both directly as bailiffs or turnkeys and indirectly as suppliers of food and ale. Even if one could somehow claim no direct or associational experience with imprisonment for debt, its physical manifestations were inescapable. In urban areas most people would walk past or close to a debtors' prison every day, being situated upon thoroughfares and bridges or – as with the Fleet – on the edge of marketplaces, reminding the shopper and shopkeeper of the potential consequences of idle transactions. Many of the fortifications which survived the English Revolution were converted into gaols, prisons becoming imposing features of the landscape which loomed over towns and were viewable for miles in the surrounding countryside. Furthermore, the number and size of prisons continued to expand as new gaols were built, some constructed to look more like stately country homes than houses of deprivation, a feature which attracted tourists who came to gaze with grim fascination upon the wraiths haunting stunning baroque architecture.[16] Even in popular culture there was no escape; the debtors' prison was the setting of plays, novels, songs, and artistic renditions, while numerous charity concerts or plays were advertised as being staged for the benefit of poor prisoners. The first performance of Handel's *Messiah* in 1742 – the composer himself having been recently financially precarious – was far from atypical when staged in Dublin 'For Relief of the Poor Prisoners in the several Gaols' with tickets costing half a guinea each.[17] The debtors' prison was not a thread which society could easily unpick, having been woven deep into its experience by constant and continued use. To conceive of eighteenth-century England without recognising the contribution of the institution of debt imprisonment is to perceive an England which did not exist. Debt imprisonment was not a fringe activity conducted solely against the destitute and it is evident that creditors regarded the ability to seize the bodies of debtors as providing them with security and personal benefit. Yet, despite their proclivity, the administration and function of the debtors' prisons, let alone why creditors made regular use of them, remain poorly understood.

Markets, no matter their level of sophistication, require regulation to function. Modern economies generally contain regulation overseen by the state though historical regulation was frequently 'fragmented and decentralised', leading some economists to fail to recognise that which was not written into law as true regulation.[18] Regardless, they both (no matter their formality) serve the same function in persuading potential members to invest their capital, time, and labour by offering protections from risk. Good regulation which protects all participants without significantly hindering the processes of capital generation will naturally allow long-term growth to flourish. However, even when regulation is less effective than assumed or is defective and merely decorative, that it exists at all encourages participation so long as commercial society continues to believe sufficient capital protections are in place. In 2008, discovery of the illusory nature of regulation shattered the world economy and participants were not protected. However, prior confidence in "safe" markets had led to exponential growth and Western economic prosperity.[19] If society saw value in the institution of debt imprisonment, then (regardless of efficiency) it should be understood as a tool of market regulation which incentivised participation, though it remains to be seen as to why they understood it as such and to what extent it was effective for participants.

Institutions have long been seen as key in encouraging economic participation in the early modern period. In the eighteenth century, Britain experienced the world's first transition to sustained market growth arising from the commercialisation and industrialisation which characterised the economy of this period.[20] The unilateral nature of this success is frequently overstated even though it has been clear since the work of Julian Hoppit in 1987 that 'prosperity ... coincided with the blossoming of business collapses'.[21] Similarly, its negative implications for workers in various sectors can be minimised and research in the last few decades has questioned real increases in standards of living for the majority before the later nineteenth century. However, it is impossible to deny that something unique happened in Britain at this time which led to previously unexperienced growth even if magnitudes, implications, and origins prove debateable.[22] Since the pioneering work of Douglass North and Barry Weingast on the greater security of private property after 1688, it has been argued that new institutions established the circumstances necessary for growth. These institutions, being 'the incentive systems that structure human interaction', North argues, reduced 'uncertainty in the world' which led to the 'creation of impersonal capital markets' and modern banking practices which provided loanable capital to fund the Industrial Revolution.[23] Subsequent research has furthered and diversified the institutional approach, arguing for multifarious mechanisms by which institutions encouraged participation and industrialisation even where demonstrating the weaknesses of North & Weingast's interpretation of the post-1688 period.[24]

The institutional approach is, however, not without its critics or obvious faults. Gregory Clark and Deirdre McCloskey in particular have demonstrated that institutions securing private property had been in place in England for centuries (as well as in other nations). If they did contribute at all, the scale of growth in what McCloskey terms 'the great enrichment' has been deemed by detractors as too vast to be explained by institutions alone.[25] A purely institutional understanding of the Industrial Revolution is clearly insufficient; however, the contribution of institutions in allowing other factors to thrive in the manner in which they did should not be underestimated. To understand the growth which actually took place in Britain during the long eighteenth century (instead of a hypothetical best-possible growth scenario), it is necessary to recognise how humans navigated the unstable and immature economic reality which they occupied.

This book demonstrates how economic actors solved problems of their commercial environment related to the transfer of goods through their interpretation and use of existing institutions. It does not claim the debtors' prisons had any role in ensuring industrialisation occurred in Britain in the eighteenth century before its European neighbours – though coincidentally the practice was much smaller in scale and regularity on the continent.[26] Rather than an account of the origins of growth, it is an examination of how growth was facilitated. It asserts that, as a result of its contemporary interpretation, the institution of debt prevented the disincentivisation of traders, ensuring that the wheels of growth were not inhibited by grit. While broad conceptions of supply and demand can be assumed as respectively prompting the Industrial and Commercial Revolutions, there existed a clear risk to their maintenance in the immature economic climate's lack of incentive to *sell*. Though the incentive and motive for selling either raw materials – such as the supplier of Hogarth's coffee beans – or finished goods – such as to the 'learned gentleman' hobnobbing in St John's Gate – appear to be clear, in reality eighteenth-century sellers frequently had cause to withhold their goods or services. The contemporary market was deeply insecure and did not simply function as a miniature of its modern counterpart where the sale of a legal chattel is essentially risk free. Few transactions in the eighteenth century resulted in the immediate compensation of the seller. Almost all exchanges – from bread and ale to the supply of luxury goods and raw materials – were based upon the use of credit due principally to the insufficiency of coinage. Unlike the credit used to secure modern purchasing, most everyday consumer credit in the eighteenth century was not tied to a banking institution or secured by specified capital reserves. Instead it was constructed out of individual reputation and secured by a buyer's honour.[27] Without a clear means of simple recovery, wise shopkeepers were motivated to sell only to those they trusted and not take on substantial credit burdens. While selective selling would ensure their own security, it could not provide a market for the voluminous supply of industrialised Britain, interrupting both the supply and demand of the market by preventing transfer of goods from manufacturers to consumers. The debtors' prison, by giving consequence to purchases on the security of the person and existing as a means through which creditors could coerce payment, mitigated the insufficiencies of credit, preventing traders from adopting overly conservative selling strategies and helping to maintain order and growth.

Key to debt imprisonment's strength as an institution was that it was not designed in the period to respond, inflexibly, to a problem perceived by a disconnected legislature. Like other institutions identified as contributing to eighteenth-century growth, debt imprisonment was not a novelty in the post-1688 period. Contemporary opponents of the prisons, fixing upon their supposed tyranny, had to reach deep into English history to find a time before the confinement of debtors. In 1788 Edward Farley returned to the days of King Alfred for evidence of lost English liberty, declaring that 'his reign in general was glorious; there was no such thing as imprisonment for debt, with all its horrid train of extortion, oppression, disease, and famine'. In Farley's view 'foreign laws and customs' lay at the heart of subsequent subversion of the common law, one of many writers claiming that imprisonment for debt was contrary to *magna carta*.[28] While the introduction of arrest for unpaid debts occurred in the post-Norman and post-Runnymede era, it was very much an English phenomenon rather than a foreign import and one which was established incrementally. At the end of the thirteenth century, the enactment of the statutes of *Acton Burnell* (1283) and *Merchants* (1285) enabled civic authorities, for the first time, to present, imprison, and (upon non-payment) seize the goods of insolvent debtors under some limiting circumstances.[29] This successful urban system was soon replicated at the manorial level to deal with rural debt.[30] In some localities debt imprisonment was even older. Borough custom occasionally allowed courts to confine those convicted of indebtedness until they or another satisfied the plaintiff. This right predated *Acton Burnell*, imprisonment for debt growing out of genuine commercial desire rather than the creativeness of legislators.[31] While the original statutes limited the right of arrest to the court, in 1352 it was extended to private creditors who were subsequently able to imprison without a debtor having first declared their financial liabilities.[32] This provided the institution of debt imprisonment the central mechanism it would rely upon until it was abolished in 1869.

Despite the long history of debt imprisonment, the eighteenth-century institution was largely distinct from its forebears, securing private property in a different fashion c.1750 than it had c.1350. The institution's place in the economic climate was defined by contemporary interpretation and use. The number of economic actors who might be and who were confined for debt remained low during the medieval era as this method of proceeding generally administered more prominent merchants rather than the mass of obligations which creditors settled informally or through manorial courts. In the sixteenth century, responding to England's growing commercial status, the mechanisms of fiscal recovery were strengthened including both the introduction of bankruptcy and a series of legal developments which made arrest available in "actions on the case". While this theoretically changed little about the underlying nature of the institution, by allowing for wider interpretations of "debt" resulting from oral promises and not just broken specified agreements it significantly escalated the potential for how creditors could approach debt imprisonment. This was furthered in the seventeenth century by the introduction of new writs that reduced the costs of arrest significantly, broadening who could make use of the system.[33] Growth in imprisonment from the middle of the seventeenth century (a century after changes to arrest but predating cheaper writs) was reliant upon centuries of legal development but was driven by a shift in the economic environment and commercial culture in which the institution was situated. Crucially, the defined nature of debt imprisonment remained hazy after 1352 – there was no specified transgression which led to confinement save displeasing a creditor nor did the courts have significant involvement in determining which trespasses deserved confinement and which did not as it was a user-driven system. While debt imprisonment is regularly described as something that *happened* to people, it should instead rightly be conceived of as something which was deliberately *done* to them by a third party. Each individual arrest was shaped by the motivations of those who enacted it, being the order of human individuals, and was therefore reflective of forces within the wider commercial world, the institution's role in society being moulded by each use. In this manner, debt imprisonment allowed unrelated economic changes to flourish – ensuring that increased desire to consume or ability to supply did not flounder due to the inherent insecurity of credit-based transacting. Economic actors made use of a pre-existing institution from a contemporary perspective to mitigate the insufficiencies of their commercial environment and regulate the market until practices and systems caught up with revolutionary growth, an activity which was more instinctive than deliberate. Understanding why it did so reveals why the ground upon which the Industrial Revolution occurred continued to be profitable despite the initial lack of modern-looking institutions at the level of everyday commerce.

It might credibly be questioned why, if the debtors' prisons were such important facilitators of market enforcement as this conceptual approach to the eighteenth-century market claims, they have not previously been recognised or taken seriously as economic institutions. Debt imprisonment has not, until recently, received much significant scholarly enquiry of any kind, the literature on personal debt being similarly sparse in comparison to that on credit. In part this arises from the slow development of the valuable and growing literature on failure in the eighteenth century.[34] However, the debtors' prisons have yet to be included in this literature due in large part to the debtor-focussed approach of the limited existing social and cultural accounts of prisons.[35] The debtor-perspective of imprisonment – usually framing those confined as victims, innocent of any crime – has been dubious about the chances of repayment and little enquiry has been made beyond the summative dismissal of Dorothy George in 1925 that 'all this misery and cruelty had no effect at all in … secur[ing] the rights of property and the sanctity of contract. It had exactly the opposite effect' and was no more than an 'alternative to murder'.[36] More recent scholars have similarly been sceptical about the ability of imprisonment to redress grievances, describing chances of repayment as 'exiguous'.[37] Principally, like the sociological or economic dismissals of the role of debtors' prisons, it has largely been seen by historians as a punitive institution, an interpretation fed by the wider literature on penal incarceration of felons.[38] Failing to engage with their practical purposes, some of the existing literature on the institution focusses entirely upon its reformers or individual notable prisoners which often minimise the system which they inhabited.[39]

Not all investigations of the prisons have been so cursory.[40] Research into the lives and conditions of debtors has illuminated the diverse cultural landscape of debt imprisonment.[41] Accounts focussing upon particular gaols, rooted in their administrative records, have provided less overtly pessimistic descriptions though their focus often lingers predominantly on felons.[42] Furthermore, study of the system of debt imprisonment itself has grown in recent years, leading to a number of studies which treat the institution more complexly than as mere tyranny upon which ground a range of forthcoming scholarship will build.[43] Most notable of these is Tawny Paul's recent *Poverty of Disaster* (2019). Her account of the pervasive insecurity of commercial life for the middling sorts explores the contribution of debt imprisonment to the economic mindset of the trading classes in depth, with particularly detailed consideration of the gendered dimension of indebtedness and its corporeal consequences as well as of "failure" in society more generally. Paul's is, in essence, the definitive social history of debt as a function of the lived experience in the eighteenth century. The prisons are, however, to some extent the site rather than the subject of her enquiry, using the gaols as a means of exploring the lives of debtors and altering conceptions of the advent of capitalism (focussing more heavily on the 'visceral experience' of debt).[44] *Credit and Debt*, acknowledging the fact that the system of imprisonment and the motivation of creditors have largely been absent from previous examination of debt, places the prison itself at its heart. While it includes discussions of the cultural aspects of confinement, it is only tangentially concerned with them largely because works like Paul's already reveal these in sharp focus upon which this economic history of the system builds.

Demonstrating how one of the most pervasive institutions in eighteenth-century Britain operated is a key facet of this book. In contrast to most existing accounts, this is a depersonalised history of the debtors' prison. It does not ask whether it was right or wrong, or whether it was cruel. It rarely asks whether debtors suffered during their confinement, either due to the conditions or the act of imprisonment itself, because it is only partially concerned with those imprisoned. Accusations that this book does not significantly acknowledge the negative corporeal consequences upon the individual might therefore be valid, though it similarly does not contend prisons were pleasant places. It is essentially focussed upon one question about debt imprisonment: "did it work?" This does not necessarily extend to "should it not have been abolished" or "was it the best possible financial system", merely "why did creditors engage in the apparently illogical process of debt imprisonment rather than another mechanism and were their objectives achieved by it?" While issues of the Commercial and Industrial Revolutions are largely in the background of this brick-by-brick deconstruction of debt imprisonment, as this institution served their needs, the revelation of the largely successful operation of debtors' prisons expands our understanding of the commercial environment in which both thrived. In answering the central question, this study investigates the debtors' prisons by conducting an economic history of the relationship between creditors, debtors, prison officials, the state, and the wider community and the institution of debt imprisonment. It demonstrates how and why it proved effective and that prisoners like Richard Hogarth should not necessarily be regarded as failures simply because they were arrested. At its core, this book seeks to rid the eighteenth-century debtors' prison of its punitive associations, emphasising its inherent nature as a site of contract enforcement, coercion, and negotiation.

The basis of this examination are the records produced by prisons themselves, many of which have not previously been discussed in detail. These include the administrative documents of a variety of institutions across the country though particularly – due largely to how records have been preserved – within the City of London and its environs. The majority of the quantitative data upon which this re-examination of debtors' prisons is based are drawn from the surviving commitment registers – detailing the confinement, obligations, and release of individual debtors – of London's Wood Street Compter and Fleet Prison as well as Lancaster Castle Gaol. These three prisons provide the most extensive statistical data on eighteenth-century imprisonment heretofore produced. The book uses these documents not only to measure effectiveness but also to demonstrate the impact of debtors' prisons upon the wider commercial economy, building upon quantitative data with the writings of reformers, theorists, prison managers, politicians, newspaper commentators, authors, and (where possible) the accounts of those who experienced imprisonment for debt first hand.

The book begins with the perspective of creditors themselves, the initiators of imprisonment. Chapter 1 discusses the economy of commercial credit which the prisons inhabited. It builds upon the substantial scholarship of early modern credit using contemporary discussion as well as the financial records of those embroiled within credit to emphasise how unstable and informal much of the market was, separating the credit of "finance" from the credit of everyday commerce. While it shows the impossibility of trading without credit, it makes clear how little practical security was offered to traders by the practice of buyers taking goods merely on the ill-defined promise "to pay". Furthermore, it explores the theoretical foundations of debt imprisonment, comparing it with other available measures of securing repayment, and demonstrating that while the prisons were far from perfect mechanisms of contract enforcement, they were essentially the least flawed option for commercial debt, emphasising that the institution was not constructed by eighteenth-century creditors but interpreted by them to solve the problems of their business reality. Chapter 2 continues the examination of the institution from the creditor perspective by evaluating – during a period of significant penal experimentation and the supposed rise of modern "enlightened" capitalism – how much use commercial people made of the powers of arrest through the surviving commitment registers. This discussion, which also sets out the irregular and informal structure of prisons (acknowledging how this complicates a study of creditor behaviour), demonstrates the overall lack of decline in arrest rates, asserting that debt imprisonment and commercial growth were not incongruous, most prisoners coming from the same commercial classes as plaintiffs.

Chapter 3 analyses the data produced from commitment registers on how prisoners were ultimately released in depth to test whether this regulation of the market was illusory or actually in operation. It represents an examination from the perspective of both creditor and debtor, revealing the likelihood and speed at which the former might expect satisfaction and the various methods by which the latter might achieve freedom including where they thwarted plaintiffs. Debtors were confined for shorter periods than is commonly assumed though the majority had far from brief experiences with confinement. Furthermore, the majority at all three prisons studied were likely to obtain their release by convincing creditors to release them, suggesting that they had managed to settle their debts in some form and that creditors were right in assuming that they had the means to pay if coerced. Discussing each mechanism of release in detail allows for a more complex understanding of the processes of imprisonment, removing suggestions that it was merely a death sentence, not least because mortality rates were lower than is usually expected.

Chapters 4 and 5 expand from the release data, exploring the processes behind the two most important ways in which debtors returned to society. Having shown that debtors were regularly able to convince their creditors to release them, discussion of the debtor economy in Chapter 4 explores the multiple strategies prisoners employed to raise capital. It demonstrates that the surprisingly liberal nature of confinement allowed debtors to engage in the wider world of commerce, manage their external affairs, and engage in productive labour from within gaol in whatever way best served their individual situation, the function of prisons being to coerce debtor-focus rather than to itself be the facilitator of payment. In Chapter 5, however, it is acknowledged that not all debtors were able (despite the significant corporeal pressures of imprisonment) to pay their debts. A minority of prisoners were genuinely insolvent and required external means to secure liberty. By studying the development of the irregularly passed Insolvency Acts which released applicants confined at a specific moment through a form of bankruptcy, this chapter explores the organic legislative responses to imprisonment for debt which prevented the institution from collapsing under its own weight without having to enact substantial reform. Furthermore, it explores how the community of creditors responded to these amnesties which undermined their coercive power as well as the motivations of debtors in deciding whether to apply for freedom.

Finally, this book examines how the national system of debtors' prisons functioned without central control, organisation, or funding, being as irregular an institution as the credit it enforced. Through official enquiries, administrative reports, and surviving records of income and expenditure, Chapter 6 investigates the role of keepers in ensuring the system was financially effective and palatable for the wider community. It suggests that keepers should not be seen simply as cruel and arbitrary exploiters of prisoners for extracting fees and rents, but as businessowners without whom debt imprisonment could not have functioned in the eighteenth century. Chapter 7 then turns to the thorny question of reform of debtors' prisons, a much discussed though little realised project in the eighteenth century. Though almost all the major reforms were features of nineteenth-century legislation, it highlights the unrecognised impact of attempts to limit imprisonment to the "right" sort of debtor. By barring the imprisonment of the poorest debtors, it is seen that the legislature unwittingly created a punitive element of what was previously a solely economic institution. This undermined the informal system of debt regulation and limited the ability of users to interpret the institution for their own needs. However, it also shows how little appetite there was, even at the end of the century, for a full abolition of this necessary system, there being no sign c.1815 that debt imprisonment would not be a feature of the next six centuries of English commerce.

Notes

1 Richard Hogarth, *Thesaurarium Trilingue Publicum; Being an Introduction to English, Latin, and Greek* (London: 1689); Ronald Paulson, *Hogarth Vol. I – The Modern Moral Subject 1697–1732* (Cambridge: Lutterworth Press, 1991), pp. 1–35; William Hogarth, *Anecdotes of William Hogarth* (London: 1833); John Ireland,

Hogarth Illustrated Vol. I (London: 1793), pp. vi–xi; *Post Man and the Historical Account*, 8th–11th January 1703/4, no. 1226.

2 Paulson, *Hogarth*, pp. 1–35; Jenny Uglow, *Hogarth – A Life and a World* (London: Faber & Faber, 1997), pp. 9–46; David Bindman, "Hogarth, William (1697–1764)", *Oxford Dictionary of National Biography* (Oxford University Press, 2004), online edition, https://doi.org/10.1093/ref:odnb/13464 (accessed 3rd December 2019); Sir John Soanes Museum, "Hogarth: 101", 20th September 2019, *The John Soane's Museum*, www.soane.org/features/hogarth-101 (accessed 3rd December 2019).

3 *Post Boy*, 20th–22nd December 1711, no. 2592; *Evening Post*, 27th–30th June 1713, no. 607; *British Mercury*, 14th October 1713, no. 432; *Post Man and the Historical Account*, 8th–10th September 1715, no. 11150.

4 *Daily Courant*, 6th February 1706, no. 1190; *Daily Courant*, 21st June 1707, no. 1671; *Post Man and the Historical Account*, 8th–11th January 1704, no. 1226.

5 "Commitment Register", 1708–1713, Fleet Prison, The National Archives, London (hereafter TNA), PRIS 1/2.

6 "Richard Hogarth", Debtors' Schedules, 1712, Court in Session – Insolvent Debtors, London Metropolitan Archives, London (hereafter LMA), CLA/047/LJ/17/018/A.

7 Julian Hoppit, "The Use and Abuse of Credit in Eighteenth-Century England", in *Business Life and Public Policy – Essays in Honour of D.C. Coleman*, eds. Neil McKendrick and R. B. Outhwaite (Cambridge: Cambridge University Press, 1986), p. 76.

8 David Graeber, *Debt – The First 5000 Years* (New York: Melville House, 2011), p. 334; see: Tawny Paul, *Poverty of Disaster – Debt and Insecurity in Eighteenth-Century Britain* (Cambridge: Cambridge University Press, 2019), pp. 95–97.

9 Craig Muldrew, "Interpreting the Market: The Ethics of Credit and Community Relations in Early Modern England", *Social History* vol. 18, no. 2 (1993), p. 163.

10 Charles Gildon, *The Post-Boy Robb'd of His Mail: or, The Pacquet Broke Open. Consisting of Letters of Love and Gallantry, and All Miscellaneous Subjects: In Which Are Discovered the Vertues, Vices, Follies, Humours and Intrigues of Mankind. With Remarks on Each letter* (London: 1706), pp. 79–80; F. A. S. Murray, *Thoughts on Imprisonment for Debt Humbly Addressed to His Majesty* (London: 1788), p. 10.

11 Charles Dickens, *Little Dorrit* (London: 1857), p. 314; see: William Holdsworth, *A History of English Law Vol. VIII* (London: Methuen & co., 1925), pp. 231–232; Colleen Lannon, "Whose Fault? The Speculator's Guilt in *Little Dorrit*", *Victorian Literature and Culture* vol. 45 (2017), pp. 413–432; Kenneth Dyson, *States, Debt, and Power – Saints and Sinners in European History and Integration* (Oxford: Oxford University Press, 2014), p. 90.

12 Matthew J. Baker, Metin Cosgel, and Thomas J. Miceli, "Debtors' Prisons in America: An Economic Analysis", *Journal of Economic Behaviour & Organisation* vol. 84 (2012), pp. 216–219; Department of State, *Papers Relating to the Foreign Relations of the United States Part II* (Washington: Government Printing Office, 1909), p. 1173.

13 "The New Debtors' Prison", *New York Times*, 6th April 2009; "Are Debtors' Prisons Coming Back?", *Wall Street Journal*, 28th August 2012; "The New Debtors' Prison", *The Economist*, 16th November 2013; "A Modern System of Debtor Prisons", *New York Times*, 28th March 2016; "Bernie Sanders' Cash Bail Bill Seeks to End 'Modern Day Debtors' Prisons'", *The Guardian*, 25th July 2018.

14 Genevieve LeBaron and Adrienne Roberts, "Confining Social Insecurity: Neoliberalism and the Rise of the 21st Century Debtors' Prison", *Politics and Gender* vol. 8 (2012), p. 26; Torie Atkinson, "A Fine Scheme: How Municipal Fines Become Crushing Debt in the Shadow of the New Debtors' Prison", *Harvard Civil*

Rights-Civil Liberties Law Review vol. 51, no. 1 (2016), pp. 202–210; Christopher D. Hampson, "The New American Debtors' Prisons", *American Journal of Criminal Law* vol. 44, no. 1 (2016), pp. 8–14.

15 Brianna L. Campbell, "The Economy of the Debtors' Prison Model: Why Throwing Deadbeats into Debtors' Prison Is a Good Idea", *Arizona Journal of International and Comparative Law* vol. 32, no. 3 (2015), pp. 867–871; "Why Hamas Jails People Who Can't Pay Their Debts", *The Economist*, 2nd August 2018; Nusrat Choudhury, "Jeff Sessions Takes a Stand for Debtors' Prisons", *American Civil Liberties Union Online*, 28th December 2017.

16 See: John Howard, *The State of the Prisons in England and Wales, with Preliminary Observations, and an Account of Some Foreign Prisons* (London: 1777); Roger Lee Brown, *A History of the Fleet Prison, London – The Anatomy of the Fleet* (Lampeter: Edwin Mellen Press, 1996); Margaret DeLacy, *Prison Reform in Lancashire, 1700–1850 – A Study in Local Administration* (Stanford: Stanford University Press, 1986); Stephanie Adele Leeman, "Stone Walls Do Not a Prison Make: The Debtors' Prison, York", *York Historian* vol. 11 (1994), pp. 23–39.

17 Donald Burrows, *Handel: Messiah* (Cambridge: Cambridge University Press, 1991), pp. 8–17; see: Margot C. Finn, "Being in Debt in Dickens's London: Fact, Fictional Representation and the Nineteenth-Century Debtors Prison", *Journal of Victorian Culture* vol. 1, no. 2 (1996), pp. 203–226; Gregory Dart, *Metropolitan Art and Literature, 1810–40 – Cockney Adventures* (Cambridge: Cambridge University Press, 2012), pp. 195–220.

18 Robert Baldwin, Martin Cave, and Martin Lodge, "Regulation – The Field and the Developing Agenda", in *The Oxford Handbook of Regulation*, eds. Robert Baldwin, Martin Cave, and Martin Lodge (Oxford: Oxford University Press, 2010), p. 10; see: Andreas Bergh and Carl Hampus Lyttkens, "Measuring Institutional Quality in Ancient Athens", *Journal of Institutional Economics* vol. 10, no. 2 (2014), p. 297.

19 Avner Grief and Joel Mokyr, "Institutions and Economic History: A Critique of Professor McCloskey", *Journal of Institutional Economics* vol. 12, no. 1 (2016), p. 32; Thomas I. Palley, *From Financial Crisis to Stagnation – The Destruction of Shared Prosperity and the Role of Economics* (Cambridge: Cambridge University Press, 2012), pp. 64–65, 148–149.

20 E. A. Wrigley, *The Path to Sustained Growth – England's Transition from an Organic Economy to an Industrial Revolution* (Cambridge: Cambridge University Press, 2016).

21 Julian Hoppit, *Risk and Failure in English Business 1700–1800* (Cambridge: Cambridge University Press, 1987), p. 176.

22 See: Paul, *Poverty of Disaster*, pp. 236–237; Joel Mokyr, "Accounting for the Industrial Revolution", in *The Cambridge Economic History of Modern Britain – Volume I: Industrialisation, 1700–1860*, eds. Roderick Floud and Paul Johnson (Cambridge: Cambridge University Press, 2004), pp. 1–2; Hans-Joachim Voth, "Living Standards and the Urban Environment", in *The Cambridge Economic History of Modern Britain – Volume I: Industrialisation, 1700–1860*, eds. Roderick Floud and Paul Johnson (Cambridge: Cambridge University Press, 2004), p. 293; Jane Humphries and Jacob Weisdorf, "The Wages of Women in England, 1260–1850", *Journal of Economic History* vol. 75, no. 2 (2015), p. 426; Stephen Broadberry, Bruce M. S. Campbell, Alexander Klein, Mark Overton, and Bas van Leeuwen, "Clark's Malthus Delusion: Response to 'Farming in England 1200–1800'", *Economic History Review* vol. 71, no. 2 (2018), pp. 639–664.

23 Douglass C. North, "The Role of Institutions in Economic Development", *United Nations Economic Commission for Europe Discussion Paper Series* no. 2003.2 (2003), pp. 1–10; Douglass C. North and Barry R. Weingast, "Constitutions and Commitment: The Evolution of Institutions Governing Public Choice in Seventeenth-Century England", *The Journal of Economic History* vol. 49, no. 4 (1989), pp. 803–832.

24 Larry Neal and Stephen Quinn, "Networks of Information, Markets, and Institutions in the Rise of London as a Financial Centre, 1660–1720", *Financial History Review* vol. 8 (2001), pp. 7–26; Carl Wennerlind, *Casualties of Credit – The English Financial Revolution, 1620–1720* (Cambridge: Harvard University Press, 2011), p. 7; Geoffrey M. Hodgson, "1688 and All That: Property Rights, the Glorious Revolution, and the Rise of British Capitalism", *Journal of Institutional Economics* vol. 13, no. 1 (2017), pp. 79–107; Joel Mokyr, "Bottom-Up or Top-Down? The Origins of the Industrial Revolution", *Journal of Institutional Economics* vol. 14, no. 6 (2018), pp. 1003–1024. See also: Avner Greif, "Coercion and Exchange – How Did Markets Evolve?", in *Institutions, Innovation, and Industrializations – Essays in Economic History and Development*, eds. Avner Greif, Lynne Kiesling, and John V.C. Nye (Woodstock: Princeton University Press, 2015), pp. 71–74; Li Tan, "Market Supporting Institutions, Guild Organisations, and the Industrial Revolution: A Comparative View", *Australian Economic History Review* vol. 53, no. 3 (2013), pp. 221–246.

25 Gregory Clark, *A Farewell to Alms – A Brief Economic History of the World* (Woodstock: Princeton University Press, 2007), pp. 147–151; Deirdre McCloskey, "Max U versus Humanomics: A Critique of Neo-Institutionalism", *Journal of Institutional Economics* vol. 12, no. 1 (2016), pp. 1–27; Deirdre McCloskey, "The Great Enrichment: A Humanistic and Social Scientific Account", *Scandinavian Economic History Review* vol. 64, no. 1 (2016), pp. 6–9.

26 Holdsworth, *English Law Vol. VIII*, p. 231; Erika Vause, *In the Red and in the Black – Debt, Dishonour, and the Law in France between the Revolutions* (London: University of Virginia Press, 2018).

27 A detailed discussion is provided in Chapter 1 of the literature on commercial credit though the key element of this interpretation is derived from: Craig Muldrew, *The Economy of Obligation – The Culture of Credit and Social Relations in Early Modern England* (Basingstoke: Macmillan, 1998).

28 Edward Farley, *Imprisonment for Debt Unconstitutional and Oppressive, Proved from the Fundamental Principles of the British Constitution and the Rights of Nature* (London: 1788), pp. 10–11; John Dunton, *Athenian Sport: or Two Thousand Paradoxes Merrily Argued to Amuse and Divert the Age* (London: 1707), pp. 66–69; Anon. *The Unreasonableness and Ill Consequence of Imprisoning the Body for Debt, Prov'd from the Laws of God and Nature, Human Policy and Interest* (London: 1729); Anon. *An Inquiry into the Practice of Imprisonment for Debt, and a Refutation of Mr James Stephen's Doctrine. To Which Is Added, A Hint for Relief of Both Creditor and Debtor* (London: 1773); Margot C. Finn, "Henry Hunt's *Peep into a Prison*: The Radical Discontinuities of Imprisonment for Debt", in *English Radicalism, 1550–1850*, eds. Glen Burgess and Michael Festenstein (Cambridge: Cambridge University Press, 2007), p. 195.

29 Christopher McNall, "The Business of Statutory Debt Registries, 1283–1307", in *Credit and Debt in Medieval England c.1180–c.1350*, eds. P. R. Schofield and N. J. Mayhew (Oxford: Oxbow Books, 2002), pp. 68–69, 82; Jay Cohen, "The History of Imprisonment for Debt and Its Relation to the Development of Discharge in Bankruptcy", *Journal of Legal History* vol. 3 (1982), p. 154; Pamela Nightingale, "The Lay Subsidies and the Distribution of Wealth in Medieval England, 1275–1334", *Economic History Review* vol. 57, no. 1 (2004), p. 10.

30 Chris Briggs, *Credit and Village Society in Fourteenth-Century England* (Oxford: Oxford University Press, 2009), p. 81.

31 Christopher McNall, "The Recognition and Enforcement of Debts under the Statutes of Acton Burnell (1283) and Merchants (1285), 1283–1307", unpublished PhD thesis, University of Oxford (2000), pp. 165–166.

32 Margot C. Finn, *The Character of Credit – Personal Debt in English Culture, 1740–1914* (Cambridge: Cambridge University Press, 2003), p. 110.

33 Neil L. Sobol, "Charging the Poor: Criminal Justice Debt & Modern-Day Debtors' Prisons", *Maryland Law Review* vol. 75, no. 2 (2016), p. 495; Cohen, "The History of Imprisonment for Debt", p. 158; Stephen J. Ware, "A 20th Century Debate about Imprisonment for Debt", *American Journal of Legal History* vol. 54, no. 3 (2014), p. 352; Matter of Morris, 12 B.R. 321 (Bankr. N.D. Ill. 1981); Holdsworth, *English Law Vol. VIII*, p. 231; Paul, *Poverty of Disaster*, pp. 35–36.

34 Hoppit, *Risk and Failure*, p. 176. See: Peter M. Solar and John S. Lyons, "The English Cotton Spinning Industry, 1780–1840, as Revealed in the Columns of the *London Gazette*", *Business History* vol. 53, no. 3 (June 2011), pp. 302–323; John Mason, "Enterprise, Opportunity, and Bankruptcy in the Early Derbyshire Cotton Industry", in *King Cotton – A Tribute to Douglas A. Farnie*, ed. John F. Wilson (Lancaster: Carnegie, 2009), pp. 149–150; C.Y. Ferdinand, "The Economics of the Eighteenth-Century Provincial Book Trade: The Case of Ward and Chandler", in *Re-Constructing the Book – Literary Texts in Transmission*, eds. Maureen Bell, Shirley Chew, Simon Eliot, Lynette Hunter, and James L.W. West III (Aldershot: Ashgate, 2001), pp. 42–56; Edward J. Balleisen, *Navigating Failure – Bankruptcy and Commercial Society in Antebellum America* (Chapel Hill: University of North Carolina Press, 2001); Jennifer Aston and Paolo di Martino, "Risk, Success, and Failure: Female Entrepreneurship in Late Victorian and Edwardian England", *Economic History Review* vol. 70, no. 3 (2017), pp. 837–858.

35 Paul, *Poverty of Disaster*, being the exception in terms of including the prisons within conceptions of failure.

36 Dorothy George, *London Life in the Eighteenth Century* (London: Penguin, 1979 (first edition 1925)), pp. 297–301.

37 Hoppit, "Use and Abuse", p. 76; Julian Hoppit, *Britain's Political Economies – Parliament and Economic Life, 1660–1800* (Cambridge: Cambridge University Press, 2017), p. 156; Joanna Innes, "The King's Bench Prison in the Later Eighteenth Century: Law, Authority and Order in a London Debtors' Prison", in *An Ungovernable People – The English and Their Law in the Seventeenth and Eighteenth Centuries*, ed. John Brewer and John Styles (London: Hutchinson, 1980), p. 255; Joel Mokyr, *The Enlightened Economy – An Economic History of Britain 1700–1850* (New Haven: Yale University Press, 2009), p. 379.

38 Paul, *Poverty of Disaster*, p. 21. See: Robin Evans, *The Fabrication of Virtue – English Prison Architecture, 1750–1840* (Cambridge: Cambridge University Press, 1982); J. M. Beattie, *Policing and Punishment in London, 1660–1750* (Oxford: Oxford University Press, 2001); Randell McGowen, "Penal Reform and Politics in Early Nineteenth-Century England: 'A Prison Must Be a Prison'", in *Imagining the British Atlantic after the American Revolution*, eds. Michael Meranze and Saree Makdisi (Toronto: University of Toronto Press, 2015), pp. 219–239.

39 Rodney M. Baine, "The Prison Death of Robert Castell and Its Effect on the Founding of Georgia", *The Georgia Historical Society* vol. 73, no. 1 (Spring 1989), pp. 67–78; Alexander Pitofsky, "The Warden's Court Martial: James Oglethorpe and the Politics of Eighteenth-Century Prison Reform", *Eighteenth Century Life* vol. 24, no. 1 (2000), pp. 88–102; Richard H. Condon, "James Neild, Forgotten Reformer", *Studies in Romanticism* vol. 4, no. 4 (Summer 1964), pp. 240–251; Gabriel Cervantes and Dahlia Porter, "Extreme Empiricism, John Howard, Poetry, and the Thermometrics of Reform", *The Eighteenth Century* vol. 57, no. 1 (Spring 2016), pp. 95–119; Pat Rogers, "Defoe in the Fleet Prison", *The Review of English Studies* vol. 22, no. 88 (November 1971), pp. 451–455; Cheryll Duncan, "'A Debt Contracted in Italy': Ferdinando Tenducci in a London Court and Prison", *Early Music* vol. 42, no. 2 (2014), p. 227; John Ginger, "New Light on Gawen Hamilton – Artists, Musicians and the Debtors' Prison", *Apollo* vol. 136 (September 1992), pp. 156–160.

40 See: Paul H. Haagen, "Eighteenth-Century English Society and the Debt Law", in *Social Control and the State – Historical and Comparative Essays* (Oxford: Basil Blackwell, 1986), pp. 222–247; Paul Hess Haagen, "Imprisonment for Debt in England and Wales", unpublished PhD thesis, University of Princeton (1986).

41 Innes, "King's Bench"; Finn, *Character of Credit*; Jerry White, "Pain and Degradation in Georgian London: Life in the Marshalsea Prison", *History Workshop Journal* vol. 68 (Autumn 2009), pp. 69–98; Jerry White, *Mansions of Misery – A Biography of the Marshalsea Debtors' Prison* (London: Bodley Head, 2016).

42 DeLacy, *Prison Reform*; Brown, *Anatomy of the Fleet*; Gary Calland, *A History of the Devon County Prison for Debtors in St Thomas* (Exeter: Little History, 1999); Eric Stockdale, *A Study of Bedford Prison 1660–1877* (Bedford: The Bedfordshire Historical Record Society, 1977); David Kelly, "The Conditions of Debtors and Insolvents in Eighteenth-Century Dublin", in *The Gorgeous Mask: Dublin 1700–1850*, ed. David Dickson (Dublin: Trinity History Workshop, 1987), pp. 98–120.

43 Vause, *Debt, Dishonour, and the Law*; Bruce H. Mann, *Republic of Debtors – Bankruptcy in the Age of American Independence* (London: Harvard University Press, 2002). Also, for the current fertile ground of prison scholarship, see the *Early Modern Prisons – Exploring Gaols, Bridewells, and Other Forms of Detention, 1500–1800* (eds. Rachel Judith Weil and Richard Bell) blog containing a range of emerging work on debtors' prisons from established and early career scholars likely to appear in the coming years as published scholarship and completed PhD theses.

44 Paul, *Poverty of Disaster*.

1 Indebtedness and insolvency in eighteenth-century England

In Southwark, on the afternoon of Thursday 30th May 1728, the trumpeter John Baptist Grano discovered his luck had finally run out. He had been arrested the previous day for his debts and carried to a tavern, probably run by an associate of the bailiff, where he attempted to raise bail while being plied with food and copious amounts of drink at an exorbitant rate. Business had not been good in recent months and Grano's inability to live within his means (his actual income as a musician being dwarfed by his own presumptions of gentility) had finally stretched the patience of his many creditors. Nevertheless, Grano was at first optimistic about his situation. Debt was not only an occupational hazard for the precariously employed court musician but a way of life to anyone living in London in the eighteenth century. As he had been able to reasonably put off his creditors for some time and had avoided previous brushes with fiscal reality, Grano was confident that his extended social circle would save him by providing sufficient cash to secure bail. However, despite sending for his friends and relatives, his only visitor that day was the bailiff who 'about 12 … came to tell me that if I was not bayl'd by 5 a Clock that Day they must carry me over to the Marshalsey'. As the clock ticked down and no 'Brother, relation or Friend came nigh me', a disappointment Grano found most 'ungrateful', he began to accept the inevitability, as so many did across the eighteenth century, of his internment in 'this hell' – a debtors' prison.[1]

Sixty-five years later in Lower Thames Street, the firm of Peirce & Tait, dealers in fish, was coming to an end and the partners embarked upon the process of settling outstanding bills. Unlike Grano, the firm had experienced thirty years of wealth and successful trading, yet the partners remained in a highly precarious position as far as their accounts stood. The firm listed all outstanding bills 1763–1793 alphabetically, assigning each to one of three columns titled simply 'Bad', 'Doubtful', or 'Good' with amounts totalling £3258 18s 7d, £1499 6s 9d, and £1265 8½d respectively. Upon accounting for its own debts, the firm calculated that 'Bonds & Notes of Hand, in joint name of Peirce and Tait' amounted to £1126 15s 2d, £64 17s 8d, and £1537 19s 1d under the same headings as their own bills. While 'good' bills were those that had apparently been or were in the process of being settled and many of those 'doubtful' had been paid in part, there still existed a significant disparity in their accounts. While they were theoretically able to settle their own debts, little would be left for the ageing partners in their retirement. However, 'Bad' did not prove irretrievable as the firm managed to reduce the total owed to them to just £648 4s 4¼d by the time the account book was abandoned. Many of these debts, both small and large, had lain unpaid for several years and accepting the unpredictability of repayment was just as much a reality of trade for Peirce & Tait as having to live on extended credit was for their customers. However, the rapid turnaround in the accounts regarding recalcitrant debtors demonstrates how effective the application of focus and a significant degree of coercion could be in finally settling accounts, particularly when customers were reminded of the imposing walls of the Marshalsea.[2]

Grano and Peirce & Tait, separated by nearly three quarters of a century, lived in an England in which vast sums of unsecured credit permeated throughout commercial life. Sometimes it moved at great speed, being settled in hours, and sometimes it accumulated in secret, piling upon itself over time until a debtor could no longer hold demands at bay or was discovered by their executors after death. Some credit transactions were based on contracts poured over by lawyers for months by which thousands of pounds of obligation were agreed. Others depended upon the buyer signing a written promise to pay by a specified date negotiated in a matter of minutes. Many more deals were agreed casually and sealed with merely a handshake or a smile. Credit depended upon reciprocal arrangements, community relations, and generous dealing but it also consisted of a great deal of confidence and bravado as self-interested parties attempted to secure the best possible terms and convince one another of perhaps grander capabilities than they truly possessed in order to compete commercially in a largely informal market. Regardless of its size, the formality of the agreement, or how long it took to settle, credit had one universal truth across the period – those who offered it expected to be paid. Securing repayment of deals inflated by bravado and without defined contracts frequently proved problematic while substantial credit entanglements, involving potentially dozens of actors, put participants at great personal risk meaning both debtor and creditor (when they could be distinguished) risked ruin. Yet it was not a system from which one could choose to abstain, princes and paupers both being beholden to credit's favours.

This chapter discusses why eighteenth-century consumers and businesspeople found credit so attractive and so inescapable, but it also demonstrates how potentially unstable and dangerous such contracting could be. It explores the scholarly well-trodden ground of the ubiquity of credit in the early modern economy while emphasising how precarious much credit was, even when supposedly supported by formal arrangements. It then turns to the problems associated with enforcing such arrangements, analysing the efficacy of available institutions by which vendors could be assured of securing their capital, demonstrating that many of the most obvious legal solutions regularly proved impractical outside of large enterprise and high finance. It was, it is argued, the debtors' prison which, before nineteenth-century advances in economic practice, represented the most effective response to debt, being (like the credit upon which it was based) innately personal. Yet this system of debt imprisonment was far from a well-designed state institution, instead functioning as a relatively nebulous system of private activity, infected with inefficiency arising from corruption, customary behaviour, and the well-meaning reforms of the "enlightened". While debtors' prisons – a medieval institution which remained largely unchanged in the eighteenth century despite revolutions in finance, commerce, industrialisation, and society – were never a perfect solution, for creditors like Pierce and Tait faced with debtors like Grano it regularly proved to be their only option in recovering everyday debt.

★★

Daniel Defoe described credit in his *Complete English Tradesman* of 1725 as the lifeblood of eighteenth-century economic society calling it 'the foundation, the life and soul of business'; it was, 'in a private tradesman, ... his prosperity'. To Defoe and his readers, credit was far more than a desirable support to trade, allowing it to grow beyond conventional limits – it was essential to the continued existence of commerce itself. Nor was this reliance on credit restricted to cash-poor workmen or international dealers waiting months for goods or payment to cross the Atlantic, Defoe claiming that 'no Tradesman can be in so good circumstances as to say he ... does not stand in need of credit'.[3] While Defoe's almost hagiographical celebration of 'Lady Credit' is perhaps the best known, he was one of many voices describing credit as the sustaining force of England's commercial world, powering the vast increase in wealth that occurred during the eighteenth century.[4] Arthur Nevil concluded in 1762 that 'Industry is reared ... by Credit and Credit is the Mover ... of Commerce', while in the 1790s William Gordon wrote that 'credit is the great foundation of commerce', and the creditors of a Bristol bankrupt declared in 1783 that 'credit is universally allowed to be the parent and life of trade' and 'indispensable in the affairs of men'.[5] Nor did Defoe's writings age poorly, being in near constant print throughout the century. When William Wright published his own *Complete Tradesman* in 1789, he lifted Defoe's comments on credit almost directly with only minor updating, *The Monthly Review* still concluding 'the young tradesman will certainly be much benefited' by Wright's book.[6]

The extension of capital on trust has an obvious role in the promotion of economic activity beyond that enabled by existing limited personal wealth in all societies. However, the era of bank loans to facilitate long-term expenditure was a distant future to most early modern businesspeople. Eighteenth-century credit generally did not consist of money lending and bank loans which were heavily restricted by usury laws, though lending capital for interest did occur in this period and particularly consumed concerns about the state's credit and public debt.[7] Most private debt instead arose from sales credit, the offering of a product with delayed payment, and almost all exchange, whether it be for goods or services, was based upon it, customers buying luxury goods and daily bread on credit, while employers even paid wages on credit.[8] This was certainly not an eighteenth-century innovation; credit had always been a feature of English commerce but had proliferated extensively from the late sixteenth century when interpersonal credit outstripped the rate of consumption and filled courts with litigation to resolve commercial disputes.[9] While the rate of litigiousness declined relatively quickly, the use of credit itself did not abate largely due to the underlying drivers of its use not being remedied, principally the deficiencies in the physical realities of the coinage, credit remaining central to economic life into the nineteenth century.[10]

Viable metal currency was in short supply across the period compared to growing commercial demand. The unfitness of the currency was partly a result of the inherent vulnerability of pre-modern coinage to counterfeiting and to clipping in particular by which the quantity of silver within an individual coin was diminished. While ordinary people were likely to take a clipped or debased coin at its face value, the merchants they bought from would not, weighing small currency to determine its true value and hoarding undamaged coins for dealings with other suppliers.[11] Where bad coin circulated much of it still might be dead weight in the pocket when attempting to purchase goods in more formal venues than the marketplace, the street, or village alehouse. Even if the coinage had remained unharmed, Craig Muldrew concludes the supply of metal was 'never anywhere near large enough to meet the needs of the economy', let alone tackle inflation as commerce began to outgrow the ores upon which it had been based for millennia.[12] Eighteenth-century consumers and vendors, however, remained suspicious of innovation. While some sectors were willing to experiment with paper money particularly in the form of circulating Exchequer bills, credit was generally seen as a substitute rather than a replacement for currency, and attempts to increase the circulation of silver and gold were frequently advocated.[13] As late as 1776, fearing the existential threat posed by 'paper-credit', Rev. Price claimed that 'the only remedy ... is an increase of coinage'. However, Price's citation of similar arguments from the 1690s and 1730s as well as his pamphlet being reprinted in 1795 emphasises how little progress was made in producing a viable gold and silver currency across the period.[14]

While the insufficiency of currency continued to drive use of credit, by the eighteenth century arguably a more significant contributor to its proliferation was the fact that credit had become self-producing as trading on credit begot yet more credit. By selling on credit (whether chattels or labour) an individual was obligated to purchase on credit as they lacked the coin (consisting both of their profit and that which covered their operational costs) from their sale. This was a trend identified in the period by

Defoe who, acknowledging that 'the land owes to the trade some million sterling', remarked that 'the tradesman having then trusted the landed men with so much, where must they have [money] but by giving credit also to one another?' It was not, however, merely a consequence of the land's slow production of rent for 'the master manufacturer himself begins' credit by his need to buy resources and then multiplied it by dealing with extended networks of warehouse owners and other suppliers before having sold anything.[15] In such a market, as Julian Hoppit observed, 'all businessmen were creditors and all businessmen were debtors' and all traders had to be willing to engage in the practical realities of credit.[16] The universality of credit extended beyond the trading classes. While some workforces may have been able to insist on cash payments, most working people experienced and expected a significant delay between labour and wage payment.[17] Some of their purchasing could similarly be delayed though most necessities had to be bought irrespective of currency reserves; this subsistence credit existed in addition to continued engagement with purchasing petty luxuries on credit.[18] Unsurprisingly, as Muldrew has shown, 'the majority of households had more debts than credits ... a large percentage of these households actually had more debts than credits *and* moveable goods combined' though this rarely proved problematic during the lifetime of the trader.[19]

Credit thus became more of a cultural norm rather than a commercial last resort. Customers came to expect its offer as a matter of course and its refusal, irrespective of their actual financial capability, as an affront. Jacob Vanderlint complained bitterly in 1734 that traders were 'forced to court and oblige [with credit] almost anybody that will take their Goods'.[20] This proclivity of credit purchasing impacted not only how but when consumers chose to purchase. As early as the 1720s Defoe described how 'men often buy cloaths before they pay for them because they want cloaths before they can spare the money'. Viewing this as a fundamental behavioural shift, a triumph of desire over fiscal conservatism arising from the Consumer Revolution, Defoe further recorded that 'we see very considerable families who buy nothing but on trust; even Bread, Beer, Butter, Cheese, Beef and Mutton, Wine, Grocery, &c. being the things which even with the meanest families are generally sold for ready money'.[21] Defoe was largely uncritical of such transacting though other writers bemoaned credit's promotion of excessive consumption, particularly in the first half of the century. An anonymous poem of 1735 railed against the false hopes of credit which, rather than enhancing wealth, threatened to consume it:

> They both do mind what some do *Credit* call, Which very hard on Citizens do fall; Though Trade be small, and Rents exceeding high, The thing call'd *Credit* must by no means die: To keep up which, all Fashions they will follow, Till Fashions sometimes all their Credit swallow.[22]

The silk dealer and economic theorist Isaac Gervaise, despite presumably being regularly involved in the national system of credit, warned that credit artificially drove up consumption, prophesising an inevitable financial collapse. Writing in 1720 shortly before the English market crashed from over speculation in South Sea stock rather than consumerism, Gervaise warned that credit, rather than being a sustaining force, originated 'from Fear and Desire' as creditors desperately sought to undersell one another.[23] Puritanical figures advocating for the return to buying nothing but in ready money, particularly finding voice during commercial panics, were generally a minority and more reflective of credit's ubiquity than cultural doubt. Even businesspeople agreeing with Gervaise could not practically avoid offering credit, Defoe warning that those who tried to offer 'No Trust by Retail' did not succeed as even 'very good customers ... who do at proper times make payments punctual enough' would be insulted and 'go away from them'.[24]

Gervaise's concern about credit representing a house of cards without firm foundation appears relatively understandable from a modern perspective, as does trader trepidation in general. Early modern credit was, by the standard of later and (arguably) earlier periods, surprisingly unstable as it was rarely based upon defined tangible collateral. Instead, credit was calculated by a socially defined and communicated system of reputation, determining whether an individual debtor was trustworthy through their estate and prior transacting but also an array of non-financial qualifiers.[25] A reputation for honest dealing and prompt payment in a commercial setting increased creditability but so did acts of charity or church attendance while public drunkenness or cruelty to one's family might detract from it, regardless of fiscal responsibility.[26] These qualities were communicated orally by rumour and neighbourly gossip, Muldrew describing how 'credit became a type of currency where a "propriety" or property of the self in terms of virtuous attributes, was circulated by word of mouth through the community'.[27] People worked hard to protect their social reputation for economic needs. The significant rate of defamation suits, alongside less formal protections of honour such as taking out advertisements in the newspaper, reflects both how actively people sought to protect their reputation but also how vulnerable it was to slight insults. Accusations of adultery, drunkenness, keeping 'bad company', or even of being a 'quack' or witch could significantly harm commercial interests.[28] While these might be seen potentially as credible measures of a person's trustworthiness, other elements of reputation deviated even further from commercial reality. Societal rank, and the presumptions of honour that came with it, possessed inherent credit which was nearly impossible for traders to question let alone refuse despite the frequent shortages of cash among the gentry.[29]

Personal wealth was not absent in the calculation of creditability. Knowledge of a customer's material goods was a significant contributor to creditability calculations and might override poor neighbourliness.[30] However, as the issue of the gentry reveals, suggestion of capability through socially defined qualities of wealth was not always a trustworthy indication of actual capacity. In an increasingly disconnected and urban economy featuring thousands rather than tens of potential customers, knowledge of any individual's wealth became heavily reliant upon sartorial appearance and personal declarations of status. This, in turn, was undermined as fashion and novelties became more affordable to less creditworthy individuals.[31] Such problems were emphasised in the period by stories of notable frauds. William Stroud, who terrorised London shopkeepers for years before finally being caught in 1752, frequently purchased expensive clothing on credit and used his 'genteel' appearance to purchase jewellery and other high-value goods, also on credit. After selling these to pawnbrokers, Stroud would disappear into 'the Crowds of London' leaving creditors out of pocket and without a means of redress.[32] While men of Stroud's cunning were far from common and most customers were not intending to defraud a shopkeeper, the reduced absolute indication of wealth from outward appearance undermined the ability of creditors to make accurate judgements on sight. Furthermore, even accurate displays of wealth provided no indication of the extent to which a potential debtor was already obligated to other creditors.

Even where accurate assessments of wealth could be made, bargains were staked not upon that which could easily be seized and sold but upon the personhood of the debtor, the body being the receptacle in which worth (i.e. reputation) was stored. One 1729 pamphleteer even denied that transactions based upon anything more substantial could be considered "credit" in the first place:

> Private credit is when one private man lends his money to another and depends entirely for his payment upon the debtor's personal security: For when a creditor takes a pledge or a mortgage for securing his repayment, I reckon he gives no credit to his debtor, but depends upon what he has in his hands for his payment.[33]

Such transacting appears remarkably insecure, not merely because it lacked defined financial elements which could be recovered if the debtor defaulted but because the agreement itself often consisted of little more than an oral promise "to pay" or face "consequences". This practice left a surprising amount of control over the process of repayment in the hands of the debtor as the creditor was merely left with an open-ended agreement "to be paid", such informality being furthered by the fact that most agreements were entirely oral.[34] Such orality promoted ease of access to credit and, in turn, the rate of commerce as the illiterate, whether customer or vendor, was not excluded. The list of seven debts totalling £18 owed in 1761 to Thomas Price, a Smithfield buckle-chape maker, demonstrates he was able to participate in diverse and extended forms of credit. Price offered credit for 'goods sold and delivered' from his business but also in delayed rent to his two lodgers and as 'Money Lent' to friends and neighbours despite Price being unable to sign his own name, suggesting his illiteracy and the probability that he lacked formal accounts.[35]

Not all sales credit was so orally or informally constructed. Particularly in urban areas where large and highly mobile populations decreased the integrity of mutual trust between neighbours, traders could insist upon deals being secured by bills of exchange or notes of hand. These were, it has been argued, legally relatively indistinct by the eighteenth century, though notes of hand were simpler constructions, usually constituting a written promise to pay under agreed terms drawn up at the moment of sale that even within the seventeenth century were used to support informal credit for dealers across the social spectrum.[36] Bills of exchange were preferred by financial institutions and – while they did spread into wider commerce during the period – were a tool associated principally with merchants dealing with one another.[37] Both might, under certain circumstances, be transferred, sold, or exchanged to third parties (sometimes at a discount) though the original signatory remained liable for the debt stated upon the note. However, these notes did little more than formalise oral agreements. As they remained rooted in the personal security of the debtor, relying on interpersonal confidence instead of defined collateral, it is unclear whether they offered any real increased security to creditors.[38] Joseph Harris, in his 1769 *An Essay upon Money and Coins*, pointed out that bills of exchange 'strictly speaking, pay no debts; they only transfer credit from one place to another'.[39] Those participating in such transfers of credit were inherently vulnerable even if they trusted the immediate members of the chain. The Birmingham jurist and historian William Hutton described being returned a bill of exchange in the 1780s 'which lately passed through my hands' from his creditor due to the original name in the bill refusing to pay. Hutton was able to return the bill to the debtor who had offered it to him and though this individual 'paid me chearfully' Hutton then informed him his chances of recovering the original sum in a similar manner were remote.[40]

When traders, who frequently made use of a mix of formal and informal contracting, tried to balance their books, distinction between the two might come to appear minimal. William Acton, a London oilman, was required to draw up a list of outstanding debts owed to him in 1755, recording that he was owed £91 15s by twenty-one customers. The majority of this was owed by thirteen unsecured 'book debts' referring to oral agreements, dominated by £20 owed by a Mr Wickham of Saville Row, the remainder owing sums between 16s and £8. However, £35 16s was owed by seven customers on notes of hand and one upon a bond. While any trader might have large amounts owed to them on formal mechanisms at a given time, it is clear that Acton's written contracts had not in practice provided much more security than his book debts. The earliest note dated back to 13th July 1727 when Richard Swinton, a potter of Grosvenor square, made his mark on an agreement to pay 'ye sum of £1 upon Demand'. The other notes of hand from across the subsequent two decades contained more specific payment plans such as David Prole in October 1741 who was to make 'all three payments quarterly by Midsummer next' or Francis Nash who agreed in March 1738 to pay 'two months after date the sum of Ten Pounds'. That they remained outstanding suggests that without defined consequences or collateral, written agreements could be little better than the oral promises they represented. Presumably Acton had possessed many more such notes of hand during his trading years which had been paid on demand, but so presumably had most of his oral book debts. While undoubtedly these written agreements carried more weight than oral promises, representing a method of confirming when a customer was in breach, they were not in themselves a guarantee of payment. Even the legal bond by which 'Alexander Statham, his heirs, Execs or Administrators doe well and truly pay or Cause to be paid unto William Acton ... the full summe of Ten Pounds ... with Interest' had exceeded the due date of the 22nd October 1733 by over twenty years.[41]

How then, considering the lack of defined payment plans, the imperfection of formal contracting, and the dominance of personhood in providing security did creditors manage to secure their businesses and recover capital? Surprisingly, the imperfections of reputation-based informal credit were regularly unproblematic as in the majority of instances a vendor's trust in customers was proved valid. Only the minority of debts ever required legal intervention, suggesting a significant separation between the potential precariousness highlighted in this system of informal personality and actual financial calamity.[42] Customers, beyond wanting to avoid formal enforcement proceedings, were motivated by cultural forces and the reciprocal bonds of community to pay their debts if they could. Eighteenth-century consumers were regularly reminded of the importance of honouring commercial promises by their local shopkeepers, in the literature they read, and every Sunday from the pulpit.[43] In 1718, the bishop of Ely, William Fleetwood, gave a far from unusual sermon to a congregation in London, based on the book of Kings, declaring God commanded money should always be put '*first*, to the payment of ... debt, and *secondly*, to the sustenance of [a debtor's] children'. Fleetwood went on to chastise those who could not pay their debts, claiming their insufficiency arose only from 'this hastening to be rich, and endeavouring to make great fortunes in a little time, by most immoderate and excessive Gains', repeatedly setting out 'the reasonableness' and 'Justice of paying Debts', the latter being a common theme of the moral debate on credit.[44] Religious exhortations also featured in secular tracts such as manuals for young tradesmen which lectured from Corinthians to promote the payment of debts promptly, cautioning against hubristic assumptions that those temporarily flushed with business success were 'out of the reach of disaster'.[45] Beyond the wrath of God, debtors had good cause to pay essential vendors promptly for fear that a penchant for delayed payments – a behaviour known in alehouses as 'long chalking' – would invoke the wrath of shopkeepers, leading them to be cut off or stricter terms set on future transactions.[46] Such threats were more palpable than the vague consequences detailed in notes of hand. An irritated watchmaker could probably be paid at a later date, but the local baker (possibly the only source of bread) had to be paid as soon as it was fiscally possible to ensure his continued positive impression of the family. However, these concerns were not restricted to the poor and the wage reliant; commercial vendors (such as watchkeepers and local bakers) could be just as likely to find payment problematic and had to keep essential suppliers of metal or grain happy, manuals warning that to continue trading upon credit beyond their own business resources was to unjustly 'trade on … the estates of creditors' and risk their ire.[47]

The likelihood of unprompted satisfaction was increased by creditors acting with a practical quantity of generosity; they did not usually demand imminent repayment, believing debtors would, for their own sake, make payment once they were able to. Joseph Spier, a dealer and chapman of London, drew up a list of customers who still owed him money 'for sundry goods sold and delivered' for the years preceding 1769. Upon investigating their circumstances he discovered that, of his 246 customers, owing on average £1 15s each, 29% had died since the initial transaction.[48] While deceased debtors owed slightly more on average (£2 3s 4d), this included Spier's only debtor obliged for more than £15, Robert Nixon who owed £38 15s 3d. When discounting Nixon, the deceased average debt fell to £1 13s, suggesting that both they and their living debtors were not paying on instalment. These numerous small commercial debts, even among the living dating back to at least before 1765, suggest that Spier was a relaxed and generous creditor willing to allow his customers to pay in their own time particularly given that so many had died since the last transaction. However, an overly generous nature was risky and probably contributed to Spier's imprisonment for his own debts earlier that year.[49] Spier's unfortunate state was probably an outlier as creditors usually tempered their generosity as circumstances required, presumably as Spier's own creditor did. While creditors could not always rely on a customer's good nature and remain passive, it was regularly only necessary to issue a simple reminder that payment was required to prompt debtors into action. Indeed, a shopkeeper physically asking for money may have been the first instance in which a debtor recognised that such payment might be due, particularly in consideration of the regularly ill-defined promise "to pay".

However, when a shopkeeper's patience expired and they demanded payment, that they would receive what they were owed was far from certain; customers who had sworn to their solvency might suddenly declare their impoverishment and inability to pay. Why this occurred was, for debtors, an important reputational argument. Debtors and pamphleteers, railing against the behaviour of callous creditors, regularly argued that distinctions should be made between 'honest debtors', who had been rendered insolvent by broader economic circumstance or the faults of others, and 'fraudulent debtors' who deliberately failed to pay.[50] One 1788 pamphlet declared emphatically: 'Reason proclaims there should be some Distinction made between the Debtor that cannot, but would if he could pay the utmost Farthing, and he who robs his Neighbour by contracting Debts, which he knew he never could … pay', seemingly refusing to acknowledge that any debtors existed in-between these two extremes.[51] This represented a stratification of unpaid debt, acknowledging cultural assumptions about the inherent nefariousness of those who delayed 'just' payments and who spent carelessly while denying one's own similarity to such 'fiends'. This framing further exacerbated the sense of injustice some debtors felt when creditors took measures against their non-payment. The complaints of James Stephen, imprisoned in the King's Bench in 1770, were typical of irate prisoners who felt their honesty had been unfairly questioned:

> Justice requires not that the person should be confined for an uncertain, unlimited time, and that the defendant must, after all, pay debt, costs, and interest, unless it could be supposed that it was in the power of the debtor to satisfy the creditor previous to his confinement ... nor can it be reconciled to justice, that the prodigal spendthrift and the unfortunate honest man should share the same fate.

Having railed against the lack of deferential treatment he experienced and the cruelty of imprisoning him while unable to pay, Stephen concluded that 'resentment is generally [a creditor's] motive for destroying his adversary (as he imagines his debtor to be)'.[52]

   The argument for treating those who were merely unfortunate with greater sympathy than those who showed open disdain to shopkeepers was far from an outlandish or unconvincing one nor were creditors, or at least their literary sympathisers, necessarily averse to the concept of stratified legal responses. Robert Holloway, writing a year after Stephen, agreed there 'ought to be a line drawn between the fraudulent and honest debtor: the one merits a more exemplary correction than the laws inflict, the other claims not only the law's protection, but the aid of humanity'.[53] However, while debtors might always feel they had behaved properly, creditors were far more likely to damn them than commiserate with them. The creditors of Joseph Pedley in 1783 were happy to acknowledge that, in hypothetical circumstances, the insolvency laws 'in general are undiscriminating. They involve the worthless Sharper and unfortunate Debtor in one common lot, and they release the wicked to whom imprisonment is no punishment, at a time they release the innocent'. They remained, however, clear that in Pedley's case, he was 'the sole author, manager, and actor, of every suffering he [and his creditors had] sustained' and complained vociferously that 'creditors [might] be condemned for their' proceeding against debtors legally.[54] Separating debtors into "honest" and "fraudulent" was an academic exercise, unlikely to be conducted outside of pamphlet literature. There certainly were a minority of deliberately fraudulent debtors, cheating lenders before absconding, who might be considered separate from the honest and unlucky.[55] But, even if a creditor had evidence of a debtor's genuine unfortunateness, this did not obscure the fact that a customer had sworn (a sacred act) that they could and would make such a payment.[56] Any failure to do so could rightly be seen as fraudulent by creditors and it was the responsibility of the so-called 'honest debtor' to find the means of completing their oath.

Credit was not a gift but a contract (even if one that was usually only orally promised) which could not be escaped even by death.[57] As J.R. Wordie argued, 'in the market place, money is never given away for nothing'; debtors understood what would be required of them when they purchased on credit and could not feign innocence due to unfortunate circumstances.[58] Indeed, debtors clearly made choices about which of their many contracts to fulfil when they had resources. Creditor and debtor priorities were regularly diametrically opposed, debtors feeling (not unreasonably) their capital was better spent on sustenance, increasing household wealth, or redeeming promises to valued acquaintances before satisfying shopkeepers, while any individual creditor felt (not unreasonably) that their particular demand should be the most pressing. Such prioritisation regularly appeared callous or nonsensical to the creditor. Jeoffry Wagstaffe complained in 1769 that

> a *man of honour* will pay no debts contracted to tradesmen, or mechanics, and does not care if they and their families starve or beg, provided he can make a genteel appearance in good company; but he is the most punctual creature alive in all gaming debts, commonly called debts of honour; and for this he is a damn'd honest fellow.[59]

While 'men of honour' were a fringe concern, there were always competing views of what actions could or could not reasonably be taken to ensure a creditor was rightly satisfied. Coercing the debtor into prioritising creditors was an inherent element of the functioning informal credit market, arguably as essential as the willingness of vendors to offer credit and the need to preserve reputation.

Creditors were far from devoid of options to recover their money. On some occasions, an uncooperative debtor could be dealt with indirectly by engaging with the larger chain of credit. During the seventeenth century, particularly in rural communities, members of credit chains might come together to swap and eventually cancel debts.[60] This system, known as 'reckoning', was more difficult to apply in eighteenth-century urban environments in which credit networks had become too extended and depersonalised, however, debt swapping still occurred if in a less direct form. Delays in payment were a frequent problem for those who worked for wages and while in most instances workers simply built up various debts until they were paid at the end of the job (probably wiping out their cash injection entirely in one afternoon as they cleared each account), in certain cases they might exchange wages (existing as debts from their employers) for goods. This restricted workers to a finite recoverable bill and allowed vendors to target single solvent organisations such as building contractors rather than the many labourers who worked for them. Adam Smith refers briefly to (and rather overlooks) in his 1776 *Wealth of Nations* 'a village in Scotland where it is not uncommon, I am told, for a workman to carry nails instead of money to the baker's shop or the ale-house'.[61] Smith, by his own admission, had not experienced the transaction first hand and presumably his witness had also been an outsider. Both men, clouded by their assumptions of primitivity in the highlands, assumed a bar-ter economy. While in a confined rural community barter is not impossible, it is more probable that these nails had been given to the illiterate workmen as a token of their delayed wages (rather than instead of them) which could be offered to select local shopkeepers who would later exchange them with the employer for actual coin.[62] It seems unlikely that nails would have been an effective token in larger urban areas, being anonymous objects that could originate from any worksite or none, but in a close-knit community where innkeepers presumably knew to whom the nails belonged, they were as ef-fective as a legal bill of exchange. They thus functioned similarly to the shop tokens produced by various traders across the period which, despite being technically only redeemable at the venue of production, circulated through confined communities as genuine small coins.[63] In 1759, a correspondent to the *Public Advertiser* detailed the circumstances by which the highland system appears to have been replicated in London. This writer observed how 'Pay tables' for 'any considerable building' project

> are always kept at some alehouse, the Landlord of which makes Interest with the Master of the Workmen to pay them at his House, for which Favour he sometimes advances the Money to the Master to pay his Men or else procures him Silver for that Purpose, … the Landlord officiating as clerk … each Man's score is first cleared along with other Stoppages, and the Journeyman receive the pitiful Balance of a Week's Wages.[64]

Furthermore, mariners or their wives regularly sold or offered credit on wage tickets long before their actual pay might be incoming and, while in this case it related to a specified sum backed by state institutions, this practice was not unrelated to trade on nails in confined communities where neighbours were aware of whom one worked for and how much they earned.[65]

Physical representations of credit, exchangeable with a third party, were, however, a method of avoiding the problems of enforcement rather than deal-ing with non-payment when it occurred. Furthermore, there was no guar-antee that by reckoning one could cancel debts in full or that third parties would still be solvent when debts needed to be exchanged. Ultimately all debts, whether formally secured or informally agreed, required a legal mech-anism to enforce their payment for the good of the individual creditor and, so Smith argued, for commercial society as a whole: 'when the law does not en-force the performance of contracts, it puts all borrowers nearly upon the same footing with bankrupts or people of doubtful credit'.[66] More recent scholars have highlighted the central importance of institutions in supporting market growth during the eighteenth century which led to the accumulation of so much debt, including development associated with the Industrial Revolution.

Though, unlike in accounts focussed upon new protections for private property, in informal contract enforcement, most of the institutions were already present before this period and outlasted it despite undergoing relatively little change.[67] Complaints from individuals such as James Stephen that 'justice should restrain and curb such violence, and not pave the way' suggests that state institutions were more than happy to provide assistance to even the cruellest of creditors.[68] William Hutton, who in his role as commissioner of Birmingham's Court of Requests regularly settled debt disputes, reflected the presiding sentiment of the legal system when he wrote that, as 'there is no trading without credit', then 'consequently every assistance should be given to the creditor' by the law.[69]

The most obvious legal remedy was the ability of creditors to proceed against those who owed them debts or had committed breach of promise at common law. However, use of common law, while regular, was in the eighteenth century far from a simple method of fiscal recovery. Proceedings could be expensive, and while costs might be awarded against the debtor this was only possible if the creditor actually won, and payment relied upon a debtor who had already failed to pay before their debt was increased to include costs (and the costs of their own defence).[70] Furthermore, until a court actually sat (a delay which could last months) debtors, feeling aggrieved by being pursued against, were largely free to defer payment – potentially waiting until the moment of the trial to offer anything to their creditors. Proceedings were further delayed as claimants were required to pursue individual cases against a single debtor, with collective judgement not permitted. Even if a claimant was successful, courts were limited to making awards of execution against the debtor's person or their 'goods and chattels'. By the eighteenth century this excluded many of the most valuable possessions (particularly for those involved in higher finance) such as shares, stock, bank notes, bonds, and copyhold land as value lay in their concept rather than their physical state. The system was therefore less than popular when it came to speedy settlement of debts where the debtor was disinclined to be helpful.[71] Even in the seventeenth century, the overwhelming majority of cases brought to court involved a written mechanism of obligation suggesting more complex deals of substantial size for which common law was an effective solution.[72] This did not mean the courts did not serve a purpose. When dealing with deals involving sums in the hundreds or thousands of pounds, or where there was a dispute over the existence or validity of a debt claim, the courts were the most effective means of legally untangling disputes.[73] However, in dealing with the majority of commercial debt – sums under £100 owed to those who needed a guarantee of payment having already been rebuffed by recalcitrant customers – common law proved slow, bureaucratic, and insufficient.

A number of accounts have highlighted bankruptcy, with its recognition of insolvency and distribution of the estate among creditors, as a swifter collective method of debt recovery.[74] Bankruptcy was a regular process in the period and the statute, which dated back to 1542, steadily became less taboo in the eighteenth century for those who went 'broke'.[75] However, comparisons between it and modern bankruptcy are unwarranted, the early modern statute being profoundly limited and rooted in the motivations of its sixteenth-century authors to protect the rights of land and property, representing a bastardisation of its continental inspiration.[76] At its heart, the prerequisites to open a commission of bankruptcy remained broadly unchanged until the early nineteenth century and though there were some modifications in the early eighteenth century these might be described as largely procedural from the perspective of creditors.[77] The reform c.1705 principally focussed on dealing with punishing fraudulent bankrupts, though it did introduce the process by which an insolvent's remaining obligations were cleared after the distribution of their estate, previously creditors being able to continue pursuing the remainder of their debt after receiving their portion.[78] Furthermore, it instituted a requirement that potential bankrupts owe at least £100 to a single creditor, regardless of the total amount they owed, though other creditors were eligible to benefit if their demands were smaller. The process could only be initiated by creditors and then at least four-fifths of the total number had to be in agreement. This represented a significant threat to the efficacy of bankruptcy. As one 1732 pamphleteer explained:

> If two Creditors of Twenty Pounds each, were to oppose ... against Seven ... to whom he owed as many Thousand Pounds each, he could not obtain his Discharge for Want of Four Fifths in Number; or if Four Creditors, to whom he was indebted One Thousand Pounds each, were inclined to Lenity, yet was another single Creditor, whose Demands should be but One Penny above One Thousand Pounds, to withstand the Rest, his Case would be the same, for Want of Four Fifths in Value ... nor was he obliged to give any Reason for so acting, being accountable to none but God for any unreasonable Severities towards the Bankrupt.[79]

If a commission of bankruptcy was thus opposed, failed at any stage of determination, or was dismissed by the whims of the Lord Chancellor, it could not proceed even if the debtor was in favour.[80]

Even more detrimental to bankruptcy's efficacy for creditors was that its use was arbitrarily restricted to debtors who were classified under the sixteenth-century statute as 'traders'. This qualifying term was rather loosely originally defined as 'any Merchant or other Person, using or exercising the Trade of Merchandise by way of Bargaining, Exchange, Rechange, Bartry, Chevisance, or otherwise, in Gross or by Retail, or seeking his or her Trade of Living by Buying and Selling'.[81] Due to this imprecision, courts adopted a simple four-part test to determine qualification for bankruptcy:

1   The individual in question had to be engaged in *both* buying and selling.
2   Purchases had to be personal chattels – i.e. those selling land, insurance, stock, etc., did not qualify.

3   Their occupation needed to be a 'general way of merchandise' –
    disqualifying those who sold exclusively to a specific clientele, such as
    military suppliers.
4   Trading had to be the primary source of the debtor's occupation –
    William Blackstone explaining: 'One single act of buying and selling
    will not make a man a trader; but a repeated practice, and profit by it'.[82]

The resulting ambiguity meant a number of small traders were eligible for
bankruptcy, while many others – despite dealing with significant lines of
credit, being subject to intense risk, and frequently becoming indebted –
were excluded.[83]

The requirement to be both buying and selling immediately disqualified
the majority of the population from servants and husbandmen to lawyers and
admirals as they 'are paid for their work and labour' rather than deriving income from trade.[84] This does not mean that the law was devoid of logic and
restricted only to those who explicitly styled themselves "merchant". From
1592, shoemakers, originally excluded as their primary focus was manual
work, were declared eligible for bankruptcy as buyers and sellers of different
leather goods.[85] Many other crafts subsequently became eligible. However,
the law remained preposterously specific about what did and did not qualify as it tried to distinguish merchants from 'servants'. Thomas Goodringe's
eighteenth-century guide to bankruptcy makes clear how narrowly the statute was applied as those doing relatively similar work were treated as entirely
alien under the law. In the case of those making clothing for clients, eligibil-
ity depended on whether the debtor had bought the cloth or been given it by
the client: 'A Clothier that buys the Wool, and hath it made up into Cloth,
may be a Bankrupt … A Taylor that makes Garments only, and as Servant to
his Customers shall not be a Bankrupt'. How land was used was another difficult issue: 'A Grazier or Drover may be a Bankrupt … if he hireth Grounds,
and feeds the Cattle … but not if he graze upon his own Freehold'. The legal
logic held that if one owned the land then the adult cow was grown out of it
while the renter bought grass and turned it into beef just as the cordwainer
bought leather and turned it into shoes. While there is a beauty to this legal
thinking (ultimately defending the interests of landed property), that according to Goodringe innkeepers and victuallers, a group which had a great need
for bankruptcy, were not normally eligible as they were not involved in general merchandise can only have been a frustration. As Goodringe explained:

> For though [the victualler] buy Provisions to be spent in his House, yet
> he doth not properly sell it, but utters it at such Rates as he thinks rea-
> sonable Gains … the Guests do not contract or take it at a certain Price,
> but they may have it, or refuse it.[86]

All of these distinctions were perfectly logical at the pen of a legal theorist
but, as a practical means of enforcing debt contracts, bankruptcy was restric-
tive, arbitrary, and ineffective.[87]

Separately, bankruptcy was an extreme measure. As a means of dividing the estate of a failed business (where that business fit the prerequisites) it could be relatively effective. Though creditors were unlikely to recover all of their money they usually received a reasonable proportion on their debt from the sale of the bankrupt's property. Nor was participation limited to high-value creditors such as investors or business partners as creditors who were owed rent or had unpaid bills from common goods could also receive recompense. However, this effectiveness made bankruptcy insufficient for the purpose of enforcing everyday contracts. Unlike in continental Europe where commissions of bankruptcy were often a stage of negotiation at the end of which the debt might be extended, in England, once the Lord Chancellor agreed to open proceedings, they could end only in one way – division of the estate of the bankrupt.[88] Most issues of non-repayment occurred when the debt was lower than the value of the debtor's estate which, fundamentally, was the *opposite* situation for which bankruptcy provided. As such, bankruptcy was the equivalent of demolishing a wall rather than opening a window to let in a breeze. Technically the desired outcome (creditors recovering what they were owed) had been achieved but this had come at a significant cost. Nor was this merely a problem for the broken debtor. Creditors who were deemed overly severe, such as by bankrupting a solvent debtor, risked losing customers; consequently, traders boasted of how compassionately they treated their debtors.[89] In most cases, the debtor needed to be cajoled into paying rather than wiped out. Bankruptcy was simply incompatible with the world of informal sales credit.

This incompatibility stretched beyond its efficacy, for its operational theory and target of recompense were not in line with the credit which it attempted to remedy. While the division of a debtor's estate was a practical method of reimbursing creditors, the credit to which commerce related, as previously stated, was rooted not in wealth or possessions but in individual personality. Under these specific circumstances, the seizure of the debtor's person was the most logical response to debt as it pursued the collateral upon which bargains were staked. Furthermore, prisons in the eighteenth century functioned largely as economic rather than punitive institutions. The principal association with criminal justice was yet to manifest and most felons confined in gaols remained for only short periods, awaiting either trial or punishment. Even at busy London prisons there may have been periods where the number of felons was negligible.[90] This did not mean no criminals were punished with imprisonment, usually for minor offences such as brawling or perjury. Between 1776 and 1781 the percentage of punishments handed out at the Old Bailey in London consisting of imprisonment briefly rose from inconsequential to 40% of all verdicts when the American Revolution interrupted transportation which previously accounted for 43% of sentences per annum.[91] However, even with this shift in practice, debtors constituted the majority of those confined.[92]

It is helpful to perceive of debtors' prisons in this period not as places of punishment as modern prisons are, but as pawnshops dealing in human flesh.[93] If an individual deposits their watch with a pawnbroker and uses the money to buy necessities, they cannot have access to their property until they return the money to the pawnbroker, completing their contract. Similarly, if an individual were to buy a watch on the credit of their personhood, logically, they should not have access to themselves (i.e. their liberty) until they pay the agreed monetary sum that the person is standing in for, the creditor requiring a method of holding the bargain's collateral hostage. In either case, there is no dispute about whether the debtor is at fault; all that matters is that they do not have the money to complete the agreed contract. This quasi-Shakespearean analogy is not incompatible with the legal theory of debt imprisonment at the time which held, not that a debtor could not pay, but (irrespective of reality) that they chose not to pay – 'being imprisoned, not for *owing* a sum of money, but till he *pays* it'.[94] Debt imprisonment was, in this model, not about punishing the lack of repayment but about compelling debtors to fulfil the terms of their unwritten contract. It coerced debtors to find a solution to obstacles of repayment by giving them something tangible to lose if they did not, just as if the pawnbroker had sold on their much loved watch.

While the prisons thus had a clearer connection with the process of everyday credit than did the legal mechanisms of common law or bankruptcy, it is clear they were far from a perfect system of financial recovery distinct from court process. The complications of being arrested might be said to be manifest for the individual debtor whose whole life was transformed (and in some cases threatened) by confinement. However, it is also clear that the system of debt imprisonment as it existed in eighteenth-century England was one beset with inefficiency for the individual creditor arising from unnecessary additions to the vast traditions of imprisonment and accepted corruption. A variety of customary practices existed that decreased the functionality if not the efficacy of the system by increasing debtor expenses which, while not strictly elements of the institution and occasionally legally prohibited, were so ingrained it is impossible to imagine eighteenth-century debtors' prisons without them. Nor was custom alone in detracting from debt imprisonment, as well-intentioned legal mechanisms further reduced the simplicity and surety of the institution for creditors who should have been the primary concern of legislators.

The most prominent issue of this type was the proliferation of what were commonly known as sponging houses. Following a bailiff's 'clap on the shoulder', an arrested debtor's first destination was regularly not the prison stated in the writ but, as with John Grano, the house of the bailiff or an accomplice such as a tavern run by his wife, designed to extract, or 'spunge', as much money as possible.[95] Here arrestees were bullied into buying food and drink for the company:

> Your Keeper forthwith calls for a Bottle of Wine, orders a Couple or Half a Dozen of Fowls to be immediately roasted, and other things suitable … a Pint of Brandy is called for, out of which, if any be left, when they are all served round, perhaps one Glass may come to your turn, or otherwise you must call for more, or go without.[96]

Eventually, debtors were carried to a secured room or cage, potentially lacking even straw to sleep upon, and for which an excessive rent was charged.[97] The potential profits were extensive and serjeants, bailiffs, and prison yeoman battled over who possessed the legal rights of arrest – implicitly giving them power over whether, how, and where to sponge.[98] Some debtors, by choice, remained in sponging houses for extended periods while they attempted to procure the aid of friends or call in their own debts; Margaret Coghlan in the 1790s 'was locked up seven weeks' in a sponging house, an unusually long stay in 'which time I employed myself in endeavouring to arrange my affairs'.[99] In this manner some debtors would avoid actual imprisonment, though there were no guarantees of aid arriving while one lost money in rent to the sponger and there were complaints that some bailiffs obstructed communications to lengthen residencies.[100] While debtors were not powerless to insist upon their removal to prison, the fear of gaol conditions – bailiffs telling horror stories of prisons being 'a horrid, terrible and dismal Place, and that you are greatly Befriended by them, in not being immediately carried thither' – frightened some into staying put.[101] A number of pamphlets claimed that conditions in prisons were actually better and the cost of living was certainly cheaper, one account calculating one day's bill as a minimum of 17s 6d in a sponging house compared to 1s 7½d even in the premium ward of Newgate.[102] In many instances, debtors so detained were only brought to the prison once their last farthing had been spent and there was nothing more to be gained by the bailiff.[103] The sponging houses posed an existential threat to the entire institution of debt imprisonment, hampering debtors, creditors, and even prison managers. In the early eighteenth century, the new keeper of the Wood Street Compter in Cheapside complained of eleven sponging houses in the streets surrounding the prison which were sapping his ability to make a living.[104] Though the houses were made illegal during the 1720s they were difficult to supress, and accounts of them appear in debtor discourse across the century.[105] In 1736, the Court of Common Pleas reaffirmed that 'the Warden [of the gaol] do take effectual Care, that every Prisoner … be conveyed to the Prison … without being carried to any publick Victualler or Drinking House', though in 1777, prison reformer John Howard was still advocating for a law declaring that 'no bailiff should be suffered to keep a public house' and the Thatched House Society complained of their impoverishing powers in 1796.[106] Even in the subsequent century, the diarist and sportsman Colonel Hawker, upon being unable to locate his local doctor in 1836, concluded snidely that he was 'most probably again in a sponging house'.[107]

The reason sponging houses represented such an issue was that they served no purpose; being imprisoned included an array of costs for debtors including prison rent though, as is discussed in detail in Chapter 6, these represented a saving for creditors and society at large by reducing administrative costs. A debtor sponged only benefited the already compensated bailiff. At least in the custom of garnish, which also impacted negatively upon creditors, other prisoners received a one-off cash injection. In this practice, the bunkmates of new arrivals to cells demanded they offer up a certain amount of money, otherwise the clothing they stood in was 'stript off his back' and sold for the use of the assembled.[108] Usually this enabled purchases of alcohol to toast the new arrival through raucous drinking, one poet describing: 'Garnish, was their general Cry, To which [he] did with them comply, And in their Cups, their Creditors defy'.[109] Some debtors were happy to comply, grateful for the company and sociability; Grano upon his arrival at the Marshalsea in 1728 having been admitted to 'a Room habited by the best People' was more than willing to purchase a 'tallBoy of Drink' and 'sate up till about 11' drinking.[110] On occasion, garnish money was put to more practical use such as paying for coal or other group necessaries, though this depended again upon customs within the particular prison and occasionally between particular cells.[111] Except in instances where gaolers meddled with or pilfered garnish money, it was a relatively harmless practice when compared with the sponging houses particularly as it reduced expenses for other prisoners.[112] It did, however, remain an issue for creditors, hampering repayment, even if extortion by prisoners was less expensive than by bailiffs.

Beyond these extrajudicial customs, certain legal facets reduced the effectiveness of imprisonment by undermining its coercive strength. One of the system's most significant potential weaknesses was also rooted in one of its greatest strengths for creditors. The majority of prisoners were confined on *mesne* process meaning that they were imprisoned on a pre-trial basis, usually (though not exclusively) through a writ of *capias ad respondendum* (an arrest to respond). In theory the purpose of this writ was to secure the 'body of the defendant ... so that [the plaintiff] may have him in court on the day of the return, to answer to the plaintiff of a plea of debt or trespass' and 'after the defendant hath appeared, the effect of these writs is taken off', the prisoner being released. Such writs were relatively easy and cheap to obtain. Creditors, upon applying to the court for an arrest swore to the indebtedness of the individual, usually stating how much was owed and how the debt had arisen. However, the importance of accuracy was relatively superficial, witnesses and evidence not being required at this stage. The most important barrier seems to have been the paying of a shilling to the court, though costs might rise if an arrestee were found to be outside of the jurisdiction or in another county. Following trial at common law, a creditor, instead of proceeding against the debtor's estate, could place their person into execution through a separate writ of *capias ad satisfaciendum*, returning them to prison 'to make the plaintiff satisfaction to his demand; otherwise ... to remain ... till he does'. Plaintiffs or any other creditors were prevented from commencing 'new executions against lands, goods, and chattels' while a debtor was confined, though these could be resumed against heirs if they died.[113] However, only a minority of debtors were imprisoned in execution and the issuing of writs of *satisfaciendum* appears to have been rare as most creditors had little interest in proceeding to trial. At Lancaster Castle Gaol, the commitment registers of which unusually record whether debtors were brought to trial, 83% of the 828 prisoners appear

to have not seen the inside of a court room (1793–1796). Only eighty-nine
debtors were re-confined in execution following a trial in court, while a further forty-eight were committed, tried, and released 'for want of execution',
the creditor proceeding against their estate. Additionally, Joseph Holmes in
1796 appears to have been found not liable for his debts of £74 at trial and
released 'for want of judgement'.[114] *Mesne* process was essentially a legal fiction for creditors seeking to confine debtors as, rather than the first stage of
recovery, in most cases pre-trial arrest was the entirety of the process, creditors having little motivation to abandon their power of unlimited detention
by proceeding to trial.[115]

Creditors had every reason to be unreasonable with debtors who were
responsible for their own upkeep within the prison including rent, bedding,
and provisions while they were held on *mesne* process though the law disrupted the totality of creditor power. As technically the nature of the writ
indicated that the debtor was merely being held to guarantee their appearance in court, there were mechanisms by which debtors could subvert and
undermine the obvious coercive power of permanent confinement involved
with *mesne* process.[116] Writs of *supersedeas* could stop the legal process of arrest
writs and discharge the prisoner if the creditor was shown to have failed to
bring the defendant to trial within sufficient time. As *An Attorney's Practice*
(1743) explained, 'If any Person be committed … in Hillary Term or Vaca-
tion, unless the Plaintiff bring such Prisoner to the Bar … and declare against
him within six Days after Trinity Term begun, such Prisoner may be discharged by *Supersedeas*'.[117] For example, a prisoner committed between 23rd
January and 22nd April 1806 would need to be brought to trial by 12th June
of that year or they would be eligible for release without having to pay their
debts.[118] As the process of the human pawnshop relied on indefinite coercion
any such mechanism undermined the institution's ability to enforce contracts
and support market functionality.

Fortunately, the practical application of such writs was more complicated
than their theory. Debtors were required to prepare and apply for *supersedeas* discharge themselves. As a Parliamentary Committee investigating
imprisonment for debt learned in 1792, the process included acquiring the
'Certificate of the Causes [a prisoner] is charged with, with an Affidavit (if
he is in a County Gaol) of the Gaoler's having signed such Certificate; he
must then take out a Summons from a Judge, for the Plaintiff to shew Cause
why a Writ of *Supersedeas* should not issue to discharge the Defendant; that
Summons he must serve on the Plaintiff's Attorney, and if the Plaintiff's
Attorney do not attend the Judge, Affidavit must be made of such Service,
and of the Attendance of the Defendant's Attorney, upon which the Judge
will grant an Order for the Defendant's Discharge'.[119] The costs of this
extended process were substantial; a 1715 satirical dictionary of law terms
translated *supersedeas* simply as 'Fresh Fees'.[120] Similarly, in 1736 the author
of *Law Quibbles* complained that, of statutes to prevent delays in trials, 'none
of them … are Effectual' and attorneys hired to procure *supersedeas*, though

they found 'Clients in the Possession of Estates, [they] seldom leave them otherwise than' with their fortune spent.[121] Legal costs affected plaintiffs as well; "John Bull" in Arbuthnot's *Law is a Bottomless Pit* (1712) discovered that in his suing he had 'paid for every Syllable and letter' of the writs and actions taken out by his attorney, 'bless me, what immense Sums'.[122] Undoubtedly though costs fell harder on the prisoner as 'the Plaintiff, who can go and come where he pleases' could therefore 'save the Charge of his Attorney or Council's Attendance on him'.[123] Furthermore, prison fees and rents were not excused by the writ and some institutions charged debtors a higher release fee if they were discharged through *supersedeas* rather than by their creditor, even though the prison itself bore no extra costs.[124] The 1792 committee made clear that 'if the Defendant is unable to defray the Expence of such Proceedings, he must remain in Prison, though legally entitled to his Discharge'.[125] For the majority of prisoners without the capital to procure *supersedeas*, and even for those with sufficient capital, it was cheaper, easier, and simpler to focus on paying debts rather than avoiding them.

Supersedeas writs were not impossible to acquire. Towards the end of the century, debtors could petition the charitable Thatched House Society to 'on a state of his case, procure his *supersedeas* for him, free of any charge'. However, they only accepted claims from 'small' debtors (those owing under £5) and the society was predominantly focussed on paying the costs and debts of said small debtors rather than dismissing suits.[126] Only four Lancaster prisoners were explicitly removed by *supersedeas*, though a further sixty-four were released due to 'want of declaration' (8%), indicating its probable use due to a lack of trial. At London's Fleet Prison, release explicitly through *supersedeas* of its wealthier prisoners was more regular though still accounted for only 12% of those released (1733–1795). Furthermore, it is not possible from prison registers to distinguish between writs of *supersedeas*, which released prisoners due to a lack of trial commencing, and those which released prisoners under other circumstances. *Supersedeas* was a general writ of stopping confinement and, as certain legal guides suggest, was in some instances the formal writ for releasing a prisoner after they had 'procured good Bail'.[127] In the records of the Fleet, four of those released by *supersedeas* were explicitly done so 'on a writ of *supersedeas* on Bail being paid', in one case the bail money being paid by a benefactor. In another case, following the issuing of a Commission of Bankruptcy, *supersedeas* was used by the court to end the confinement while after one debtor escaped, the writ was entered to clear him from the prison's records.[128]

The problems associated with procuring the right of *supersedeas* release were also faced by prisoners entitled to an allowance known as the groats. Following the statute commonly called the Lord's Act of 1758, debtors could offer up their estate to 'make satisfaction to the creditor or creditors ... in like manner as assignees of commissioners of bankrupts' in return for their release. The creditor was able to block the release though they were thereupon required to pay debtors a groat a day (4d) in upkeep, though if there were more than one of them the sum was distributed among them.[129] Failure to keep up with the payments for six weeks would lead to a prisoner's release and the clearing of the debt.[130] In 1792, one creditor learned that even adhering to payment was not sufficient if it was regarded as irregular when he was sued in King's Bench for paying the groats frequently after the prisoners had been locked up for the night, his debtor not receiving them until the next day for which the justices released him.[131] The futility of this exercise on the part of creditors was a topic both of disgust but also of amusement, one collection of witticisms suggesting creditors should release debtors but continue to pay them 'eighteen-pence a week' while 'the other ten-pence shall go towards the discharge of the debt'.[132]

However, as with *supersedeas*, release under these terms had to be procured by the debtor whose entire wealth had just been handed over; the expense for suing for groats in the first place, let alone release, regularly cost at least between 'two and three guineas'.[133] At Lancaster, just seven were released after non-payment of groats though at least thirteen other prisoners were awarded them at some stage, the register not recording whether they were properly paid.[134] Howard claimed this 'mode of obtaining redress ... is attended with difficulty', reporting that according to the keeper of Carlisle gaol, during his fourteen year tenure, 'no more than four or five had received' groats and that 'not one debtor had the ailment in York Castle, Devon, Cheshire, Kent, and many other counties'.[135] The 1792 House of Commons committee, having concluded that groats covered less than half a debtor's probable weekly expenses, were informed that at the Fleet just eighteen of the over two hundred prisons received groats, at the Giltspur Street Compter there were eight, and at Ludgate just six.[136] Fourpence a day was regularly seen as not even necessarily being worth suing for; Quaker societies provided members with four shillings a week before groats were awarded and subsequently continued to supply 2s 6d a week in addition 'until he has his liberty'.[137] Like *supersedeas*, groats were an occasional hinderance to creditors and while their existence did undermine the totality of coercive power they never threatened the institution as a whole.

★★

In eighteenth-century England's commercial world, uncertainty was a matter of course and external displays of confidence essential to the ability to transact. If one could not declare "trust me" to a business acquaintance and they satisfy you with goods based on no more evidence or persuasion, then one's ability to survive economically, let alone profit, was dubious at best. It was also a system which resisted formality and balked at progress in which the precarious ability to enforce trust in others represented a perpetual fiscal sword of Damocles. Debt imprisonment was far from a theoretically perfect system of recovery (whether it worked in practice is a matter for subsequent chapters) as it allowed numerous mechanisms to persist by which debtor capital was spent unprofitably or potentially allowed their release without any satisfaction to creditors. However, unlike bankruptcy, its faults did not reside in the underlying institutional theory by limiting access only to the creditors of trader debtors. Furthermore, regardless of these differing defects, the prisons as tools of contract enforcement were rooted in the reality of daily commerce in a fashion that bankruptcy (responding to failures in large enterprise) could not. In large part their issues lay in that they were not an institution designed to tackle a wider economic problem, but an older system re-interpreted through use to mitigate financial challenges. However, this was also their strength as it allowed debtors' prisons to function as society needed them to rather than being rigid and immoveable. This imperfect (or lack of) design allowed further deficiencies such as *supersedeas* to flourish, but simultaneously undermined *supersedeas* by failing to ensure it provided realistic redress for debtors.

The prisons, despite being a medieval innovation, were a product of their economic reality enabling commercial activity based upon fast moving, informal, reputation-based credit by offering creditors like Pierce & Tait a chance to place debtors like Grano in between them and the descending sword of insolvency. Daniel Defoe, who had experienced debt imprisonment first-hand in 1692, was well attuned to this situation as with many other aspects of the debt economy. In 1729, defending the rights of creditors and the commercial world they fed, he concluded:

> What is the Reason why in Scotland, and in other Countries, they have so little Trade? Tis because you cannot enforce your Demand of Debt, you can't send the Debtor to Prison; and therefore no Man buys till he has Money to pay.[138]

In an economy where few had easy access to money regardless of wealth, such circumstances were fatal to growth.

Notes

1 John Grano (John Ginger ed.), *Handel's Trumpeter – The Diary of John Grano* (Stuyvesant: Pendragon Press, 1998), p. 27.
2 Peirce and Tait, "Bad and Doubtful Debt Book 1763–1793", [1793?], Businesses: Small Collections, LMA, CLC/B/227/MS31573; Anon. *The London Directory for the Year 1792* (London: 1792), p. 113.
3 Daniel Defoe, *The Complete English Tradesman in Familiar Letters* (London: 1726), pp. 408–423.
4 Paula R. Backscheider, "Defoe's Lady Credit", *Huntingdon Library Quarterly* vol. 44, no. 2 (1981), pp. 89–100; Marieke de Gooede, "Mastering 'Lady Credit'", *International Feminist Journal of Politics* vol. 2, no. 1 (2000), pp. 58–81; Natasha Glaisyer, "A Due Circulation in the Veins of the Publick: Imagining Credit in Late Seventeenth- and Early Eighteenth-Century England", *The Eighteenth Century* vol. 46, no. 3 (2005), pp. 277–297.

5 Arthur Nevil, *Some Hints on Trade, Money, and Credit* (London: 1762), pp. 9–12; William Gordon, *The Universal Accountant and Complete Merchant Vol. II* (1796), p. 7; Anon. *The Case of the Creditors of Joseph George Pedley, A Bankrupt of Bristol, and Now a Prisoner in that City … With Cursory Thoughts on Credit, and the Conduct of Bankers* (Bristol: 1783), pp. 1, 6.

6 William Wright, *The Complete Tradesman: Or, a Guide in the Several Parts and Progressions of Trade* (London: 1789), pp. 84–86; Anon. *The Monthly Mirror Vol. 81 – July to December 1789* (London: 1789), pp. 374–375.

7 Craig Muldrew, *The Economy of Obligation – The Culture of Credit and Social Relations in Early Modern England* (Basingstoke: Macmillan, 1998), p. 114; Julian Hoppit, "Financial Crises in Eighteenth-Century England", *Economic History Review* vol. 39, no. 1 (February 1986), p. 43; Lorna Ewen, "Debtors, Imprisonment and the Privilege of Girth", in *Perspectives in Scottish Social History*, ed. Leah Leneman (Aberdeen: Aberdeen University Press, 1988), pp. 55–57; Judith M. Spicksley, "'Fly with a Duck in Thy Mouth': Single Women as Sources of Credit in Seventeenth-Century England", *Social History* vol. 32, no. 2 (May 2007), pp. 198–200; Peter Temin and Hans-Joachim Voth, *Prometheus Shackled – Goldsmith Banks and England's Financial Revolution after 1700* (Oxford: Oxford University Press, 2013), pp. 15, 73, 93; Anon. *A Common Law Treatise of Usury and Usurious Contracts* (London: 1710); John Cary, *A Discourse on Trade and Other Matters Relative to It* (London: 1745); Anon. *Law Quibbles: Or, a Treatise of the Evasions, Tricks, Turns and Quibbles, Commonly Used in the Profession of the Law to the Prejudice of Clients* (London: 1736), p. 25; Wright, *Complete Tradesman*, p. 14; F. A. Windsor, *Prosperity of England Midst the Clamours of Ruin* (1799).

8 Muldrew, *Economy of Obligation*, pp. 95, 118; Craig Muldrew, "From Credit to Savings? An Examination of Debt and Credit in Relation to Increasing Consumption in England (c.1650 to 1770)", *Quaderni Storci* vol. 137 (August 2011), pp. 402–407.

9 Muldrew, *Economy of Obligation*, p. 96; Chris Briggs, *Credit and Village Society in Fourteenth-Century England* (Oxford: Oxford University Press, 2009); Christopher McNall, "The Business of Statutory Debt Registries, 1283–1307", in *Credit and Debt in Medieval England c.1180–c.1350*, eds. P. R. Schofield and N. J. Mayhew (Oxford: Oxbow Books, 2002), pp. 68–88; Pamela Nightingale, "The Lay Subsidies and the Distribution of Wealth in Medieval England, 1275–1334", *Economic History Review* vol. 57, no. 1 (2004), pp. 1–32.

10 Nicola Phillips, *Women in Business 1700–1850* (Woodbridge: The Boydell Press, 2006), p. 82; David A. Kent, "Small Businessmen and Their Credit Transactions in Early Nineteenth-Century Britain", *Business History* vol. 36, no. 2 (1994), pp. 47–64; Muldrew, *Economy of Obligation*.

11 Craig Muldrew, "'Hard Food for Midas': Cash and Its Social Value in Early Modern England", *Past and Present* no. 170 (2001), pp. 78–120; see: Walter Merrey, *Remarks on the Coinage of England from the Earliest Times to the Present Times, with a View to Point Out the Causes of the Present Scarcity of Silver* (Nottingham: 1789).

12 Muldrew, *Economy of Obligation*, pp. 3, 98, 101; See: David Graeber, *Debt – The First 5000 Years* (Brooklyn: Melville House, 2011), pp. 308–327; Bruce G. Carruthers, "The Sociology of Money and Credit", in *The Handbook of Economic Sociology – Second Edition*, eds. Neil J. Smelser and Richard Swedberg (Princeton: Princeton University Press, 2005), p. 362.

13 Aaron Graham, "Credit, Confidence, and the Circulation of Exchequer Bills in the Early Financial Revolution", *Financial History Review* vol. 26, no. 1 (2019), pp. 63–80.

14 Rev. Price, *Funds. A Just and Impartial View of the Funds of England … First Printed in the American War: 1776* (London: 1795), p. 9.

15 Defoe, *Complete English Tradesman*, pp. 410–414.

16 Julian Hoppit, "The Use and Abuse of Credit in Eighteenth-Century England", in *Business Life and Public Policy – Essays in Honour of D.C. Coleman*, eds. Neil McKendrick and R. B. Outhwaite (Cambridge: Cambridge University Press, 1986), p. 66.

17 Judy Z. Stephenson, "Real Wages? Contractors, Workers, and Pay in London Building Trades, 1650–1800", *Economic History Review* vol. 71, no. 1 (2018), p. 116; Temin and Voth, *Prometheus Shackled*, p. 15; Muldrew, "Credit to Savings?", p. 407.

18 Julian Hoppit, "Attitudes to Credit in Britain, 1680–1790", *The Historical Journal* vol. 33, no. 2 (June 1990), p. 313; T. S. Ashton, *An Economic History of England – The Eighteenth Century* (London: Methuen, 1955), p. 207.

19 Muldrew, *Economy of Obligation*, p. 118; Defoe, *Complete English Tradesman*, p. 412.

20 Jacob Vanderlint, *Money Answers All Things: Or, an Essay to Make Money Sufficiently Plentiful Amongst All Ranks of People* (London: 1734), p. 66.

21 Defoe, *Complete English Tradesman*, pp. 410, 413. On Consumer Revolution see: Neil McKendrick, John Brewer, and J. H. Plumb, *The Birth of a Consumer Society – The Commercialization of Eighteenth-Century England* (Bloomington: Indiana University Press, 1982); Natasha Glaisyer, *The Culture of Commerce in England 1660–1720* (Woodbridge: Boydell Press, 2006); Lorna Weatherill, "The Meaning of Consumer Behaviour in Late Seventeenth- and Early Eighteenth-Century England", in *Consumption and the World of Goods*, eds. John Brewer and Roy Porter (London: Routledge, 1993), pp. 206–227; T. H. Breen, "The Meaning of Things: Interpreting the Consumer Economy in the Eighteenth Century", in *Consumption and the World of Goods*, eds. John Brewer and Roy Porter (London: Routledge, 1993), pp. 249–260.

22 Anon. *The Credit and Interest of Great Britain Considered, or the Way to Live above Want* (London: 1735).

23 Isaac Gervaise, *The System or Theory of the Trade of the World* (London: 1720); J. M. Letiche, "Isaac Gervaise on the International Mechanism of Adjustment", *Journal of Political Economy* vol. 60, no. 1 (1952), pp. 35–36.

24 Defoe, *Complete English Tradesman*, pp. 412–413.

25 Kent, "Small Businessmen", p. 58. Muldrew, *Economy of Obligation*, p. 3.

26 Craig Muldrew, "Class and Credit: Social Identity, Wealth and the Life Course in Early Modern England", in *Identity and Agency in England, 1500–1800*, eds. Henry French and Jonathan Barry (Basingstoke: Palgrave Macmillan, 2004), p. 148.

27 Muldrew, *Economy of Obligation*, p. 156.

28 Muldrew, "Hard Food for Midas", p. 83; Tawny Paul, "Credit, Reputation, and Masculinity in British Urban Commerce: Edinburgh, c.1710–70", *Economic History Review* vol. 66, no. 1 (2013), pp. 226–248; Glaisyer, *Culture of Commerce*, pp. 21, 37–38; Natasha Glaisyer, "Calculating Credibility: Print Culture, Trust and Economic Figures in Early Eighteenth-Century England", *The Economic History Review*, New Series, vol. 60, no. 4 (November 2007), p. 686; Julia Rudolph, *Common Law and Enlightenment in England 1689–1750* (Woodbridge: Boydell Press, 2013), pp. 137–140; Alexandra Shepard, *Accounting for Oneself: Worth, Status, and the Social Order in Early Modern England* (Oxford: Oxford University Press, 2015), p. 279; Graeber, *Debt*, p. 328.

29 Lamar M. Hill, "'Extreame Detriment': Failed Credit and the Narration of Indebtedness in the Jacobean Court of Requests", in *Law and Authority in Early Modern England – Essays Presented to Thomas Garden Barnes*, eds. Buchanan Sharp and Mark Charles Fissel (Newark: University of Delaware Press, 2007), p. 137.

30 Alexandra Shepard, "Minding Their Own Business: Married Women and Credit in Early Eighteenth-Century London", *Transactions of the Royal Historical Society* vol. 25 (2015), p. 65.

31 McKendrick, Brewer, and Plumb, *Consumer Society*, p. 2.
32 Anon. *The Life of the Famous William Stroud, Who Was Convicted at the Last Quarter Sessions for the City and Liberty of Westminster, as a Rogue and a Vagabond* (London: 1752); William Stroud, *The Genuine Memoirs of the Life and Transactions of William Stroud* (London: 1752).
33 Anon. *An Honest Scheme for Improving the Trade and Credit of the Nation* (London: 1729), pp. 3–4.
34 Muldrew, *Economy of Obligation*, p. 96.
35 "Thomas Price", Debtors Schedules: Wood Street Compter & Borough Compter, 1761, LMA, CLA/047/LJ/17/045.
36 K. H. Burley, "An Essex Clothier of the Eighteenth Century", *The Economic History Review* vol. 11, no. 2 (1958), p. 299; James Muir, *Law, Debt, and Merchant Power – The Civil Courts of Eighteenth-Century Halifax* (Toronto: University of Toronto Press, 2016), p. 194; Patricia Wyllie, "Reassessing the English Financial Revolution: Credit Transferability in Probate Records of Sedbergh and Maidstone, 1610–1790", in *Faith, Place, and People in Early Modern England – Essays in Honour of Margaret Spufford*, eds. Trevor Dean, Glyn Parry, and Edward Vallance (Woodbridge: Boydell Press, 2018), p. 139.
37 Wright, *Complete Tradesman*, pp. 89–95; Muldrew, *Economy of Obligation*, pp. 111–114; Larry Neal and Stephen Quinn, "Networks of Information, Markets, and Institutions in the Rise of London as a Financial Centre, 1660–1720", *Financial History Review* vol. 8 (2001), p. 9; Mina Ishizu, "Boom and Crisis in Financing the British Transatlantic Trade – A Case Study of the Bankruptcy of John Leigh & Company in 1811", in *The History of Bankruptcy – Economic, Social, and Cultural Implications in Early Modern Europe*, ed. Thomas Max Safley (London: Routledge, 2013), pp. 146, 153; L. Anderson, "Money and the Structure of Credit in the Eighteenth Century", *Business History* vol. 12, no. 2 (1970), p. 96; Julian Hoppit, "Attitudes to Credit in Britain, 1680–1790", *The Historical Journal* vol. 33, no. 2 (1990), p. 307; Temin and Voth, *Prometheus Shackled*, p. 15; Amanda Bailey, *Of Bondage – Debt, Property, and Personhood in Early Modern England* (Philadelphia: University of Pennsylvania Press, 2012), pp. 5–7.
38 Julian Hoppit, *Risk and Failure in English Business 1700–1800* (Cambridge: Cambridge University Press, 1987), p. 133; Ellen Hartigan-O'Connor, *The Ties that Buy – Women and Commerce in Revolutionary America* (Philadelphia: University of Pennsylvania Press, 2009), p. 83.
39 Joseph Harris, *An Essay upon Money and Coins Part 1* (1757), p. 120.
40 William Hutton, *Courts of Requests: Their Nature, Utility, and Powers Described, with A Variety of Cases, Determined in that of Birmingham* (Birmingham: 1787), pp. 80–81.
41 "William Acton", Debtors Schedules: Fleet Prison, 1755, LMA, CLA/047/LJ/17/096.
42 Muldrew, *Economy of Obligation*, p. 195.
43 See: Margot C. Finn, *The Character of Credit – Personal Debt in English Culture, 1740–1914* (Cambridge: Cambridge University Press, 2003).
44 William Fleetwood, *The Justice of Paying Debts. A Sermon Preach'd in the City* (London: 1718), pp. 1–12. Much of Fleetwood's text appears in William Scott, *A Sermon on Bankruptcy, Stopping Payment, and the Justice of Paying Our Debts* (London: 1773). On 'justice' and debt, see: Richard Allestree, *The Whole Duty of Man, Laid Down in a Plain and Familiar Way for the Use of All, But Especially the Meanest Reader* (London: 1704), p. 243; Anon. *The Performance of Fair and Legal Contracts, the Surest Method to support Publick and Private Credit* (1721), p. 1; Thomas Secker, *Sermons on Several Subjects, by Thomas Secker, LL.D. Late Lord Archbishop of Canterbury Vol. III* (London: 1770), p. 274; Mathew Wheelock, *Reflections Moral and Political on Great Britain and Her Colonies* (London: 1770), p. 9; Robert Nelson, *The Whole Duty of a Christian, by Way of Question and Answer* (London: 1774), p. 58.

45 Corinthians: 'Let him that thinketh he standeth, take heed lest he fall'. George Whitmore, *The Duty of Not Running in Debt* (London: 1800); Wright, *Complete Tradesman*, p. 43.

46 Richard Brathwaite, *Barnaby's Journal, under the Names of Mirtilus and Faustulus Shadowed* (London: 1774), p. 9; Charles Caraccioli, *Chiron: Or, the Mental Optician Vol. II* (London: 1758), p. 71; Wright, *Complete Tradesman*, p. 13.

47 Wright, *Complete Tradesman*, p. 18.

48 "Joseph Spier", Debtors Schedules: Wood Street Compter, 1769–1770, LMA, CLA/047/LJ/17/058.

49 "List of Prisoners Handed over by the Sheriffs to Their Successors on 28 Sept Annually, with Notes of Occurrences during the Subsequent Year", 1768–1769, Wood Street Compter later Giltspur Street Compter, LMA, CLA/028/01/014.

50 A. Grant, *The Progress and Practice of a Modern Attorney* (London: 1795), p. 9; Anon. *The Christian's Gazette* (London: 1715), p. 27; James Burges, *Consideration on the Laws of Insolvency* (London: 1783), p. 15; Daniel Defoe, *Some Objections Humbly Offered to the Consideration of the Hon House of Commons, Relating to the Present Intended Relief of Prisoners* (London: 1729); John Adams, *A Sermon Preach'd at the Cathedral-Church of St Paul, before the Right Honourable Sir Samuel Garrard, Bar. Lord Mayor of the City of London, and the Court of Aldermen. On Tuesday, November 22 1709. Being the Day Appointed by Her Majesty's Royal Proclamation, for a Publick Thanksgiving* (London: 1709), p. 8; Arthur Ashley Sykes, *The Scripture Doctrine of the Redemption of Man by Jesus Christ. In Two Parts* (London: 1755), p. 9; Samuel Paterson, *Joineriana: Or the Book of Scraps Vol. I* (London: 1772), pp. 119, 149; Thomas Delamayne, *The Rise and Practice of Imprisonment in Personal Actions Examined* (London: 1772), p. 64. The apparent unfairness of failing to distinguish between honest and fraudulent debtors is echoed by later scholarship, see: Thomas Babington Macaulay, *The History of England from the Accession of James II – Vol. III* (London: J.M. Dent & Sons, 1955), p. 516; Gustav Peebles, "Washing Away the Sins of Debt: The Nineteenth-Century Eradication of the Debtors' Prison", *Comparative Studies in History* vol. 55, no. 3 (2013), pp. 707–708; V. Marksham Lester, *Victorian Insolvency – Bankruptcy, Imprisonment for Debt, and Company Winding-up in Nineteenth-Century England* (Oxford: Clarendon Press), p. 101; Richard Grassby, *The Business Community of Seventeenth-Century England* (Cambridge: Cambridge University Press, 1995), p. 217; Hoppit, "The Use and Abuse", p. 77; Gillian Selley, "Charles Lanyon, Merchant of Penzance: Victim of Cruelty and Corruption in the County Debtors Prison in Exeter", *The Devon Historian* vol. 83 (2014), p. 39; Richard H. Condon, "James Neild, Forgotten Reformer", *Studies in Romanticism* vol. 4, no. 4 (Summer 1964), p. 243.

51 F. A. S. Murray, *Thoughts on Imprisonment for Debt Humbly Addressed to His Majesty* (London: 1788), p. 11.

52 James Stephen, *Considerations on Imprisonment for Debt* (London: 1770), pp. 18–19.

53 Robert Holloway, *A Letter to John Wilkes, Esq; Sheriff of London and Middlesex; In Which the Extortion and Oppression of Sheriffs Officers, with Many Other Alarming Abuses, Are Exemplified and Detected; And a Remedy Proposed* (London: 1771), p. 34.

54 Anon. *The Case of the Creditors*, pp. 7–9.

55 Anon. *William Stroud*; James Bolland, *Memoirs of James Bolland Formerly a Butcher Then Officer to the Sheriff of Surry, Afterwards Officer to the Sheriff of Middlesex, and Lately a Candidate for the Place of City Marshal; Executed at Tyburn, March 18. 1772, for Forgery* (London: 1772), p. 3; Richard King Esq, *The Frauds of London Detected; or, a Warning Piece against the Iniquitous Practices of that Metropolis* (London: 1779); Emily Kadens, "The Last Bankrupt Hanged: Balancing Incentives in the Development of Bankruptcy Law", *Duke Law Journal* vol. 59, no. 7 (April 2010), pp. 1229–1319.

56 Karen A. Macfarlane, "'Does He Know the Danger of an Oath?': Oaths, Religion, Ethnicity and the Advent of the Adversarial Criminal trial in the Eighteenth Century", *Immigrants & Minorities* vol. 31, no. 3 (2013), pp. 317–345.

57 Gideon Yaffe, "Promises, Social Acts, and Reid's First Argument for Moral Liberty", *Journal of the History of Philosophy* vol. 45, no. 2 (April 2007), p. 276; William Holdsworth, *A History of English Laws Vol. VI* (London: Methuen, 1924), pp. 655–656;

> where two men are condemned in debt, and one was taken and died in execution, yet the taking of the other is lawful. So also if a defendant in debt dies in execution, the plaintiff may have a new execution.

Anon. *A Law Grammar: Or, and Introduction to the Theory and Practice of English Jurisprudence* (1791), p. 25.

58 J. R. Wordie, "Deflationary Factors in the Tudor Price Rise", *Past & Present* vol. 154 (1997), p. 33.

59 Jeoffry Wagstaffe, *The Batchelor: Or, Speculations Vol. II* (London: 1769), p. 5; also see Anon. *Modern Honour: A Poem in Two Cantos* (London: 1760), p. 41 and Joseph Dorman, *The Rake of Taste. A Poem* (London: 1735), p. 6.

60 Craig Muldrew, "Interpreting the Market: The Ethics of Credit and Community Relations in Early Modern England", *Social History* vol. 18, no. 2 (1993), p. 173.

61 Adam Smith, *An Inquiry into the Nature and Causes of the Wealth of Nations. Vol. I* (Dublin: 1776), pp. 34–35.

62 Graeber, *Debt*, pp. 21–41; William Baxter, "Observations on Money, Barter, and Bookkeeping", *The Accounting Historians Journal* vol. 31, no. 1 (2004), pp. 129–139; Garry Carnegie, "Re-Examining the Determinants of Barter Accounting in Isolate Communities in Colonial Societies", *Accounting History* vol. 9, no. 3 (2004), pp. 73–87.

63 Harris, *Essay upon Money*, p. 65; Graeber, *Debt*, p. 327; Carruthers, "Sociology of Money", p. 355.

64 *Public Advertiser*, 24th March 1759, no. 7610, p. 2.

65 Thomas Thorisby, *An Humble Proposal for Advancing the Credit of Seamens Wages, and for Preventing Their Fraudulent Selling the Same* (1710); Margaret Hunt, "Women and the Fiscal-Imperial State in Late Seventeenth- and Early Eighteenth-Century London", in *A New Imperial History: Culture, Identity and Modernity in Britain and the Empire, 1660–1840*, ed. Kathleen Wilson (Cambridge: Cambridge University Press, 2004), pp. 29–47; Jennine Hurl-Eamon, "The Fiction of Female Dependence and the Makeshift Economy of Soldiers, Sailors, and Their Wives in Eighteenth-Century London", *Labour History* vol. 49, no. 4 (2008), pp. 481–501.

66 Smith, *Wealth of Nations*, p. 141.

67 Douglass C. North and Barry R. Weingast, "Constitutions and Commitment: The Evolution of Institutions Governing Public Choice in Seventeenth-Century England", *Journal of Economic History* vol. 69, no. 4 (1989), pp. 803–831; Douglass C. North, "Institutions", *Journal of Economic Perspectives* vol. 5, no. 1 (1995), pp. 97–112; Avner Grief and Joel Mokyr, "Institutions and Economic History: A Critique of Professor McCloskey", *Journal of Institutional Economics* vol. 12, no. 1 (2016), pp. 29–41.

68 Stephen, *Considerations*, p. 19.

69 Hutton, *Courts of Requests*, p. 232.

70 Ian P. H. Duffy, *Bankruptcy and Insolvency in London during the Industrial Revolution* (London: Garland Publishing, 1985), p. 59; Cheryll Duncan, "New Purcell Documents from the Court of King's Bench", *Royal Musical Association Research Chronicle* vol. 47, no. 1 (2016), p. 6.

71 Ian P. H. Duffy, "English Bankrupts, 1571–1861", *American Journal of Legal History* vol. 24 (1980), p. 285.

72 Craig Muldrew, "Credit and the Courts: Debt Litigation in a Seventeenth-Century Urban Community", *The Economic History Review* vol. 46, no. 1 (February 1993), p. 24.

73 Rudolph, *Common Law*, pp. 137–139.

74 See: Hoppit, *Risk and Failure*; Richard Grassby, *The Business Community of Seventeenth-Century England* (Cambridge: Cambridge University Press, 1995); Kadens, "Last Bankrupt", pp. 1229–1319; Kent, "Small Businessmen", pp. 47–64; Jay Cohen, "The History of Imprisonment for Debt and Its Relation to the Development of Discharge in Bankruptcy", *Journal of Legal History* vol. 3 (1982), pp. 153–171.

75 Cohen, "The History of Imprisonment for Debt", pp. 154–156; Wright, *Complete Tradesman*, pp. 15–19.

76 See: Joel Mokyr, *The Enlightened Economy – An Economic History of Britain 1700–1850* (New Haven: Yale University Press, 2009), pp. 379–381 ('who could not or *would not* be declared bankrupt'); Hoppit, *Risk and Failure*, pp. 18–28.

77 William Holdsworth, *A History of English Law Vol. XIII* (London: Methuen & Co., 1952), pp. 264, 318–320, 376–412; Kadens, "Last Bankrupt".

78 Dave de Ruysscher, "Bankruptcy, Insolvency, and Debt Collection among Merchants in Antwerp (c.1490 to c.1540)", in *The History of Bankruptcy – Economic, Social, and Cultural Implications in Early Modern Europe*, ed. Thomas Max Safley (London: Routledge, 2013), p. 195; Jérôme Sgard, "Bankruptcy, Fresh Start and Debt Renegotiation in England and France (17th to 18th century)", in *The History of Bankruptcy – Economic, Social, and Cultural Implications in Early Modern Europe*, ed. Thomas Max Safley (London: Routledge, 2013), p. 228.

79 Philanthropos, *Proposals for Promoting Industry and Advancing Proper Credit* (London: 1732), p. 30.

80 Duffy, *Bankruptcy and Insolvency*, pp. 7–55; Cohen, "The History of Imprisonment for Debt", pp. 159–163; Duffy, "English Bankrupts, 1571–1861", pp. 283–305.

81 "An Act touching Orders for Bankrupts", 1571, 13 Elizabeth, c.7.

82 William Blackstone, *Commentaries on the Laws of England – Vol. II* (Oxford: 1770), p. 476.

83 Cohen, "The History of Imprisonment for Debt", pp. 159–163; Duffy, "English Bankrupts, 1571–1861", pp. 83–305; Duffy, *Bankruptcy and Insolvency*, pp. 7–55.

84 John Paul, *A System of the Laws Relative to Bankruptcy. Shewing the Whole Theory and Practice of that Branch of the Law, From the Issuing the Commission to the Final Dividend and Writ of Supersedeas for Dissolving the Same* (London: 1776), pp. 13–14.

85 Duffy, "English Bankrupts, 1571–1861", p. 295.

86 Thomas Goodringe, *The Law against Bankrupts: Or a Treatise Wherein the Statutes against Bankrupts Are Explain'd, by Several Cases, Resolutions, Judgments and Decrees, Both at Common Law and in Chancery* (London: 1713), pp. 11–16.

87 See: Cohen, "The History of Imprisonment for Debt", pp. 159–163; Duffy, "English Bankrupts, 1571–1861", pp. 283–305; Duffy, *Bankruptcy and Insolvency*, pp. 7–55; Goodringe, *The Law against Bankrupts*.

88 Sgard, "Bankruptcy in England and France", p. 224.

89 Jane Elizabeth Moore, *Genuine Memoirs of Jane Elizabeth Moore. Late of Bermondsey, in the County of Surry. Written by Herself. Vol. III* (London: 1786), pp. 186–187; Tawny Paul, *Poverty of Disaster – Debt and Insecurity in Eighteenth-Century Britain* (Cambridge: Cambridge University Press, 2019), pp. 204–205.

90 Paul Langford, *A Polite and Commercial People – England 1727–1783* (Oxford: Clarendon Press, 1998), p. 158.

91 Results obtained from search of all guilty verdicts 1720–1815 in: Tim Hitch-cock, Robert Shoemaker, Clive Emsely, Sharon Howard, and Jamie McLaugh-lin, et al., *Old Bailey Proceedings Online 1674–1913*, www.oldbaileyonline.org (accessed 11th September 2017).

92 Robin Evans, *The Fabrication of Virtue – English Prison Architecture, 1750–1840* (Cambridge: Cambridge University Press, 1982), p. 19.

93 See: Finn, *Character of Credit*, pp. 10–11.

94 Anon. *The Debtor and Creditor's Assistant; or, a Key to the King's Bench and Fleet Prisons* (London: 1793), p. 83; Mokyr, *Enlightened Economy*, p. 379; Cohen, "The History of Imprisonment for Debt", p. 155; Paul H. Haagen, "Eighteenth-Century English Society and the Debt Law", in *Social Control and the State – Historical and Comparative Essays*, eds. Stanley Cohen and Andrew Scull (Oxford: Basil Blackwell, 1986), p. 225.

95 Francis Grose, *A Classical Dictionary of the Vulgar Tongue* (London: 1796), pp. 57, 215; Rodney M. Baine, "The Prison Death of Robert Castell and Its Effect on the Founding of Georgia", *The Georgia Historical Society* vol. 73, no. 1 (Spring 1989), p. 70; Duffy, *Bankruptcy and Insolvency*, p. 61; Tim Hitchcock and Robert Brink Shoemaker, *London Lives – Poverty, Crime and the Making of a Modern City, 1690–1800* (Cambridge: Cambridge University Press, 2015), p. 102.

96 Anon. *An Accurate Description of Newgate. With the Rights, Privileges, Allowances, Fees, Dues, and Customs Thereof* (London: 1724), pp. 19–20; Anon. *A Trip to a Spunging-House, or, The Spend Thrift Caught in the Powdring-Tub of Affliction* (London: 1709).

97 Anon. *Accurate Description*, p. 23; Anon. *The Case of Richard Richards* (London: 1726), p. 12; Anon. *The Amours and Adventures of Two English Gentlemen in Italy* (Worcester: 1795), p. 134; Anon. *The Prisoner's Advocate, or a Caveat against under Sheriffs, and Their Officers; Jayl-Keepers, and Their Agents* (London: 1726), p. 19.

98 "Petition against Yeoman Being Allowed to Make Arrest without Serjeants", c.1710, Poultry Compter, LMA, CLA/025/PC/04/005; "Swordbearers to En-quire into Character of Yeomen or Serjeants", 1707, Poultry Compter, LMA, CLA/025/PC/04/004.

99 Margaret Coghlan, *Memoirs of Mrs Coghlan* (Cork: 1794), pp. 93–94.

100 Anon. *The Arbitrary Punishments and Cruel Tortures Inflicted on Prisoners for Debt* (London: 1729), p. 10;

101 Anon. *Accurate Description*, p. 19; Anon. *The Kingston Atlantis: Or, Woodward's Miscellany* (London: 1731), p. 26.

102 Anon. *Accurate Description*, pp. 30–32; Anon. *Arbitrary Punishments*, p. 10.

103 Anon. *The Life and Uncommon Adventures of Capt. Dudley Bradstreet* (Dublin: 1755), p. 98; Simon Wood, *Remarks on the Fleet Prison: or, Lumber-House for Men and Women. Written by a Prisoner on the Common-Side, Who Hath Lain a Prisoner Near Three Years, on the Penalty of a Bond. No Debtor* (London: 1733), pp. 12–13.

104 "The Humble Petition of Herbert Pinchon Keeper of Woodstreet Compter within the Said Citty", c.1700, Petitions of Prisoners and Others Relating to Prisons, LMA, CLA/032/01/021, xlviii.

105 Charlotte Charke, *A Narrative of the Life of Mrs Charlotte Charke* (London: 1755), p. 91; Anon. *The Compulsive Clause in the Present Act of Insolvency, Fully Considered* (London: 1761), pp. 24–31; Anne Bailey, *Memoirs of Mrs Anne Bailey* (London: 1771), p. 5; Jane Elizabeth Moore, *Genuine Memoirs of Jane Elizabeth Moore. Vol. II* (London: 1786), p. 339; Elizabeth Gooch, *The Life of Mrs Gooch. Written by Her-self. Dedicated to the Public. In Three Volumes. Vol. III* (London: 1792), pp. 57–59; Mary Wells, *Memoirs of the Life of Mrs Sumbel, Late Wells; of the Theatres-Royal, Drury-Lane, Covent-Garden, and Haymarket. In Three Volumes. Written by Herself. Vol. I* (London: 1811), pp. 180–182.

106 Anon. *A Compleat Collection of the Rules and Orders of the Court of Common Pleas at Westminster* (London: 1736), p. 244; John Howard, *The State of the Prisons in England and Wales, with Preliminary Observations, and an Account of Some Foreign Prisons* (London: 1777), pp. 10–11; Anon. *An Account of the Rise, Progress, and Present State of the Society for the Discharge and Relief of Persons Imprisoned for Small Debts throughout England* (London: 1796), p. 12.

107 Peter Hawker, *The Diary of Colonel Peter Hawker 1802–1853. Vol. II* (London: Greenhill, 1988), p. 105.

108 Hutton, *Courts of Requests*, pp. 140–141; McConville, *English Prison Administration*, p. 52; Anon. *The Bee Reviv'd: Or, the Prisoners Magazine* (London: J. Lewis, 1750), p. 4; Gary Calland, *A History of the Devon County Prison for Debtors in St. Thomas* (Exeter: Little History, 1999), pp. 26–27.

109 Anon. *A Trip*, p. 6; Howard, *State of the Prisons*, pp. 25–26.

110 Grano, *Handel's Trumpeter*, pp. 27–28.

111 Anon. *Accurate Description*, pp. 3–10; Margaret DeLacy, *Prison Reform in Lancashire, 1700–1850 – A Study in Local Administration* (Stanford: Stanford University Press, 1986), pp. 31–32, 50; "List of Fees and Garnish by Ward", c.1700, Miscellaneous Papers, Newgate Prison – Administration, LMA, CLA/035/02/026(i).

112 Philip Woodfine, "Debtors, Prisons, and Petitions in Eighteenth-Century England", *Eighteenth Century Life* vol. 30, no. 2 (Spring 2006), p. 10.

113 Richard Burn, *A New Law Dictionary: Intended for General Use, as Well as for Gentlemen of the Profession Vol. I* (London: 1792), p. 117; George Crompton, *Practice Common Placed: Or, the Rules and Cases of Practice in the Courts of King's Bench and Common Pleas, Methodically Arranged Vol. I* (London: 1786), p. xlii; Duffy, *Bankruptcy and Insolvency*, p. 61; Philip Burton, *Practice of the Office of Pleas in the Court of Exchequer Both Antient and Modern Vol. I* (London: 1791), pp. 99–100.

114 "Lancaster Gaol Register of Debtors and Plaintiffs", 1793–1796, Home Office and Prison Commission Records: Prison Records Series 1, TNA, PCOM 2/440.

115 Paul Hess Haagen, "Imprisonment for Debt in England and Wales", unpublished PhD thesis, University of Princeton (1986), pp. 8–10, 33–34.

116 Haagen, "Imprisonment for Debt", pp. 1–39; V. Marksham Lester, *Victorian Insolvency – Bankruptcy, Imprisonment for Debt, and Company Winding-up in Nineteenth-Century England* (Oxford: Clarendon, Press, 1995), p. 90; Duffy, *Bankruptcy and Insolvency*, pp. 61–64; Sean McConville, *A History of English Prison Administration – Volume I 1750–1877* (London: Routledge & Kegan Paul, 1981), pp. 49–56; Anon. *The Gentleman, Merchant, Tradesman, Lawyer, and Debtor's Pocket Guide, in Cases of Arrest* (Bath: 1785), p. 60; Joanna Innes, "The King's Bench Prison in the Later Eighteenth Century: Law, Authority and Order in a London Debtors' Prison", in *An Ungovernable People – The English and Their Law in the Seventeenth and Eighteenth Centuries*, ed. John Brewer and John Styles (London: Hutchinson, 1980), p. 255; Peter J. Coleman, *Debtors and Creditors in America – Insolvency, Imprisonment for Debt, and Bankruptcy, 1607–1900* (Madison: The State Historical Society of Wisconsin, 1974), p. 4; Hoppit, "The Use and Abuse of Credit", p. 76.

117 Attorney at Law, *An Attorney's Practice Common-Placed* (London: 1743), p. 51.

118 Term Date List 1806–1807, "List of Prisoners Handed over by the Sheriffs to Their Successors on 28 Sept Annually, with Notes of Occurrences during the Subsequent Year", 1805–1806, Wood Street Compter later Giltspur Street Compter, LMA, CLA/028/01/035.

119 Journal of the House of Commons, *Report for the Committee Appointed to Enquire into the Practice and Effects of Imprisonment for Debt* (1792), pp. 7–8.

120 Thomas Burnett, *A Second Tale of Tub* (London: 1715), p. 103.

121 Anon. *Law Quibbles*, p. 19.

122 John Arbuthnot, *Miscellanies: Containing the History of John Bull* (Dublin: 1746), p. 24.

123 Philanthropos, *Proposals for Promoting Industry*, pp. 10–11.

124 John Mackay, *A True State of the Proceedings of the Prisoners in the Fleet Prison* (London: 1729), pp. 15–16, 26; William Hargreave, *History and Description of the Ancient City of York. Vol. II* (York: William Alexander, 1818), p. 234.

125 House of Commons, *Committee into Imprisonment for Debt*, p. 8.

126 Anon. *Debtor and Creditor's Assistant*, p. 25; 'The Society for the Discharge and Relief of Persons imprisoned for Small Debts, [now] known by the Name of the Thatched House Society' (Anon. *An Account of the Rise, Progress, and Present State of the Society for the Discharge and Relief of Persons Imprisoned for Small Debts throughout England* (London: 1799), p. 70.), the name derived from the 'Thatched House Tavern' where they held early meetings (Anon. *Genuine Memoirs of Dr Dodd* (London: 1777), p. 57).

127 John Lilly, *Modern Entries, Being a Collection of Select Pleadings in the Courts of King's Bench, Common Pleas and Exchequer* (London: 1723), p. 788.

128 "Commitment Registers", 1733–1795, Fleet Prison, TNA, PRIS 1/5-16.

129 "An Act for the Relief of Debtors with Respect to the Imprisonment of Their Persons", 1758, 32 George II, c.28; William Hands, *A Selection of Rules Occurring in the Prosecution and Defence of Personal Actions in the Court of King's Bench* (London: 1795), pp. 108–109.

130 Thomas Macdonald, *A Treatise on Civil Imprisonment in England* (London: 1791), pp. 108–110; Haagen, "Imprisonment for Debt", p. 12.

131 Charles Durnford and Edward Hyde East, *Reports of Cases Argued and Determined in the Court of King's Bench … Vol. V* (London: 1794), pp. 36–37; Hands, *Personal Actions*, p. 111; Anon. *The Devil: Containing a Review and Investigation of all Public Subjects Whatever* (London: 1786), p. 146.

132 John Croft, *Scrapeana: Fugitive Miscellany* (York: 1792), p. 318.

133 Anon. *Debtor and Creditor's Assistant*, p. 34; Calland, *Devon County Prison*, pp. 19–20; Josiah Dornford, *Seven Letters to the Lords and Commons of Great Britain, upon the Impolicy, Inhumanity, and Injustice of Our Present Mode of Arresting the Bodies of Debtors* (London: 1786), p. 74.

134 "Lancaster Register", PCOM 2/440.

135 Howard, *State of the Prisons*, pp. 10–11.

136 House of Commons, *Committee into Imprisonment for Debt*, pp. 31–32, 51–54, 76–79.

137 Anon. *Rules and Orders to Be Observed by the Industrious Protestant Society of Friends, United for the Mutual Support of Each Other: Instituted at the House of Mr Samuel Warren, the Three Jolly Butchers, Hoxton Market-Place, Begun April, 1784* (London: 1794), p. 8; Christopher Johnson, *Considerations on the Case of the Confined Debtors in the This Kingdom* (London: 1793), p. 32.

138 Daniel Defoe, *Some Objections Humbly Offered to the Consideration of the Hon House of Commons, Relating to the Present Intended Relief of Prisoners* (London: 1729), p. 20; Pat Rogers, "Defoe in the Fleet Prison", *The Review of English Studies* vol. 22, no. 88 (November 1971), p. 452.

2 Enlightened capitalism

Use and structure of debtors'
prisons

The last 500 years of English law have witnessed ever increasing use of imprisonment. Through much of the early modern period, judicial vengeance
focussed primarily upon physical punishments of the body such as whipping,
branding, removal and mutilation of body parts, or execution. Almost all
felons who were imprisoned were merely within gaol awaiting their trial or
punishment. This did not mean no societal undesirables were imprisoned
as a punishment and, from the sixteenth century, the gaol was increasingly
used as a tool of punishment for groups such as religious prisoners or offences
against the court. Real innovation emerged with the growth of bridewell
prisons which, following the example of their London namesake, combined
imprisonment as penalty alongside forced labour. This significant experiment
in English law spread slowly from correcting the behaviour of the disorderly
poor receiving parish support to the penalising of petty crimes.[1] In the seventeenth and eighteenth centuries, the escalating use of transportation rather
than execution to punish felons can also be construed as a tacit societal move
towards modern imprisonment strategies, offenders being held in an area (the
colonies) against their will from which, after a specified number of years,
they could return to English society. When considered in this light, the regular detention of felons for a set time when transportation was interrupted by
revolution in America was a relatively short psychological leap particularly as
many were stored on hulks in the Thames. The law became less and less of a
spectacle in the two centuries following 1775 building upon sixteenth- and
seventeenth-century developments and, as a result, reformative or punitive
imprisonment grew to dominate the consequences of prosecution, shadow-
ing all others following the abolition of the death penalty in 1965.[2]

While in the nineteenth century prisons came to be understood as institutions of punishment – a development Foucault called the 'new age of
penal justice' as both the law and prisons were redefined legally and in the
public mindset – throughout the eighteenth century they remained principally associated with the detention of debtors.[3] These prisoners constituted
more than half of gaol inhabitants – vastly outnumbering the fraction of
experimental punitive confinements – and their detention was not construed
as a punishment experience.[4] The subsequent primacy of "punishment" for

gaols and the decline of debt imprisonment have, however, led to suggestions that their use by creditors declined from the eighteenth century into abolition in the nineteenth century due to a cultural shift not concerning prisons but attitudes towards debtors. It has been posited that the emergence of enlightened capitalism led traders to cease punishing those who had merely committed the crime of insolvency, a theory relying in part upon an anachronistic emphasis on detention as penance. The anthropologist Gustav Peebles has, for example, explicitly linked the decline of debt imprisonment to the development of the civilisation of 'nascent capitalism' by which the prisons came to be seen as a 'barbarous indulgence'. Based on the writings of reformers and philosophers he asserted that as the economy developed in speed, sophistication, and size 'the prison's ritualistic capacity to nullify the power of monetary obligations' – Peebles depicting gaols solely as places of exile or 'a zone of keeping-to-oneself' rather than vehicles of repayment – 'and endorse the present-orientation of economic traditionalism [became] far more dangerous than it had been in the past'. While Peebles stopped far short of explicitly claiming capitalism ended debt imprisonment, he stated that its abolition in England constituted 'pro-creditor legislation', that the gradual spreading of capitalist 'attitudes … managed to shutter all the debtors' prisons of Europe', and that the 'shuttering of the debtors' prison … underscores the well-established claim that liberal, capitalist ideology relied upon the commensurate and simultaneous construction of a supposedly barbaric Other [i.e. the debtors' prison]'.[5]

By an extension of this logic, it might appear that the end of debt imprisonment was an inevitable consequence of economic growth – that from the moment the English began to dabble in financial markets or construct steam powered machinery, the debtors' prisons were doomed. That the prisons ceased to be relevant even before the Debt Act of 1869 which essentially closed them is undeniable. It is easy to overlook that Charles Dickens's *Little Dorrit*, written in the late 1850s and focussing on the debtors' prisons, was conceived as a historical novel discussing an essentially bygone practice. Dickens introduces the Marhsalsea prison to his readers early in the novel with 'it is gone now, and the world is none the worse without it'.[6] However, their lack of relevance in the reign of Queen Victoria speaks nothing of inevitability and even if an emergence of enlightened capitalism from the end of the eighteenth century is accepted, relying upon the attitudes of pamphleteers, philosophers, and reformers to indicate the everyday practice of proto-capitalist creditors seems questionable. Overall, the contribution or lack thereof of capitalism to changing use of debt imprisonments is difficult to deny or affirm principally as existing knowledge of the rate of use of debtors' prisons (even from contemporaneous assessments) is highly limited.

There exist different interpretations of what creditors wanted out of an act of debt imprisonment – setting aside momentarily the theoretical underpinning of 'being imprisoned, not for *owing* … but till he *pays*' – but there is also no common understanding of how many creditors were making use of the practice and whether the rate of using it to achieve objectives changed over the period.[7] While there have been some pioneering attempts to estimate prison population size, previous efforts have largely only achieved general suggestions of those imprisoned at a given moment.[8] An indication of the changing rate at which creditors used debtors' prisons is of fundamental importance in attempting to assess the role the gaols played in commercial society during an era of wide-ranging economic change. This chapter explores the available material to indicate rates of imprisonment and suggest how arrest rates reflected economic activity. However, it also reveals the uneven structure of debtors' prisons (operating not as a national system but a conglomeration of local institutions) and the role of debtors in securing their own confinement which complicates any study of the behaviour of individual creditors as well as acknowledging that commercial motivations in rural Cumberland could be diametrically opposed to those in Smithfield. Finally, *who* creditors were arresting (and by implication who they were not arresting) is examined, revealing that any association of the prisons with the punishment of the insignificant poor is based on a faulty understanding of the role of debt imprisonment in society.

★★

The paucity of quantitative study on the use of debt imprisonment has arisen primarily from the surprisingly poor survival rate of prison records. Debtors' prisons functioned as institutions owned and governed by either the state or local authorities with courts of quarter sessions regularly enquiring into practices within gaols under their jurisdiction and making orders concerning specific debtors or in response to legislative changes.[9] These orders – such as when, in October 1729, the court in Cambridge 'pursuant to a Late Act of Parliament … doth … Order Limitt and direct that' only a specified list of 'Fees … Shall for the future be paid to the Severall Bailiffs' – were made with a sense of detachment.[10] This disconnection was a result of the governance of the courts having little to do with the everyday reality of the prisons. Their regular involvement was limited to the payment of salaries to doctors and ministers or covering the unusual expenses of officers, the Cambridge court dutifully paying in 1719 'unto Edward Yorke Keeper of the Gaoler … the sume of Forty Shillings for and towards the Expences … in providing for and relieving the Poor Prisoners … being sick of the Small Pox'.[11] Court payments belie the fact that almost all prisons were run as private institutions, the right being purchased by keepers who ran the institutions for as much profit as could be extracted. Accordingly, prison records were the property of the keeper and if Edward Yorke kept the Cambridge gaol records after he departed, he would have been far from unusual, keepers continuing to charge those who might need to read their registers, such as when checking on the financial history of a potential business partner.[12]

This does not mean that no details of prison administration have survived, however, due to the need for court involvement, surviving documents tend to privilege moments of crisis such as disease or corruption. Various records exist relating, for example, to the investigation of the Marshalsea and Fleet prisons in 1729 due to particularly corrupt keepers, or of Newgate following an outbreak of typhus which spread into the Old Bailey killing sixty (including jurists, judges, sheriffs, lawyers, and the Lord Mayor) in 1750.[13] Occasionally one-off lists survive of prisoners present in specific gaols on a specific day, produced either for the irregularly passed Insolvency Acts, in response to crises like the sacking of prisons in the Gordon Riots of 1780, or by reforming visitors such as John Howard and James Neild.[14] Having been produced in isolation and without context such documents provide little useful evidence about creditor activities.[15] Even taken as a national whole, they only provide evidence of what populations of prisons were rather than arrest rates, however, in many cases they remain the sole record of imprisonment at an individual institution. Despite the long history of London's Poultry Compter (c.1393–1817), the only surviving record of its prisoners for debt is a list prepared for the Court of Aldermen in December 1724.[16]

In a small number of cases, usually arising from happy accidents of document storage, the records produced by individual prisons of their charges are preserved, recording prisoners as they arrived and departed the prison. These documents, generally known as commitment registers, still do not give a full view of arrest as many potential prisoners avoided ever stepping inside a gaol. In 1663, Samuel Pepys's dinner was interrupted by 'Thomas of the Poultry [Compter]' bearing a writ concerning £30 10s Pepys owed on behalf of the Admiralty. Rather than submitting to his confinement, Pepys merely sent Thomas with his servant Griffin 'to tell [the money] out to him in the office', subsequently declining to accompany Thomas to the compter for evidence of the settling of the case as 'I have good witness of the payment of it'.[17] While Pepys was probably unusual in his casual privilege, many other debtors, hearing of warrants out for their arrest, will have rushed to settle their bills before a bailiff caught up with them. Though the totality of warrants issued cannot be measured through commitment registers, they do allow for a unique indication of the rate at which debtors were actually confined at individual gaols, suggesting creditor activity in a manner population counts cannot. Commitment registers are referred to for prisons across the period – some with ominous and grand titles such as the register for London's Wood Street Compter before the Great Fire known as 'the Black Book' – though only a select handful of surviving examples have been identified.[18] While it is possible that further examples may eventually be discovered, surviving eighteenth-century commitment registers have currently only been identified for London's Fleet Prison, the Wood Street Compter in Cheapside (which became the Giltspur Street Compter in 1791), Surry's King's/Queen's Bench Prison, and Lancaster Castle (the county gaol of Lancashire).[19] Additionally, records for the Borough Compter in Southwark exist between 1811 and 1830 and some prisons such as the Marshalsea in the 1760s have fragmentary lists recording commitment dates which might be seen as a poor relation of the registers though providing little contextual data beyond arrivals in a given year.[20] Surviving registers vary in detail and in how fragmentary a series is preserved. For example, the Fleet Prison's fifty-one volumes are spread between 1686 and 1842 (two years before it closed) with all records lost between 1748 and 1777 due to the burning of the prison during the Gordon Riots in 1780.[21]

To provide comparable data, the analysis in this book focusses upon the available records of three prisons. The core of this study is the long-running, near complete series of Wood Street Compter commitment registers (1741–1815). Each of the forty volumes records the debtors present at Michaelmas, then entering new commitments over the following year before drawing up another Michaelmas list, repeating the process until a new volume was needed. Some volumes cover a single year while others were used for longer durations of up to five years. The listing process was theoretically to allow the newly appointed sheriff to acquaint themselves with the composition of the prison for which he was now responsible, the designation "compter" deriving from the medieval Latin *vice comes* (sheriff) there accordingly being two compters in London. However, the sheriffs had little involvement with prison management by this era and there is no indication the registers were taken out each year, the lists presumably only being drawn up and interrupting the natural flow of the register to comply with legislation.[22] In 1791 the prison became the Giltspur Street Compter[23] when the ageing gaol was rebuilt on a larger site less than 300 metres away. This was, in effect, the same institution, the clerk merely recording between two commitments in the register 'New Compter this Second of April 1791'.[24] In total 10,166 commitments were recorded including forty-three debtors who were imprisoned prior to Michaelmas 1741. Only eight years of records have been lost though, due to the eccentricities of the listing process and occasional laxities in clerk rigour, details of debts or how prisoners were released are lost at a greater rate than other prisons studied. In 88% of commitments, the debt size was recorded and 87% had surviving release details. The Fleet Prison series is more fragmentary, though the six volumes covering 1733–1748 and a further six for the period 1778–1795 detail 7,670 commitments of debtors. These registers also contained a significant subset of prisoners committed for contempt of court or for crimes related to the excise, usually suffering forfeiture of their estate to the crown. As these individuals cannot be said to have been confined for the repayment of privately held debts, the nearly 400 additional cases have not been included in the data. The large Fleet registers functioned as more formal documents than their Wood Street equivalents, lacking the idle doodling by clerks – the 1766 Wood Street register is adorned with a large self-portrait sketched in ink presumably by an idle prison officer on a quiet afternoon – or updates on procedure exhibited in the compter files, and details on debts (99%) or release (91%) were thus kept with greater consistency. Unfortunately, only one volume survives from Lancaster Castle Gaol covering 1793–1796 though the formulaic lined volume, dividing data into columns, clearly was once part of a longer series. As the only known example of an English debtors' prison commitment register outside London, even the comparatively small number of commitments recorded (828) represents a significant regional comparator to the more voluminous London material with 93% listing their debts and 99% recording release.

These three prisons were far from equal or even necessarily similar, being part of a hierarchical national system. The majority of this stratification did not arise from a deliberate legalised tiering of responses to debt, rather it was the natural consequence of the nationwide social structure and its corresponding variations in wealth upon local areas. Prisons in regions of declining importance or sparse populations tended to be of a lower quality than those within booming urban areas where citizens might expend wealth on rebuilding gaols in grand styles as an emblem of civic pride. In London the city expended significant sums rebuilding the gaols after the destruction of 1666 as well as on the 'purchase [of] contiguoss Grounds for inlargement' suggesting their desire to not simply restore the prisons to their former state. Similarly, when the prisons were rebuilt a century later, while no expense was spared, focus was less upon the comfort of prisoners than the city, the architects constructing luxurious façades to testify to the refinement of the civic officials who paid for them.[25] The York County Gaol, functioning as the chief prison of the wealthy city and its surrounding area, was a particularly striking and early example of civic pride expressed through penal constructions. Its impressive baroque styling which cost over £8,000 in 1705 was intended primarily for the glorification of its builders. This grandeur was testified to both by contemporary admirers (becoming a common tourist spot) and by it being one of the only eighteenth-century prisons still standing. Its inhabitants undoubtedly did benefit from the replacing of the old castle, particularly the better sort of debtors who were separated into a more luxurious wing by design, though the expenditure on external beauty reveals civic priorities.[26]

By contrast, debtors in more provincial areas were frequently housed in ageing castles made redundant by the Civil War or in cramped, poorly upkept medieval gaols.[27] At Leicester County Gaol in 1777, the prison reformer John Howard found the debtors in 'a long dungeon' which was 'damp [with] two windows', noting that the problems associated with the prison were of 'long standing' as they echoed complaints from the gaol dating back to 1690.[28] Similarly, he recorded the prisoners at Gloucester Castle were 'always ... sick' there being a 'large Dunghill ... constantly ... near the stone steps', their condition was worsened further as 'the floor is so ruinous, that it cannot be washed'.[29] However, there was not a simple divide between town and countryside. Newer prisons were far from perfect and there were regular complaints about the internal state of the prisons of London between the fire and the delayed late eighteenth-century rebuilding.[30] Similarly, some larger castle prisons offered higher quality confinement than gaols housed in glorified former keeps such as that containing Cambridge gaol, which was close to complete structural collapse by 1770.[31] Lancaster Castle (continuing to function as a prison until 2011) was a relatively comfortable example even prior to its continued improvement in line with the county's growing wealth. Margaret DeLacy's 1986 study details a prison which overcame its deficiencies such as its rambling design and age through the court's willingness to expend capital on providing each cell with a fireplace and to make repairs when prisoners complained of issues such as leaking roofs for which debtors at other county gaols had little remedy. Furthermore, its relatively recent role as a fortification designed to hold out for months under siege contributed a supply of clean water from a well within the walls and generously sized rooms.[32]

It is false to describe every provincial prison as dilapidated and solely confining the poor who could not afford to have lived in cities where their indebtedness would have resulted in greater comfort once confined. Lancaster was still relatively unique however, and it is clear some prisons were simply better than others, their population reflecting increased quality. While such stratification was not designed, the increased rate of poorer prisoners in certain gaols was occasionally a consequence of formal legal process. *Mesne* process was limited to those who owed at least £2 of debt after 1725; however, the proliferation of the Courts of Requests throughout the century from the middle of the eighteenth century allowed for the regular confinement of "small" debtors whose obligations could be counted in pennies.[33] Such prisoners tended to be confined in smaller urban prisons, sometimes even in bridewells, or occasionally in dank unpleasant specially constructed institutions, more reminiscent of workhouses.[34] In the Birmingham town gaol, known locally as 'the Dungeon', Howard found the prisoners from the Court confined in a room with 'only one window eighteen inches square' damning the prison as 'very offensive'.[35] To be confined in a specially constructed Court of Requests prison was, therefore, to be held at the bottom of the national system of debt imprisonment, having been placed there not directly by a creditor but by a court. While most Court of Request debtors were lucky enough to be held in a traditional debtors' prison, their presence will have detracted from the attractiveness of such gaols, offending the sensibilities of higher status prisoners. Wood Street held increasing numbers of such debtors who briefly dominated the intake in the early 1780s, further reducing the quality of life for members of the middling sorts at a prison already in dire need of refurbishment.

Despite this apparent stratification, the quality of where one was imprisoned reveals little about the actions of creditors. Beyond the contribution of the Court of Requests, differentiation between use of prisons within a given administrative area (such as in a city with multiple gaols) should reflect, on a macro scale, little more than capacity. For example, a debtor seized by the bailiff while walking down Coney Street in York was legally powerless to ensure they were taken to the comfortable castle prison rather than the dreaded nearby Kidcotes gaol on the bridge over the Ouse – Howard writing 'it were in vain to offer any hints of improvement ... [as] this Gaol cannot be made a good one'.[36] However, at the highest end of the national structure in the superior court gaols, evidence of creditor activities was blurred by the ability of debtors to select their place of incarceration, one 1793 pamphlet commenting suggestively that 'no place in the universe abounds so much with *character* as the King's Bench and the Fleet'.[37] This distortion was enabled by writs of *habeas corpus* which allowed debtors to subvert the near absolute coercive power of creditors by transferring their case to a superior court. This did not mean their case came to trial any quicker. Like the legal fiction of procuring *capias ad respondendum* when creditors had no intention of bringing debtors to court, the motivation behind *habeas corpus* writs was in moving the location of the prisoner, as by transferring the case to a superior court the debtor was required to move to its corresponding prison. The process was expensive; the price of procuring the writ alone amounted to at least 'five or six pounds' by 1736 with costs later rising to over twenty pounds.[38] Nor was the writ the sole expense. Once arrested, debtors seeking *habeas corpus*, alongside paying for coaches, coachmen, food, and lodging, were liable for the expenses and salaries of the guards who were required to accompany them between prisons. Those obtaining the writ from distant locations would therefore need to be able to pay significant amounts in hard cash up front to cover the days or weeks it would take for them to be carried from their prison of origin to London.[39]

Some debtors clearly regarded such costs worth paying, commitment to a superior court prison offering significant benefits. It has been suggested that, if a creditor could not afford to travel the same distance to bring the debtor to trial or negotiate with them, cases defaulted.[40] However, for most prisoners the purpose of the move was motivated by more direct personal benefit. The travel writer and former spy John Macky, on a visit to York in the first decades of the eighteenth century, was profoundly struck by the recently rebuilt debtors' prison. He marvelled at the modern building and its spacious yard remarking that

> the Air [is] so good, that one would wonder that any Prisoner should take a *Habeas Corpus* to remove himself from thence. ... There is only this Difference, that at York a Prisoner never goes without the Walls; but from the Fleet and King's Bench, in a Hackney Coach, one may go privately anywhere.[41]

While almost all debtors' prisons were porous in terms of who they let in, the Fleet and King's Bench were remarkably open in who they let out, prisoners having access to a specifically defined area surrounding the prison known confusingly as "the *rules*". These were notorious regions of legal ambiguity; before the 1750s a significant percentage of London marriages occurred within the Fleet's *rules* because Church regulations were less strictly enforced, costs low, and banns did not need to be issued.[42] For debtors, they were an area in which, though imprisoned in name, 'a prisoner … lives at large'. The Fleet's *rules*, about half a mile in circumference, covered most of the Fleet market reaching Ludgate Hill, while at the King's Bench, before a restriction in 1790, they extended 'upwards of three miles in circumference' including several notable 'places of public entertainment'.[43] Technically, prisoners were barred from entering public houses within the *rules* at the King's Bench but it was almost impossible to prevent them, many living therein while there were no such restrictions at the Fleet.[44]

As with *habeas corpus*, obtaining *ruler* status was not cheap. At the King's Bench, the Marshall charged seven and a half guineas if the debtor owed up to £50, rising to ten guineas for those owing £100, adding another five guineas for each subsequent £100 of debt. The keeper of the Fleet was practically generous in only charging 'five per cent for the first £100, and two and a half per cent for every other £100'.[45] While fees were therefore technically lower for those owing smaller amounts, it can be assumed the wealthiest were the principal inhabitants of the *rules* as those owing less than £50 probably had more meagre resources and were unable to meet even the lowest entry charge. Furthermore, debtors were expected to find and pay for their own lodging in the *rules* and could be subjected to further charges by prison administrators.[46] For those who could not afford permanent residency, it was possible to obtain *day rules* 'to enable [prisoners] to dispatch their necessary Affairs abroad'.[47] These allowed a prisoner to walk free in the city so long as 'he should return … at, or before nine o'clock in the evening'. *Day rules* were limited by the 1790s to only three days a term at the King's Bench, the prison charging 4s 2d for days one and three and 3s 2d for the second. At the Fleet they remained unlimited though at the slightly higher expense of 5s for the 'first and last day, and 4s 6d every intermediate day'.[48] As such, a prisoner at the Fleet with *day rules* was essentially only under curfew.

A German visitor to London in the 1790s reflecting on the *rules* commented that 'prisoners may not only ramble but even live within these whenever he can find security that he will not escape. It is remarked that no nation is so credulous as the English'.[49] Creditors frequently complained about lax enforcement, claiming that some debtors obtained a writ of *habeas corpus* and then acquired the *rules* solely in order to escape, taking a ship to Ireland or the continent.[50] When the Fleet's *rules* were examined in 1753 only twenty-eight of the eighty-eight "*rulers*" were found; however, there is no indication they had actually fled and may have been elsewhere in the capital at the time as there was little to stop rulers from straying beyond the set boundaries.[51] The majority do not seem to have been attempting to escape, having had to submit a substantial security in order to obtain the *rules* in the first place, the Fleet registers only recording four instances of escaped *rulers*.[52] Nor were the escapes that happened swift; John Suffell, who had originally been committed to Wood Street in May 1781, moved himself to the Fleet in November of that year but it was not until February 1784 that the register recorded

'Mr Suffell having been seen out of the Rules the Warden assigned over the Bond for the benefit of the Plaintiff in this Cause'.[53] Rather than flight, the purpose of obtaining the *rules* for most debtors was that it allowed them to live normal lives. There were over 200 private houses alongside thirty to forty public houses and inns within the Fleet's *rules* where debtors could take lodgings.[54] Living therein amounted to not truly being imprisoned and while one still had fewer rights and abilities than a non-imprisoned individual, many of these were subjective. *Rulers* returned to their trades, free from the possibility of being re-arrested for their debts.[55] John Everett, arrested in the 1720s for £60, described how, after giving 'Security to the Warden for the Liberty of the Rules, which cost me upwards of sixteen Guineas', he returned to his trade of alehouse keeping: 'I took the Thistle and Crown in the Old Bailey, ... and afterwards took the Cock in the Old-Bailey, there I lived for three years'.[56] It is not possible to determine from the registers how many prisoners obtained the *rules* but of 237 Fleet debtors who died with the register recording their location of residence, 40% were *rulers*. While this should be seen as an upper limit on the confined population with access to the *rules* it certainly suggests that significant numbers of Fleet debtors were imprisoned only in name across the century.

Besides the *rules*, *habeas corpus* offered prisoners with remaining assets seeking a higher quality of life a variety of methods to waste money.[57] The quality of rooms was significantly better at the superior court prisons, the rent being accordingly higher. The *Debtor and Creditor's Assistant* complimented the 'airy and commodious' rooms at the King's Bench in particular, praising the 'pleasing view of the Surry and Kentish hills' offered by third floor rooms.[58] Surgeon and theologian Clement Cruttwell favoured the Fleet remarking that it was 'reckoned the best prison ... for good rooms and other conveniences, having the benefit of an open yard'.[59] The spacious rooms and well-maintained yards, functioning as hives of leisure, were a far cry from the dilapidated county prisons as Samuel Keimer made clear in 1781: 'Was mov'd from Rules of Fleet, a prison spacious, To Gatehouse, where all things were bad, and most vexatious'.[60] The increased likelihood that superior court prisons contained wealthy or genteel debtors exacerbated and perpetuated the distorted nature of their population as those with trappings or presumptions of gentility sought to be imprisoned in the "right" institution. When the actress Mary Wells was arrested watching her friend Frederick Reynolds's play *How to Grow Rich* in 1796, she seemed not to have even considered paying her debts. She spent three weeks in a sponging house refusing to be taken to the 'county gaol' while organising her writ of *habeas corpus*, travelling out into Surrey under guard there being 'no judge in town to sign' her writ, eventually gaining admittance to the Fleet. Throughout, her concern was in establishing her social position, rebuking servants or officers who treated her like the prisoner she was, wasting money on the sponging house, the writ, and the coach and guards who carried her out into the country as well as to her prison of choice.[61]

Both superior court prisons also contained significant numbers of what might be called "normal" prisoners for debt, those who might easily have been confined in Wood Street or Lancaster, carried there through no agency of their own. It is difficult to determine from the registers the rate at which prisoners arrived through direct arrest or via *habeas corpus* though Paul Hess Haagen has claimed 'the numbers able to' remove were 'smaller than eighteenth-century pamphlets and debates would lead one to believe'.[62] Those applying for relief through the variously passed Insolvency Acts were required to submit their name, occupation, and last address to the *London Gazette*; based on these applications, Haagen asserted that only between '16% and 18%' of London prisoners originated outside the city, taking this as an indication of those removed by *habeas corpus*. However, this statistic fails to distinguish between all London prisons. When prisoner origins are separated by institution, clear variation arises. Of the 4,025 prisoners applying for relief from the Fleet (1725–1797), 74% originated in Middlesex (rising to 79% when including Surrey). However, 85% of the 1,123 prisoners at Wood Street originated in Middlesex, rising to over 90% when including London's environs. While the population of the Fleet was therefore not entirely made up of rural squires, the variation in the background of prisoners at institutions half a mile apart is more significant than Haagen's merging of all London prisons allows. Furthermore, *habeas corpus* was not as simple as removing from a great distance meaning that the number who arrived at the prison through it was probably greater than the one-in-five rate suggested by a study of their origins. Most of those who moved, like Mary Wells, already lived in London as it was the peculiarities of these prisons, rather than merely being in the capital, which made them attractive. Acquiring a writ to either superior court prison was the second most significant method of leaving the Wood Street Compter. Accordingly, a report produced in 1729 for the City of London on prisoners currently remaining in the Fleet who had arrived via *habeas corpus* found that every single one had previously been confined either in London or Southwark.[63] The lower transportation cost over a short distance must have contributed to making *habeas corpus* less prohibitively expensive for debtors within the capital.

Even when already housed in a superior court prison, debtors might still acquire writs; the Marshal of the King's Bench in 1792 complained that 'there have been Instances of Prisoners residing regularly at the King's Bench Prison during the Summer, and in the Fleet during the Winter'.[64] Of the 819 prisoners recorded as leaving the Fleet through *habeas corpus*, 38% would later return from the King's Bench on a subsequent writ. John Austen, a victualler living in St Pancras Wells in London, was committed to Wood Street in October 1792 owing £200 though he was removed to the Fleet on the 3rd November having only spent four days in the compter. A year later, by which time his debts had increased to £377 when three additional creditors pressed charges, he again acquired a writ of *habeas corpus* to take him to the King's Bench though quickly acquiring a third writ to return him to the Fleet, possibly having not found Southwark to his liking. When he was finally released by the 1794 Insolvency Act after nearly four years in three different prisons, he had managed to reduce his debts to under £300 though if he had been content to remain in the compter, this would presumably have been achieved much earlier and to a greater degree.[65]

The over selection of the upper tier of debtors, present to some extent in all prisons, as well as those who, thanks to the privileges of the *rules*, were lacking in motivation to work towards a speedy release must be borne in mind when observing any figures obtained from the superior court prisons. This also applied to the rate of commitment though it is unclear by what rate *habeas corpus* inflates the actual behaviour of creditors. Any account relying solely upon the records of superior court prisons, particularly if describing them as representative, should be treated with caution. Statistically these prisons provide an example of what might be assumed to be the least efficient prisons, an ill-fitting cog in the system, crying out for reform which never sufficiently materialised though they cannot be ignored because, as is clear from the size of their commitment registers, their admission rates dwarfed all other gaols.

★★

The rate of commitment at each prison is detailed in Figure 2.1 excluding years without full coverage in the registers such as the twelve debtors recorded for 1749 at the Wood Street Compter. Additionally, to extend the Fleet data, a count was made of commitments in surviving registers from 1725 to 1727

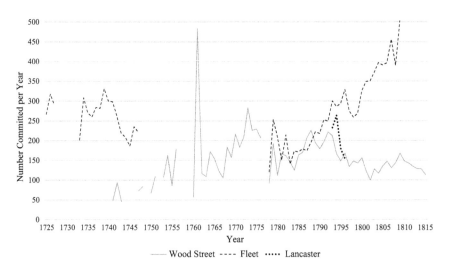

Figure 2.1 Annual Commitment Rate 1725–1815 at Wood Street Compter, Fleet Prison, and Lancaster Castle.

and 1796 to 1809 (reducing the total by twenty per year to reflect the average number of commitments for contempt or forfeiture), contributing a further 5,937 commitments not within the wider data. The totals are referred to as commitments rather than as unique debtors as there are occasional instances of individuals returning to the prison. While there are some specific case studies of recidivism that might be drawn from the registers, particularly at the Fleet, it is impossible to measure the rate at which this occurred both because separating common names is not feasible – Wood Street featuring twenty-five debtors called William Smith (1754–1813) – and as the vast majority of prisons to which these individuals might have been previously or subsequently committed are lost. Furthermore, at the Fleet, some debtors might appear multiple times in the same year. The overwhelming majority of the 308 prisoners who removed to the King's Bench and eventually returned to the Fleet did so within six months, resulting in a slight inflation of the number of individual commitments per year across the period.

Use of debtors' prisons by creditors underwent significant variation in the eighteenth century though not all fluctuation was a result of changes in the rate or style of commercial activity as was demonstrated at Wood Street in 1761. While this year was relatively mundane in terms of economic activity, a slight but significant addition to the 1760 Insolvency Act caused a spike in imprisonment unmatched across the period. From 1736 legislators had included mechanisms within the variously passed Insolvency Acts by which creditors could compel prisoners to apply for release within twenty days (on pain of death) in an attempt to tackle a perceived problem with debtors who were content to remain in prison indefinitely, possessing sufficient capital to support their lifestyle.[66] The addendum to the 1760 Act, commonly known as the Compulsive Clause, removed the requirement that prisoners be confined before a specified date meaning that creditors now had the power to compel future debtors from the moment of confinement on a permanent basis.[67] Newspaper fear about the potential for fraud and misunderstanding of how the Clause operated led to a crisis of creditor confidence in the summer of 1761 (particularly in London). Traders rushed to imprison and compel debtors before they could do so fraudulently leading to significant numbers who would not normally have been arrested finding their way into suddenly overcrowded debtors' prisons. In September, one newspaper reported to shocked readers that 'there are upwards of 300 prisoners in the Poultry Compter, and two thirds of that number in … Wood-Street, the greatest part whereof are … upon the Compulsive Clause'.[68] The crisis was short lived however, Parliament abolishing the Clause upon its return in November 1761, and few compelled debtors spent more than a month within gaol. Without this addendum, the annual commitment total was likely to have been a quarter of the 483 actually confined at Wood Street. How the crisis unfurled is a valuable window onto the frailty of interpersonal trust though is of only minor relevance to creditor attitudes towards confinement as a whole in the eighteenth century.

More sustained trends than in 1761 indicate patterns within the broader in-formal economy. There was no sustained period of decline in use by creditors in line with expanding wealth and economic complexity or modernity. By contrast, use of Wood Street – being a first destination prison where debtors had been arrested in the days preceding commitment – appears to have grown after 1740. This image of growth is slightly exacerbated by the loss of data from the 1720s when the national population of debtors' prisons was almost certainly at its highest rate. The indicative Fleet data suggests commitment rates c.300 while in a surviving list drawn up of the 321 debtors held at Wood Street on the 15th December 1724, 104 had been committed in the previous twelve months.[69] This decade experienced a significant disruption to the informal credit market as a result of the South Sea Bubble, other fragmentary data suggesting higher than average commitments.[70] The number of applica-tions to Insolvency Acts in this decade grew to c.4,500 from pre-Bubble rates of c.2,000, less conservative estimates rating this growth from c.2,500 to over 8,000 applications in the same period.[71] While studies of bankruptcy have downplayed the effects of the Bubble, this pinnacle of debt imprisonment testifies to the significant impacts which cash shortages and lost confidence in the informal credit market had upon the unbankruptable population.[72] Lower numbers applying for the 1736 and 1743 Insolvency Acts indicate that high commitment rates probably dissipated relatively quickly at non-superior court prisons. The Fleet commitment rate in the 1730s, mirroring that of the mid-1720s, may have represented the final ripples of the Bubble, with prisoners arriving via *habeas corpus* having been arrested several years prior or being involved in complicated cases which were still unresolved. Isaac Levy was committed to the Fleet more than a decade after the Bubble in July 1734 owing a total of £3806 10s arising from still ongoing disputes related to mutually owned South Sea stock.[73] The 1740s represented a level of commit-ment that was probably on a par with the pre-Bubble era (when accounting for the lost ability to confine those owing under £2) and with most prisons in the 1730s, suggesting that subsequent growth represented an actual shift in non-crisis committing.

Some accounts have previously posited that as revolutions in commerce, finance, and particularly consumption led to increased indebtedness, use of debt imprisonment may have similarly risen. Margot Finn, for example, suggested that the beginning of the reform movements in the early 1770s reflected increased use of debtors' prisons in the previous two decades fol-lowing consumptive growth.[74] While bankruptcy rates, based on Julian Hoppit's 1987 assessment, began to grow from c.200 per year to c.400 in the late 1760s, it appears arrest rates had already been growing for two decades.[75] Annual commitment rates at Wood Street grew from under hundred a year to c.140 in the mid-1750s, a figure to which average commitments at the prison frequently returned over the following six decades, suggesting that new commercial behaviour did, as predicted by Finn, lead to increased debt imprisonment (at least in London), particularly if the 55% increase in annual commitments across fifteen years was replicated in other gaols. Commitments increased again from around 1768 (183) and climbed to an overall peak in 1773 (283). However, this increase was short lived, rates swiftly returning to the c.140 standard established in the 1750s. There was another brief period of increased annual commitment 1786–1793 when entries to the prison averaged 201 debtors per annum. Commitment patterns soon reverted to the earlier standard, the remainder of the period averaging 139 commitments per annum. Changes in the Lancaster rate were on a par with the compter for the three years available suggesting the broader applicability of the non-superior court data. There was some gradual decline in commitment rates at the compter after 1813, but rather than represent any drop in the number of committed debtors in the capital, it instead reflects the construction and opening of the new Debtors' Prison for London and Westminster, the compter ceasing to take debtors after 1815.[76] While commitments fell from 148 in 1810 to 128 in 1814, rates remained on a par with those over the previous half-century. Even with the prison closing at the end of the year, 114 debtors were committed to Giltspur Street in 1815, Wynifred Griffiths entering the compter less than two weeks before it shut.[77]

The relative consistency of commitments to Wood Street of c.140 was partly a consequence of the physical limitation on the number of debtors who could reasonably be committed to the gaol in a given year. Potential prisoners, excluding those tied by the process of their arrest to a particular gaol (such as through the Court of Requests), were probably committed by courts and bailiffs to specific local prisons at a commensurate rate to which existing residents were released. Arrests were thus distributed relatively evenly across prisons in a city such as London with numerous gaols; a high commitment rate at one was therefore probably reflected at other institutions. For example, in the unusual year of 1761 when 424 were released from Wood Street by the Compulsive Clause, other prisons saw similarly high rates of release: 605 debtors at the Poultry Compter, 396 at the Marshalsea, 115 at the Borough Compter, and 111 from Ludgate were compelled.[78] It seems unlikely based on the size of the Common Side at both the Wood Street and Giltspur Street compters, the number of Master's Side apartments, and assuming that a proportion of prisoners brought families with them, that the gaol could have comfortably held more than one hundred debtors at a time, even this figure probably being an overestimation of realistic capacity before 1791.[79] Figure 2.2 presents the monthly population at each of the prisons studied, calculated[80] from release dates and estimating missing dates based upon stated release methods. The regular commitment rate of c.140 apparently maintained the compter's population at capacity. During the period 1795–1800 when the annual commitment rate ranged between 134 and 168, the monthly population did not drop below 49, while it also peaked at 90 and averaging c.70; these might be called typical years. By contrast, increases in the annual rate such as that 1769–1775 – in which annual commitment totals rose above 200 five times – led to a commensurately higher population between 75 and

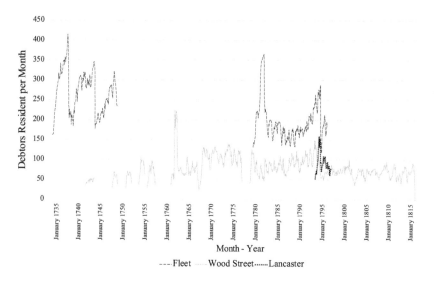

Figure 2.2 Calculated Monthly Population of the Fleet, Wood Street Compter, and Lancaster County Gaol, 1735–1815.

139, averaging 110. This undoubtedly was a period of overcrowding at the compter. It can also be assumed that other prisons in the vicinity of Wood Street were similarly crowded as one would expect these gaols to otherwise dilute the intake of the compter and prevent overcrowding, suggesting that the compter commitment figures are broadly indicative of patterns at other London prisons and the overall behaviour of arresting creditors.

Commitment rates at the Fleet were always likely to be higher than those at other prisons due not only to the prison's attractiveness but also to its size, being able to contain hundreds of debtors and their families at a time as is clear in 2.2. Its low commitment rate c.1780, placing it on an apparent par with the compter, is therefore striking. This appears to have been a consequence largely of the Gordon Riots rather than reflecting change in the behaviour of creditors. In 1780, the gates of the prison were forced open and, after the inhabitants had been given 'time to remove their goods', the 'mob ... set fire [to] different apartments' in the gaol and 'the whole was [soon] entirely consumed'.[81] The prison was repaired relatively quickly though in 1781 the site was still described as a memorial of 'the devastations committed by the populace ... [in] the sacred name of religion'.[82] This reduced the number who could be committed to the Fleet before full reconstruction as well as its attractiveness to potential debtors arriving via *habeas corpus*. Given these events, the decline from 253 commitments in 1779 to 150 in 1781 (Wood Street experiencing 192 and 167 commitments in the same period, only suffering minor damage during the riots) appears as perhaps a shallower decline than might have occurred. Furthermore, while annual commitment totals may have been similar, as is clear in 2.2 the actual population at the Fleet remained far higher than at the compter.

Following the increase in commitment 1740–1760 at Wood Street, rates continued to increase reflecting increased commercial activity though were also frequently interrupted, growth being exhibited at the compter 1764–1775, at all prisons 1784–1793, and at the Fleet 1795–1809 (and possibly beyond). The period between the end of the Seven Years War and the outbreak of conflict with American colonists represented the sharpest growth in and highest rates of commitment to the compter. While it is difficult to attribute this alteration directly to military action, it is certainly notable that an era of increasing imprisonment leading to overcrowding of London gaols was bookended by two moments of global instability which returned monthly populations rates to manageable proportions. The passage of seven Insolvency Acts 1765–1781 consistently failed to return the compter's monthly population to its traditional average of below seventy, suggesting other factors were aggressively driving confinement. Growth in commitment following the end of Atlantic conflict was briefly interrupted in 1789 and then ended following the resumption of struggle in Europe in 1793 at all three prisons. In direct contrast to the post South Sea experience, commitment rates fell when moments of instability occurred. In part this reflects the seriousness for general commerce of the 1720s as well as the increased likelihood that business failure would result in bankruptcy after c.1770 due to the lower barrier of entry the £100 debt requirement represented. Victims of outright business failure were more likely to be included in bankruptcy proceedings than in debtors' prisons seventy years after the South Sea Bubble, emphasising debt imprisonment's role (from a creditor's perspective) in tackling failure to pay debts rather than dispensing of those completely unable to pay them. The Fleet did hold significant numbers of those experiencing business collapse and its commitment rates continued to grow during periods of instability such as after 1793. It thus represented a middle ground between normal debt imprisonment of the merely unhelpful and bankruptcy of the insolvent. However, it was still a debtors' prison and patterns of use were more closely aligned with similar institutions overall. Outbreaks of war created spikes in bankruptcy, totalling 1,276 in 1793 (more than double the previous year's rate), which reflected similar growth in superior court commitments while decreasing them at standard prisons. However, economic crises such as that in 1797 which had a measurable impact on bankruptcy did not increase superior court confinement.[83] At the Fleet 1797 heralded a decline in commitments which was not reversed until after 1800. Decreased use of arrest in this era therefore probably indicates contractions in credit rather than reduced failure; when the market was unstable and confidence low, traders lent to a smaller share of their customer base with whom they were more familiar or refused to lend further to already heavily indebted business contacts, reducing the number of potential imprisonable debtors. By contrast, when imprisonment rates were high it reflected periods of prosperity when traders were able to take more significant risks by lending widely and generously which led both to increased profitability and default rates, creditors being able to survive extended, uncertain, or even failed repayments.[84]

Continued growth in bankruptcy cases across the eighteenth century has been previously qualified in the context of population increase. The low level of increase at the Wood Street and Fleet gaols might therefore be seen as overall decline when rated against London's commensurate population growth from 675,000 in 1750 to almost one million by 1800.[85] However, due to the physical limitations of gaol size, it was impossible for commitment rate growth to match population increase, an issue reflected by the construction of new and larger prisons after 1780. This data can be extrapolated to a national comparison which indicates creditor use of prisons was not significantly declining. Assessing the national population of prisons is fraught with caveats and complexities. John Howard's various prison visits in the 1770s and 1780s detailed 2–2,500 resident debtors at a time, a figure far smaller than contemporary estimates such as Dr Johnson's in 1759 'that more than twenty thousand are at this time prisoners for debt'. Johnson's figure is almost certainly too high; he himself in a 1767 collected edition of *The Idler* essays noted 'this number was at that time confidently published, but the author has since found reason to question the calculation'.[86] However, Howard's is also a poor representation of the extent of debt imprisonment being an assessment of those resident at a particular moment. Monthly populations outside of the superior court prisons, as is clear in Figure 2.2, were frequently around half the total committed in a given year, suggesting annual prison commitments c.1777 based on Howard's observations closer to five thousand. The irregularly passed Insolvency Acts, while freeing a minority of debtors across the period, provide a more effective tool for assessing the population over time. Haagen used the acts to assess the population of prisons in 1700 and 1800, concluding there was a decline in arrest rates from 1 in every 375–700 to 1 in every 500–1,000 adult males based on the number committed to the Fleet and King's Bench in specific years.[87] Tawny Paul has also recently used totals applying for the Acts to roughly estimate that 'in London between 1710 and 1770 … 570 to 1,549 individuals' were imprisoned each year based on the number committed to the Fleet and the King's Bench in selected years.[88] It is clear, however, from sustained examinations of commitment registers that the rate of prisoners who were released by an Act (particularly outside the superior courts) varied over the period as well as the raw numbers applying varying widely between types of prison. Even by conducting assessments based on the registers drawing on different prison types, any calculation (including this one) is likely to be crude and problematic as well as based on incomplete material. The following is therefore intended only to indicate general trends (to determine whether there is still a case for eighteenth-century imprisonment decline) and not as a calculation of the exact prison population, an objective that is almost certainly unachievable.

National population estimates are here produced for 1725, 1743, 1781, and 1794, each year selected based on the availability of data on Act application rates. These are far from perfect samples; 1725 is not based upon commitment registers, instead using surviving lists of prisoners present at Wood Street and the Poultry Compter in 1725, and Lancaster can only provide data for 1794. Initial surveys of the *London Gazette* indicated that in the years studied 2,977, 2,248, 1,355, and 1,394 unique debtors applied for relief in the year of the Act (not including fugitives or duplicate applications), suggesting a significant decline in debt imprisonment not evident in the commitment registers even beyond changing population rates. For the years after 1725, the percentage of debtors released that year who took the Act was calculated at Wood Street (44%, 8%, 11%), the Fleet (80%, 61%, 48%), and Lancaster (27%), excluding those who applied but were unsuccessful or were released in a subsequent year. Each gaol was taken as a representative of three broad categories of institutions, borough or civic prisons, the superior courts, and county gaols into which all prisons returning debtors to the *London Gazette* were divided, the categories representing 141, 2, and 61 institutions respectively. While Lancaster could only represent county gaols properly in 1794, a rate following the decline exhibited at the Fleet was roughly applied providing 67% and 47% for 1743 and 1781. Finally, in 1725, based on those who appeared in the lists for the Wood Street and Poultry compters provided to the Court of Aldermen who subsequently appeared in the *Gazette*, a general rate of 40% was arbitrarily applied to each category though if the Fleet was closer to its 1743 rate the total applying is reduced by c.600.

By multiplying application rates by the value needed to bring register rates to 100% of release in a given year, new national figures were devised of 7,443, 3,550, 5,803, and 6,069 debtors released from prisons in 1725, 1743, 1781, and 1794. These figures reinforce the assertion that the 1720s represented a high point of debt imprisonment as a result of the South Sea Bubble. In London 0.3% of the population might have been imprisoned in borough gaols or roughly,[89] when accounting for the c.20% of London debtors who were female, one in every hundred economically active adult males. It also removes the suggestion that imprisonment declined dramatically. In 1776, one newspaper reported 'there are upwards of 8,000 debtors in the different prisons waiting to take the benefit of the expected Act'; while this might previously have been dismissed as an exaggeration it accords largely with these figures and is possibly therefore based in some fact.[90] The percentage of the population experiencing debt imprisonment per year appears to have been largely stable between 1743 and 1794 at roughly three in five thousand nationally or, when only examining adult males, three in every thousand. This consistency largely reflected increased imprisonment rates in cities but decreased rates in provincial areas, ensuring that in the most capitalist areas creditors made more rather than less use of debt imprisonment. However, applying these figures outside of the benchmark years is complicated by the fact that the number released was higher in years of Acts than in the preceding year. The total released from the Fleet rose from 235 to 345 in 1742–1743 and 266 to 368 in 1793–1794. While the Wood Street total fell from 85 to 72 in 1742–1743, it increased from 86 to 96 in 1781–1782 and 175 to 181 in 1793–1794; at Lancaster the number released exploded[91] from 123 to 292. Nevertheless, even if the rate was reduced by a thousand debtors in non-Act years, this would still indicate that up to 5,000 individuals (a quarter of Johnson's but double Howard's estimate) were released from debtors' prisons every year in the late eighteenth century, with commensurate numbers therefore being committed. Considering that, after 1780, 95% of debtors in London were adult males (female imprisonment having declined significantly since the 1720s due to demographic changes), this arrest figure represents an even more significant fraction of the potential imprisonable group. In 1794, roughly 1,800 debtors were released from London borough gaols based on the above extrapolation. Even reducing this by 20% to provide a lower level of 1,500 in non-Act years (according with Tawny Paul's estimate's upper boundary), this still might represent 0.7% of all adult males being arrested in the capital every year. As it was suggested in 1792 that only 10–15% of writs issued resulted in an actual imprisonment, debts being satisfied in the interval, the total adult male population *facing* imprisonment each year may have been closer therefore to 4%, or one in every twenty-five men.[92]

These indicative population estimates demonstrate that prisoners were too numerous to have been a fringe element of the population nor did creditors cease to use the prisons in a considerable fashion during the eighteenth century. In part, that a supposed rise of enlightened capitalism failed to end the prisons is not surprising as the prisons were not being used to punish debtors but to facilitate justly owed repayments. Furthermore, this false assertion relies on an unstated assumption that imprisoned debtors constituted the impoverished underclasses who were punished by creditors for their poverty. By contrast, as the details of who was being arrested show (and thus by implication who creditors were not arresting), those whom creditors chose to arrest were frequently drawn from those most engaged in commercial and particularly proto-capitalist activity.

There was no unitary "debtor". Creditors targeted a broad swath of individuals across the period and the quantity of debt individual prisoners owed varied significantly. While William Snagge arrived at the compter in July 1800 owing an eye watering £40,000 to John Drummond of the prominent Drummond's banking house, William James Borroughs (committed 26th February 1789 and 'discharged' the same day) was one of three debtors in the compter registers committed for just a shilling, though Borroughs's obligations were more than trebled by court costs to 3s 10d alongside gaol fees.[93] At the Fleet sums were even more distorted; while £3 16s 8d represented the smallest commitment, James Baker was committed in 1746 owing the impossibly large sum of £300,000, a second smaller debt of £20 soon also being sued for demonstrating the breadth of debts even for an individual debtor, one presumably being a business obligation and the other personal.[94]

Table 2.1 Debts Owed at the Fleet Prison, Wood Street Compter (Without Court of Request Debtors), and Lancaster Castle Gaol, 1735–1815

Debt Range	Fleet		Wood Street		Lancaster	
<£10	115	2%	1,632	26%	48	6%
£10–20	713	9%	1,220	19%	207	27%
£20–30	649	9%	719	11%	126	16%
£30–40	628	8%	525	8%	97	13%
£40–50	494	7%	344	5%	62	8%
£50–60	420	6%	238	4%	42	5%
£60–70	271	4%	138	2%	26	3%
£70–80	329	4%	163	3%	26	3%
£80–90	183	2%	75	1%	21	3%
£90–100	392	5%	211	3%	17	2%
£100–200	1,329	18%	461	7%	58	8%
£200–500	1,049	14%	321	5%	28	4%
£500–1,000	507	7%	133	2%	10	1%
>£1,000	484	6%	175	3%	5	1%
Total	7,563	100%	6,355	100%	773	100%

However, as is clear from Table 2.1 depicting the distribution of debts owed at the three prisons exempting those committed by the Court of Requests who were confined through a court order rather than directly by a creditor, the majority owed smaller, more manageable though by no means meagre sums. That only c.15% of debtors outside of the superior court prisons owed enough to go bankrupt suggests further that the bankruptcy laws lacked the capability to deal with everyday debt. That 45% of Fleet debtors did qualify (if they were also "traders") equally suggests that creditors continued to favour this method of coercion over the legal settlement offered by application to the Lord Chancellor. The majority of values exhibited here generally do not imply business collapse or insolvency – rather they reflect the sums that commercially active individuals would have on their books at any time and probably also had debts of similar sizes owing to them. This situation only became problematic when financial strategy was disrupted by death, economic downturn, or when a creditor made an unexpected demand. It suggests that creditors used debtors' prisons against those with assets – those who were also in trade – rather than impoverished wage labourers who would not have accrued debts of this size. While this disrupts the traditional image of prisoners as poor consumers, it accords precisely with the image Daniel Defoe (who had first-hand knowledge of what led one to debtors' prison) provided of the operation of credit:

> A country clothier, … though [he] cannot have credit for spinning and weaving, he buys his Wooll at the Staplers or Fellmongers, and he gets two or three months credit for that; he buys his oil and soap of the country shopkeeper, or has it sent down from his factor at London, and gets

longer credit for that, and the like of all other things so that a Clothier of any considerable business, when he comes to die, shall appear to be four or five thousand pounds in debt.[95]

While Defoe suggests his clothier is safe due to the value he is, in turn, owed, if his stapler or factor had lost patience over the £30 or £40 he owed for individual goods then an arrest was not unlikely if he could not recover his own debts quickly enough. Proto-capitalism, leading to an overextension of credit, thus had all the probability of increasing use of debtors' prisons as abolishing them while the credit market remained so irregular.

Despite their general association with the middling sorts, it is clear that the populations of these three prisons, based upon their debts, were far from identical groups. While the Fleet would always be distinct – this data further revealing the significant number of wealthy prisoners owing sums it might take even the well-to-do middling sorts imprisoned in the compter a lifetime to accrue – those confined at Wood Street and Lancaster were not as similar as the commitment rates exhibited above imply. While comparable shares owed less than £50 (in itself a not inconsiderable sum for most working and trading people), a significantly larger group of debtors at Wood Street owed the smallest sums which amounted to barely more than subsistence credit. Even without the Court of Request debtors (who increase the share owing less than £10 to 43%), at Wood Street 18% owed less than £5 compared to only four debtors at the Fleet and one at Lancaster. The compter therefore potentially contained a more regular minority of poor, subsistence credit debtors though such sums were not necessarily inconsequential as they appear and may have still represented debts from trade. A labourer working on the building of the Giltspur Street Compter in c.1791 earned, at most, just 2s 4d per day. It would have taken such a worker forty-three days to accumulate £5, assuming they did not have to spend any of their wages. Even if able to obtain work at this rate on every single day of the year (an obviously impossible task even discounting the need to rest or take off holy days) they could barely have earned more than £40.[96] It seems unlikely that such individuals would have been lent sufficient credit to have been confined regularly in the compter. Rather the lower debts at Wood Street reflect the faster pace of trade in London than in disparate Lancashire. In the bustling shops of Cheapside surrounding the compter, traders (having wide customer bases all having purchased on credit) expected to be paid as quickly as possible in case their own suppliers or those they bought their own everyday and luxury goods from decided that payment was due. These individuals spent short periods in prison, an arrest being used as a blunt tool of ensuring payment was made immediately. Additionally, the process of procuring an arrest was faster and cheaper where the courts were local as in London. While those in Lancaster itself may have had recourse to easy justice, those residing in Bolton, Manchester, or Macclesfield may have only confined those with more pressing debts. Wood Street therefore combined those owing strictly business debts (such as Defoe's Clothier) alongside those who had made commercial purchases. If one examined the debtors' prison in Liverpool, the population would likely be more akin to that in Wood Street than at Lancaster Castle.

The impression that debtors were as likely to be traders engaged in the credit market as their creditors is furthered by Table 2.2's depiction of their occupational structure. Applicants to Insolvency Acts were required to submit a declaration of their status or occupation to the *London Gazette*. The table details the submissions of the 5,916 applicants to Insolvency Acts between 1725 and 1797 from the three prisons matched to the Wrigley *et al.* Primary, Secondary, Tertiary system of occupational coding (PST), though titled individuals have been extracted from the tertiary sector.[97] Additionally, 764 applicants stated more than one occupation. These secondary trades, such as the industrially polymathic Joseph Brinton confined in Wood Street in 1755 who described himself as a 'Locksmith, Bell-hanger, Kiln Plate Worker, and Innholder', have not been included in the table. Many cited occupations which involved similar trades and skills, Francis Harper at the Fleet in 1774 being a 'Spring maker and Tyre smith' while other bi-employed debtors had lesser work which supported their primary occupation (such as being both a farmer and butcher), which probably did not change their principal societal

Table 2.2 Occupations of Insolvency Act Applicants (1725–1797)

	Fleet	*Wood Street*	*Lancaster*
Total	4,025	1,123	768
Primary	4.2%	2.0%	15.2%
Secondary	41.2%	45.0%	46.4%
Tertiary	37.7%	37.8%	29.6%
Other	17.0%	15.2%	8.9%
Agriculture	4.2%	2.0%	15.2%
Food & Drink	6.2%	4.7%	7.4%
Clothing	6.5%	7.8%	4.3%
Footwear	1.9%	3.0%	2.7%
Textiles	3.1%	4.2%	18.5%
Woods	3.3%	4.4%	1.3%
Metals	9.5%	10.3%	3.5%
Building & Construction	4.3%	4.0%	3.9%
Other Manufacturing	6.3%	6.5%	4.8%
Dealers & Sellers	18.2%	18.4%	15.9%
Victualling & Innkeeping, etc.	9.8%	6.3%	13.8%
Financial Services	0.9%	0.8%	0.8%
Other Services	1.8%	1.9%	0.5%
Professions	3.8%	2.8%	1.6%
Transport & Communications	3.2%	7.5%	3.1%
Labourer	0.3%	1.6%	2.9%
Gentleman etc.	12.7%	6.9%	2.9%
No Occupation	4.0%	6.7%	3.1%

status. The 159 applicants who described themselves as a victualler in addition to another occupation might suggest, given that only two were female, that secondary occupations regularly represented a wife's business which was technically a husband's property under coverture.[98]

The occupational structure of the prisons was, as implied by the debts they owed, not identical due principally to their locations and entrance procedures. The Fleet contained significant numbers who listed themselves with some form of title. While Peers of the Realm were protected from imprisonment, their households including heirs were vulnerable and it was not unusual for those with statuses ranging from minor gentry to landed aristocracy to be arrested when necessary.[99] Numerous French titled names appear in the Fleet commitment registers after 1789, following their flight across the channel. In 1755, even the former King of Corsica, Theodore von Newhoff, was released from the King's Bench by an Insolvency Act and though described in the *Gazette* as a 'Baron ... from Westphalia' he reputedly 'registered his Kingdom ... for the use of his creditors' under the amnesty.[100] The clustering of such prisoners in the superior courts testifies further to their distinct status though the 7% of Wood Street prisoners identified as gentleman are also significant considering that they only constituted around 3% of Londoners.[101] Wood Street's inhabitants were therefore not entirely eclipsed by the superior courts in terms of prisoner status. The compter's gentlemen were poorer on average as while they had been lent double the average sum of their fellow prisoners released by an Act (c.£54), the average Fleet gentry debt of c.£420 was nearly four times the compter equivalent. Similarly, while all those at the compter were recorded as either a gentleman or gentlewoman alongside one esquire, the Fleet released seven baronets, the Marquis de Massiac, and Lady Ann Onslow through the Acts.

That the two London prisons differ from industrialising though still relatively rural Lancashire is to be expected. The predictably higher rate of agricultural occupations and of those working in textiles – even two of those identified as metal workers in Lancashire were involved in the textile trade, being 'cotton machine manufacturers' – suggests that prison populations did reflect the occupational foundations of surrounding areas. Lancaster Gaol also contained a higher degree of debtors who might be said to be engaged in work which could have been waged. Eighty of Lancaster's 141 textile professions were described as some form of 'weaver' who were probably distinct from the sixteen described as textile 'manufacturers'. These figures are distorted somewhat by the South Sea Bubble as 39% of the weavers were cleared in the 1720s along with 55% of Lancaster's labourers, the textile industry subsequently being dominated by manufacturers (particularly of cotton), dyers, and clothiers. Most of those, however, in the agricultural sector in this provincial gaol across the period were described as 'husbandman' compared to London's 'farmer' debtors, implying that more prisoners in Lancaster were of comparatively lower social statuses. While the Lancaster debtors should not be described as inherently "poorer" than those from London, they were drawn from a less wealthy pool of traders even if that wealth was only implied by the reputation (and credit) of their societal rank; it is also likely their arresting creditors were similarly poorer than those in London.

When examining the overall sectoral distribution of the Primary agricultural, Secondary manufacturing, and Tertiary service occupations there was a surprising amount of similarity between the three prisons. These shares are not in line with estimations of the national distribution of work. Estimates by Jacob Field (based upon declared statuses of grooms marrying in the *rules* of the Fleet) suggest a PST breakdown in 1751 of 7%, 60%, and 34% for London and 50%, 33%, and 17% for England as a whole.[102] When excluding debtors who were described as labourers or with non-occupational statuses (including titles, marital status, and racial identities such as the two Wood Street prisoners who identified themselves only as 'a Jew' in 1725) the prisons still underrepresent agriculture even for urban London and overrepresent the tertiary sector by a striking margin. Even in 1851 the tertiary sector was just 22.8% of the national distribution compared (when removing "other" occupations) to 53%, 49%, and 34% at the Fleet, Wood Street, and Lancaster in the eighteenth century.[103]

Strikingly, in London the manufacturing sector, while being overrepresented in Lancaster, constituted a smaller section of the prison population than they did within the city as a whole. This skewing of expected occupational structure indicates that prisoners were not drawn evenly from across the population and that certain trades were more likely to experience the credit difficulties that could see them imprisoned. Debtors were, as their debts suggest, predominantly middle class even in Lancaster. For example, in Field's 1751 data, Dealer & Seller business owners constituted only 3.9% of the population, while Transport & Communications (generally wage earners) contributed 21.1%, having inverse relevance at the prisons. Wage earners were less likely to appear at the prisons, their credit being dominated by subsistence or minor luxury purchases. They did always constitute a minority of prisoners, but their place was significantly lesser than their frequency within the urban polity and that the insecurity of their economic status would suggest. Instead the largest groups were those involved in vending or dealing – the crux of the credit market – being those who by necessity offered and took on more credit than any other occupation (achieving profit through risk). Similarly, professionals represented only a small subset due to their lesser reliance on credit. Those involved in medicine, representing 41% of imprisoned professionals, were an exception as unlike architects, rectors, and schoolmasters, they regularly relied on credit, one newspaper commentator asking 'how would it be possible for an Apothecary to [avoid credit] for many of their patients seem to be affronted if a bill be sent in once in a year'.[104] While many were educated and thought themselves distinct from common shopkeepers, in terms of the processes of trade, they were subject to the same strictures and calamities as the local fruiterer.

Despite their wealth and social important, businesses such as alehousekeepers or Defoe's clothier which were reliant upon extended credit both to customers and from suppliers, dominated those imprisoned while also being more likely to arrest those they had more in common with economically than their customers. This distinction in who was being arrested is key to why debt imprisonment was not antithetical to enlightened capitalism. While the arrest of wage labourers by gentlemen might fairly be seen as unproductive and a form of punishment, a brewer imprisoning an innkeeper (who he was legally incapable of bankrupting) was merely ensuring that the needs of capital were met. Debt imprisonment operated as a coercive mechanism of contract enforcement – it relied on debtors being able to actually make payment when pressed. Creditors understood the differences between their debtors and would not have proceeded against every debtor; lost debt was the price of doing business. However, throughout the period there were those who needed to be faced with tangible consequences to convince them it was necessary to make payment, the advancement of the Industrial Revolution failing to change this fact. If it had any impact, it may have been in an increased protection of the manufacturing classes from imprisonment as small independent workshops lost out to mechanisation and joined the ranks of the waged.

★★

The increased use of imprisonment as a mechanism of punishment did not, within the eighteenth century, lead to a substantial decrease in creditor use of debtors' prisons as a means of securing financial recovery. While further alignment of prisons with corrective confinement of felons – even the death penalty ceasing to be a spectacle once it was moved within gaols – was largely concurrent with the nineteenth-century collapse of debt imprisonment, the two developments were not necessarily symbiotic. Though debt imprisonment peaked in the 1720s due to the wide-ranging South Sea shocks, following a return to pre-Bubble confinement rates the raw numbers and potentially the percentage of the population imprisoned per year grew alongside increased commercialism. From the evidence of commitment registers alone, there was no sign in 1800 that the prisons would not still be operating regularly in 1900 as they had in 1700. Furthermore, creditors were not merely lashing out at the impoverished victims of capitalist activity – instead they took out writs against their fellow Smithians to protect the integrity of their business reliant upon the undeveloped informal credit market. The most likely contribution of capitalism to reducing prison intake was not its "enlightened" status therefore but in consigning those in the lower middling sorts to wage labour –being unable to compete as independent tradespeople – and thus being unlikely to accrue enough debt worth imprisoning. The prisons did remain diverse institutions even if those at bottom of the economic pile became safer from *mesne* process both through demographic and legal changes. The population and experience of being confined within any given gaol was far from unitary even within a single city though largely reflecting the hierarchical nature of England at this time. This institution was then as informal (in terms of being centrally administered or designed) as the credit market it served.

The scholarship of "enlightened capitalism" does reflect a real change in societal attitude towards debt imprisonment at least within the pamphlet literature. Particularly in the later eighteenth century, there emerged significant numbers of new charitable societies and a growing sense that the 'cruelties' of debt imprisonment could be mitigated. This almost certainly arose from the increased population of prisons observed within commitment registers. As elderly prisons struggled to cope with populations exceeding their seventeenth-century construction, the suffering of inhabitants became difficult to ignore. However, this change in literature did not mandate that change occurred in actual practice, not least because while creditors were happy to confine their debtors, they were less likely to willingly boast about it in the public print. In this sense then, without the epithet "enlightened", the attribution of 'capitalist' to the debtors' prison can be seen as accurate in generalities. A socially stratified system, which prioritised interests of the individual creditor's capital over the well-being of any individual member of society about which much was written but little done to reform – it is hard to find a better definition of eighteenth-century debt imprisonment than capitalist.

Notes

1 John Howard, *The State of the Prisons in England and Wales, with Preliminary Observations, and an Account of Some Foreign Prisons* (London: 1777), p. 8; Prison Committee of Bridewell Hospital, *Propositions for Reform* (London: 1793), p. 1; House of Commons, *Second Report from the Committee on the Prisons within the City of London and Borough of Southwark* (1818), pp. 254–255; Robin Evans, *The Fabrication of Virtue – English Prison Architecture, 1750–1840* (Cambridge: Cambridge University Press, 1982), p. 21; J. M. Beattie, *Policing and Punishment in London, 1660–1750* (Oxford: Oxford University Press, 2001), p. 24; Bruce Watson, "The Compter Prisons of London", *London Archaeologist* vol. 5, no. 5 (1993), p. 120; Paul Griffiths, "Contesting London Bridewell, 1576–1580", *Journal of British Studies* vol. 42, no. 3 (2003), p. 286.

2 See: Randell McGowen, "Penal Reform and Politics in Early Nineteenth-Century England: "A Prison Must Be a Prison"", in *Imagining the British Atlantic after the American Revolution*, eds. Michael Meranze and Saree Makdisi (Toronto: University of Toronto Press, 2015), pp. 219–239; James Sharpe, "Civility, Civilizing Processes, and the End of Public Punishment in England", in *Civil Histories – Essays Presented to Sir Keith Thomas*, eds. Peter Burke, Brian Harrison, and Paul Slack (Oxford: Oxford University Press, 2000), pp. 228–230; Simon Devereaux, "The Making of the Penitentiary Act, 1775–9", *The Historical Journal* vol. 42, no. 2 (1999), pp. 405–433; W. Chalkin, "The Reconstruction of London's Prisons, 1770–99: An Aspect of the Growth of Georgian London", *London Journal* vol. 9, no. 1 (1983), p. 20.

3 Michel Foucault, *Discipline and Punish – The Birth of the Prison* (New York: Vintage Books, 1995), p. 7.

4 Evans, *Fabrication of Virtue*, p. 19.

5 Gustav Peebles, "Washing Away the Sins of Debt: The Nineteenth-Century Eradication of the Debtors' Prison", *Comparative Studies in Society and History* vol. 55,

no. 3 (2013), pp. 701–724; Gustav Peebles, "Whitewashing and Leg-Bailing: On the Spatiality of Debt", *Social Anthropology* vol. 20, no. 4 (2012), pp. 432, 435; Gustav Peebles, *The Euro and Its Rivals: Currency and the Construction of a Transnational City* (2011), pp. 124–126; see: Gustav Peebles, "The Anthropology of Credit and Debt", *Annual Review of Anthropology* vol. 39 (2010), pp. 225–240.

6 Charles Dickens, *Little Dorrit* (London: 1857), p. 41.

7 Anon. *The Debtor and Creditor's Assistant; or, a Key to the King's Bench and Fleet Prisons* (London: 1793), p. 83.

8 Paul Hess Haagen, "Imprisonment for Debt in England and Wales", unpublished PhD thesis, University of Princeton (1986), pp. 54–80; Tawny Paul, *Poverty of Disaster – Debt and Insecurity in Eighteenth-Century Britain* (Cambridge: Cambridge University Press, 2019), pp. 43–44.

9 Philip Woodfine, "Debtors, Prisons, and Petitions in Eighteenth-Century England", *Eighteenth Century Life* vol. 30, no. 2 (Spring 2006), pp. 1–31.

10 "Order Books", 1715–1738, Cambridgeshire Quarter Sessions Records: Court in Session, Cambridgeshire Archives, Cambridge, Q/SO/4, 195.

11 "Order Books", Q/SO/4, 6.

12 See: Henry Brooke, *The History of Henry Earl of Moreland Vol. I* (London: 1781), p. 263.

13 Jerry White, "Pain and Degradation in Georgian London: Life in the Marshalsea Prison", *History Workshop Journal* vol. 68 (2009), pp. 69–98; Anon. *A Report from the Committee Appointed to Enquire into the State of the Gaols of This Kingdom. Relating to the Marshalsea Prison; and Farther Relating to the Fleet Prison* (London: 1730); Roger Lee Brown, *A History of the Fleet Prison, London – The Anatomy of the Fleet* (Lampeter: Edwin Mellen Press, 1996); Watson, "Compter Prisons", p. 118; Woodfine, "Debtors, Prisons, and Petitions", p. 18; Philippa Hardman, "Fear of Fever and the Limits of the Enlightenment – Selling Prison Reform in Late Eighteenth-Century Gloucestershire", *Cultural and Social History* vol. 10, no. 4 (2013), pp. 511–531; "Ventilation … Gaol Fever and Its Prevention, the Substance of Information Given to a Committee", 1747–1753, Newgate Prison: Administration, LMA, CLA/035/02/049.

14 See: Howard, *State of the Prisons*; James Neild, *Account of Persons Confined for Debt, in the Various Prisons of England and Wales; Together with Their Provisionary Allowance during Confinement: As Reported to the Society for the Discharge and Relief of Small Debtors, in April, May, June &c 1800* (London: 1800); "List of Prisoners in the Compter Made Per out of the Ct of Ald", 15th December 1724, Wood Street Compter later Giltspur Street Compter, LMA, CLA/028/01/043; "Draft Report on State and Number of Prisoners", 1802, Newgate Prison: Miscellaneous Papers, LMA, CLA/035/02/026, (vi); William Holdsworth, *A History of English Law Vol. XIII* (London: Methuen & co., 1952), p. 377; Woodfine, "Debtors, Prisons, and Petitions", pp. 1–31.

15 Brown, *Anatomy of the Fleet*, pp. 154, 170–171; Jay Cohen, "The History of Imprisonment for Debt and Its Relation to the Development of Discharge in Bankruptcy", *Journal of Legal History* vol. 3 (1982), pp. 158–159; Matthew J. Baker, Metin Cosgel, and Thomas J. Miceli, "Debtors' Prisons in America: An Economic Analysis", *Journal of Economic Behaviour & Organisation* vol. 84 (2012), pp. 218–219.

16 "List of Prisoners in the Poultry Compter 16 Dec 1724 with Original Causes of Detainer, None Being Detained for Fees Only", Poultry Compter, LMA, CLA/030/02/006. For non-debtor prisoners see fragmentary surviving Charge and Commitment Books, 1782–1823, Poultry Compter, LMA, CLA/030/01.

17 Samuel Pepys (Henry B. Wheatley ed.), *The Diary of Samuel Pepys … Transcribed from the Shorthand Manuscript … Edited with Additions by Henry B. Wheatley. Vol. III* (London: George Bell & Sons, 1893), pp. 379–380.

18 Walter Thornbury, *Old and New London: A Narrative of Its History, Its People, and Its Places Vol.1* (London: Cassell, Petter, & Galpin, 1873), p. 368; W. Stubbs, *The Crown Circuit Companion … Vol. I* (London: 1749), p. 18; Anon. *The Debtor's Pocket Guide, in Cases of Arrest* (London: 1776), p. 137; Anon. *Considerations on the Laws between Debtors and Creditors* (London: 1779), p. 21; Anon. *A Concise Abstract of the Most Important Clauses in the Following Interesting Acts of Parliament Passed in the Sessions of 1781* (London: 1781), p. 91; Anon. *The Gentleman, Merchant, Tradesman, Lawyer, and Debtor's Pocket Guide, in Cases of Arrest* (Bath: 1785), p. 107; Corporation of London, *The Names and Address of the Several Officers of the City of London* (1789), p. 65; Anon. *Copy of the Resolutions Agreed to at a Meeting of the Magistrates of the Three Divisions of the County of Lincoln* (1791), p. 4.

19 Fleet Prison Commitment Books 1686–1842, Records of the Fleet Prison, TNA, PRIS 1; "List of Prisoners Handed over by the Sheriffs to Their Successors on 28 Sept Annually, with Notes of Occurrences during the Subsequent Year", 1741–1815, Wood Street Compter later Giltspur Street Compter, LMA, CLA/028/01/001-040; King's (Queen's) Bench Prison Commitment Books 1719–1862, Records of the King's Bench Prison, TNA, PRIS 4; "Lancaster Gaol Register of Debtors and Plaintiffs", 1793–1796, Home Office and Prison Commission Records: Prison Records Series 1, TNA, PCOM 2/440.

20 "List for Marshalsea", 1769, Surrey Quarter Sessions – Records Relating to the Release of Debtors, Surrey History Centre, Woking, QS3/2/20-21.

21 John Timbs, *Curiosities of London* (London: 1867), p. 345.

22 Corporation of London, *The Names and Address of the Several Officers of the City of London* (1789), p. 65.

23 For the sake of simplicity, I refer to both gaols by the general moniker of "Wood Street" or "the compter" unless the institution's latter incarnation is particularly relevant.

24 "List of Prisoners Handed over by the Sheriffs to their Successors on 28 Sept Annually, with Notes of Occurrences during the Subsequent Year", 1788–1791, Wood Street Compter later Giltspur Street Compter, LMA, CLA/028/01/027.

25 T. F. Reddaway, *The Rebuilding of London after the Great Fire* (London: Jonathon Capt Ltd, 1940), p. 189; "Wood Street Compter", 1666–1676, Rebuilding of London after the Great Fire, Corporation of London, LMA, COL/SJ/03/027; Dorothy Stroud, "The Giltspur Street Compter", *Architectural History* vol. 27 (1984), p. 127; Arthur Stratton, "Two Forgotten Buildings by the Dances", *The Architectural Review* vol. xl (1916), pp. 21–24.

26 Stephanie Adele Leeman, "Stone Walls Do Not a Prison Make: The Debtors' Prison, York", *York Historian* vol. 11 (1994), pp. 23–39; T. P. Cooper, *The History of the Castle of York – From Its Foundation to the Present Day with an Account of the Building of Clifford's Tower* (London: Elliot Stock, 1911), pp. 209–222; William Hargreave, *History and Description of the Ancient City of York, Vol. II* (York: William Alexander, 1818), pp. 232–244; the prison's main building now contains the York Castle Museum – while other buildings used as gaols such as Lancaster Castle still stand, very few purpose built debtors' prisons survived the nineteenth century.

27 Eric Stockdale, *A Study of Bedford Prison 1660–1877* (Bedford: The Bedfordshire Historical Record Society, 1977), pp. 36, 45–49; Gillian Selley, "Charles Lanyon, Merchant of Penzance: Victim of Cruelty and Corruption in the County Debtors Prison in Exeter", *The Devon Historian* vol. 83 (2014), pp. 39–48; Gary Calland, *A History of the Devon County Prison for Debtors in St. Thomas* (Exeter: Little History, 1999).

28 Howard, *State of the Prisons*, p. 277.

29 Howard, *State of the Prisons*, p. 344.

30 Chalkin, "The Reconstruction of London's Prisons", pp. 21–34; Woodfine, "Debtors, Prisons, and Petitions", pp. 1–31; Petitions of Prisoners, Offices of Newgate and the Compters, and Other Persons relating to Prison Life, Repair of Prisons, Collections, Ill Health, Abuse by Officers, for Discharge, &c", 1675–1700, Prisons and Compter – General, LMA, CLA/032/01/021.

31 Howard, *State of the Prisons*, pp. 248–249.

32 Margaret DeLacy, *Prison Reform in Lancashire, 1700–1850 – A Study in Local Administration* (Stanford: Stanford University Press, 1986).

33 Joanna Innes "The King's Bench Prison in the Later Eighteenth Century: Law, Authority and Order in a London Debtors' Prison", in *An Ungovernable People – The English and Their Law in the Seventeenth and Eighteenth Centuries*, ed. John Brewer and John Styles (London: Hutchinson, 1980), p. 253; Ian P. H. Duffy, *Bankruptcy and Insolvency in London During the Industrial Revolution* (New York: Garland Publishing Inc, 1985), pp. 106, 112; A. F. Pollard, "The Growth of the Court of Requests", *The English Historical Review* vol. 56, no. 222 (April 1941), pp. 300–303; W. H. D Winder, "The Courts of Requests", *The Law Quarterly Review* vol. 52, no. 207 (1936), p. 373; Margot Finn, "Debt and Credit in Bath's Court of Requests, 1829–39", *Urban History* vol. 21 (October 1994), p. 213; Michele Slatter, "The Norwich Court of Requests – A Tradition Continued", *Journal of Legal History* vol. 5, no. 3 (1984), p. 97; Margot C. Finn, *The Character of Credit – Personal Debt in English Culture, 1740–1914* (Cambridge: Cambridge University Press, 2003), p. 202.

34 William Smith, *State of the Gaols in London, Westminster, and Borough of Southwark. To Which Is Added, an Account of the Present State of Convicts Sentenced to Hard Labour on Board the Justitia upon the River Thames* (London: 1776), p. 33; Anon. *Debtor and Creditor's Assistant*, p. 67.

35 Howard, *State of the Prisons*, pp. 274–276.

36 Howard, *State of the Prisons*, p. 405.

37 Anon. *Debtor and Creditor's Assistant*, p. 42.

38 Anon. *Law Quibbles: Or, a Treatise of the Evasions, Tricks, Turns and Quibbles, Commonly Used in the Profession of the Law to the Prejudice of Clients* (London: 1736), pp. 27, 72; Brown, *Anatomy of the Fleet*, p. 158; Anon. *Debtor and Creditor's Assistant*, p. 38.

39 Haagen, "Imprisonment for Debt", p. 65; T. Pearce, *The Poor Man's Lawyer: Or, Laws Relating to the Inferior Courts Laid Open* (London: 1755), p. 62.

40 Brown, *Anatomy of the Fleet*, p. 158.

41 John Macky, *A Journey through England in Familiar Letters from a Gentleman Here, to His Friend Abroad in Two Volumes, Vol. II* (London: J. Pemberton, 1722), p. 208.

42 Roger Lee Brown, "The Rise and Fall of the Fleet Marriages", in *Marriage and Society – Studies in the Social History of Marriage*, ed. R. B. Outhwaite (London: Europa Publications Ltd, 1981), pp. 117–136.

43 Anon. *Debtor and Creditor's Assistant*, pp. 7–11.

44 Brown, *Anatomy of the Fleet*, p. 267; Anon. *London and Its Environs Described* (London: 1761), p. 309.

45 Anon. *Debtor and Creditor's Assistant*, p. 12.

46 Journal of the House of Commons, *Report for the Committee Appointed to Enquire into the Practice and Effects of Imprisonment for Debt* (1792), p. 46.

47 John Mackay, *A True State of the Proceedings of the Prisoners in the Fleet-Prison, in Order to the Redressing Their Grievances, before the Court of Common-Pleas* (London: 1729), pp. 5–6.

48 Anon. *Debtor and Creditor's Assistant*, pp. 10, 11.

49 Johann Wilhelm von Archenholtz, *A Picture of England: Containing a Description of the Laws, Customs, and Manners of England ... Translated from the French* (Dublin: 1791), p. 168.

50 Cheryll Duncan, "'A Debt Contracted in Italy': Ferdinando Tenducci in a London Court and Prison", *Early Music* vol. 42, no. 2 (2014), p. 225; Nigel Stirk, "Arresting Ambiguity: The Shifting Geographies of a London Debtors' Sanctuary in the Eighteenth Century", *Social History* vol. 25, no. 3 (October 2000), p. 319; Simon Wood, *Remarks on the Fleet Prison: or, Lumber-House for Men and Women. Written by a Prisoner on the Common-Side, Who Hath Lain a Prisoner Neat Three Years, on the Penalty of a Bond. No Debtor* (London: 1733), p. 12.

51 Brown, *Anatomy of the Fleet*, p. 235.

52 Johann Wilhelm von Archenholtz, *A View of the British Constitution and, of the Manners and Customs of the People of England* (Edinburgh: 1794), p. 278 (while this is an updated version of the Archenholtz tract cited above, his two accounts of the *rules* differ in detail and disdain).

53 "List of Prisoners Handed over by the Sheriffs to Their Successors on 28 Sept Annually, with Notes of Occurrences during the Subsequent Year", 1780–1781, LMA, CLA/028/01/023; "Commitment Registers", 1778–1782, Fleet Prison, TNA, PRIS 1/11.

54 Brown, *Anatomy of the Fleet*, p. 267.

55 Innes, "King's Bench", p. 256.

56 John Everett, *A Genuine Narrative of the Memorable Life and Actions of John Everett* (London: 1730), pp. 12–13.

57 Anon. *The Ambulator; or, the Stranger's Companion in a Tour Round London* (London: 1782), p. xvi.

58 Anon. *Debtor and Creditor's Assistant*, p. 2.

59 Clement Cruttwell, *A Tour through the Whole Island of Great Britain; Divided into Journeys. Interspersed with Useful Observations, Vol. I* (London: 1801), p. 101.

60 Samuel Keimer, *A Search after Religion, among the Many Modern Pretenders to It* (London: 1718), p. 22; Smith, *State of the Gaols*, pp. 32–33; Woodfine, "Debtors, Prisons, and Petitions", pp. 1–31; Richard Britnell, "Town Life", in *A Social History of England, 1200–1500*, eds. Rosemary Horrox and Mark Ormrod (Cambridge: Cambridge University Press, 2006), p. 141; William Paget, *The Humours of the Fleet. A Poem* (Birmingham: T. Aris, 1749); Anon. *Debtor and Creditor's Assistant*, p. 45.

61 Mary Wells, *Memoirs of the Life of Mrs Sumbel, Late Wells; of the Theatres-Royal, Drury-Lane, Covent-Garden, and Haymarket. In Three Volumes. Written by Herself. Vol. I* (London: 1811), pp. 180–188.

62 Haagen, "Imprisonment for Debt", p. 66.

63 "A List of Such Persons Who Appear by the Fleet Commitment Books to Have Been Removed from Other Prisons by Habeas Corpus", 1724–1729, Prisons and Compters – Individual Prisons, LMA, CLA/032/04/010.

64 House of Commons, *Committee into Imprisonment for Debt*, p. 39; Paul, *Poverty of Disaster*, p. 228.

65 "List of Prisoners Handed over by the Sheriffs to Their Successors on 28 Sept Annually, with Notes of Occurrences during the Subsequent Year", 1792–1793, Wood Street Compter later Giltspur Street Compter, LMA, CLA/028/01/028; "Commitment Registers", 1790–1795, Fleet Prison, TNA, PRIS 1/14 – PRIS 1/15; *London Gazette*, 17th–21st June 1794, no. 13674, p. 588.

66 "An Act for the Relief of Insolvent Debtors", 1736, 10 George II, c.26; "An Act for the Relief of Insolvent Debtors", 1742, 16 George II, c.17; "An Act for the Relief of Insolvent Debtors", 1747, 21 George II, c.31; "An Act for the Relief of Insolvent Debtors", 1755, 28 George II, c.13.

67 "An Act for Relief of Insolvent Debtors", 1760, 1 George III, c.17.

68 *Lloyd's Evening Post*, 9th–11th September 1761, no. 649, p. 253.
69 "List of Prisoners in the Compter Made Per out of the Ct of Ald", 15th December 1724, Wood Street Compter later Giltspur Street Compter, LMA, CLA/028/01/043.
70 "List of Prisoners in the Poultry Compter", CLA/030/02/006; "List of Prisoners in the Compter", CLA/028/01/043; Daniel Defoe, *Some Objections Humbly Offered to the Consideration of the Hon. House of Commons, Relating to the Present Intended Relief of Prisoners* (London: 1729), p. 6; Haagen, "Imprisonment for Debt", p. 54.
71 *London Gazette*, 16th–19th July 1720, no. 5869 – 15th–19th July 1729, no. 6796; estimates of John Levin, forthcoming.
72 Julian Hoppit, "The Myths of the South Sea Bubble", *Transactions of the RHS* vol. 12 (2002), pp. 141–165; Julian Hoppit, "Financial Crises in Eighteenth-Century England", *Economic History Review* vol. 39, no. 1 (1986), pp. 47–49; Ann M. Carlos and Larry Neal, "The Micro-Foundations of the Early London Capital Market: Bank of England Shareholders during and after the South Sea Bubble, 1720–25", *Economic History Review* vol. 59, no. 3 (2006), pp. 498–538; see: Carl Wennerlind *Casualties of Credit – The English Financial Revolution, 1620–1720* (Cambridge: Harvard University Press, 2011), p. 238.
73 "Commitment Registers", 1733–1735, Fleet Prison, TNA, PRIS 1/5.
74 Finn, *The Character of Credit*, pp. 109–124, 154–162; Duffy, *Bankruptcy and Insolvency*, p. 372. Finn's projected increase was later and more dramatic than depicted here though this is because she misrepresented Ian Duffy's figures for 1798, 1808, and 1818, respectively, claiming they were for 1759, 1769, and 1779. Her accidental mistake lies in Duffy's confusingly laid out table that has two columns of dates. By identifying an increase on the far right of the table and tracing to the date on the far left, one receives an answer forty years earlier than Duffy intended.
75 Julian Hoppit, *Risk and Failure in English Business 1700–1800* (Cambridge: Cambridge University Press, 1987), pp. 182–183.
76 House of Commons, *Committee on the Prisons*, p. 247.
77 "List of Prisoners Handed over by the Sheriffs to Their Successors on 28 Sept Annually, with Notes of Occurrences during the Subsequent Year", 1813–1815, Wood Street Compter later Giltspur Street Compter, LMA, CLA/028/01/040.
78 *London Gazette*, 31st March–4th April 1761, no. 10092 –1st–5th December 1761, no. 10162.
79 Howard, *State of the Prisons*, pp. 174–177; Neild, *Account of Persons Confined*, pp. 13–16; "Plan of Two Pair of Stairs. Showing Use of Rooms", 1780, Surveyor's Department: Plans – Justice, LMA, COL/SVD/PL/08/0092; "Plan of the Ground Floor of the Giltspur Street Compter", 1800, Surveyor's Department: Plans – Justice, LMA, COL/SVD/PL/08/0108.
80 Calculated by totalling commitments in any given month, deducting the total removed in that month, and adding the remainder to the total result for the previous month (*month* (b) = ($\sum committed - \sum released$) + *month* (a)). Release dates were estimated for all those not specifying it in a register based upon available existing data. For example, where a method was stated such as 'discharged' the average of those released by this method for the year was taken while those released by Insolvency Acts were assumed to have taken the next Act passed. Those without release methods were taken at the period average.
81 Anon. *The Remembrancer; or, Impartial Repository of Public Events for the Year 1780, Part Two* (London: 1780), p. 12; Anon. *The Proceedings at Large on the Trial of George Gordon, Esq.* (London: 1781), p. 19.

82 Anon. *The Complete Modern London Spy, For the Present Year, 1781* (London: 1781), p. 36.

83 Hoppit, *Risk and Failure*, pp. 122–139.

84 See: T. S. Ashton, *Economic Fluctuations in England 1700–1800* (Oxford: Clarendon Press, 1959), p. 110.

85 Hoppit, *Risk and Failure*, p. 47; E. A. Wrigley, "A Simple Model of London's Importance in Changing English Society and Economy 1650–1750", *Past & Present* vol. 37 (1967), pp. 44–46.

86 Samuel Johnson, *The Idler in Two Volumes. Vol. I* (London: 1767), p. 211; Haagen, "Imprisonment for Debt", p. 53.

87 Haagen, "Imprisonment for Debt", pp. 58–62.

88 Paul, *Poverty of Disaster*, pp. 43–44.

89 Assuming that adult economically active males comprised roughly one in four of the population. Wrigley, "Simple Model", pp. 44; E. A. Wrigley, *The Path to Sustained Growth – England's Transition from an Organic Economy to an Industrial Revolution* (Cambridge: Cambridge University Press, 2016), pp. 47–49.

90 *London Evening Post*, 16th–18th May 1776, no. 8450.

91 Numbers of those released from the Fleet c.1777–1780 are minimised by the loss of previous registers while the increase at Lancaster from 1793–1794 is probably an overestimation based on lost registers prior to 1793.

92 Innes, "King's Bench", p. 254; Paul, *Poverty of Disaster*, p. 113.

93 "List of Prisoners Handed over by the Sheriffs to Their Successors on 28 Sept Annually, with Notes of Occurrences during the Subsequent Year", 1795–1800, Wood Street Compter later Giltspur Street Compter, LMA, CLA/028/01/030; "List of Prisoners", 1778–1791, CLA/028/01/027.

94 "Commitment Registers", 1735–1737, Fleet Prison, TNA, PRIS 1/6; "Commitment Registers", 1745–1748, Fleet Prison, TNA, PRIS 1/10.

95 Daniel Defoe, *The Complete English Tradesman in Familiar Letters* (London: 1726), pp. 413–415; Pat Rogers, "Defoe in the Fleet Prison", *The Review of English Studies* vol. 22, no. 88 (November 1971), p. 452.

96 "Papers of a Committee concerned with the rebuilding of the Compter", 1785–1789, Giltspur Street Compter, LMA, CLA/029/02/001 – the papers suggest a wage of between 2s and 2s 4d *per diem* based on tasks undertaken, not how much the contractor was paid. See: Judy Z. Stephenson, "Real Wages? Contractors, Workers, and Pay in London Building Trades, 1650–1800", *Economic History Review* vol. 71, no. 1 (2018), pp. 106–132; Robert C. Allen, "The High Wage Economy and the Industrial Revolution: A Restatement", *Economic History Review* vol. 68, no. 1 (2015), pp. 1–22; Judy Z. Stephenson, "Mistaken Wages: The Cost of Labour in the Early Modern English Economy, a Reply to Robert C. Allen", *Economic History Review* vol. 72, no. 2 (2019), pp. 755–769; Peter Earle, *The Making of the English Middle Class: Business, Society and Family Life in London, 1660–1730* (London: Methuen, 1989), pp. 329–330.

97 E. A. Wrigley, "Occupational Coding – The PST System", *The Cambridge Group for the History of Population and Social Structure* (2010), www.campop.geog.cam. ac.uk/research/occupations/datasets/coding/

98 Sebastian Keibek and Leigh Shaw-Taylor, "Early Modern Rural by-Employments: A Re-Examination of the Probate Inventory Evidence", *Agricultural History Review* vol. 61, no. 2 (2013), pp. 244–281; Amy Louise Erickson, "Married Women's Occupations in Eighteenth-Century London", *Continuity and Change* vol. 23, no. 2 (2008), pp. 267–307; Tawny Paul, "Accounting for Men's Work: Multiple Employments and Occupational Identities in Early Modern England", *History Workshop Journal* vol. 85 (2018), pp. 26–46.

99 Haagen, "Imprisonment for Debt", pp. 13–15.

100 *London Gazette*, 3rd–6th May 1755, no. 9473, p. 4; Horace Walpole, *An Epitaph in the Churchyard of St Anne, Soho* (1757); Anon. *The Freemason's Magazine Vol. V* (London: 1793–5), p. 104.

101 Jacob Field, "Clandestine Weddings at the Fleet Prison c.1710–50: Who Married There?", *Continuity and Change* vol. 32, no. 3 (2017), pp. 365, 374. Field does not record the percentage of gentleman, etc., in his table though does note in a footnote the '334 in c.1751 who gave their occupation/status as "gentleman" or "esquire"' who he excluded. This would represent 2.7% if included in his Table 3.

102 Field, "Clandestine Weddings", p. 365.

103 Wrigley, *Sustained Growth*, p. 69.

104 *Lloyd's Evening Post*, 12th–15th June 1761, no. 611, pp. 560–561.

3 Coercive contract enforcement

Debtors' prisons as economic institutions

'A prison pays no debts' was a phrase repeated consistently throughout the latter era of English debt imprisonment. Its most notable expression was that in 1777 of the prison reformer John Howard: 'it is often said, "A prison pays no debts"; I am sure it may be added, that a prison mends no morals'.[1] In the decades following, Howard's words were echoed regularly, often with direct reference to the old reformer though they were nothing new, Edward Farley in 1788 calling the phrase an 'adage, which is an old one, [that] remains in full force'.[2] In 1787, William Huntington provided an almost unusual variation on the theme by commenting 'laying in prison, you know, pays no debts' while the same year another writer declared

> as it is true to a proverb that a jail pays no debts, so an act that authorises an arrest ... appears to inflict an unequal punishment, to the detriment of creditors, who, ninety-nine times in an hundred ... lose their money.[3]

Josiah Dornford meanwhile asked rhetorically in 1785 'is the old adage reversed which says that a gaol pays no debts? I cannot find one good reason for it, and there are many against it'.[4] A 1792 pamphlet entitled *A Candid Statement of the Case of the Insolvent Debtors of the Kingdom of Ireland* declared slightly sardonically 'that a prison pays no debts is an aphorism not more trite than true'. The truth of this phrase, as *A Candid Statement* went on to assert, was obvious to all observers and required no evidence ('perpetual imprisonment operates with unerring certainty to support my assertion') while another writer similarly declared 'it is so well known a truth ... that it is become proverbial'.[5] Howard, by his own admission, was not the originator of this phrase and while his printing of this aphorism appears to have sparked a flurry of its use, variations on the phrase 'a prison pays no debts' were common across the eighteenth century, whether in reference to debtors' prisons, familiar touchstones in literature, or in religious works as analogies to Hell.[6] Seven years before Howard's *State of the Prisons*, James Stephen's pamphlet *Considerations on Imprisonment for Debt*, written from his cell in the King's Bench, declared 'it is generally confessed, that a prison pays no debts'. Even a pamphlet directly written in opposition to Stephen's, seeking to defend civil arrest, admitted 'it is most certainly true, that a prison pays no debts ... the debtor squanders, when in confinement, what ought to satisfy the creditor'.[7]

The earliest printed appearance of the phrase still presented it essentially as a piece of common, universally accepted knowledge. John Vernon's 1678 guide to young tradesmen cautioned readers against the use of the prisons, providing a qualifier (which was apparently not necessary for Howard's readers) for the adage:

> Still [have] regard to these old and good Maxims, That a Prison pays no Debts. That the first Offer [a debtor makes] is generally the best [and] when the first is refused, it seldom rises higher. Besides, of ten Men that are put into Prison, nine of them either die there, or besot themselves so much, that when they come out, they are fit for nothing but Gaming or Drinking. And if this be the way to pay Debts, let any reasonable Man judge; whereas if they were out, and had a little respit, they might be able to pay every Man in some time.[8]

Here Vernon encapsulated the perceived problems of debt imprisonment for the debtor, society at large, and the creditor which have remained largely unchallenged since. The malaise and unproductivity experienced by confinement led inevitably to the debtor being made degenerate (or deceased) and thus unserviceable to the community once they were released while the creditor who had caused this situation gained nothing from it making the whole endeavour foolhardy. Vernon advised the young tradesman to be compassionate and patient, recommending they believe that their customers would honour commitments once they were able to even though not all debtors, as many creditors learnt in practice, acted as honourably as Vernon had promised they would.

Vernon's advice appeared to be still relevant to an audience of an 1857 novel which remains the definitive depiction of debtors' prisons and, twinned with Shakespeare's *Merchant of Venice*, the most important rumination on the justice – or injustice – of debt in English literature. The setting of Charles Dickens's *Little Dorrit*, the Marshalsea Prison of the 1820s, was one with which the author was intimately familiar, his own father John having been confined therein. As in Vernon's, Dickens's account depicts the only outcomes of debt imprisonment as perpetual confinement until death, with aid only coming from external saviours while debtors and their families (with the exception of sainted "Little" Amy) become debauched. Even though William Dorrit is released after twenty years confinement, it is solely through *deus ex machina*.[9] Dickens's account, reliant on a societal repetition of the 'old and good Maxim', has had an evocative impact upon subsequent scholarly discussion of debtors' prisons.[10] The great legal historian William Holdsworth described, only five decades after the passing of the Debtors Act which essentially ended debt imprisonment, how 'constraint of the debtor's person thus became in England a more general method of execution than in many other countries in Europe ... The results can be read in the pages of Dickens'.[11] While more recent scholars have been less likely to directly invoke *Dorrit*, the ghost of the 'old and good Maxim' is evident in a variety of accounts such as in declarations that 'when debtors held out against their creditors long enough to be imprisoned, the chances of their paying were exiguous'.[12]

Despite the apparently universally accepted wisdom that to imprison a debtor was simultaneously a fool's errand on the part of the plaintiff and a death sentence for the defendant, creditors continued to make use of the prisons across the period and country. That writers felt inclined to repeat the adage suggests that it appeared to be falling upon deaf ears. As was demonstrated in the previous chapter, rather than "capitalist enlightenment" bringing about the demise of debtors' prisons, prison populations increased following the Consumer Revolution while confinement rates at the superior court gaols grew into the nineteenth century.[13] Furthermore, rather than being impoverish paupers, the majority of debtors were the tradesman which works like Vernon's aimed to advise.

Scholars, and some contemporaries, have sought to explain what role debtors' prisons – not apparently paying debts – served within commercial society. The majority of accounts have depicted the prisons as a very visible deterrent to overly risky commercial behaviour. Paul Langford, highlighting the flexible and informal system of contemporary credit, concluded that 'without the deterrent of imprisonment that system would collapse'.[14] Joel Mokyr similarly claimed 'obviously that draconian measure was effective primarily through deterrence rather than actual punishment'.[15] Meanwhile, Peter Coleman, described the operation of the debt law in English controlled colonial America evocatively as 'let the borrower beware'.[16] One of the few quantitative accounts of debt imprisonment focussing on their decline in the early United States of America, conducted by Mathew Baker, Metin Cosgel, and Thomas Miceli, also concluded the role of prisons was primarily as a deterrent. As well as a method of checking the ambition of traders and encouraging them to keep within their means, they argue the 'primary function [of prisons] was to deter default in the first place by giving borrowers an incentive to disclose hidden assets' when creditors demanded payment.[17] The prisons, looming over towns and marketplaces, certainly acted as a deterrent (implied by every transaction on personal credit) but this does not necessarily explain why individual creditors went to the trouble of imprisoning those who had defaulted other than as a warning to others. Not all examinations of the commercial role of prisons has seen them in such a passive state. Craig Muldrew has, for example, argued 'imprisonment was primarily intended to keep chronically untrustworthy people out of credit networks'. Confinement broke an individual's credit standing, publicly demonstrating their untrustworthiness, thus preventing them from being able to trade again and further inhibit trade.[18] This view also appeared in the period. In the satirical dialogue between *Mr Trader and Mr Cheator* of 1702, a creditor declared when faced with his unscrupulous debtor 'truly, I think they had better keep you close

Confin'd, than discharge you, and give you the opportunity of playing over the same Game'. The debtor, reminding the reader that 'a prison pays no debts' and asking 'Why, would you have us confined for ever?' is informed 'Ay, by all means; and then you'll be prevented from Tricking us anymore'.[19] While this conception of the gaols does consider why they were used and not just why they existed, it still fails to discern the motivation of thousands of creditors who went to the trouble and expense of actually confining debtors beyond a sense of communal duty of preventing others from losing out.

Possibly the only discussion which manages to provide a theory for the driving desire behind arrest was that produced by James Stephen in 1770. Imprisoned in the King's Bench he asserted that 'resentment is generally [a creditor's] motive for destroying his adversary (as he imagines his debtor to be)'.[20] In this view that a prison paid no debts was irrelevant for the purpose of detention was gaining the satisfaction of vanquishing the customer who had the temerity to cause a creditor to lose wealth. While it is possible that all creditors were vindictive and sought nothing but the satisfaction of destroying their opponents, this seems unlikely. Instead, despite the repeated assertions of historians and contemporary pamphleteers, creditors were motivated because the 'old and good maxim' appears to have been largely false. The prisons when viewed through the logic of the contemporary credit market functioned as inherently economic institutions in their role as coercive contract enforcers. In an economy where the fulfilment of obligations was reliant upon good will, a method of compelling debtors through legal intimidation was necessary for the survival of informal contracting. Beyond the theoretical logic of their use, this chapter shows through an examination of the end process of imprisonment revealed in the commitment registers of the Fleet Prison (1733–1748, 1778–1795), the Wood Street Compter (1741–1815), and Lancaster Castle Gaol (1793–1796), that the debtors' prisons were a practical tool of recovering money. Having first explored the surprisingly short duration of the majority of imprisonments, this discussion analyses the diverse mechanisms by which prisoners secured their freedom. While it is shown that there were always those who left prisons with their creditors still out of pocket, it demonstrates the overall picture of successful blackmail through confinement of the person, protecting the vast informal credit market upon which commerce depended.

★★

Far from inescapable tombs, debtors' prisons operated as institutions with revolving doors, the frequency of departure not being limited to those prisoners permitted to journey during the day into the *rules*. Table 3.1 details the distribution of commitment lengths based on prisoners with declared release dates at the Fleet Prison (91% of prisoners), the Wood Street Compter (87%), and Lancaster Castle Gaol (99%). The number of prisoners who were held for long stretches of time was surprisingly low. At Wood Street only eleven

Table 3.1 Distribution of Commitment Lengths at the Fleet Prison, Wood Street Compter, and Lancaster Castle Gaol, 1735–1815

Length of Commitment	Fleet		Wood Street		Lancaster	
	Num	*%*	*Num*	*%*	*Num*	*%*
Same Day	129	1.9	60	0.7	2	0.2
1–100 Days	2279	33.5	2223	27.3	354	42.9
101–200 Days	1233	18.1	3726	45.8	216	26.2
201–365 Days	1238	18.2	1409	17.3	152	18.4
1–2 Years	1036	15.2	575	7.1	90	10.9
2–5 Years	749	11.0	140	1.7	11	1.3
5–10 Years	129	1.9	8	0.1	0	0.0
> 10 Years	20	0.3	3	0.0	0	0.0
Total	*6813*		*8144*		*825*	

prisoners were held for more than five years, the longest residency being that of James Hamilton who was committed in July 1769 and did not leave the compter until May 1786.[21] Longer imprisonments did represent a more distinct category at the Fleet though the 149 prisoners held for over five years remained a tiny minority – even if they had all been held at once the gaol would still have been half empty. The commitment of Hannah Barber, who spent almost thirty-two years in the Fleet where she died in 1821, is particularly striking. Barber was later cited by the radical MP Joseph Hume in his campaign against the Exchequer, she having been separately charged with contempt for refusing to pay her debt following a court order.[22] Lancaster, possibly in part due to the low survival rate of registers, exhibited no imprisonments reaching the five year mark, the longest being that of John Lowndas who spent four and a half years in the castle from September 1795 on a paltry £14 1s debt.[23] Lowndas was a distinct figure in the castle, the second longest confinement, lasting 292 fewer days, arriving and departing during his tenure. At either of the London prisons, Lowndas would have still represented a relatively long-term commitment as only seventeen Wood Street and 196 Fleet debtors experienced longer confinements.

The dearth of long commitments suggests that the concept of "friendly arrest" – prevalent both in contemporary debate and in subsequent scholarly literature – was largely mythical.[24] Debtors who had asked friends to commit them could, in theory, hold on to their property until death, spending it liberally or allowing it to pass to their heirs relatively unmolested. The only course of action available to genuine creditors was to bring in their own actions as once a debtor was held in prison, no creditor could proceed against their estate.[25] Joanna Innes, for example, based on the plentiful contemporary discussion of such fraud suggested in 1980 that as 'imprisonment actually offered the debtor protection for his property, some men chose to have themselves imprisoned by friendly actions ... the debtor could retain everything he owned and spend it as he pleased'.[26] The 1792 Parliamentary Committee investigating debt imprisonment, describing those committed on friendly actions, similarly declared that 'to Debtors of the worst Description a Prison is no Punishment; but on the contrary that such Persons find an Interest, or a Gratification in remaining in a Situation full of Misery to the Honest'.[27]

The only probable candidate for "friendly arrest" at the compter is its longest commitment, James Hamilton, who owed just £15 4s 5d to one creditor. The remarkably long commitment coupled with a relatively small debt might indicate the potentially fraudulent nature of his arrest. The second longest commitment was that served by Samuel Plaisted (1804–1815) who, though held for ten years, eight months, and twenty-five days, was arrested to answer debts totalling £784 13s 7d. Hamilton was thus resident six years longer than Plaisted for a sum sixty-six times smaller.[28] However, Hamilton did not die in the compter indicating that any other creditor had been satisfied as well as the original "friendly action". Even if they had not brought claims, they or (if they had died) their executors could now proceed against Hamilton's property or arrest him again. In the records of the Fleet Prison, arguments for the possible existence of friendly action appear more persuasive. This might be expected given the relative liberty provided by the gaol for those who chose to have themselves confined. Of the ten longest remaining prisoners (some of whom may have been previously imprisoned elsewhere before being removed there through a writ of *habeas corpus*), one died in the *rules* and a further four died within the prison. These prisoners also tended to owe significant amounts. Hannah Barber owed £406 17s 7d to one creditor, Stephen Welch (dying in 1770 after twenty-three years in the Fleet) owed £400 to four individuals, and Philip Hall was committed from 1786 to 1801 owing eight creditors £2358 12s. However, while one of those who died was committed without debts being recorded, the debts of David Boyes, who died in the *rules* in 1755 after thirteen years, were detailed as only £24 19s among three creditors. This does not discount friendly action, particularly as he moved out into the *rules*, but it seems a remarkably low sum for which to defer freedom considering the expenses of Fleet imprisonment not experienced in Wood Street. It is possible that Boyes had undeclared creditors owed larger sums who were declining to press action after hearing of his false imprisonment in the hope he would eventually leave, allowing them to charge him subsequently on their own terms.

Two debtors within this group were released by a parliamentary Insolvency Act, meaning that their debts were cleared in exchange for turning over their remaining property. Creditors were occasionally suspicious of debtors who took advantage of such acts of clemency particularly when reading about cases such as James Bolland, eventually executed for forging a promissory note in 1772, who supposedly 'threw himself into a goal' after making large purchases out in the country. When he 'took the benefit of an Act of Insolvency' his rural creditors were not promptly made aware and so lost their debts by not applying to the court in time.[29] The regularity of this behaviour is questionable though, while it can be said to be a minority of examples, it remains a possibility. It is notable that the two debtors among this group taking the Act both apparently declined to take earlier Acts. William Gray, a London tailor, took the 1755 Act but qualified for Acts in 1743 and 1748 while George leDouble, a ringmaker also from London, avoided Acts in 1748, 1755, and 1761 before being released in 1765. Debtors who qualified were not necessarily inclined to take the benefit of an Act automatically and these two were far from isolated examples of debtors who declined the benefit before changing their minds at a subsequent statute. However, it is possible that Gray and leDouble had waited for creditors to die or leave London to minimise the number of individuals paid out of their estate at the Act, thus retaining a higher percentage of their property. At the other end of the confinement spectrum, only eighteen out of 1,029 debtors released by an Act had spent less than one hundred days in the Fleet suggesting that friendly action, while still possibly at work, was not a significant driver of commitment in advance of Acts with debtors hoping, like Boland, to clear themselves before creditors were organised. While "friendly action" possibly occurred in the eighteenth century, scant evidence of its regularity outside pamphlet literature suggests the concept should be dismissed largely as contemporary fearmongering by panicky tradesmen.

Rather than fraudulent activity, the principal revelation of Table 3.1 is that debtors spent relatively short amounts of time within prison. Figures like Dickens's William Dorrit, spending over twenty years in the tiny Marshalsea prison, were few and far between.[30] Even Dickens's father spent only three months in the Marshalsea when committed in 1824, though presumably this felt like an inordinate period of time to the twelve-year-old Charles, forced to leave school and go out to work.[31] Like John Dickens, debtors in these prisons were likely to obtain their freedom relatively quickly with 72% of Fleet, 88% of Lancaster, and 91% of Wood Street debtors being released within one year. At both Lancaster and Wood Street, more prisoners were released on the same day of their confinement than were held for longer than five years and, while the same cannot be said of the Fleet, debtors released there within a day actually constituted a more significant category. Except at Wood Street which experienced a surprising density of debtors held roughly between three and six months, the single largest group were debtors who spent up to one hundred days in prison. Mean commitment lengths of 355 days, 184 days, and 172 days at the Fleet, Wood Street, and Lancaster respectively emphasise that not all prisoners had such a fleeting relationship with confinement, though these results are largely distinct from the remaining data particularly as the prisons recorded lower median commitments of 178, 127, and 117 days respectively.

While the compter and castle's prisoners almost entirely fell into the categories of shorter confinement, at the Fleet there were a range of experiences. Those who were held for longer than one year were not merely confined to those who – due to the unusual luxuries of the Fleet in both the freedom of the *rules* and the comforts of the Master's Side – elected to expend capital on their lifestyle rather than on liberty. Uncooperative genuine prisoners were certainly present at the Fleet though the relatively even distribution across the admittedly arbitrary categories of Table 3.1 suggests that other factors contributed to longer commitments than at other prisons. Not all cases were heard in superior courts due solely to removal by *habeas corpus* as numerous substantial debts or complex financial entanglements were heard there appropriately. Such cases simply took longer to settle, particularly those that involved complications concerning wills or annuities of dubious ownership. However, these individuals while making the population of the Fleet distinct from non-superior court prisons did not significantly extend the median commitment length as the majority of prisoners were able to leave the prison after a similar duration as their compatriots down the road at Wood Street. While release was not immediate and an imprisonment lasting around six months certainly would have had a significant impact on individual debtors, it was far less damaging physically, emotionally, or economically than the previously presumed permanent confinement. Committing a debtor to prison was therefore not a fool's errand as the dispute appears usually to have been resolved in a timely – though far from instant – manner.

Rapid release alone does not necessarily establish the effectiveness and usefulness of debt imprisonment. Reasons for release recorded by the clerks of the various prisons were extensive, ranging from the frequent instances of mundane processes such as 'Discharged by the Plaintiff's Attorney' to the unique. At Wood Street, Joseph Howell was committed on the 20th August 1785 but 'not being the right Defendant he was discharged 22nd about noon' and Thomas Geale, having been confined since 1739, was recorded as gone from the prison in 1743 inexplicably as he had 'Escaped from Guildhall at the time when he was to be Discharged from his Debts'.[32] Robert Jacques only spent thirty-six days at the Fleet in 1790 before he 'was taken by Writ of Habeas Corpus to the Old Bailey' as he had been 'convicted of Conspiracy against the Warden' of the Fleet.[33] Additionally, outside of the data under study here, the release of fifteen prisoners confined to the Fleet for crimes against the excise represent one of the clearest uses of imprisonment as a tool of extortion. Having been charged with impossible forfeitures to the crown reaching up to £9,000, they were in 1743 'Discharged by *Supersedeas*' having agreed to 'Entry aboard one of his Majesty's Ships of War'.[34] Even without such outlier examples, examination of release methods across time and prisons mandates some elements of simplification. Thirteen broad categories of release type were devised, some comprising numerous unique descriptors of a common type such as "Court Process" and others constituting a singular description which did not accord with any broad grouping as with the "Compulsive Clause" group who were released by legislation but in an unusual manner that only applied in 1761, being a generally solvent group who spent less than a month in gaol. At the Fleet, multiple methods of release were frequently recorded by the clerks, for example, a debtor may have been discharged of some claims though died before all their creditors were satisfied while at other gaols only the final mechanism was detailed. In this data only the method which actually allowed them to leave has been recorded which may underestimate some mechanisms such as *supersedeas* in particular. However, generally, if a debtor was released by the plaintiff, most of their other charges had been cleared similarly. The categories and their rate of use at the prisons are detailed in Table 3.2.

The category of "Discharged" includes all indications that creditors acquiesced to the release of the prisoner. At Wood Street, in almost all the over seven thousand cases this refers to a simple recording of 'Discharged' though these were supplemented by thirty-two releases providing more detail such as 'Settled', 'Plaintiff Satisfied', 'Discharged by the Plaintiff', 'Money Paid', and the one debtor explicitly 'Bailed'. Securing bail was a more passive involvement of the creditor than in situations where they had been 'Satisfied' and did not necessarily indicate the end of the suit. However, it did represent the debtor having been released after the creditor had been able to extract something, in this case security (either rooted in wealth or a third party), which had not been part of their previous informal arrangement and so has here been associated with suit completion as an example of successful coercion particularly as a creditor could reject the security offered. At Lancaster only two debtors were 'discharged' but this was due to the register providing specific detail on release in almost all cases. Of the "Discharged" category 18% were bailed, 26% were released 'by Plaintiff's Order', and 47% were released 'by order of the Plaintiff's Attorney'. A further 9% were released 'for want of

Table 3.2 Categories of Release at the Fleet, Wood Street Compter, and Lancaster Castle, 1733–1815

Release Category	Fleet			Wood Street			Lancaster		
	Num	%	Avg Days	Num	%	Avg Days	Num	%	Avg Days
Discharged	3332	43.4	272	7390	72.7	179	518	62.5	132
Legislation	1181	15.4	721	431	4.2	413	194	23.4	294
Moved	819	10.7	87	495	4.9	103	7	0.9	52
Dead	486	6.3	599	88	0.9	264	3	0.4	160
Supersedeas or Creditor Inaction	902	11.8	276	1	0.0	401	73	8.8	153
Charity	76	1.0	379	37	0.4	130	0	0.0	
Court Process	115	1.5	335	7	0.1	5	25	3.0	162
Escape	24	0.3	296	4	0.0	561	0	0.0	
Compulsive Clause	2	0.0	1073	215	2.1	36	0	0.0	
Expiration of Time	0	0.0		152	1.5	93	0	0.0	
Bankruptcy	58	0.8	218	0	0.0		0	0.0	
Other	5	0.1	945	31	0.3	235	2	0.2	276
(Release Details Not Specified)	670	8.7	530	1315	12.9	123	6	0.7	61
TOTAL	7670		348	10166		183	828		172

execution' following trial though whether notice was posted by the creditor, their lawyer, or the court is unclear. At the Fleet, only two debtors who were explicitly 'Discharged … on putting in bail to the warrant' were included in this category. However, another four were released by writ of '*supersedeas* on putting in bail'. As it was impossible to separate these from others bailed through the writ where only '*supersedeas*' was recorded in the register, they were defined by the use of the writ. Even excluding these bailed debtors, the Fleet "Discharged" category experienced greater diversity reflecting the more complex cases raised in superior courts. Only 2% were simply 'discharged' while 42% were 'discharged by the plaintiff' and 56% by their lawyer. The remainder were released by an array of other methods such as William Gardner who was 'Discharged by Payment of Debt & Costs to the Warden' in 1790.[35]

It is possible that the share of those discharged from Wood Street represents an exaggeration considering the unspecific nature of the 'discharged' description used, the significantly higher share it comprises than the Fleet, and the general absence of those released by *supersedeas* or similar creditor inaction which survey studies of the King's Bench suggest was more prevalent than observed here.[36] The only Wood Street debtor who fell into the inaction category was Edward Lindon who spent over a year at the compter before being released in October 1807 though no writ of *supersedeas* was involved. Lindon, after turning over all his property in line with the Lord's Act of 1758, had secured the payment of groats (4d a day) from his creditor who had opposed his release from gaol on the condition that if these were delinquent for six weeks Edward could sue for his release. Considering the £16 debt which was partially cleared by the sale of Lindon's property, it is not a great surprise that his creditor failed to make these payments.[37] Only one other prisoner is noted in the frequently taciturn compter registers as receiving groats when Lieutenant John Upton sued over a defect in his groats while imprisoned between 1791 and 1794. Upton's creditor, who was owed £240, appears to have acquiesced to payment of the groats, calculating that 4d a day was an acceptable cost in recovering this large sum though Upton was eventually released by an Insolvency Act.[38]

While I previously argued that *supersedeas* and release for the non-payment of groats were rarer than pamphlet literature suggests, this does not mean they were non-existent. At the Fleet and Lancaster Castle, creditor inaction represented the third most significant way in which prisoners left suggesting that some degree of obscuring occurred in Wood Street's registers as it seems improbable that nobody ever secured *supersedeas* from the compter. However, it is unlikely that the rate comprised more than 5–10% of prisoners, with Wood Street and Lancaster probably experiencing a relative parity. The rate at the Fleet may have been a result of the use of *supersedeas* being higher in the first half of the eighteenth century for which comparable commitment register data is sparse. At the Fleet, use of the writ more than halved from 14.3% of releases 1733–1748 to 6.5% of debtors by 1778–1795. Despite this decline, the writ was certainly more widespread at elite prisons like the Fleet due to various contributing factors such as the wealthier nature of prisoners, the use of *habeas corpus* to deliberately cause defaults in proceedings by removing cases far from a creditor's location, and the costs of procuring *supersedeas* being lower at superior court prisons than other London gaols.[39] At the Fleet, 43% of those acquiring the writ owed at least £100 and 66% owed at least £50. Predominantly this data supports the impression produced by contemporary disgust at the costs involved that these rights were frequently prohibitive. While it must have occurred in some form at Wood Street, it would not have significantly reduced the share discharged by creditor consent. Writs enabled the release of a minority of debtors though were far from regular enough to trouble creditors or to preoccupy the concerns of most debtors.

Figure 3.1, which illustrates the percentage of debtors at each prison who experienced confinement of at least a certain length up to 500 days (i.e. meaning that a debtor released after one hundred days would be included in each day-category up to one hundred and one), reveals a significant disparity in the first months of confinement between prisons. It provides a further demonstration of the Fleet's slower rate of release caused by larger more complicated debts and removal of motivations to pursue release. Separately, it indicates that, after roughly five months of confinement, expectations for Lancaster and Wood Street prisoners were essentially on a par. However, it also reveals a delay at Wood Street indicating that, in the first three months it was actually the prison from which one was least likely to be released. Of Wood Street prisoners, 90% remained at least ninety days as opposed to 67% and 60% at the Fleet and Lancaster respectively. The sudden and brief acceleration in release after ninety days might be regarded as evidence of significant use of *supersedeas* being roughly three months after their confinement. Writs

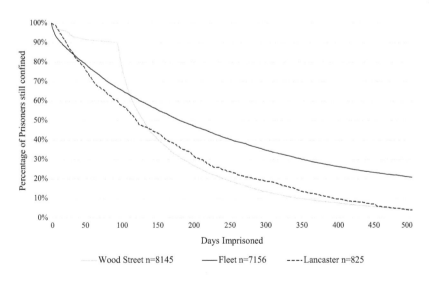

Figure 3.1 Share of Prisoners for Debt Held for a Minimum Number of days (1735–1815).

were supposed to be used if a prisoner had been committed in the previous legal term and not been brought to trial by the ensuing term. However, for the decline to be so steep, significant numbers of debtors would have to be committed across the period in the second half of each term and then procure writs almost immediately in its successor at a rate unrepeated in either the Fleet or Lancaster where evidence of such release was regular. While a hidden rate of *supersedeas* possibly contributed to decline it does not explain it or the high rate remaining up to ninety days. Factors largely unique to Wood Street such as the Compulsive Clause of 1761 or the poorer Court of Requests debtors are similarly unhelpful as they do not, if removed from the model, affect the pattern. Instead it seems likely that this delay in release suggests a surprisingly high rate of prisoners being brought to trial, writs of *supersedeas* thus not being applicable. Lancaster is the only register which regularly records debtors taken to trial. Of this admittedly small sample of 138 debtors, 92% still remained confined after ninety days (largely reflecting the Wood Street delay) in stark contrast to those who were never apparently tried of whom only 54% remained. This does not mean that the majority of Wood Street prisoners were taken to trial or that trials even led to the release of many debtors as the subsequent decline – while significant – is not a cliff-edge. It indicates that a sizeable minority of debtors and creditors at the compter proved intransigent before trial even with arrest. The act of taking the debtor to court may have been necessary to convince some debtors that there was no other option than making just payments while some creditors may either have felt that execution offered more bargaining power or refused to entertain compromise payment plans prior to a court's verdict. It is not immediately clear why this sub-segment of Wood Street debtors was more likely than at other prisons to see trial though it was probably a result of closer proximity to the relevant court, a greater regularity of hearings, lower costs, and London creditors being more likely to possess demonstrable evidence of their debts through notes of hand or bills of exchange which made them more confident of success in the courtroom.[40]

The higher rate of prisoners being taken to trial does not change the interpretation of 'discharged' at Wood Street. Following trial debtors followed one of a few limited paths. Some of those who were placed into execution were released by another method (though none obviously by *supersedeas*) and so the designation of 'discharged' would not have been applied to them in the register, while those who did eventually satisfy creditors were 'discharged'. This latter group were no different from the majority on *mesne* process who paid their debts without being summoned to court. Other debtors were 'discharged' immediately after a trial as their creditors elected to proceed against their goods (as occurred in 34% of instances of Lancaster trials). However, just as with those bailed, the conclusion of the process of imprisonment had been the satisfaction of the creditor to some extent even if they had not simply been paid in cash. In these instances, the system of debt imprisonment had functioned in line with the letter of the law and not just as a force of coercion.

Debtors had been held to ensure they did not abscond before trial and, particularly if they were unmarried and without families, to prevent them from continuing to spend money and accrue debts.[41] A small minority were occasionally acquitted at trial though they were statistically immeasurably small in number – happening only once at Lancaster – as only creditors confident of success would risk trial, the institution of debt imprisonment essentially giving them unlimited power of determining how to proceed.

Even when accounting for a potential over-estimate at Wood Street, this data reveals that the primary reasons debtors did not spend a long time in prison and why creditors made such regular use of debt imprisonment was that the majority appear to have paid their debts. In other words, debtors' prisons proved a consistently effective method of enforcing informal credit contracts across the period. These were not punitive but economic institutions as debtors were not destroyed. The coercive power of confinement, even at the less efficient Fleet Prison, gave debtors an active motivation to pay their debts in a manner not previously provided by passive threats to reputation or the ability to procure further credit in the future. This new impetus was particularly evident in the cases of those released within a week of their confinement of whom, when exempting those who simply moved to another gaol, 86% of Wood Street, 76% of Fleet, and 64% of Lancaster debtors satisfied their creditors. The majority required some time to organise their affairs so as to satisfy creditors (the processes of which are discussed in the following chapter); however, the majority were still discharged relatively quickly compared with probable delays without coercion.

Figure 3.2 details the percentage of those released rounded to the nearest whole hundred days up to 1,600 days who were discharged at each prison until the total number released became insignificant. It demonstrates greater

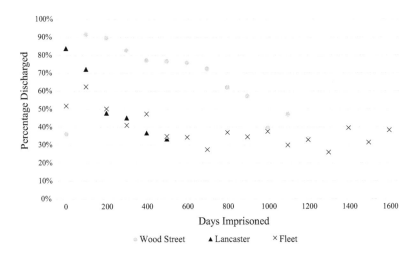

Figure 3.2 Percentage of those Released to the Nearest Hundred Days Who Were Discharged.

disparity between the prisons in terms of the possibility of creditor satisfaction over time. The chance that a debtor being released from Lancaster would be discharged fell relatively quickly though this partially reflected the high rate of swift debt payment at the castle. Of those discharged from Lancaster, 34% did so in under forty-nine days – another 37% in the hundred days following – suggesting that many of those imprisoned were delinquent at the moment of arrest but probably actually capable of making payments or at least of securing bail. Additionally, 76% of all prisoners at Lancaster were released within 249 days suggesting that the minority remaining were likely to have experienced greater difficulty in obtaining their release and secured freedom through a different path. Similarly, Wood Street experienced a consistent decline in the likelihood of discharge over the first three years of confinement though degradation was far slower and followed a much lower rate of release for debtors experiencing the shortest confinements. The reasons behind its decline are largely similar to Lancaster though the decreased severity indicates that Wood Street debtors, possibly due to their location in London which maintained their access to capital generation schemes, retained the potential to secure their own release for longer. The increased decline after two years of confinement represents the reduced share of the population who could ever have paid their debts. The largely flat rate experienced by the Fleet reflects the distortions created by the prison's unique situation. The Fleet contained a higher percentage of prisoners who were unable, or unwilling, to make swift payment due to the contribution of *habeas corpus* on the makeup of the population – those able to make swift payment while confined elsewhere being unlikely to relocate there. The liberties and luxuries of the Fleet probably also demotivated prisoners from ensuring a swift exit, being less willing to disclose assets or sell property immediately after arrest. However, the maintenance of discharge at the Fleet over time also suggests the contribution of more complex cases which, even in instances of enthusiastically co-operative and solvent debtors, required many more months and years to unpack. While a debtor entering their second year at the compter was increasingly unlikely to ever make full satisfaction, a creditor of a Fleet debtor, as long as they were patient and had received a portion of their demand, could be as optimistic about payment as they had during the first year following arrest.

While it was the most important outcome of debt imprisonment, not all debtors were released having settled their accounts. In some instances, leaving the prison did not even mean release as significant numbers were merely transferred to another gaol. Not all of those moved were taken to a superior court prison. Those Free of the City of London as well as widows of Freemen were able, on arrest, to demand to be taken to the more favourable prison of Ludgate. Many were confined before this was requested (or were ignored by the bailiff) and so were required to apply for a *duce facias* from within prisons like the compter, the added expenses amounting to 'many a Pound to poor Men' according to one 1742 pamphlet.[42] Twenty-seven debtors were taken from Wood Street to Ludgate across the period, seven taking longer than thirty days to secure their upgrade. The rate of transfer may have been higher in the period pre-dating the registers as the majority removed to Ludgate before the original prison's demolition in 1760, at which point it was moved into the Bishopsgate Street Workhouse. In 1794, Ludgate again relocated to separate buildings within the Giltspur Street Compter effectively ending movement to it except in the case of Daniel Magenis in 1810 who was taken across the prison yard the same day he was confined in the compter.[43] Not all movement was voluntary as, occasionally, prisoners for debt who became embroiled in felonious matters might be taken to a gaol such as Newgate. While the registers do not usually record the nature of their crime, it is clear that debtors were tried both for cases committed before their imprisonment, such as forgery or perjury, as well as crimes committed in gaol particularly arising from brawling. For example, in 1796 John Proctor was removed from the Fleet to stand trial 'for feloniously killing & slaying Henry Rede a Prisoner for Debt in the Fleet Prison against his Majesty's Peace'; as the witnesses 'were called but did not appear' (being prisoners) he was acquitted.[44] Such instances were rare – not occurring at all at Lancaster and for only thirty-eight Fleet and twenty-three Wood Street prisoners.

Very few prisoners were able to pay for writs of *habeas corpus* to remove to the superior court prisons from Lancaster, reflecting both the added expense of travelling to London from the north as well as the generally poorer nature of its prisoners, with only seven being transferred to the King's Bench. A small but notable cohort of Wood Street debtors possessed both the means and inclination to seek better accommodation, contrasting with the majority middling sort prisoners. There does not appear to have been a significant preference for the neighbouring Fleet Prison with 227 debtors carried there compared to 194 to the King's Bench alongside a minority 'removed by *habeas corpus*' to destination unknown. These individuals were unlikely to have made a significant contribution to compter life as few remained long, thirty-three of the 495 debtors moving to another prison on the same day they arrived at the compter while another eighty-five left in the following fortnight.

Those removing from the Fleet reflect a greater range of motivations than seeking the advantages of a superior court prison which they already possessed. The administrators of the King's Bench reported to the House of Commons committee investigating debt imprisonment in 1792 that

> by an expensive Abuse of the Writ of *Habeas Corpus*, Prisoners frequently procure themselves to be removed from One [superior court] Prison to another; and there have been Instances of Prisoners residing regularly in the King's Bench Prison during the Summer, and in the Fleet during the Winter.

Habeas corpus removal from the Fleet was not evenly distributed over the year as only four months accounted for more than 7% of departures each lending some credence to this assertion. Furthermore, 28% left in May and June though other prisoners preferred the inverse practice as 24% headed south in November and 17% in February, preferring to winter or welcome spring in Southwark. This minority, selecting the optimum prison based upon the season or overcrowding, was clearly content not to pay their debts and remain confined.[45] However, movement was also a process inflicted upon debtors. Significant numbers of those moving to the King's Bench did so within days of their commitment to the Fleet and might return on another writ shortly after suggesting that in some cases *habeas corpus* was used by creditors as a method of denying wealthy debtors the ability to comfortably settle.[46] Of the 781 prisoners issued writs of *habeas corpus*, 311 returned to the Fleet and ninety-five moved at least once more. Robert Taylor, first committed in May 1782 owing £600 to John Castleman moved regularly and, while it is not impossible that he procured these writs himself, the frequency of *habeas corpus* implies creditor coercion. Taylor was transferred after only a week to the King's Bench although he returned the next day, his debt having risen to £850 when two other creditors brought in charges. In June, thirty-three days after his second commitment to the Fleet, he was again removed for two days, returning for only four days before he was dragged back to the King's Bench for a matter of hours, returning by the end of the day. Taylor then spent a comparatively long period of 151 days at the Fleet until he was taken back across the Thames in November, returning the next day. He subsequently remained at the Fleet seventeen days until 3rd December when, in one day, he was taken to the King's Bench, back to the Fleet, and then back to the King's Bench again where he remained until February 1783. His debts fluctuated across this period, rising and falling, suggesting that this coercion had encouraged him to try and settle with his most aggressive creditors. However, when he returned for the final time on the 8th February, he now owed £1353 10s to five creditors. Castleman appears to have been the driving force of this tactic as he was now only owed £97 10s which may have been subsequently satisfied as Taylor ceased his travels and died in the prison nearly ten years later in August 1792.[47] Movement by *habeas corpus* between superior court prisons thus represents a diverse tapestry of strategies by both debtors and creditors, in contrast to the largely singular intention behind removal from traditional prisons. However, figures like Taylor were an exception with the majority moving just once probably doing so for convenience or preference (perhaps their place of business or residence being south of the water).

Ultimately, the imprisonment of Taylor might be described as unsuccessful as he died with obligations outstanding. Those removing as quickly as possible from close confined gaols to the airier superior court prisons may have been partially motivated by the dreaded and much spoken of gaol fever.[48] John Howard in the opening of his account described how, upon his first visits to the prisons, 'my attention was principally fixed by the gaol-fever, and the small-pox, which I saw prevailing to the destruction of multitudes, not only of felons in their dungeons, but of debtors also'.[49] Doctor and reformer William Smith similarly encapsulated the prevailing view of the inevitability of disease and death within the prisons in 1776:

> The sober, virtuous, and industrious prisoner ... deprived of liberty, and rendered totally incapable of relieving himself or doing justice to others ... when sickness visits him, weighed down with anguish and a load of woe, he meets death with pleasure.[50]

Despite hopes of escaping to "safer" gaols, inevitably the longer one remained in prison the higher chances were of death, a concern that should have worried creditors as well. At Wood Street the percentage of prisoners "released" who had died tripled from 0.9% in the first year to nearly 3% subsequently, the Fleet experiencing a similar increase from 5% in the first year to 8.6% thereafter. However, despite this increase the percentage who died in prison is surprisingly low considering the general rhetoric and the uncleanliness of many early modern prisons.[51] Death rates were not just low overall but sparse across the period as is clear in Figure 3.3 detailing the number of debtors who died per year, excluding the seventy-four Fleet and four Wood Street prisoners whose date of death went unrecorded. At Lancaster, the death rate was almost non-existent, confirming Margaret DeLacy's impression of the castle being a relatively healthy prison particularly benefited by 'a clean water supply from its own wells'.[52] All three deaths occurred in the first year of confinement. In March 1795, William Barnes died after just nine days in the castle suggesting that which killed him may have already been at work before his arrest. It is possible to observe moments of mortality crises within the prisons,

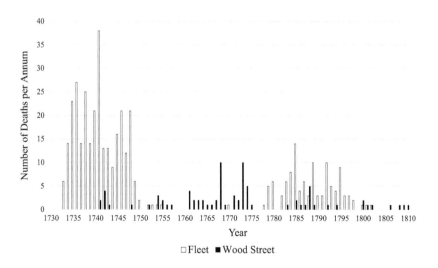

Figure 3.3 Annual Death Rates at the Fleet Prison and Wood Street Compter.

potentially resulting from prisoners like Barnes bringing diseases contracted prior to arrest to the isolated gaol communities. Indeed, one of the most high-profile eighteenth-century prison deaths, that of Robert Castell in 1728 (which led to the Oglethrope Inquiry's demands for prison reform) resulted from his sleeping in a bed previously occupied by a debtor who had arrived suffering from smallpox.[53] At the Fleet in 1741 when thirty-eight prisoners died, eight perished between the 7th May and the 11th June suggesting that one of their number – possibly Peter Mallendain who was committed on the 8th April and died on the 12th May – infected the other occupants of the cell.[54] In 1767, the keeper of Wood Street, John Kirby, petitioned the Court of Alderman for aid, stating 'that the Prisoners were afflicted with a very serious fever; that he had at his own Expence paid an Apothecary, but many being ther sick, he prayed the Court to appoint an Apothecary' which they promptly did.[55] That Kirby bothered the court with this issue testifies to the level of disease in the prison at this time being unusual – two prisoners committed in 1766, four from 1767, and seven of the 1768 commitments dying between September 1766 and February 1769.

The majority of deaths appear to have been isolated, reflecting the normal pattern of life and death in the eighteenth century, the prison just happening to be the location where they died rather than its cause. This was particularly true for the ninety-three Fleet prisoners who died in the *rules* and the eight who died after having fled in the Gordon Riots of 1780. Prison conditions may have exacerbated the risk to life, mortality being slightly higher in the winter months between October and March but not noticeably so with 52% of Fleet and 57% of Wood Street deaths during this time, February and March accounting for 20% and 25% of all deaths at the respective prisons. Some prisoners explicitly did not die of disease. At the Fleet, Henry Rede in 1795 'died in prison by means of fighting' while William Payne in 1797 was recorded as 'dead in prison by a blow from David Williams a fellow prisoner'.[56] In 1744, Ephraim Davis, owing £30 to one creditor, was found after 105 days 'Hanged ... within the prison' apparently by his own hand.[57] These men, particularly Ephraim, were killed by their imprisonment though not in a fashion usually ascribed to the gaols. The numbers dying other than by disease or natural causes may have been higher as no detail of how a prisoner died was given in most instances and only one prisoner was recorded explicitly as dying of 'small-pox in the house' at the Fleet in 1739.[58]

It is possible that the number who died of disease *acquired* in prison was significantly higher if including those who expired after release. Many prisoners spent relatively short amounts of time within gaol, possibly shorter than the time a condition would need to kill them particularly if it was acquired towards the end of their confinement. In 1753, Dr John Pringle submitted a report to the Philosophical Society on work to replace the Newgate ventilators in which he described the impact on workers, several of whom died after the completion of work. Thomas Wilmot, one of the journeymen interviewed, 'said his disorder had come on gradually ... but that he was then so very ill, he could work no longer'. While Wilmot recovered, he spread 'the contagion' to his daughter who then passed it to her mother, subsequently infecting her sister and the Wilmots' son.[59] This pattern was occasionally repeated by released prisoners, whose death (and the deaths of family members) following confinement would not have been noted in the registers.[60] While the impact on public health of close confinement should not therefore be underestimated, from the purely economic perspective of creditors, those who died *after* paying their debts had no impact upon the effectiveness of imprisonment as a means of enforcing contracts and the fear of demise may have been a powerful tool of debtors trying to settle as quickly as possible on any available terms.

The death rate observable in the surviving registers (privileging the post-1740 period) may represent a distortion of the period as a whole. Deaths at the Fleet were higher in the early period as is clear in Figure 3.3 when 10% of prisoners with stated release methods died, representing just 4% after 1778. While this might have been a reflection of the higher commitment rate at this time it also predates an era of healthcare reform in London following an outbreak of typhus spreading to the Old Bailey in 1750 which killed jurists and prisoners alike. Pringle, in a letter on his report to a committee created to investigate the outbreak, declared

> from the account I have had of other jayls in this city, I suspect they are all unhealthful, in being either too small for the number of prisoners, ill situated for air, ill provided with fresh water, & in having no areas, ventilators or other means for renewing the air; and that they are all very foul & offensive ... I can only declare [Newgate] to be remarkably faulty in all these respects; and that as long as it remains in the present condition it must be a perpetual nuisance & a source of distempers.[61]

The work conducted to improve cleanliness and ventilation at London's various prisons appears therefore to have been relatively successful as the post-1750 period exhibited a markedly lower death rate. Crowded gaols were still uncomfortable but no longer inherently deadly. During the high period of prison reform on the cusp of the nineteenth century, the city again organised an investigation of the prisons – presumably expecting details of death and disease. However, reports from Newgate were positive. In 1798 the court commended the keeper as '506 were in custody, and not one of them were the least indisposed'.[62] Four years later a Dr Pavel reported from his visit to Newgate that

> he did not think it a great Number to have the low Fever, there being a great many Patients and the Prisoners very numerous he believes there might have been as many ill if they had been at their own habitation, considering the Description of People.

Pavel concluded, in stark contrast to his 1750 predecessor, 'that the Goal has been as healthy under all Circumstances as could be expected'.[63]

Awareness of the potential for death, as well as motivating payment, prompted prisoners to take steps to improve their habitation and protect their health while prison keepers worked to protect their stock from destruction. Prisoners appointed from among their number stewards responsible for the upkeep of the gaol, collecting funds from each inhabitant to pay for the necessary work of cleaning and washing.[64] When conditions became particularly unpleasant, remedy being not in their individual power, debtors organised petitions to local officials for redress, such as in repairing broken pipes to bring clean water.[65] Petitions were also used by keepers to recover funds spent on taking care of sick prisoners after moments of crisis, such as that of John Kirby in 1767. Other prisons employed apothecaries on a regular basis to tend to diverse complaints, both serious and mundane. One surviving list of treatments at Wood Street from 1675 reveals an apothecary bleeding, providing cordials, enemas, cough syrups, and repeat prescriptions of 'a mixture for the Foote' for one debtor among other treatments, billing not just for prisoners but also staff such as 'Martin the cook'.[66] In this manner, while gaols remained unsanitary, mortality was at the very least controlled and restricted, a circumstance which protected the interests of creditors.

The health of prisoners was aided by the gifts of food and visits made by the numerous charitable organisations. While charity (either by the court or by individuals) explicitly released only a minority of prisoners in the registers, this represents a significant underestimation of the role of charitable acts in enacting debtor release. The reform movement frequently boasted of the number of prisoners they discharged per year. James Hallifax in a sermon published for 'the [third] Anniversary of the Society for the Discharge and Relief of Persons imprisoned for Small Debts' in 1775 saluted the number who had already been released by the reformers:

> A clear insight into the unhappy case of this species of sufferers, put it into the hearts of a few well-disposed gentlemen to attempt their relief ... from the first commencement of this undertaking, in the year 1772, to the present time, upwards of 2,700 debtors have been discharged from ... loathsome prison[s].[67]

Margot Finn also later praised the work of the society in releasing 'tens of thousands of petty debtors ... from prison between 1772 and 1831', amounting to 51,250 prisoners according to the society by 1832.[68] However, as the society was focussed exclusively on releasing "small debtors" (those owing under £5, particularly debtors committed by the Court of Requests) they judged as "innocent" victims, the high numbers they boasted of only represented a small fraction of the total prison population. The lack of Court of Request prisoners at the Fleet and Lancaster further explains the comparative lack of charity while such prisoners made up 26% of Wood Street debtors, rising to 32% or 2,237 debtors in the period in which the society was in operation. The society's work is still underestimated in the register as the term 'Discharged by the Thatched House Society' only appears in 1802–1803. Hallifax's sermon was published with an appendix report on the society's work for the year beginning 30th March 1774; this claimed that 122 Wood Street prisoners had been released by the society in the preceding year.[69] In the registers fifty Court of Request debtors and another eighty-three normal debtors owing less than £5 were released in this period, many presumably by the society. The prison may have not recorded the operation of the charity as, technically, since the debts had been paid, they were no different from other prisoners leaving with their creditor's permission. Charity, and charitable societies, may thus have been one element of securing release rather than a method. For example, begging at the grate, as was common at all debtors' prisons in this period, must have remained a significant way of accruing capital, as were other gifts and donations of a charitable nature.[70] In this way, charity, though usually external, enabled internal relief. The percentage of debtors who were released by charitable means was still probably lower than might be expected from the boasting of the reformers. At the Fleet, the court only started to discharge poor debtors 'as a pauper' in the second half of the period and the number who were freed in this way remained small as well as being generally restricted to long-term prisoners such as William Elmslie who was eventually 'discharged as a pauper' from his debt of £40 in 1791 after seven years confinement.[71] Meanwhile, specific charitable bequests to prisoners tended to aim at improving the quality of life in the prison, such as food or free sermons, rather than facilitating release. Wood Street debtors, as a City of London prison, were entitled to funds designed to release prisoners, however, these appear rarely in the registers. The Draper's Company are only cited as having released prisoners twice in the registers while a bequest known as Fuller's Charity ceased to release prisoners after 1756 with money being more regularly used to provide food and heating.[72]

One of the most significant means of release after discharge was the intervention of the state in disputes through legislation. The majority were released by the Insolvency Acts which were irregularly passed across the eighteenth century, their freedom following the turning over of their remaining property to their creditors. The development of these Acts and the reasons why individual's took advantage of them (and why others did not) are detailed in Chapter 5, though that parliament was required to intervene to end certain disputes testifies to the fact that there were some cases where debts simply could never be paid and that no degree of coercive action could procure payment. The existence of such amnesties insured that debtors did not remain imprisoned indefinitely, contributing further to the decreased mortality rate. A minority in this category were released by a statute commonly known as the Lord's Act, passed in 1729 and reissued in 1758, which functioned effectively as an ongoing Insolvency Act, the passage of which were usually time limited to those confined before a specified date. Under the Lord's Act debtors could offer up their entire estate to creditors to sat-isfy their debts, creditors opposing the release being required to provide the prisoner with maintenance payments of 4d *per diem*, a stipend known as the groats.[73] While this has from snapshot examinations of particular prisons been seen as a regular mechanism for releasing the destitute, from the broader examination of commitment books undertaken here it would seem, as other scholars have noted, 'never to have been effective'. Even in the eighteenth century the Lord's Act was described as a 'miserable refuge' that offered little recompense to either creditor or debtor.[74] The first statute cleared less than 4% of prisoners committed before 1749 while its second incarnation freed just 0.4% of Fleet debtors. Though the Lord's Act had a wider role in clearing some of a debtor's obligations, it was rarely the mechanism which ultimately returned them to the world. Similarly, at Wood Street the two Acts only cleared seven and eight debtors respectively. At Lancaster Castle however, the rate of debtors whose release was recorded as under '32 Geo II c28' (the 1758 Lord's Act) was much higher and accounted for 54% of those released by leg-islative means and 13% of all prisoners. As taking the Act required submitting a petition this may have proved simpler for Lancashire debtors as the court was held in the building they resided in, reducing the costs of hiring legal representatives. Additionally, the poorer provincial debtors may simply have been more in need of such relief and their creditors more willing to accept any form of payment available particularly as the payment of groats proved difficult to enforce.

Occasionally debtors, having been arrested by their creditors, had articles of bankruptcy brought against them demonstrating the ability of some credi-tors to be flexible and diverse in their attempts to recover wealth. Some may have imprisoned debtors they planned to bankrupt to prevent them from accruing further debts or spiriting away property, particularly the fifty-eight Fleet debtors released by bankruptcy within two months.[75] Ten debtors at Wood Street were made bankrupt during their commitment though were not released – in some cases they were not 'discharged' until several years later – suggesting that unlike at the Fleet a commission of bankruptcy did not end their confinement. Bankrupt debtors owed larger sums than on average – Simon Moritz Bethman at Wood Street owing £8,500 – making them some-what distinct from other prisoners.[76] Similarly distinct were those prisoners committed by the Court of Requests who were released at the 'Expiration of time' after reform in 1786 limited the duration such prisoners could be held to twenty days per pound of debt they owed, effectively meaning that coercion had utterly failed to enforce payment as debts were dissolved upon release.[77]

A range of prisoners were released by court processes. The reason behind such release is unclear in the majority of cases, usually simply being recorded as 'Released by Rule of Court', 'Judge', or 'the Sheriff' (the latter accounting for 36% of such release at Lancaster). It is possible that these debtors represent those who, having been brought to trial, triumphed over their creditor or lost and had their estates proceeded against. However, only three such debtors from Lancaster were recorded in the register as being summoned to trial. It is also possible that some, particularly at the Fleet, might indicate commissions of bankruptcy, 'rule of court' being a shorthand for 'By rule of the Lord Chancellor on the issuing of a Commission of Bankruptcy'. In instances where there is clarity in the registers, release by the court reflects specific administrative procedure such as Richard Williams of Wood Street who in 1781 was 'Discharged by the Court, he being a Soldier'.[78] These debtors have been kept largely separate in this category due to it being unclear what the court's reasoning behind release was, though it probably contains a high number of creditors being disappointed in their pursuit of payment. Similarly, some prisoners were released by unique methods not associated with the court or by mechanisms which are not entirely clear, the largest segment of these "Other" debtors being the thirty taken from Giltspur Street in 1815 when the debtors were moved to the New Debtors' Prison for London and Westminster in Whitecross Street.[79]

Just as with the low number fleeing from the *rules*, so too escapes from prison were generally isolated and rare which is to be expected considering the likelihood of swift release observed in this study. Wardens and keepers were keen to prevent absconding or recover debtors where possible as in the event of a gaol break they were liable to the escapee's creditors for the debt.[80] William Lindon, who managed to flee the Fleet on his first day in 1788, was eventually recovered on the 3rd September 1790 paying the full debt to the warden in just twelve days.[81] Lindon was not recorded as 'escaped' until he had been recovered making it possible that more prisoners escaped with exit details left blank as they were never retaken. Twenty debtors were explicitly described as escaping the Fleet along with four *rulers* and four non-debtor prisoners including Henry Wilson, owing £2,512 in forfeit to the excise, who boldly 'Escaped over the Prison Wall into an Empty House in Fleet Lane' after six years imprisonment in the 1740s, a notable achievement considering the height of this barricade.[82] At least three debtors recorded as 'escaped' were returned to the Fleet (including Isaac Meure who returned to the prison without the Warden noticing) while three more were taken to Newgate.[83] Burton Brace was recorded as 'Escaped & Hanged' in 1735, committing highway robbery during his flight possibly in an attempt to pay his debts of £65.[84] Prisoners were clearly aware that the burden of their escape was likely to fall on the keeper. In 1790, a conspiracy attempted to take advantage of the law on escapes by falsely imprisoning one of their number, Francis Shanley for £2,670, and then, having 'dress[ed] him in the habits of a woman', Shanley simply walked out the front gate. Ultimately the conspirators were caught though the delay in raising the alarm and the ease at which Shanley escaped suggests others may have taken advantage of the Fleet's porosity.[85]

While escapes were rare the impact of the Gordon Riots of 1780 perhaps indicates most clearly the efficacy of debt imprisonment. After the breaking open of the London prisons, at which time there were roughly 200 debtors in the Fleet and more than sixty in Wood Street, large numbers of prisoners disappeared into the city. However, while three prisoners explicitly never returned to the Fleet after the riots, in the months after the burning of the prison the majority of those who fled appear to have returned (being noted in the registers as 'Surrenders agreeable to the Acts of the 20 & 21 K Geo 3').[86] Only one prisoner explicitly escaped from Wood Street in the riots though twenty of the forty-one prisoners who had been committed in the previous six months lack any release detail in the register suggesting they may have also fled, two explicitly noted in the margin as 'set at large by the Rioters & ... given Notice persuant to the Act of Parliament'.[87] However, even before parliament offered rioters clemency, not all prisoners participated in the benefits of chaos. At Wood Street, a group of petitioners wrote to the Court of Aldermen informing them that after the mob pulled down the prison wall, they had remained in custody 'not chusing to avail themselves of so unjust a proceeding'. These prisoners observed their freedom and declined, confident that such criminality was not their only chance of freedom. Subsequently, they appear to have felt aggrieved that those who had fled were to benefit from undermining their creditors through parliament's pardon and therefore they too, as law-abiding citizens, begged to be 'released from their confinement' by statute as the escapees had.[88] While their pleading fell on deaf ears and were all still in gaol in 1781, in most cases their initial confidence was borne out. The majority (86%) satisfied their creditors by 1782 with only one of their number taking the 1781 Insolvency Act. Only John Pearce, imprisoned since 1778 and dying in the compter in 1783, might have had course to regret his decision.[89] Presumably, once the court rejected their petition, they simply went back to accumulating capital to pay the reasonable demands of their creditors as the prison walls were carefully rebuilt around them.

★★

The 'old and good maxim' that 'a prison pays no debts', despite its near constant repetition, was essentially false. While some creditors across the eighteenth century may have felt the desire to imprison their debtors to satisfy some sense of personal vengeance, they probably represented a tiny fragment of those bothering to engage in the process of arrest. Instead, debtors' prisons proved a popular recourse across the period for the trading classes quite simply because in the majority of cases they offered a degree of financial recompense. They functioned effectively as the prisons themselves were essentially passive in the process – they operated merely as places of detention holding debtors rather than performing actions of repayment and certainly not of punishment. Just as the process of debt accumulation and credit contracting was largely informal and oral in the eighteenth century, so too was the method by which it was enforced. By applying coercion, debtors were forced into prioritising the needs of their creditors and, as the data in this chapter shows, they did so relatively quickly and generally to the benefit of the plaintiff even if it was only at the hand of charity or of the legislature. Prisons were intended for dealing with those who had not paid, rather than those who could not pay. Indeed, a far better maxim might be that suggested to debtors in a poem of 1750 that when 'other Strategems were crost' to effect release there was 'none so good as paying Debt and Cost'.[90]

Notes

1 John Howard, *The State of the Prisons in England and Wales, with Preliminary Observations, and an Account of Some Foreign Prisons* (London: 1777), p. 20.
2 Edward Farley, *Imprisonment for Debt Unconstitutional and Oppressive, Proved from the Fundamental Principles of the British Constitution, and the Rights of Nature* (London: 1788), p. 148.
3 William Huntington, *The Modern Plasterer Detected and His Untempered Mortar Discovered* (1787), p. 78; Manasseh Dawes, *Commentaries on the Laws of Arrests in Civil Cases* (1787), p. 3.
4 Josiah Dornford, *Seven Letters to the Lords of the Privy Council, on the Police* (1785), p. 34.
5 Anon. *A Candid Statement of the Case of the Insolvent Debtors of the Kingdom of Ireland* (Dublin: 1792), p. 8; Anon. *Observations on the Bill Now Depending in Parliament for the Relief of Debtors* (London: 1780), p. 21.
6 See: Anon. *The Cries of the Poor Prisoners, humbly Offered to the Serious Consideration of the King and Parliament* (1716), p. 5; Delarivier Manley, *Memoirs of Europe towards the Close of the Eighth Century* (1720), p. 100; Thomas Baston, *Observations on Trade, and a Publick Spirit* (London: 1732), p. 89; William Notcutt, *The Everlasting Love and Delights of Jesus Christ with the Sons of Men* (London: 1735), p. 77; Anon. *The Attempt; or, An Essay towards the Retrieving of Lost Liberty* (1751), p. 13; P.R. *A Letter to a Friend in America* (Edinburgh: 1754), p. 109; Anon. *The Irretrievable Abyss; Humbly Addressed to both Houses of Parliament* (1757), p. 4; Anon. *Essays on Several Subjects* (1769), p. 99.
7 James Stephen, *Considerations on Imprisonment for Debt* (1770), p. 72; Anon. *An Inquiry into the Practice of Imprisonment for Debt, and a Refutation of Mr James Stephen's Doctrine* (1773), pp. 39–40.
8 John Vernon, *The Complete Countinghouse* (London: 1678), p. 180; also see Moses Pitt, *The Cry of the Oppressed* (London: 1691), p. xxv.
9 Charles Dickens, *Little Dorrit* (London: 1857).
10 Margot C. Finn, *The Character of Credit – Personal Debt in English Culture, 1740–1914* (Cambridge: Cambridge University Press, 2003), p. 51; Julian Hoppit, "The Use and Abuse of Credit in Eighteenth-Century England", in *Business Life and Public Policy – Essays in Honour of D.C. Coleman*, eds. Neil McKendrick and R.B. Outhwaite (Cambridge: Cambridge University Press, 1986), p. 76; Arthur Stratton, "Two Forgotten Buildings by the Dances", *The Architectural Review* vol. XL (1916), p. 24; Neil L. Sobol, "Charging the Poor: Criminal Justice Debt & Modern-Day Debtors' Prisons", *Maryland Law Review* vol. 75, no. 2 (2016), p. 493; Alexander H. Pitofsky, "'What Do You Think Laws Were Made For?' – Prison Reform Discourse and the English Jacobin Novel", *Studies in Eighteenth-Century Culture* vol. 33 (2004), p. 303.
11 William Holdsworth, *A History of English Law Volume VIII* (London: Methuen & co., 1925), pp. 231–232.
12 Joanna Innes, "The King's Bench Prison in the Later Eighteenth Century: Law, Authority and Order in a London Debtors' Prison," in *An Ungovernable People – The English and their Law in the Seventeenth and Eighteenth Centuries*, eds. John

Brewer and John Styles (London: Hutchinson, 1980), p. 255; Tim Hitchcock and Robert Brink Shoemaker, *London Lives – Poverty, Crime and the Making of a Modern City, 1690–1800* (Cambridge: Cambridge University Press, 2015), pp. 102–106; Hoppit, "Use and Abuse", p. 76; Julian Hoppit, *Britain's Political Economies – Parliament and Economic Life, 1660–1800* (Cambridge: Cambridge University Press, 2017), p. 156; Gustav Peebles, *The Euro and Its Rivals: Money and the Construction of a Transnational City* (Bloomington: Indiana University Press, 2011), p. 124; William Holdsworth, *A History of English Law Volume X* (London: Methuen & co., 1938), p. 181; Julian Hoppit, *Risk and Failure in English Business 1700–1800* (Cambridge: Cambridge University Press, 1987), p. 21.

13 Gustav Peebles, "Washing away the Sins of Debt: The Nineteenth-Century Eradication of the Debtors' Prison", *Comparative Studies in History* vol. 55, no. 3 (2013), pp. 701–724.

14 Paul Langford, *A Polite and Commercial People – England 1727–1783* (Oxford: Clarendon Press, 1998), p. 490.

15 Joel Mokyr, *The Enlightened Economy – An Economic History of Britain 1700–1850* (New Haven: Yale University Press, 2009), p. 379.

16 Peter J. Coleman, *Debtors and Creditors in America – Insolvency, Imprisonment for Debt, and Bankruptcy, 1607–1900* (Madison: The State Historical Society of Wisconsin, 1974), p. 5.

17 Matthew J. Baker, Metin Cosgel, and Thomas J. Miceli, "Debtors' Prisons in America: An Economic Analysis", *Journal of Economic Behaviour & Organisation* vol. 84 (2012), p. 228. Also see: Brianna L. Campbell, "The Economy of the Debtors' Prison Model: Why Throwing Deadbeats into Debtors' Prison Is a Good Idea", *Arizona Journal of International and Comparative Law* vol. 32, no. 3 (2015), pp. 849–876.

18 Craig Muldrew, *The Economy of Obligation – The Culture of Credit and Social Relations in Early Modern England* (Basingstoke: Macmillan, 1998), pp. 286–287; Carl Wennerlind, *Casualties of Credit – The English Financial Revolution, 1620–1720* (Cambridge: Harvard University Press, 2011), p. 2; Tawny Paul, *Poverty of Disaster – Debt and Insecurity in Eighteenth-Century Britain* (Cambridge: Cambridge University Press, 2019), pp. 191–193.

19 Anon. *The Case of the Traders and Dealers of England, set forth in a Dialogue between Mr Trader and Mr Cheator* (London: 1702), pp. 2–3.

20 Stephen, *Considerations*, p. 19; Paul, *Poverty of Disaster*, pp. 191–193; Roger Lee Brown, *A History of the Fleet Prison, London – the Anatomy of the Fleet* (Lampeter: Edwin Mellen Press, 1996), p. 142.

21 "List of Prisoners Handed over by the Sheriffs to their Successors on 28 Sept Annually, with Notes of Occurrences During the Subsequent Year", 1768, Wood Street Compter later Giltspur Street Compter, LMA, CLA/028/01/014; "List of Prisoners Handed over by the Sheriffs to their Successors on 28 Sept Annually, with Notes of Occurrences During the Subsequent Year", 1784–1785, Wood-Street Compter later Giltspur Street Compter, LMA, CLA/028/01/025.

22 "Commitment Registers", 1786–1790, Fleet Prison, TNA, PRIS 1/13; T.C. Hansard, *The Parliamentary Debates Vol. XIV* (London: 1826), p. 1180.

23 "Lancaster Gaol Register of Debtors and Plaintiffs", 1793–1796, Home Office and Prison Commission Records: Prison Records Series 1, TNA, PCOM 2/440.

24 See: William Penrice, *The Extraordinary Case of William Penrice, Late Deputy Marshal or Upper Turnkey of the King's Bench Prison* (London: 1768), p. 35; Richard King Esq, *The Frauds of London Detected; or, a Warning Piece against the Iniquitous Practices of that Metropolis* (London: 1779), p. 45; Farley, *Imprisonment for Debt Unconstitutional and Oppressive*; Anon. *The Debtor and Creditor's Assistant; or, a Key to the King's Bench and Fleet Prisons; Calculated for the Information and Benefit of the Injured Creditor, as well as The Unfortunate Debtor: Including Newgate, Ludgate, and*

the Three Compters. To Which Are Added, Reflections on Perpetual Imprisonment for Debt; and Outlines of a Bill for Abolishing the Same (London: 1793), p. 42; Richard H. Condon, "James Neild, Forgotten Reformer", *Studies in Romanticism* vol.4, no.4 (Summer 1964), p. 243; Margaret DeLacy, *Prison Reform in Lancashire – A Study in Local Administration* (Stanford: Stanford University Press, 1986), p. 46; John Sainsbury, "John Wilkes, Debt, and Patriotism", *Journal of British Studies* vol. 34, no. 2 (April 1995), p. 168; John Sainsbury, *John Wilkes – The Lives of a Libertine* (Aldershot: Ashgate, 2006), p. 214; Esther Sahle, "Quakers, Coercion, and Pre-modern Growth: Why Friends' Formal Institutions for Contract Enforcement Did Not Matter for Early Modern Trade Expansion", *Economic History Review* vol. 71, no. 2 (2018), p. 425.

25 See: Paul Hess Haagen, "Imprisonment for Debt in England and Wales", unpublished PhD thesis, University of Princeton (1986), pp. 1–39.

26 Innes, "King's Bench", p. 256.

27 Journal of the House of Commons, *Report for the Committee appointed to Enquire into the Practice and Effects of Imprisonment for Debt* (1792), p. 22.

28 "List of Prisoners Handed over by the Sheriffs to their Successors on 28 Sept Annually, with Notes of Occurrences During the Subsequent Year", 1804–1805, Wood Street Compter later Giltspur Street Compter, LMA, CLA/028/01/034.

29 James Bolland, *Memoirs of James Bolland Formerly a Butcher then Officer to the Sheriff of Surry, Afterwards Officer to the Sheriff of Middlesex, and Lately a Candidate for the Place of City Marshal; Executed at Tyburn, March 18. 1772, for Forgery* (London: 1772), p. 3; "Trial of James Bolland", 19th February 1772, *Old Bailey Proceedings Online*, t17720219–46.

30 Mokyr, *Enlightened Economy*, pp. 379–380; Innes, "King's Bench", p. 255; Hoppit, "Use and Abuse", p. 76; Hoppit, *Britain's Political Economies*, p. 156.

31 Michael Slater, "Dickens, Charles John Huffam (1812–1870)", *Oxford Dictionary of National Biography* (Oxford University Press, 2004), online edition, doi: 10.1093/ref:odnb/29016 (accessed 31st May 2018).

32 "List of Prisoners", 1784–1785, CLA/028/01/025; "List of Prisoners Handed over by the Sheriffs to their Successors on 28 Sept Annually, with Notes of Occurrences During the Subsequent Year", 1742, Wood Street Compter later Giltspur Street Compter, LMA, CLA/028/01/002.

33 "Commitment Registers", 1790–1793, Fleet Prison, TNA, PRIS 1/14; "Trial of Robert Jaques, John Tronson, Richard Bailey, Elizabeth Tronson, and Francis Shanley", *Old Bailey Proceedings Online*, t17900710–1.

34 "Commitment Registers", 1737–1745, Fleet Prison, TNA, PRIS 1/7–9.

35 "Commitment Registers", PRIS 1/13.

36 Paul, *Poverty of Disaster*, p. 104.

37 "List of Prisoners Handed over by the Sheriffs to their Successors on 28 Sept Annually, with Notes of Occurrences During the Subsequent Year", 1805–1806, Wood Street Compter later Giltspur Street Compter, LMA, CLA/028/01/035.

38 "List of Prisoners Handed over by the Sheriffs to their Successors on 28 Sept Annually, with Notes of Occurrences During the Subsequent Year", 1788–1791, Wood Street Compter later Giltspur Street Compter, LMA, CLA/028/01/027; *London Gazette*, 17th–21st June 1794, no. 13674, p. 591.

39 Anon. *The Attorney and Agent's New and Exact Table of Costs, in the Courts of King's Bench and Common Pleas* (London: 1786), pp. 95–97.

40 Anon. *The London Guide* (London: 1782), p. 82.

41 Gustav Peebles, "Whitewashing and Leg-Bailing: On the Spatiality of Debt", *Social Anthropology* vol. 20, no. 4 (2012), p. 431; Haagen, "Imprisonment for Debt", pp. 33–34.

42 Anon. *A New and Compleat Survey of London in Ten Parts. In Two Volumes. Vol. I* (London: 1742), p. 65.

43 Jonathan Gil Harris, "Ludgate Time: Simon Eyre's Oath and the Temporal Economies of *the Shoemaker's Holiday*", *Huntingdon Library Quarterly* vol. 71, no. 2 (March 2008), pp. 22–23; Richard Byrne, *Prisons and Punishments of London* (Grafton: London, 1992), pp. 22–24; Bruce Watson, "The Compter Prisons of London", *London Archaeologist* vol. 5, no. 5 (1993), p. 116; "List of Prisoners Handed over by the Sheriffs to their Successors on 28 Sept Annually, with Notes of Occurrences During the Subsequent Year", 1809–1810, Wood Street Compter later Giltspur Street Compter, LMA, CLA/028/01/038.

44 "Commitment Registers", 1795–1796, Fleet Prison, TNA, PRIS 1/16; "Trial of John Proctor", 13th January 1796, *Old Bailey Proceedings Online*, t17960113–98.

45 House of Commons, *Committee into Imprisonment for Debt*, p. 36.

46 Brown, *Anatomy of the Fleet*, p. 195.

47 "Commitment Registers", 1782–1786, Fleet Prison, TNA, PRIS 1/12.

48 Watson, "Compter Prisons", p. 118; Philip Woodfine, "Debtors, Prisons, and Petitions in Eighteenth-Century England," *Eighteenth Century Life* vol. 30, no. 2 (Spring 2006), p. 18; Philip Woodfine, "The Power and Influence of the Gaolers: Life and Death in York Castle Gaol," *Yorkshire Archaeological Journal* vol. 78 (2006), pp. 159–175; Jerry White, "Pain and Degradation in Georgian London: Life in the Marshalsea Prison", *History Workshop Journal* vol. 68 (Autumn 2009), p. 69; Gillian Selley, "Charles Lanyon, Merchant of Penzance: Victim of Cruelty and Corruption in the County Debtors Prison in Exeter", *The Devon Historian* vol. 83 (2014), pp. 39–48; Campbell, "Deadbeats", p. 854.

49 Howard, *State of the Prisons*, p. 2.

50 William Smith, *State of the Gaols in London, Westminster, and Borough of Southwark. To Which Is Added, An Account of the Present State of Convicts Sentenced to Hard Labour on Board the Justitia upon the River Thames* (London: 1776), p. 2.

51 Paul, *Poverty of Disaster*, p. 197; Philippa Hardman, "Fear of Fever and the Limits of the Enlightenment – Selling Prison Reform in late Eighteenth-Century Gloucestershire", *Cultural and Social History* vol. 10, no. 4 (2013), pp. 522–526; C. W. Chalklin, "The Reconstruction of London's Prisons, 1770–1799: An Aspect of the Growth of Georgian London", *The London Journal* vol. 9, no. 1 (1983), p. 21; Haagen, "Imprisonment for Debt", p. 69; Langford, *Polite and Commercial People*, p. 490.

52 Margaret DeLacy, *Prison Reform in Lancashire, 1700–1850 – A Study in Local Administration* (Stanford: Stanford University Press, 1986), pp. 24, 28–29, 183–184.

53 Rodney M. Baine, "The Prison Death of Robert Castell and Its Effect on the Founding of Georgia", *The Georgia Historical Society* vol. 73, no. 1 (Spring 1989), pp. 68–70.

54 "Commitment Registers", 1739–1741, Fleet Prison, TNA, PRIS 1/8.

55 "Extracts relating to the Prisoners in Gaols being attended by Medical People" in "Order of Ct. of Alderman for Payment of Apothecary's File for Medicines Delivered to a Great Number of Poor Sick Prisoners in Ludgate and the two Compters 1770", 1748–1775, Prisons and Compters – Prisons General, LMA, CLA/032/01/032, 1r.

56 "Commitment Registers", 1793–1795, Fleet Prison, TNA, PRIS 1/15.

57 "Commitment Registers", 1741–1745, Fleet Prison, TNA, PRIS 1/9.

58 "Commitment Registers", 1737–1739, Fleet Prison, TNA, PRIS 1/7.

59 "Account of several persons seized with the gaol distemper, working in Newgate, and its transmission to their families, by John Pringle, M.D., L.R.S., read to the Philosophical Society", 1753, Newgate Prison – Administration, LMA, CLA/035/02/049(iv).

60 See: Anon. *The Tryal of William Acton, Deputy-Keeper and Lessee of the Marshalsea Prison in Southwark, at Kingston Assizes* (London: 1729), p. 15 (death after confinement from abuse not gaol fever).

61 Letter from John Pringle to Alderman Jansen as to Gaol Fever and its Prevention, the Substance of Information Given the Committee, 1750, Newgate Prison – Administration, LMA, CLA/035/02/049(i).

62 *Whitehall Evening Post*, 23rd – 25th October, 1798, no. 8095.

63 "Draft report on state and number of prisoners", 1802, Newgate Prison – Administration, LMA, CLA/035/02/026(vi).

64 Anon. *An Accurate Description of Newgate. With the Rights, Privileges, Allowances, Fees, Dues, and Customs thereof* (London: 1724), pp. 9, 34–38; "Rules and Orders for the Better Government of the Debtors' Side of the Gaol of Newgate", 1808, Newgate Prison – Administration, LMA, CLA/035/02/031; "Rules and Orders for the Better Government of Ludgate", 1808, Ludgate Prison – Administration, LMA, CLA/033/01/001.

65 See: "Petitions of Prisoners, Offices of Newgate and the Compters, and Other Persons relating to Prison Life, Repair of Prisons, Collections, Ill Health, Abuse by Officers, for Discharge, &c", 1675–1700, Prisons and Compter – General, LMA, CLA/032/01/021, e.g. "The Humble Petition of the Prisoners in Wood-street Coompter" (xiii) 'That your Petitioners at present [lie] under very great distress for want of Water to drink, the Pipes being so decayed and broken which conveyed the Water'.

66 "Apothecary's Bill for the Prisoners in Wood Street Compter", 1675, Wood Street Compter later Giltspur Street Compter – Administration, LMA, CLA/028/03/002; Thomas R. Forbes, "Medical Supplies for Prisoners in 1675", *Bulletin of the New York Academy of Medicine* vol. 49, no. 7 (1973), pp. 592–593.

67 James Hallifax, *A Sermon Preached at the Parish Church of St Paul, Covent-Garden, On Thursday, May 18, 1775, For the Benefit of Unfortunate Persons Confined for Small Debts. Published by Request of the Society* (London: 1775), p. 7.

68 Finn, *Character of Credit*, p. 162.

69 Hallifax, *Unfortunate Persons*, p. 15.

70 White, "Pain and Degradation", p. 82; Eric Stockdale, *A Study of Bedford Prison 1660–1877* (Bedford: The Bedfordshire Historical Record Society, 1977, p. 45; Woodfine, "Debtors, Prisons, and Petitions", 10; Smith, *State of the Gaols*, p. 4; Hitchcock and Shoemaker, *London Lives*, p. 103.

71 "Commitment Registers", PRIS 1/12.

72 Howard, *State of the Prisons*, pp. 176, 229; House of Commons, *Committee into Imprisonment for Debt*, p. 79; John Entick, *A New and Accurate History and Survey of London, Westminster, Southwark, and Places Adjacent; Containing Whatever Is Most Worthy of Notice in their Ancient and Present State* (London: 1766), p. 48; City of London Livery Companies Commission, "Charitable accounts of the Mercers' Company", in *City of London Livery Companies Commission Report: Volume 4* (London: Eyre and Spottiswoode, 1884), pp. 68–96; "Petition of Prisoners in Wood-Street Compter for the paying of John Fuller Esq's Charity", no date, Debtors Petitions, LMA, CLA/040/08/009, ii; Paul, *Poverty of Disaster*, p. 101.

73 Haagen, "Imprisonment for Debt", p. 12; Paul H. Haagen, "Eighteenth-Century English Society and the Debt Law", in *Social Control and the State – Historical and Comparative Essays* (Oxford: Basil Blackwell, 1986), p. 225.

74 Paul, *Poverty of Disaster*, pp. 42, 106, 108, 117, 125; Haagen, "Imprisonment for Debt", p. 12; Anon. *New, Candid, and Practical Thoughts on the Law of Imprisonment for Debt, With a View to the Regulation of it* (London: 1788), pp. 27–33.

75 Emily Kadens, "The Last Bankrupt Hanged: Balancing Incentives in the Development of Bankruptcy Law", *Duke Law Journal* vol. 59, no. 7 (April 2010), pp. 1229–1319.

76 "List of Prisoners Handed over by the Sheriffs to their Successors on 28 Sept Annually, with Notes of Occurrences During the Subsequent Year", 1795–1799, Wood Street Compter later Giltspur Street Compter, LMA, CLA/028/01/030.

77 See: William Hutton, *Courts of Requests: Their Nature, Utility, and Powers Described, with A Variety of Cases, Determined in that of Birmingham* (Birmingham: 1787); Finn, *Character of Credit*, pp. 218–219; Margot Finn, "Debt and Credit in Bath's Court of Requests, 1829–1839", *Urban History* vol. 21, pt. 2 (October 1994), p. 214; W.H.D Winder, "The Courts of Requests," *The Law Quarterly Review* vol. 52, no. 207 (1936), pp. 392–393; Anon. *The Debtor and Creditor's Assistant; or, a Key to the King's Bench and Fleet prisons; Calculated for the Information and Benefit of the Injured Creditor, as well as the Unfortunate Debtor* (London: 1793), p. 67.

78 "List of Prisoners Handed over by the Sheriffs to their Successors on 28 Sept Annually, with Notes of Occurrences During the Subsequent Year", 1780–1781, Wood Street Compter later Giltspur Street Compter, LMA, CLA/028/01/023.

79 House of Commons, *Second Report from the Committee on the Prisons within the City of London and Borough of Southwark* (1818), p. 247.

80 William Holdsworth, *A History of English Law Volume VI* (London: Methuen & Co., 1924), p. 407.

81 "Commitment Registers", 1786–1790, Fleet Prison, TNA, PRIS 1/13.

82 "Commitment Registers", 1739–1741, Fleet Prison, TNA, PRIS 1/8.

83 "Commitment Registers", 1733–1735, Fleet Prison, TNA, PRIS 1/5; Anon. *The Practical Register of the Common Pleas* (London: 1743), pp. 199–203.

84 "Commitment Registers", 1735–1737, Fleet Prison, TNA, PRIS 1/6; "Trial of Burton Brace", 10th December 1735, *Old Bailey Proceedings Online*, t17351210–24.

85 "Commitment Registers", 1786–1790, Fleet Prison, TNA, PRIS 1/13; Trial of Robert Jaques, John Tronson, Richard Bailey, Elizabeth Tronson, and Francis Shanley", *Old Bailey Proceedings Online*, t17900710–1.

86 "Commitment Registers", 1778–1782, Fleet Prison, TNA, PRIS 1/11.

87 "List of Prisoners Handed over by the Sheriffs to their Successors on 28 Sept Annually, with Notes of Occurrences During the Subsequent Year", 1778–1780, Wood Street Compter later Giltspur Street Compter, LMA, CLA/028/01/022.

88 Debtors in Wood-Street Compter, "The Humble Petition of the undermentioned persons whose Names are hereunto subscribed Debtors in Wood Street Compter", 1780, City of London Courts of Law – Debtors Petitions, LMA, CLA/040/08/009, iii.

89 "List of Prisoners", CLA/028/01/022.

90 William Paget, *The Humours of the Fleet. A Poem* (Birmingham: 1749), p. 2.

4 The debtor economy

Obtaining release from debtors' prisons

The debtors' prison, an institution which touched the lives of almost every family in England, was a regular feature of literature and art in the eighteenth century. By far the most evocative depiction is that contained in William Hogarth's *A Rake's Progress* series, produced first as paintings and later in a widely published printed form. The desolate "Tom" trapped within London's Fleet Prison appears symptomatic of the suffering of debt imprisonment both to modern scholars and in the period, views of the image being encapsulated early in its life by an anonymous 1735 poem: 'At last he's hurried to a Jail. Dismal retreat, a second Hell, Whose Pains none know but those that feel. In Durance bound, no Money left, And even of Hope itself bereft'.[1] Tom is depicted generally as 'a man lost' trapped in a 'nightmare'; his gaunt, downcast eyes and spread hands, ranged alongside his collapsing true love, characterising the despair at the concept of ever managing to find a way out of Hell. The facial expression is familiar to all those coming to the end of a series of failed plans asking, with no inspiration forthcoming: "what now?".[2] Beyond Tom, however, is a scene of furious activity. He is sat still but the prison is alive with furious commercial motion around him. A boy emerges from beneath carrying in one hand a fresh and frothy ale – a mug full enough to allow the head to flow over its edge – which was presumably far from Tom's first, the boy's free hand outstretched demanding payment. The ale-boy might be the child of an imprisoned innkeeper and is conducting the same work he would have at home in better times. Nor is he Tom's only vendor, the turnkey leans over him pointing to a prison book which presumably lists Tom's mounting gaol bills. Elsewhere in the cell, a shabby prisoner drops his manuscript on the state of the nation's credit, a scroll he has evidently been working on for some time, that is intended more for its value as a commercial publication than for its social purpose. Unconnected to all the commotion is the figure working at his homemade forge and even if, as is usually suggested, he is attempting to turn lead into gold, this man's quiet productivity is a far cry from Tom's indolent despair. Many upon their arrival in debtors' prison certainly shared Tom's moments of sheer panic but in the days ensuing prisoners applied their newfound free time more productively. In this satirical scene of ridiculous exploits there is a clear focus on procuring freedom. Even the Icarian wings hanging above the bed speak more of optimism and industry than lethargy.

The supposedly sedentary experience of eighteenth-century debt imprisonment arises from the assumption that the prisons were not effective mechanisms of financial recovery but also the limited contemporary recording of prisoner activities. Cultural histories of debt imprisonment have clearly depicted the everyday life of the gaols as vibrant, debtors organising themselves into "colleges" of self-governance, with thriving alehouses in which those from across the social spectrum might hob-nob and indulge.[3] While such descriptions reflect a truism of the debtor nightlife which helps to overcome the absolute despair of some gaol descriptions, research has largely overlooked the equally vibrant though more productive world of the prison during the day in which the inhabitants worked to settle their accounts as well as to fund their late-night socialisation. The world of debtor labour is, however, a murky one that has been far harder to observe than formal prisoner organisations which has limited the possibility of prior investigation. Little documentary evidence of the debtor economy has survived beyond where it strayed into acts construed as illegal such as the improper import and sale of alcohol. While courts administering gaols were keen to make orders limiting social activities such as dancing or 'assembl[ing] for the purpose of [singing] Tippling [Songs] … or Gaming' they were unlikely to restrict (and thus comment upon) the labour of prisoners. Rhetorical pamphlet literature meanwhile was more concerned with forcing the poor prisoners into labour benefiting the state to combat their supposed 'habitual indolence, filth and vice' than recognising the industry of actual middling sort debtors. Furthermore, those who had been imprisoned were frequently keen not to advertise their former uncreditworthiness by publishing detailed accounts of their confinement activities beyond depicting themselves as humble and deserving of sympathy or declaring they had achieved freedom by paying all their debts without comment on how they had managed this.[4]

It is clear from the data drawn from debtors' prison commitment registers that prisons did regularly pay debts, with the majority of creditors being satisfied in some form within a year of arrest, implying that debtors were regularly engaged in pursuing their own liberty rather than meekly sat waiting for death. This chapter explores how debtors achieved discharge, providing general context to the statistical data. It uses an array of material providing momentary glimpses into the world of the debtor economy, from the moment of arrest to release, to reveal the diverse strategies employed by prisoners. Where possible it relies on investigations into prisons which cite the evidence of confined witnesses (such as the extensive enquiry conducted by a parliamentary committee in 1792) as well as personal accounts of imprisonment published in memoirs and particularly on the diary of John Grano, written during his residency at the Marshalsea in 1728–1729. It also explores the accounts of visitors to prisons, though recognising these were based on momentary rather than persistent experience of prison life and the similarly brief details mentioned in criminal trials. Additionally, evidence of the general characteristics of the debtor economy are drawn from literary depictions of the prisons – written by and for those likely to experience the real thing – which have previously been shown to be representative or at least illustrative of actual confinement to compensate for the rarity of autobiographical or administrative evidence.[5] While this does not amount to a rigorous quantitative assessment of labour, it provides necessary context which suggests conclusions on the effectiveness of prisons are tenable. Having first shown that, for most debtors, the size of their obligation did not determine the length of their confinement, owing sums they could reasonably be expected to pay, discussion turns to their methods of doing so. Some prisoners were either able simply to pay upon demand once coerced or to negotiate a settlement with their creditors. However, the most important way out is shown to be productive exertion such as that exhibited in Hogarth's depiction of the Fleet, an institution he had experienced alongside his father as a child. The prisons functioned as vibrant commercial environments, the institutions therefore producing payment through indirect means as well as being an important and previously overlooked contributor to local commerce.

★★

As generally impersonal administrative documents, the surviving commitment registers of debtors' prisons provide little detail on how individual prisoners managed to convince their creditors to discharge them. However, they do imply that those owing vastly different sums experienced similar spells within debtors' prison, suggesting that an individual debtor's ability to raise capital was proportional to what creditors had judged they could probably repay when pressed. Figure 4.1 depicts the average commitment length at each prison by the value of debt owed. Having rounded total debts owed to the closest whole pound, a £5 moving average of commitment lengths by debt owed was produced for each prison. Due to the small number of debtors at Lancaster Castle Gaol owing over £100, the prison is somewhat underrepresented. Variation between individual commitment lengths was erratic particularly as some debt categories might contain small numbers of prisoners (such as the one debtor owing £167 at the Fleet) or unusual individuals contained for very short or very long periods. However, principally Figure 4.1 does not indicate any strong correlation between the size of debt one was imprisoned for and the subsequent length of confinement. While the moving average at each prison rose slightly between £1 and £25, for larger debts there was a relatively flat general trend. At Lancaster and Wood Street, between £20 and £200, most debtors endured an average commitment of c.150–250 days, and while this length was regularly doubled at the Fleet this reflected the greater complexity of cases which still did not experience linearly increased confinement. The data suggests that those owing larger sums had been lent a comparable sum relative to their personal capacity as those owing small debts and therefore that creditors were not being overly risky when lending. Individuals with an annual income of c.£20 were not being lent debts measured

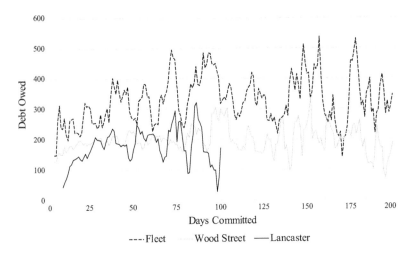

Figure 4.1 £5 Moving Average of Commitment Length by Debt Owed at the Fleet Prison, Wood Street Compter, and Lancaster Castle Gaol (1730–1815).

in the hundreds of pounds but an amount they could reasonably be expected to pay when asked. This process was generally not instantaneous as an individual's credit threshold went beyond personal wealth to include what they could expect to rely on from family, friends, their goods, their own debtors, and future income. The largely uniform commitment length for prisoners of different fiscal capacities suggests that, across the board, creditors rightly felt debtors could pay if pressed. While the *laissez-faire* institution had almost no direct involvement with securing payment, debt imprisonment's multiple impacts (on prisoners and the public) and conceptions (as threat or tangible wounding) were clear contributors to procuring repayment as the various strategies that emerge from related material reveal.

The power of debt imprisonment in securing repayment was on occasion so great as to ensure payment was, if not immediate, certainly prompt as the system did not begin only once the hapless debtor was pushed through the prison doors. While as an existential deterrent debtors' prisons could be said to always be in operation, as an active system of ensuring payment the institution commenced from the moment a writ was secured as is revealed by the various interactions debtors had with bailiffs. In 1735, William Phillips claimed to have run away 'from the Constable' arresting him for horse theft as he 'was going into the Country to receive fourteen Pound ... I thought he had been a Bailiff, and I, being in debt, was afraid of being arrested'. While Phillips was obviously lying, that he thought this a reasonable excuse indicates that numerous non-criminals, hearing their creditor had lost patience, rushed out under the cover of night to raise capital to satisfy debts, avoiding the supposed mortal dangers of confinement and protecting their reputation.[6]

A House of Commons committee investigating imprisonment for debt – its members including current and future Prime Ministers William Pitt and Charles Grey – reported in 1792 that 'in Middlesex ... there are issued annually ... exclusive of London, about 9,500 bailable Writs, that is, Writs on which the Defendant must be imprisoned if he do not find Bail; and that between 5 and 6,000 arrests, on such Writs of *Mesne* Process, are actually made' suggesting a significant number of debtors were able to pay their debts before the formal action of arrest occurred even if the bailiff caught up with them.[7] Samuel Pepys, when confronted with a bailiff during dinner in 1663, was never served with the writ, sending his servant 'to tell [the money] out to him in the office'.[8] Such a privilege was not confined to the rich and powerful as in 1796 Thomas Spurling, a suburban baker, was also able to talk his way out of arrest. The bailiff, Charles Scoldwell arrived at Spurling's home in Bedfont in Middlesex at about ten o'clock at night and 'informed him ... he had a writ against him' for £16 7s though never formally arrested Spurling. The baker attempted to escape but the ageing debtor was quickly 'caught by the collar' and agreed to settle the debt against him to avoid being carried to Newgate at his own expense. 'I have £15 in the house; you shall have that, and I will give you something else as a security for the payment of the balance, £1 7s' for which Spurling eventually turned over his watch.[9]

Even those who were formally arrested might pay without delay. In 1726 John Nevitt, was arrested at home but never made it to gaol, instead he was 'carried ... to Mr Cross's House ... at whose suit he was Arrested' there satisfying the claim against him.[10] The 1792 committee further reported that while 'not one in five [settled] the Debt on the Arrest' only 'about 900 of the Defendants so Arrested in Middlesex [15–18%], exclusive of London, are supposed to actually go to prison' and of the '3,055 bailable Writs ... issued into London, ... nearly the same Proportions as in Middlesex' were arrested and imprisoned. Indeed, while the sponging houses were a general detractor on the system of debt imprisonment, many debtors (having the capacity to pay) did settle their accounts from within them. The actress Charlotte Charke was allowed upon her arrest in the first half of the eighteenth century to wander at liberty for a few days after a friend stood security. Her attempts to raise capital were unsuccessful and she was incarcerated within a sponging house though never made it to the Marshalsea as 'all the ladies who kept Coffee Houses in and about [Covent] Garden, each offering Money for my Ransom' visited her, in turn. This, along with donations from other friends, meant Charke 'was set at Liberty' only a day after her arrival in the sponging house.[11] Though such debtors had the existential threat of imprisonment hanging over them from the moment of their first contracting, it was only its tangible reality which coercively compelled them into making payment or raising the necessary capital.

Of those who did not escape formal confinement, some endured imprisonments equally as short as Charke. Commitment registers reveal that a small group of debtors were able to settle their bills on the same day they were formally confined. While most of those leaving on the same day they arrived simply moved gaols, twenty-five Wood Street Compter, two Lancaster Castle, and twelve Fleet Prison debtors were discharged or bailed by night fall. The sums such debtors managed to pay ranged widely from a Wood Street debtor who was only required to locate a shilling to James Patten at the Fleet in 1779 who managed to drum up £860. In total, 2% of those discharged from Wood Street were freed within two weeks of their confinement along with 8% of Fleet and Lancaster prisoners. These individuals may have had coinage near or on hand when they were imprisoned, the explorer Henry Timberlake's memoir offering a clear example of this behaviour. Planning to sail to America, Timberlake settled his debts but was arrested just before departure for a bill 'which in my confusion I forgot'. He described how he

> was carried immediately to Wood Street Compter, where I wrote to a friend for money ... but being disappointed, I was obliged to pay away the little I had reserved for my expences, so that I had but two shillings left.[12]

Having to discharge what he actually owed placed Timberlake's finances in a perilous standing but his creditor was satisfied and the debt concluded. While his failure to pay before arrest was accidental, it is interesting that his initial reaction was not to pay despite having the required sum. As he might have need of this money during his voyage, he determined to ask a friend for aid, in essence moving his debt from one creditor to another. Timberlake's experience, as well as of others who paid quickly such as Thomas Spurling, demonstrates the crucial reason why the debtors' prison was such an effective tool of coercing payment: imprisonment helped restore fungibility to capital. While in theory money is an obviously transferable receptacle of wealth which can be put to any use, humans (across time) regularly relate to their money as if parts of it are sacrosanct in their purpose. Different pots of money are intended to pay for rent, food, enterprise, or the needs of children and while money hoped to be used for luxuries can be diverted, key categories (being equally pressing) cannot substitute one another.[13] As such, from the view of a creditor, debtors had the capability to pay but from the perspective of the debtors they did not as their holdings could not be multipurpose. Imprisonment smashed cash-pots, forcing an unwanted combination of pecuniary resources as ongoing needs were replaced by a new more pressing need – liberty.

Some debtors with access to currency or financial support from third parties were freed through bail rather than concluding their obligations. The possibility of securing bail has previously been questioned or suggested to have been confined to the wealthy, with indications from contemporary pamphlet evidence that an arrested debtor required security 'four times the amount that his creditor claimed he was owed'.[14] However, though most of those procuring bail acquired it before their confinement, it is clear that a minority of debtors of a variety of backgrounds were able to secure their discharge from within gaol through bail.[15] In the Fleet registers, where the amount that would be required is sometimes recorded at commitment, bail was generally set at half the charge or, at most, three quarters of the sum and almost never more than the total debt. At Lancaster, between 1793 and 1796, 11% of prisoners managed to obtain bail for debts across the spectrum of obligations, more than half taking over a month and one up to six months, suggesting that similar if not greater numbers managed to obtain it in London. Most secured bail by another 'standing security' for them. Advice books for young tradesmen cautioned against this activity without significant forethought as 'though the man were honest' if they defaulted the security 'may be obliged to pay the debt' or even arrested, although they could then potentially also arrest their bailee. Despite this sensible caution, acting as bail was a regular and expected activity, suggesting a societal confidence in the ability of those arrested to pay eventually, whether bailed or not.[16] This general optimism might even stretch to individuals standing security for strangers. George Wilkie, a London bookseller, claimed he was furious to find out he had unwittingly acted as bail for Thomas Paine, 'the author of the Seditious Writings Entitled Rights of Man'. Paine, who had been arrested for debts 'which he contracted formerly as a staymaker', secured bail through a friend, Joseph Johnson, who had persuaded his neighbour Wilkie to stand as a security 'to oblige' Johnson a favour. George Wilkie maintained that he was not aware of the debtor's identity and subsequently 'manfully disavowed in the Newspapers, that he had any connection with such a character as Paine'.[17] For a creditor to accept a third party standing security (rather than paying the debt) probably required a much higher degree of confidence in the capability and imminence of repayment than had been necessary at the initial purchase. In Tobias Smollet's 1753 novel *Adventures of Ferdinand Count Fathom*, Fathom's creditor upon being presented with those willing to stand 'absolutely rejected his personal security; and threatened him with all the horrors of a goal, unless he would immediately discharge the debt, or procure sufficient bondsmen'.[18] To manage this issue of trust, the antinomian preacher William Huntingdon suggested in 1787 that creditors should locate sureties themselves for debtors of whom they could be more confident:

> he represents my wretched case to a friend of his own; who, to gratify the affection of my creditor, delivers me from a prison; and, to lay me under an eternal obligation, both to my creditor and to himself, he steps forth and becomes my surety.[19]

In essence, this act (similar to Timberlake's strategy) changed the prisoner's creditor from one who was in imminent need of capital to one who could afford to be more patient.

Most prisoners, as was evident in 4.1, required time to secure release implying they could not pay at the moment of confinement, the prison being, for them, a general mechanism of forcing an alteration of personal priorities. Numerous prisoners attempted to sell valuable (and probably much loved) possessions and property in order to raise capital.[20] Oliver Goldsmith sold the manuscript for *The Vicar of Wakefield* when bailiffs arrived in the late 1750s, the threat of a gaol forcing him to instruct his friend Samuel Johnson to find a publisher at whatever value the novel could fetch perhaps before Goldsmith was really satisfied it was complete.[21] In William Linley's novel *Forbidden Apartments* (1800), a central character resorts to the sale of his estates in Devonshire and while he is thereby relieved, it is implied the 'purchaser, who was ready to snatch it from the hands of the auctioneer, to whom the Baronet had determined to consign it' was able to buy it at a relative discount as he promised to pay 'for it without much trouble'.[22] Most debtors disposed of much less dramatic property, both not possessing and not being required to sell land to clear their commercial obligations. A biography of James Bolland executed for forgery in 1772 records how his imprisoned debtor Mrs Blake 'impatient of confinement … gave Bolland her gold watch, and several pieces of plate, by which means she obtained her liberty', having evidently not been willing to do so until having been imprisoned 'for some time'.[23] Theoretically, Blake could have sold these items herself to pay Bolland, though by turning them over she probably got a better price for their value. Other debtors, whose creditors were not willing to accept a trade, had to take whatever rates they could acquire. The fictional Baron D'Astie in Jeanne-Marie de Beaumont's *The New Clarissa* (1768) attempted, for example, to raise capital through the clothes off his back (exchanging them for cash and cheaper habits) but was offered 'no more than thirty-six shillings for my cloaths and shirt; the lace of my waistcoat alone was worth more' by dealers on one of their regular visits to the gaol.[24] The sale of goods was not without consequence beyond emotional loss. In 1738, Michael Dicq complained to the Westminster Quarter Sessions that his master, 'Andrew Halak … jeweller' having 'failed in the world … is now a prisoner for debt … in Wood Street Compter' and had 'sold all his tools and goods' to raise capital. Michael, reliant on Halak's tools, was therefore made destitute by his inability to continue training or work for himself. Resorting to sleeping on the ground and 'almost starved', Dicq begged the court to release him from his indenture so that he could find a more solvent master.[25] While an apprentice or servant suffering from a master's disposal of estate might find relief, family members similarly deprived of means of supporting themselves might have to throw themselves upon the parish even after the debtor's release from gaol.

Prisoners also disposed of less tangible estate. The experience of arrest was certainly inspirational and led prisoners to pursue debtors who might otherwise have been allowed longer to pay – one act of imprisonment causing ripples across the credit network. As the majority of those in debt (whether ever imprisoned or not) could pay when asked, calling in obligations was probably a rapid method of raising capital. This process can be glimpsed through the administration of the Insolvency Acts. Prisoners seeking the benefit of the

Act were required to submit a schedule of their remaining estate including debts which were owed to them. By the time a debtor applied to an Insolvency Act, usually more than a year after their initial arrest, only a minority retained outstanding debts. Surviving schedules from Wood Street applicants to the 1748, 1755, 1769, 1772, and 1774 Acts record that only 30% of the 191 petitioners still had debtors of their own. These debts were large and prisoners on average were owed over £500 at c.£71 per demand. Being much higher than their own average debts (c.£55), these obligations reflected those that they had themselves struggled to recover, unwise loans which exceeded a prisoner's debtor's actual capacity as well as contracts – such as from wills, overseas debts, or cases in Chancery – which were simply difficult to remedy in haste particularly from within gaol. Those cleared by the Compulsive Clause of 1761 reported significantly different accounting as this group had spent less than a month in gaol. This experimental legislation (abolished in November 1761) allowed creditors, from the moment of imprisonment, to compel debtors to take advantage of the Act within twenty days upon pain of death. Applicants to normal Insolvency Acts were likely to have experienced repayment and recovery difficulties (already dissolving their estates to the best of their ability) while those in 1761 had barely had time to acclimatise to the gaol before being released. These two groups can therefore be taken as a proxy for a prisoner's financial state upon arrival at the prison and if remaining after a year.[26] In more than 60% of the 257 schedules studied from 1761, prisoners had at least one individual who owed them money. Outstanding debts were also smaller in 1761, averaging at c.£3 for each demand and the total owed was below £30 largely due to the higher number of debtors, being owed by an average of thirteen individuals in 1761 (18% recording at least twenty debtors) compared to just six in other years where Acts were passed. If these individuals had not been compelled and their estate turned over to creditors, they would have called in such debts themselves relatively quickly. Pressing debtors usually resulted in payment as such small obligations were absent by the time of an application to a normal Act. While such sums were still too meagre for some who were forced to apply for an Act with nothing left to cite, many of those successfully 'discharged' will have relied on their wealth stored in other persons rather than goods. Even if collecting from within gaol proved more complicated it was far from impossible particularly as the option of imprisonment was also open to them. While prisoners may have confined their own debtors in a variety of London gaols, sixty-four Wood Street prisoners can be reliably identified as imprisoning debtors alongside themselves during the tenure of their confinement. Samuel Plaisted, himself owing nearly £800 when arrested in 1804 and eventually discharged in 1815, confined at least six of his debtors in the compter who owed him a total of £126 11s 6d, allowing him to keep close tabs on their activity. Samuel probably proceeded against more than just these six as he waited nine months before confining the first of them, implying others had paid more promptly when pressed.[27] Other imprisoned creditors were far quicker to confine. In 1763, Margaret Gyles imprisoned Mary Jones the day after she was herself arrested; Margery Prudence had actually been in the process of calling in her debts when confined, arriving at Wood Street just four days after her debtor Henry Bailey.[28]

It was not only the debtor who became more willing to sacrifice their assets once the threat of imprisonment had been realised. Friends, family, and even loose acquaintances who had declined to provide further aid were likely to relent following imprisonment. John Grano, a trumpeter arrested for his debts in 1728, experienced a stark contrast in aid received based upon his confined status. Upon his initial arrest and internment in a relatively comfortable sponging house, no 'Brother, relation or Friend came nigh me', this being far from the first time his social circle had received requests for money from the spendthrift musician. However, once Grano was actually imprisoned in the Marshalsea, aid arrived from a number of quarters in the form of money, clothing, food, and alcohol. A few days after his initial commitment two acquaintances brought 'a little Coat and leather Breaches to wear while I have the Misfortune to lye here' and the next day a 'Capt Aislabie' sent him 'Six Guineas'. Four months later he was still receiving financial gifts when he was sent 'a Guinea which I suppose came from my Parents'. In Grano's case the amounts he received were small and infrequent; they were also used poorly, spent in the prison coffeehouse rather than on settling debts. When he wrote of a fellow prisoner 'the Reason I judge his Friends chuse rather to Send him Victuals than Money, is that he Seems to have no government over him Self', he may unwittingly have echoed the feelings of his own friends.[29] Other prisoners received more substantial gifts or were entirely cleared. Mary Wells, an actress who had a habitual relationship with the debtors' prison, was freed from the King's Bench by a former fellow prisoner she had befriended when he came into great wealth after his release.[30] Aid might come unprompted as in Wells's case or as a direct response to requests, Grano receiving gifts both spontaneously and in response to his letters. One pamphlet writer in 1761 described the practice of debtors 'send[ing] to his Friends [to] acquaint them with his Misfortune, in hopes of their Assistance' as a matter of expected and typical behaviour.[31] Not all such requests were successful. Elizabeth Foote after her confinement in Truro gaol in 1741 wrote to her son Samuel in London for aid: 'Dear Sam, I am in prison for debt. Come and assist your loving mother'. Samuel's reply coming from the Fleet ('Dear Mother, so am I') presumably brought little comfort though he did send his attorney to assist her and his 'hope for better days'.[32]

The general association of the institution of debt imprisonment with cruelty and suffering enhanced its utility as a system of debt recovery in soliciting aid, a debtor's social network being more willing to help when their life was potentially at risk. The societal necessity of aiding the imprisoned, whether they be familiar or not, was enforced through instructive and sympathetic literature which frequently described debtors being freed by despairing friends or even strangers concerned about their mortality.[33] In *Horatio; or, The Sincere*

Friend (1759) it was an old school friend who 'having been informed of your misfortunes … I came to town as fast as I could', in Maria Barrell's *The Captive* (1790) it was both a family friend and the creditor of another debtor inspired by 'this sad suffering family', while in *The History of Charlotte Summers* (1750) relief came from the bailiff 'who began to have a very high Opinion of his Prisoner, and but a despicable Notion of the Creditor'.[34] Beyond fears of increased mortality, the reality of imprisonment, by bringing the impoverished or flagrant commercial behaviour of a relation into public view, embarrassed aid out of unwilling relations. In an anonymous short story entitled *Cordelia*, a mother upon hearing that one of her sons had 'spent all his Fortune, disposed of his Goods, [&] run in Debt' to save the family's tarnished reputation, being 'a Woman of the strictest Honesty, she gave Orders to her eldest Son to discharge his Brother's Debts, which was immediately performed', the author portraying this behaviour as both commendable and expected.[35] Some debtors actively encouraged awkwardness. According to Dr Johnson, the writer Richard Steele asked bailiffs arresting him to wear his livery and wait on him until after a party he was hosting that evening, revealing their true identity after dinner 'when wine and mirth had set them free from the observation of a rigid ceremony', the general embarrassment leading his guests to pay all his debts 'having obliged Sir Richard to promise that they should never again find him graced with a retinue of the same kind'.[36] More flagrant still was Elizabeth Gooch who published *An Appeal to the Public, On the Conduct of Mrs Gooch, the Wife of William Gooch Esq.* from her Fleet cell in 1788. This short autobiography culminated with a description of her imprisoned state: 'oppressed by Mr Gooch, forsaken by my family, and destitute of friends', Elizabeth hoped that 'my name may be remembered with pity' upon her imminent and inevitable demise. The principal aim of this publication was to embarrass either her estranged husband, one of her recent lovers ('friends'), or her family into paying her debts, the latter being the first to snap despite having had little contact with Elizabeth for several years. Though aid in most cases arose from genuine charity and goodwill, as Gooch's targets discovered, the danger and coercive power of debtors' prisons could tarnish those at liberty by association.[37]

Most creditors expected a delay in payment and therefore used the prisons as sites of negotiation, extracting payment over time through regular contact with their debtors. Grano frequently witnessed creditors visiting prisoners during his time at the Marshalsea. In July 1728, "Indiana",[38] whom Grano had been trying to court, was visited by her creditor after which Grano observed from a distance that 'Indiana's Plaintiff had fill'd her so full about I do not know what' reflecting her joy at their mutually beneficial discussion; within a week she was discharged.[39] Grano himself experienced more obstinate creditors. That September he 'was attended by one Shepherd … who has a Note of Mine of about 50 shillings' which Grano informed him he could not pay except by instalments. At this Shephard 'us'd me very ill … and murmur'd exceedingly when I gave him once two shillings out of four, a second time two shillings out of three and lastly half a Crown out of six or seven. He follow'd me up to my Room where I had much ado to get rid of him and where he insulted me highly ... and went away in a very threatening manner'.[40] While some creditors were evidently aggrieved by delays and partial payments, insisting on every farthing, the majority were not necessarily intransigent.[41] Negotiated settlements might consist of a simple swap of obligations. A manual for formal letter writing from 1780 details how a debtor declared his creditor his 'true and lawful attorney ... in part of discharge of a debt due from me to him' by which he was impowered to pursue the prisoner's own debtors.[42] While this did not bring immediate cash into the plaintiff's pocket, by pursuing several small debts rather than one large burden, he was more likely to quickly obtain a percentage of his full demand. Even if several of the new debtors could not pay immediately, it was more satisfactory than the existing state of total non-payment. Negotiated settlements also consisted of the creation of new, defined contracts replacing existing informal ones. Mary Robinson noted in her memoir how her husband's imprisonment in the Fleet was ended in 1776 only partially by 'setting aside some debts'. The remainder of his creditors accepted 'fresh bonds and fresh securities' for his debts, presumably on more stringent or defined terms should he default again.[43] Confinement gave plaintiffs clear leverage over debtors meaning they could strike more fitting terms than their prior arrangements which had failed to produce payment. At the King's Bench, a debtor owing £221 complained to the parliamentary committee in 1792 that his creditor had refused his offer that 'if she would give me my Discharge, to work out the Debt at £10 a Year'. Although he concluded this was due to her being unwilling to 'come to any Agreement', his plaintiff held sufficient power over him not to accept a twenty-two-year delay on payment and insist on better terms.[44] Sometimes, offers to pay a portion or by instalments came from creditors. In Henry Brooke's novel *The Fool of Quality* the protagonist meets a debtor imprisoned in the Fleet whose creditors had unsuccessfully 'offered to accept ten shillings, and some of them to accept five shillings in the pound' so as to recover something.[45] The concept of debtors paying by instalments or of creditors accepting negotiated percentage payments was frequent enough to have become mundane. Mathematics textbooks provided examples on the potentially complex procedure of calculating instalment payments while it was even a topic for humourists:

> As a young blood and Mr Quin were taking an airing on horseback, they came to a pond, when he pulled a shilling out of his pocket and threw it in the pond ... replied Quin, that's as you'll pay your creditors, one shilling in the pond.[46]

Arriving at the stage where a creditor would accept portions or new bonds may have taken some time and is likely to account for those discharged after longer periods, Mr Robinson having been imprisoned for at least nine months.

Probably the most important function the institution served though was as a spectral auditor which constantly reminded prisoners of the need to focus all their efforts on satisfying creditors. This was highly dependent upon the generally detached relationship between the prison and the debtor. Beyond detention in one location, debtors (compared with other prisoners such as felons) had a surprising degree of liberty within the gaol to conduct normal lives. Most were able to continue working and to spend their profits as they saw fit including on small comforts (Grano using income to renovate his cell) though the gaol was an ever-present reminder of why they were labouring and to whom spare capital should properly be directed.[47] Some gaols provided structured work such as the Devon County Prison where poor debtors were set to sorting cotton and wool for 3d a day making them hardly distinct from bridewell prisoners, a circumstance untenable to debtors of status.[48] Direct provision of labour was rare for this reason although some keepers might intercede actively on behalf of prisoners to provide more appropriate opportunities. At York Castle Gaol in the early nineteenth century there was no specified workroom and

> no employment provided by the county … but Mr Staveley [the keeper was] very active in procuring it for shoemakers, weavers, wool-combers, tailors, and other men accustomed to similar employments; and when work of this kind cannot be met with, the prisoners are taught to make laces, garters, purses, &c., which articles they expose for sale in the castle-yard.[49]

Other prisons had specified areas for prisoners to conduct their work, the reformer John Howard advocating for the more general provision in gaols of 'a large Work-shop' having observed these in 'some few Gaols' and that 'in them I have seen chair-makers, shoe-makers, &c. employed in their several trades'.[50]

It is clear from Staveley's actions and Howard's observations that, while farmers and mariners may have found their usual skills difficult to apply while confined, for many craftspeople prison did not inhibit their ability to work apart from in the smallest, oldest, borough gaols and dungeons. The ability to labour was, however, conditional for most craftspeople upon capital. The Marshal of the King's Bench reported to the committee investigating imprisonment for debt that 'Prisoners who are of Trades work in the Prison, provided they have Money to procure Implements for carrying on their Trade', noting that accordingly of the 'about 500' prisoners, roughly one hundred worked at their trades.[51] Those aware they could not currently meet their full demands may thus have refused to turn over what they had up-front when arrested, though those lacking capital with existing tools could certainly have had them brought to the gaol. Space, as Howard noted, was also a particular issue and the majority of products being produced that he and commentary on Mr Staveley cited were small. John Stanley, a silk-weaver in the King's Bench, complained to the House of Commons committee that 'I can't carry on my Trade here for Want of Room; a Gentleman of the Trade would have employed me ... [but] when he came to see the Situation of the Place, he could not employ me, as the Trade in which I was employed requires ... much Length and Light; twelve Feet of Light is the least in which I could do any Thing'. While his work was interrupted, the specificity of his complaint implies that, had he been held in a larger cell, there would have been no obstruction to his installing a loom in the prison to manufacture broadcloth, also suggesting that prisoners might still be able to procure goods and work from a factor on credit.[52]

Space was itself, generally conditional upon capital. Almost all prisons were split into at least two wards, the Master's and Common Sides, though some further derived into Keeper's Sides or Charity Wards. This division represented rent paying and free accommodation, those willing to pay being housed in apartment cells rather than open wards. The privacy and space of the Master's Side was necessary for most businesses and its comparative absence on the Common Side, enhanced by a lack of investment in the upkeep of such wards, diminished labour opportunities, in turn. Aggrieved silk-weaver John Stanley was housed in the Common Side of the King's Bench, contrasting his lack of space with the apartments elsewhere in the gaol.[53] John Kirby, the keeper of the Giltspur Street Compter, reported to the House of Commons committee in 1792 that on the day of the inquiry the prison held eighteen male Master's Side debtors of whom 'Persons employed in Trades are – One Attorney, a Carver, a Taylor, a Pattern Drawer, and a Cabinet Maker. On the Men's Common Side, none work at Trades'.[54] The larger single- or double-occupancy master's side rooms not only clearly afforded a space advantage for manufacturers – it is hard to conceive of cabinet making in the crowded Common Side – but also offered the privacy and comfort necessary for dealing with customers. For tailors and attorneys in particular the concept of hosting clients in communal wards was unthinkable. The reformer James Neild commented that those acquiring the Master's Side were 'saved from the necessity of being suddenly plunged into the interior of the prison, among persons who it may sometimes happen are not of the purest manners', indicating it was unfit for hosting genteel clientele.[55] Wealthier prisoners were also more likely to be allowed (and to afford) day passes which let them leave the gaol under guard to conduct business. Grano even organised and performed in a benefit concert at Southwark Town Hall while theoretically restricted to the Marshalsea.[56] Failure to provide all debtors with sufficient accommodation (due largely to the gaols being run as private, profit-generating enterprises) was always an inhibitor of labour and the complete effectiveness of the prisons.

This did not mean those on the Common Side without capital were unable to conduct productive work, particularly if they were able to craft items smaller than cabinets. Daniel Defoe, for example, observed at York Castle Gaol the 'small Manufactures the Prisoners work up for Subsistence' on the

Common Side.[57] Furthermore, Kirby's testimony that 'none work at trades' is illustrative particularly as he followed this statement directly with 'the Women [on the Common Side] Wash and Work'. Kirby may have not regarded service work – implicitly assumed to be "just" women's work – as a fitting response to the committee's question which asked: 'how many there are ... working at their Trades'. The Marshal at the King's Bench similarly focussed on 'Implements for carrying on their Trade'. It is difficult to tell from this curt statement what the women were washing and for whom – possibly the gaol itself, the laundry of other prisoners, or garments solicited from external customers – but it is clear they were thus able to find productive work. Poorer prisoners on the Common Side, particularly though not exclusively women, sometimes acted as servants to those on the Master's Side – either increasing their comfort or aiding in their business ventures.[58] Some prison architects actively expected wealthier debtors to take servants; the first-class debtors' rooms in York were fitted with servants' quarters not apparent in the 'second-class' rooms.[59] Grano, whose writing almost exclusively focussed on genteel friends, remarks little on his servants at the Marshalsea though it is clear he had at least one. Eleven months into his imprisonment in April 1729 he finally explicitly described 'My Maid Molly' though it is unlikely Grano previously looked after himself.[60] In September 1728, when still sharing a cell with his friend Mr Elder, he wrote 'our Linnen was brought Home, and then we Shifted and about one hour after went to Dinner on the Goose' – aside from changing his shirt it seems Grano was entirely passive in these chores of carrying and cooking implying the presence of a maid as prison staff did not conduct menial work.[61] A Common Side prisoner called 'Hannah' appears frequently in the diary, almost always bringing Grano messages. While he never termed her his servant, she was the maid of his friend Mr Elder. She may thus, by virtue of his occupying the same room, have also acted as Grano's maid. In October 1728 Grano was calling her 'our Hannah' and by February 1729 she was 'the Girl that goes arrends for me'.[62]

Becoming a servant was simply one method by which debtors, if they could not ply their traditional trade, adapted their skills into new prison-appropriate ventures, reflecting the adaptability of the eighteenth-century workforce.[63] For example, Stanley the silk-weaver had resorted, while he waited for a proper room for his loom, to 'getting a Job at Whitewashing'.[64] This work provided only subsistence income though others commenced new trades with substantial profits in mind. Many prisoners with a range of educations turned to writing to clear their debts, and while some had prior experience many embarked upon a literary career for the first time. Samuel Foote, later a comedic actor and theatre manager but then an impoverished lawyer, first entered the printed world from his Fleet cell in 1742, producing an account of his uncle's murder.[65] One debtor in Wood Street c.1780 reportedly 'subsisted ... by writing essays for the public prints' until 'a bookseller ... employed him on a work of consequences, and ... advance[d] the money ... to pay the debt and costs'.[66] Meanwhile, in 1750 a debtor in Whitechapel

gaol published twelve issues of *The Bee Reviv'd: Or the Prisoners Magazine.*
Though it featured almost no original content, it represented an impressive
compendium of other publications which must have required a significant
amount of work and access to material within a cramped and poorly maintained gaol.[67] Prisoners frequently turned to their own situation for inspiration, writing accounts of the gaols which exaggerated the suffering and poor
conditions or focussed upon the unjustness of the law. While prisons were
uncomfortable, this literature, fed upon by an eager public, distorted the reality of confinement which was far less fatal or appalling than these pamphlets
suggest.[68] However, imprisonment was not the only topic for amateurs and
many writers produced texts such as memoirs they might have done at their
liberty. James Burton, for example, applied himself while confined in York
Castle in 1752 to drafting his *The Warning: A Recourse and Divine Poem upon
the Contageous Distemper amongst the Horned Cattle of This Kingdom.*[69]

While writing was evidently not limited to university educated individuals such as Foote, it was far from a guaranteed path to freedom. Two of the
figures in William Hogarth's *Rake's Progress* are depicted as engaged in this
activity – the elderly figure usually seen as a representation of the artist's father drops a proposal for increasing the nation's credit similar to that which
Richard Hogarth produced during his own confinement.[70] Neither Richard
nor the shabby figure saw a profit from their tracts. "Tom", whose play lies
abandoned before him, was equally unsuccessful learning, like most amateur
writers, that enthusiasm was no substitute for talent: 'The Man returns, the
Play is brought, And all his Hopes are come to Nought: Tis answered in a
Line or two, With, Sir, I've read it, and twon't do'.[71] While those who wrote
about imprisonment probably had a better chance of publication than those
who decided to write grand theatre, securing a publisher from within gaol
was not simple as is revealed in the opening 'Advertisement' of Maria Barrell's
The Captive, written from the King's Bench in 1790:

> This little production the Authoress wished to have appeared much ear-
> lier … various were her applications to several printers for the immediate
> publication, but in vain; she found that a condemnation to the sad regions
> of a living grave, was a sufficient apology for a refusal. Happily she has
> obtained one in the present, nor will (she hopes) her gratitude be wanting
> to express a sense of the obligation.[72]

Writing as a form of raising capital therefore encapsulates many of the complexities that were involved in revenue generation from within prison. While
imprisonment did not inhibit wealth creation entirely, it is impossible to deny
that a prisoner could not conduct business as they were able to at their liberty
or negotiate with the same strength. They were thus forced to turn to work
they had little expertise in which they could not guarantee anyone would wish
to pay them for even if they were able to locate potential customers. However,
the restriction of liberty by further disincentivising individuals from spending

unwisely probably outweighed these potential detractions for creditors. While it was far from simple to trade within gaol, it was entirely the prisoner's responsibility to figure out how they were going to alleviate such issues, amateur writing reflecting the entrepreneurial spirit of the debtor economy.

In-prison service work was not limited to acting as prisoner valets. Grano reported having his ablutions taken care of by fellow prisoner 'Trim' the barber; it is unclear whether this was the man's usual trade.[73] Such activities also appeared in fictional depictions of imprisonment, suggesting they would have been unsurprising to eighteenth-century audiences. In Jeanne-Marie de Beaumont's novel *The New Clarissa* (1768), the Baron D'Astie describes working for Master's Side debtors at the King's Bench:

> there were in this prison several persons who lived in an expensive manner … these people had neat apartments … I offered my service to one of them, who spoke a little broken French, and promised to perfect him in this language in a very little time.

even offering 'to dress' the client's daughter's hair which 'was quite out of curl' having been caught in the rain.[74] Many other debtors extracted wealth from those on the Master's Side through trade, the prisons containing vibrant irregular and black markets. Grano once invited a friend to his room to drink 'two pints of Wine I bought of a fellow Prisoner out of Charity'; to the seller this was surely no act of charity but a business transaction.[75] However, the casual sale does imply this was not the prisoner's main activity; rather they had probably been gifted the wine and then sold it to aid release rather than drinking it. Other prisoners in Grano's Marshalsea vended professionally. Sarah Bradshaw ran *The Oak* from her rooms throughout Grano's confinement, possibly even after being released. *The Oak* (also the nickname of the female quarters as a whole) functioned as a coffeehouse, though sold food and liquor as well, providing a social space in which daily Grano flirted with female prisoners, drank tea, played backgammon, or merely passed the time.[76] Sarah may even have sold to imprisoned customers on credit.[77] 'Mother Bradshaw' did not have a monopoly; prisoner Richard McDonnell and his wife ran a restaurant above *The Oak* known as *Titty Doll's*. Judging by Grano's decline in usage of the McDonnells after moving in with Hannah (who cooked), they offered a finer and more expensive service than Bradshaw.[78] To stay competitive, beyond her cheaper service, Sarah vended directly to cells; Grano, sat in his room early in his imprisonment, records that Bradshaw 'came to inform me she had an excellent Ham'.[79] Even the competition of an official prison taproom did not deter debtor-vendors, particularly those providing goods not officially available. The 'whistling shops', immortalised in Charles Dickens's *The Pickwick Papers* (1831) and Pierce Egan's *Life in London* (1821), were 'rooms in the … prison where drams are privately sold'.[80] In the second half of the eighteenth century, 'a rule of court' in London prohibited 'the [sale] of spirituous liquors' in prisons, creating an obvious opportunity for prisoners with access to spirits, particularly if they had wives who could smuggle in gin or brandy against whom keepers waged a constant battle.[81] At the superior court prisons 'not only the sale, but the use [of spirits] is chiefly forbid' and, as a result, a complex system of communicating through whistling was devised to facilitate the exchange of spirits, the prisoners 'being afraid to *ask* for anything of the kind'.[82]

Through petty exchange of craft goods and service sector work, a microcosm of the external economy was generated in gaols which new arrivals would have found hauntingly familiar. Debtors did not merely trade with one another, also having extensive commercial contacts outside of the prisons. The debtor economy thus contributed to wider lower value commerce in communities local to the prisons, further demonstrating that the economic world of debt imprisonment was a constantly relevant one in the eighteenth-century market. As well as business opportunities for local victuallers, prisoners constituted cheap alternative access to services which local residents may otherwise have not had access to. Grano's most notable and consistent capital generation scheme was in offering trumpet lessons, the keeper of the prison providing him a room specifically for the purpose.[83] While he recorded little detail of his 'scholars', these children of local tradesmen were surely receiving an education from a notable and (musically) successful individual on the cheap.[84] It is far from surprising that the attorney, resident on the Master's Side of the Giltspur Street Compter, was able to find an income while confined – presumably taking any possible client (who didn't need court representation) at whatever rate he could extract. Similarly, the regular presence of tailors in prisons provided access to bespoke clothing for those normally restricted to the second-hand market, though the prisons also represented an excellent source of second-hand goods to those seeking them either for their own use or for re-sale, debtors, as noted above, being forced to accept below market rates.[85] Defoe, visiting York gaol, describes how the products made within the gaol were generally bought by 'Strangers, who visit the Inside of it' describing these as 'a trifling Purchase' suggesting the discounted price of prison made goods.[86] In 1742, the warden at the Fleet estimated that as many as 3,000 non-prisoners might visit the prison every day, many making use of the sporting and drinking facilities. While this reflected the liberalities of the *rules* and occurred at the height of its use as a site of clandestine marriages, prisons without these qualities also received visitors every day.[87] At Whitechapel Prison, John Howard 'was surprized to see … ten or twelve noisy men at skittles … the Turnkey said they were only visitants. I found they were admitted here as at another public house'.[88] Evidently, the prisons did not merely represent places to secure cheap goods for commercial purposes but also cheaper sites of sociability, debtors being happy to oblige and wait upon guests.

Using the prisons as a source of cheap labour even extended to external work. In 1728, Grano was recruited by 'honest Tom Cuthbert' an old friend and fellow musician who had been contracted to provide music for the Grocer's Company barge during the Lord Mayor's procession to Westminster. While this might seem like charity, Cuthbert was clearly outsourcing his own work to one who would accept small compensation and could not afford to say no. Cuthbert was paid £14 13s 6d by the Grocers; of this, despite preparing the music, conducting on the barge, and doing the lion's share of the work, Grano received two guineas.[89] Additionally, it is probable that third parties agreed to pay the debts of prisoners in full in exchange for what amounted to indentured servitude or a second apprenticeship. The Baron in *New Clarissa* was eventually released by a peruke-maker 'seeking a journeyman' who paid the 20 guinea debt 'on condition that I should article myself to him for two years'.[90] While it is difficult to measure the direct contribution debtor economies made to local communities, that most borough gaols were constructed either in poorer regions of the city like the Marshalsea or, as in the case of the Fleet, adjoining market places suggests these institutions had far more complex contributory roles to the informal economy of the eighteenth century than simply enforcing credit.

★★

Not all of those confined in the eighteenth-century debtors' prison were able to participate in the debtor economy. There were always comparatively destitute prisoners whose only access to capital, and hope of release outside of an Insolvency Act, was through begging from visitors to the prison, from other debtors in the taproom, or at 'the grate' from passers-by. Nor did the relatively good chances of securing release alleviate the inherent suffering of being detained for no crime in unpleasant conditions – for all its industry, Hogarth's Fleet is dark and filthy, a hell in which one would not wish to remain. However, the reason so few are identified as dying in the prison in the commitment registers is clearly that this hell hurried debtors to pay up, liquidate their effects, or labour their way to freedom as soon as possible. Even "Tom" was 'at length discharged' despite Hogarth hurrying him to his final internment in Bedlam, a truly inescapable institution.[91] Perhaps what is most striking about the strategies by which debtors satisfied their creditors is how little changed they were by the imprisoned status of members of the debtor economy. Not only did they employ strategies they might have at their liberty – pursuing their own debtors, selling goods, imploring friends for aid, or attempting to negotiate with creditors – but they also conducted the activities which had landed them in gaol by continuing at their businesses, even occasionally dealing on credit. The eighteenth-century debtors' prison was then a coercer, not a facilitator, of payment. It proved effective as it forced a debtor to shift their priorities into satisfaction of the creditor and away from personal need, leading them to make financial decisions such as the sale of property they would otherwise have been loath to do. It was nothing but a detractor to the economic health of the prisoner – selling hard-won goods at below market-value or working on exploitative terms – but by the institution's lack of involvement in directing how payment was to be achieved, it allowed the individual to solve their own problems in whatever fashion best suited them.

Notes

1 Anon. *The Rakes Progress; or, the Humours of Drury-Lane. A Poem* (London: 1735), pp. 47–51.

2 See: Jenny Uglow, *Hogarth – A Life and a World* (London: Faber & Faber, 1997), p. 255; Peter Temin and Hans-Joachim Voth, *Prometheus Shackled – Goldsmith Banks and England's Financial Revolution after 1700* (Oxford: Oxford University Press, 2013), pp. 11, 22; Barbara Horby, "The Prodigal Rector in the Fleet," *Northamptonshire Past and Present* vol. 60 (2007), p. 72.

3 Joanna Innes, "The King's Bench Prison in the Later Eighteenth Century: Law, Authority and Order in a London Debtors' Prison," in *An Ungovernable People – The English and their Law in the Seventeenth and Eighteenth Centuries*, eds. John Brewer and John Styles (London: Hutchinson, 1980), pp. 250–298; Margaret DeLacy, *Prison Reform in Lancashire, 1700–1850 – A Study in Local Administration* (Stanford: Stanford University Press, 1986), pp. 29–32; Margot C. Finn, *The Character of Credit – Personal Debt in English Culture, 1740–1914* (Cambridge: Cambridge University Press, 2003), pp. 140–147; Jerry White, *Mansions of Misery – A Biography of the Marshalsea Debtors' Prison* (London: Bodley Head, 2016).

4 "Rules and Orders … Debtors side", 1808, Newgate Prison – Administration, LMA, CLA/035/02/031; William Smith, *State of the Gaols in London, Westminster, and Borough of Southwark. To Which Is Added, An Account of the Present State of Convicts Sentenced to Hard Labour on Board the Justitia upon the River Thames* (London: J. Brew, 1776), pp. 65–80.

5 See: Finn, *Character of Credit*.

6 "Trial of William Phillips", 11th September 1735, *Old Bailey Proceedings Online*, t17350911–72; see: Anon. *The Adventures of a Valet. Vol. II* (London: 1752), p. 154.

7 Journal of the House of Commons, *Report for the Committee Appointed to Enquire into the Practice and Effects of Imprisonment for Debt* (1792), pp. 19, 82–83; John Debrett, *The Parliamentary Register; or History of the Proceedings and Debates of the House of Commons … During the Second Session of the Seventeenth Parliament of Great Britain Vol. XXXIII* (London: 1792), p. 17; Alexander Stephens, *Public Characters. Of 1805. Vol. VII* (London: 1805), pp. 99–100.

8 Samuel Pepys (Henry B. Wheatley ed.), *The Diary of Samuel Pepys … Transcribed from the Shorthand Manuscript … Edited with Additions by Henry B. Wheatley. Vol. III* (London: George Bell & Sons, 1893), pp. 379–380.

9 "Trial of Charles Scoldwell", 14th September 1796, *Old Bailey Proceedings Online*, t17960914–6.

10 "Trial of John Hall & Anthony Newel", 31st August 1726, *Old Bailey Proceedings Online*, t17260831–38.

11 Charlotte Charke, *A Narrative of the Life of Mrs Charlotte Charke, (Youngest Daughter of Colley Cibber, Esq.)* (London: 1755), pp. 89–94.

12 Henry Timberlake, *The Memoirs of Lieut. Henry Timberlake, Who Accompanied the Three Cherokee Indians to England in the Year 1762* (London: 1765), pp. 138–139. Timberlake claims to have been taken to Wood Street sometime between August 1762 and January 1764 though he does not appear in a commitment register. It is possible his entry has been lost due to the registers occasionally suffering from pages being torn or removed entirely. It is also possible he paid while in the office of the compter (or in a sponging house associated with the gaol) without being formally committed or that Timberlake, who spent only a few months of his life in London, mistook the Poultry for the Wood Street Compter. Regardless, it seems unlikely he would invent financial insufficiency and debt imprisonment in an otherwise self-congratulatory memoir.

13 See: Richard Thaler and Cass Sunstein, *Nudge – Impowering Decisions about Health, Wealth, and Happiness* (New Haven: Yale University Press, 2008), p. 50.

14 Paul Hess Haagen, "Imprisonment for Debt in England and Wales", unpublished PhD thesis, University of Princeton (1986), p. 4; Roger Lee Brown, *A History of the Fleet Prison, London – the Anatomy of the Fleet* (Lampeter: Edwin Mellen Press, 1996), p. 141.

15 See: Ian P.H. Duffy, *Bankruptcy and Insolvency in London During the Industrial Revolution* (New York: Garland Publishing Inc, 1985), Craig Muldrew, *The Economy of Obligation – The Culture of Credit and Social Relations in Early Modern England* (Basingstoke: Macmillan, 1998) pp. 61–63; pp. 275–276, 282–283; Julian Hoppit, *Risk and Failure in English Business 1700–1800* (Cambridge: Cambridge University Press, 1987), p. 33; A.M. Qasem, "Bail and Personal Liberty", *Canadian Bar Review* vol. 30, no. 4 (1952), pp. 380, 385; Finn, *Character of Credit*, p. 117; James Peller Malcolm, *Londinium Redivivum, Or an Ancient History and Modern Description of London Compiled from Parochial Records, Archives of Various Foundations, the Harleian Mss and Other Authentic Sources. Vol. IV* (London: 1807), p. 597; House of Commons, *Committee into Imprisonment for Debt*, pp. 3–11, 19–21.

16 William Wright, *The Complete Tradesman: Or, a Guide in the Several Parts and Progressions of Trade* (London: 1789), p. 31; William Blackstone, *Commentaries on the Laws of England. In Four Books – Vol. II Book 2* (Boston: 1799), p. 464; Samuel Vaughan, *A Refutation of A False Aspersion* (London: 1769), p. 15.

17 Francis Oldys, *The Abridged Life of Thomas Pain, The Author of the Seditious Writings, Entitled Rights of Man* (London: 1793), p. 24.

18 Tobias Smollett, *The Adventures of Ferdinand Count Fathom. Vol. II* (London: 1753), p. 14.

19 William Huntingdon, *The Modern Plasterer Detected, and His Untempered Mortar Discovered* (London: 1787), p. 78.

20 On importance of possessions, see: Judith S. Lewis, "When a House Is Not a Home: Elite English Women and the Eighteenth-Century Country House", *Journal of British Studies* vol. 48, no. 2 (2009), pp. 341–342.

21 John Hawkins, *The Life of Samuel Johnson* (Dublin: 1787), p. 373; James Boswell, *The Life of Samuel Johnson Vol. I* (London: 1791), p. 225.

22 William Linley, *Forbidden Apartments. A Tale. Vol. II* (London: 1800), p. 181.

23 James Bolland, *Memoirs of James Bolland, Formerly a Butcher then Officer to the Sheriff of Surry, Afterwards Officer to the Sheriff of Middlesex, and Lately a Candidate for the Place of City Marshal; Executed at Tyburn, March 18, 1773, for Forgery* (London: 1772), p. 3.

24 Jeanne-Marie de Beaumont, *The New Clarissa Vol. II* (London: 1768), p. 263.

25 "Michael Dicq (1738)", in *Petitions to the Westminster Quarter Sessions, 1620–1799*, ed. Brodie Waddell, *British History Online*.

26 "Debtors Schedule: Fleet Prison, Ludgate Prison, Poultry Compter, Wood Street Compter", 1748, LMA, CLA/047/LJ/17/027/72-77; "Debtors Schedules: Wood Street Compter", 1755, CLA/047/LJ/17/042; "Debtors Schedules: Wood Street Compter A-N", 1761, CLA/047/LJ/17/044; "Debtors Schedules: Wood Street Compter P-Y", 1761, CLA/047/LJ/17/045; "Debtors Schedules: Wood Street Compter", 1769–1770, CLA/047/LJ/17/058; "Debtors Schedules, Fleet Prison, Ludgate Prison, Newgate Prison, Wood Street Compter", 1772, CLA/047/LJ/17/061; "Debtors Schedules, Fleet Prison, Ludgate Prison, Wood Street Compter", 1774, CLA/047/LJ/17/063.

27 "List of Prisoners Handed over by the Sheriffs to their Successors on 28 Sept Annually, with Notes of Occurrences During the Subsequent Year", 1803–1812, Wood Street Compter later Giltspur Street Compter, LMA, CLA/028/01/033-039.

28 "List of Prisoners Handed over by the Sheriffs to their Successors on 28 Sept Annually, with Notes of Occurrences During the Subsequent Year", 1763, Wood Street Compter later Giltspur Street Compter, LMA, CLA/028/01/010; "List of

Prisoners Handed over by the Sheriffs to their Successors on 28 Sept Annually, with Notes of Occurrences During the Subsequent Year", 1761–1762, Wood Street Compter later Giltspur Street Compter, LMA, CLA/028/01/009.

29 John Grano (John Ginger ed.), *Handel's Trumpeter – The Diary of John Grano* (Stuyvesant: Pendragon Press, 1998), pp. 27, 31, 32, 112, 120.

30 Mary Wells, *Memoirs of the Life of Mrs Sumbel, Late Wells; of the Theatres-royal, Drury-lane, Covent-garden, and Haymarket. In Three Volumes. Written by Herself. Vol. I* (London: 1811), p. 178.

31 Anon. *The Compulsive Clause in the Present Act of Insolvency Fully Considered. With Its Good and Bad Consequences Plainly Stated, and Clearly Answered. To Which Is Annexed, Proposals for the More Effectual Recovery of Debts, and Without Arrests. With the Evils of Goals for Debtors Reasonably Exposed* (London: R. Davis & C. Henderson, 1761), p. 25.

32 Elizabeth N. Chatten, *Samuel Foote* (Boston: Twayne Publishers, 1980), p. 14.

33 Finn, *Character of Credit*, pp. 318–320.

34 Anon. *The Theatre of Love. A Collection of Novels* (London: 1759), p. 56; Maria Barrell, *The Captive. By Maria Barrell, at the King's Bench* (London: 1790), pp. 28–31; Anon. *The History of Charlotte Summers Vol. II* (London: 1750), p. 278.

35 Anon, *Theatre of Love*, p. 74.

36 Samuel Johnson, *An Account of the Life of Mr Richard Savage* (1774), pp. 14–15.

37 Elizabeth Gooch, *An Appeal to the Public, On the Conduct of Mrs Gooch, the Wife of William Gooch Esq.* (London: 1788), pp. 66–68; see: Alexander Wakelam, "Coverture and the Debtors' Prison in the Long Eighteenth Century", *Journal for Eighteenth-Century Studies* (forthcoming 2021); Julie Steenson, "Life Lessons: Self-Defence and Social Didacticism in Elizabeth Gooch's Life-Writing and The Contrast", *Women's Writing* vol. 18, no. 3 (2011), pp. 405–422.

38 Grano often recorded fellow prisoners in his diary under nicknames he provided for them, a practice particularly applied to female prisoners unfortunate enough to become the object of his affections.

39 Grano, *Handel's Trumpeter*, p. 60.

40 Grano, *Handel's Trumpeter*, p. 86.

41 Tawny Paul, *Poverty of Disaster – Debt and Insecurity in Eighteenth-Century Britain* (Cambridge: Cambridge University Press, 2019), pp. 103–105.

42 George Brown, *The New English Letter-Writer; or, Whole Art of General Correspondence* (London: 1780), p. 231.

43 M.J. Levy (ed.), *Perdita – The Memoirs of Mrs Robinson* (London: Peter Owen, 1994), pp. 79–84.

44 House of Commons, *Committee into Imprisonment for Debt*, p. 63.

45 Henry Brooke, *The Fool of Quality; or, The History of Henry Earl of Moreland. Vol. II* (Philadelphia: 1794), pp. 71–72.

46 Francis Walkingame, *The Tutor's Assistant: Being a Compendium of Arithmetic. And a Complete Question-Book* (London: 1770), p. 146; Jeremy Squib, *The Cracker; or Flashes of Merriment: A Collection of Humorous Fire-Works Never Play'd off before* (London: 1770), p. 9; Paul, *Poverty of Disaster*, p. 104.

47 Grano, *Handel's Trumpeter*, p. 133.

48 Gary Calland, *A History of the Devon County Prison for Debtors in St. Thomas* (Exeter: Little History, 1999), p. 25.

49 William Hargreave, *History and Description of the Ancient City of York, Vol. II* (York: William Alexander, 1818), p. 244; T. P. Cooper, *The History of the Castle of York – From Its Foundation to the Present Day with an Account of the Building of Clifford's Tower* (London: Elliot Stock, 1911), p. 221.

50 John Howard, *The State of the Prisons in England and Wales, with Preliminary Observations, and an Account of some Foreign Prisons* (London: 1777), p. 47.

51 House of Commons, *Committee into Imprisonment for Debt*, pp. 44, 69–71.

52 House of Commons, *Committee into Imprisonment for Debt*, p. 63.

53 House of Commons, *Committee into Imprisonment for Debt*, pp. 62–63.

54 House of Commons, *Committee into Imprisonment for Debt*, pp. 78–80.

55 James Neild, *An Account of the Rise, Progress, and Present State, of the Society for the Discharge and Relief of Persons Imprisoned for Small Debts Throughout England and Wales* (London: 1802), p. 135.

56 Grano, *Handel's Trumpeter*, pp. 51–83.

57 Daniel Defoe, *A Tour Thro' the Whole Island of Great Britain … Vol. III* (London: 1742), p. 155.

58 DeLacy, *Prison Reform*, p. 30.

59 Stephanie Adele Leeman, "Stone Walls Do Not a Prison Make: The Debtors' Prison, York", *York Historian* vol. 11 (1994), p. 28.

60 Grano, *Handel's Trumpeter*, p. 242.

61 Grano, *Handel's Trumpeter*, p. 111.

62 Grano, *Handel's Trumpeter*, pp. 58, 72, 76, 85–86, 89–90, 93, 111, 114, 139, 147–148, 155, 191.

63 Tawny Paul, "Accounting for Men's Work: Multiple Employments and Occupational Identities in Early Modern England", *History Workshop Journal* vol. 85 (2018), pp. 26–46.

64 House of Commons, *Committee into Imprisonment for Debt*, p. 62.

65 Samuel Foote, *The Genuine Memoirs of the Life of Sir John Dinely Goodere Who Was Murdered by the Contrivance of His Own Brother on Board the Ruby Man of War, in King Road near Bristol, Jan 19 1740* (London: 1742).

66 Anon. *The Complete Modern London Spy, for the Present Year, 1781* (London: 1781), pp. 42–43.

67 Anon. *The Bee Reviv'd: or, The Prisoners Magazine. Containing the Greatest Curiosities in Prose and Verse, from All the Other Magazines, and the Politest Books and Papers Now in being. For the Benefit of the Compiler a Prisoner for Debt in Whitechapel Jail. … Printed and Sold by J Lewis in Pater-Noster Row, near Cheapside* (London: 1750); Howard, *State of the Prisons*, pp. 189–190.

68 Anon. *Trick Upon Trick, Being an Account of all the Cheats of Both Prisons, the Queen's Bench and Fleet … Written by one that Was a Prisoner in Both Places* (London: 1703); Anon. *The Mourning Poet; or The Unknown Comforts of Imprisonment … Written by a Poor Brother in Durance* (London: 1703); Samuel Byrom, *An Irrefutable Argument Fully Proving, That to Discharge Great Debts Is Less Injury, and More Reasonable than to Discharge Small Debts … By Samuel Byrom … Now Confined within the Walls of the Fleet* (London: 1726); Simon Wood, *Remarks on the Fleet Prison; Or, Lumber-House for Men and Women. Written by a Prisoner on the Common-Side, Who Hath Lain a Prisoner near three Years, on the Penalty of a Bond* (London: 1733); Anon. *The Attempt: Or, An Essay towards the Retrieving Lost Liberty, Reforming the Corrupt and Pernicious Laws of this Nation, and Rendering the Recovery of Debts Easy and Effectual … By a Prisoner in the Poultry-Compter* (London: 1751); Anon. *The Oppressed Captive … Wrote by the Author and Sufferer in the Fleet Prison* (London: 1757); Anon. *A Narrative of the Late Disturbances in the Marshalsea Prison* (London: 1768); James Stephen, *Considerations on Imprisonment for Debt* (London: 1770). This sample does not include the bounteous literature written by condemned felons or prisoners for religion.

69 Gooch, *Appeal to the Public*; Jane Elizabeth Moore, *Genuine Memoirs of Jane Elizabeth Moore. Late of Bermondsey, in the County of Surry. Written by Herself: Containing the Singular Adventures of Herself and Family. Her Sentimental Journey through Great Britain: Specifying the Various Manufactures Carried on at each Town. A Comprehensive Treatise on the Trade, Manufactures, Navigation, Laws and Police of this*

Kingdom, and the Necessity of a Country Hospital (London: 1786); Robert Ker, *An Account of the Disorderly Way Some of the Ministers of this Present Church, and their Way of Baptizeing Children without Consent of the Father … Robert Ker (Wright) Composed these Following Lines in the Prison House of Dalkeith* (Edinburgh: 1711); James Burton, *The Warning: A Recourse and Divine Poem upon the Contageous Distemper amongst the Horned Cattle of this Kingdom … by James Burton, A Prisoner, In York Castle, for a small Debt. Published for the benefit of the Author* (York: 1752); Anon. *Anecdotes, Tales &c. Selected by a Debtor during his Confinement in Durham Jail* (Durham: 1800).

70 Uglow, *Hogarth*, p. 42.
71 Anon. *Rake's Progress*, p. 50.
72 Barrell, *Captive*, p. vi.
73 Grano, *Handel's Trumpeter*, p. 110.
74 de Beaumont, *New Clarissa*, pp. 264–266.
75 Grano, *Handel's Trumpeter*, p. 131.
76 Grano, *Handel's Trumpeter*, passim.
77 White, *Mansions of Misery*, pp. 63–65.
78 Grano, *Handel's Trumpeter*, pp. 44, 57, 66, 98, 131, 139.
79 Grano, *Handel's Trumpeter*, p. 33.
80 Francis Grose, *A Classical Dictionary of the Vulgar Tongue* (London: 1793), p. 231.
81 "Rough Minutes of Committee to Examine the Allegations of the Petitions of the Keepers of Newgate, Ludgate, and the Two Compters as to the Act for Taking away Liquor Taps in the Prisons", 1787, LMA, COL/CA/PCA/01/003, 1v.
82 Anon. *The Debtor and Creditor's Assistant; or, a Key to the King's Bench and Fleet Prisons* (London: 1793), pp. 49–50.
83 Grano, *Handel's Trumpeter*, 88.
84 Grano (Ginger), *Handel's Trumpeter*, 3–11, 13–14, 18–19, 24–26; John Ginger, "New Light on Gawen Hamilton – Artists, Musicians and the Debtors' Prison", *Apollo* vol. 136 (September 1992), 156–160.
85 See: John Styles, "Clothing the North: The Supply of Non-élite Clothing in the Eighteenth-Century North of England", *Textile History* vol. 25, no. 2 (1994), pp. 139–166; Beverly Lemire, "Second-hand Beaux and "Red-armed Belles": Conflict and the Creation of Fashions in England, c.1660–1800", *Continuity and Change* vol. 15, no. 3 (2000), pp. 391–417; Miles Lambert, "'Cast-off Wearing Apparel': The Consumption and Distribution of Second-hand Clothing in Northern England During the Long Eighteenth Century", *Textile History* vol. 35 (2004), pp. 1–26. On prison as market for goods: de Beaumont, *New Clarissa*, pp. 262–264; Maria Smyth, *The Woman of Letters; or, the History of Miss Fanny Belton. Vol. II* (London: 1783), pp. 213–225.
86 Defoe, *Tour*, p. 155; DeLacy, *Prison Reform*, pp. 32–33.
87 Roger Lee Brown, "The Rise and Fall of the Fleet Marriages," in *Marriage and Society – Studies in the Social History of Marriage*, ed. R.B. Outhwaite (London: Europa Publications Ltd, 1981), p. 120; Jacob Field, "Clandestine Weddings at the Fleet Prison c.1710–1750: Who Married There?", *Continuity and Change* vol. 32, no. 3 (2017), p. 351.
88 Howard, *State of the Prisons*, p. 190.
89 Grano, *Handel's Trumpeter*, pp. 118–124, 138.
90 de Beaumont, *New Clarissa*, pp. 266–268.
91 Anon. *Rake's Progress*, p. 52.

5   The Insolvency Acts

When debtors' prisons failed

In 1789, Henry New wrote with exasperation to 'the worshipful the magistrates at the general quarter sessions of the peace' of Staffordshire. New's story was largely unremarkable nor was it uncommon given the precarious and insecure nature of commercial life in the eighteenth century.[1] A hatter from the market town of Evesham in Worcestershire, Henry had apparently taken on a variety of debts including £35 to Richard Stevens. To the enterprising hatter this probably seemed a meagre amount at the time of agreement, sure to be raised from the inevitable profits coming his way. However, whether by his own failures or falling victim to the realities of provincial commerce, New 'met with many heavy losses in trade, which', when Stevens demanded the money he had been promised, 'rendered him utterly incapable of satisfying the plaintiff's debt'. Stevens, presumably feeling aggrieved by New's pleas of impoverishment had the hatter confined in Stafford Gaol, confident that the businessman had estates which could be dissolved, friends he could seek aid from, or debts of his own that could be called in. Sixteen months later, the debtors' prison had failed to produce payment, Richard Stevens having died waiting for the hatter to fulfil his promises. Henry had not been as inactive as Richard or his executor, who continued to demand full repayment of the £35, may have assumed. By 1789 New, 'having tried every effort for that purpose' and 'by the bounty of his friends' had managed to raise money 'nearly suffeshant to procure his discharge' though without a final three guineas he was 'utterly incapable of advancing' his release as no further exertion could procure further capital. Out of options and fearing he may – due to 'the horrors of gaol' – soon follow Stevens's path, he petitioned the court to 'condescend to his relief' by furnishing him the three guineas as this comparatively small donation would 'be the means of restoring your petitioner again to society'.[2] It is far from unreasonable to imagine the court taking pity on the unfortunate Henry New. However, while the occasional petitioner might be granted such favour, as men and women like New – trapped in debtors' prisons and unable to pay their debts despite their best efforts, many requiring sums far greater than three guineas to relieve them – were far from rare, the charity of magistrates was never enough to provide remedy when debtors' prisons failed.

At its heart the act of imprisonment was (as well as a coercion) a test of financial reality – at the moment of arrest a creditor believed in a debtor's original declaration that they could pay, a statement which was shown to be valid or false only through confinement. A certain minority were always bound to fail this test no matter how long they were confined or how earnest their efforts due to an initial overestimate of their capacity, a significant downturn in fortunes, or having been burdened with creditors who were unwilling to negotiate in any manner, all three appearing to apply to Henry New. At the start of the century Daniel Defoe claimed those who could not pay their debts 'had no Hopes of ever being delivered, but by the general Jayl Delivery of the Grave'.[3] Nor were debtors the only ones concerned as creditors were hurt financially by the impossibility of liberty, one 1793 writer arguing that 'perpetual imprisonment for debt, besides that it is cruel and monstrous in itself, is no less ruinous to the creditor than the debtor. It actually defeats the very end it pretends to answer'.[4] In this aspect, the institution of debt imprisonment appears to have been fatally flawed as it was unable, in its hands-off functionality, to enable the satisfaction of creditors whose debtors were simply unable ever to pay. Furthermore, it thus denied their productive return to the commercial environment which (even by eighteenth-century standards) was unjust, failure in business not necessarily indicating fraud or extravagance.

When the unsupervised institution failed, direct intervention was required to ensure it did not collapse under the weight of the insolvent. However, the ability of mechanisms which were defined features of the institution such as *supersedeas* to enable release outside of the superior courts has already been shown to be limited.[5] Instead, direct external intervention was irregularly required, taking the form of a series of statutes passed by Parliament known as the Insolvency Acts. The limited scholarly attention which such Acts have received has portrayed them largely as simple amnesties, the operation of legislation to counter the worst impulses of uncontrollable plaintiffs: 'Creditors may have been able to throw recalcitrant debtors into jail, but as soon as the prisons were full so Parliament emptied them'.[6] However, the doors of gaols were not merely held open, prisoners had to confer something to their creditors, paying out of their remaining estate which they had heretofore been unwilling to part with, at a rate of shillings in the pound. These Acts forced compromise; they functioned, as Defoe put it, as 'a kind of Truce between Debtor and Creditor' by requiring plaintiffs be compensated but that they accept a lesser return than their full demand.[7] They thus appear antithetical to the creditor focussed bent of the law and the coercive nature of debtors' prisons which promised no relief until full satisfaction.

This chapter focusses on one of the most notable ways, according to the commitment registers, in which debtors escaped imprisonment. While the majority throughout the period quietly settled their debts, the most visually striking method of release was an Insolvency Act which foiled creditors *en masse*. It details how such legislation developed from its mid-seventeenth-century origins of limited relief to become a regular mechanism of facilitating the continued efficacy of the prisons, exploring legislative innovation and subsequent conservatism, assessing the infrequency of their passage. It also explores how creditors reacted to the undermining of their rights and assesses the uptake of Insolvency Acts, emphasising that not every debtor regarded such clemency as worth seeking.

★★

Legislation which released large numbers of insolvent debtors at a specific moment was far from innovative by the eighteenth century, even though reformers continued to push for more permanent relief statutes into the nineteenth century. General amnesties or state attempts to settle disputes in a variety of forms occurred throughout the seventeenth and eighteenth centuries, motivated (in theory) by a desire to relieve the impoverished who were trapped in debtors' prison. Some state relief efforts took the form of crown charity such as the issuing of Royal Bounties to relieve debtors from specific prisons, though the funds available were diluted by extension to the general poor in surrounding parishes.[8] From the early seventeenth century, possibly arising from the increased rate of credit litigation after c.1580, the state began to intercede formally in the process of debt imprisonment. In 1624, James I's government instituted a Commission of Judges with the power to 'treat, perswade, mediate, and procure compositions, and agreements with the Creditors' of insolvent prisoners which aimed to produce mutually beneficial solutions.[9] It was however, the pressures of the English Revolution which generated the first legislative attempt to enact large-scale immediate, if time limited, relief. In the late 1640s, the issue of debt imprisonment became an increasingly prescient one both to pamphleteers and petitioners. Some authors – writing to both Parliament and the Crown – called for the general abolition of the 'inhumane slavery of imprisonment for debt' which they felt had been promised by the Petition of Right and the Solemn League and Covenant (such claims being legally dubious) while most simply argued for the release of poor prisoners (potentially including themselves).[10] In September 1649, Parliament passed the first of what came to be known generally as the Insolvency Acts, though it is unclear whether this arose more from the reforming spirit of the English Republic or the pressures of gaols visibly packed with debtors after a decade of instability. Regardless, it proved to be one of the longest lasting innovations of the Commonwealth, with Acts being regularly passed until the 1820s.

The 1649 Act was a fundamentally different beast to eighteenth-century legislation though it represented the foundations upon which all subsequent statutes were built. It ordered the release of

> any person now ... imprisoned ... where the Cause of Action was originally for Debt, upon the request of such party, and taking his or her Oath ... that *bona fide* he or she is not worth in Possession, Reversion, or

Remainder of any Estate Real or Personal to the value of Five Pounds, besides necessary wearing Apparel, and Bedding for himself, his Wife and Children, and Tools necessary for his Trade or Occupation, not exceeding the value of Five Pounds; and hath not directly or indirectly conveyed or intrusted his or her Estate, thereby to expect and Profit, Benefit, or Advantage.

The Act, on its face, offered little to creditors if they 'cannot deny the truth of the said Oath' though neither did it actually clear debtors. While prisoners were released and could not be imprisoned again for the same debts,

all and every former Judgement and Execution had or taken forth against such Debtor, shall be and stand good against the Goods and Chattels of the said Debtor … And that it shall and may be lawful … to take out any new Execution against any other the Lands, Goods, and Chattels.

Furthermore, characteristic of the era of its passage, the Act did not 'extend to any person or persons, who have been in arms against the Parliament, or have adhered to the Forces raised against the Parliament'.[11] Despite its partisan limitations, the lack of specified recompense to creditors who had procured arrests, the failure to culminate disputes (debtors still being liable after release), and its restriction to the most impoverished, this statute represented a significant advance. It acknowledged fundamentally at a legislative level that some debtors were unable to procure freedom independently and that some creditors could never be persuaded to behave in a realistic fashion by accepting compromise, with or without the intervention of state sanctioned commissions. Nor were its limitations particularly unusual given that seventeenth-century bankruptcy similarly did not free debtors from their obligations.[12]

Subsequent seventeenth-century amnesty statutes, passed by both Protectorate and Restoration governments, built upon these initial developments. In 1653, panels of judges were set up to 'hear and determine the Causes of such Persons Imprisonment', seizing the estates of escapees, to 'sell and dispose of the estate' belonging to any 'Merchant or Tradesman' who had 'done or suffered any thing for which he might be adjudged a Bankrupt', and (among other investigative tasks) to settle the debts of those who 'hath made or caused to be made a voluntary settlement of any of his own Estate'.[13] This reflected an attempt to tackle the two key issues of 1649, the failure to compensate creditors and bring suits to culmination. However, the laborious process of the appointed courts seems unlikely to have proved a practical remedy nor did the innovations survive the return of monarchical rule. The passage of the 1670 'Act for the Releife and Release of Poore Distressed Prisoners for Debt' ignored developments since 1649, releasing those who swore 'That I have not any Estate Reall or Personall in Possession, Reversion or Remainder of the value of ten pounds in the whole, or sufficient to pay the

Debt or Dammages for which I am imprisoned' with judgements related to debts still standing against their estate. Creditors were able to insist upon a prisoner's continued detention though were required subsequently to 'at his and their owne proper costs and charges allow and pay weekely a reasonable Maintenance to the said prisoner or prisoners such as the said Commissioners ... shall order and appoint not exceeding eighteen pence a weeke'.[14] It is notable that the legislative innovation of a time-limited Insolvency Act (first passed within less than a year of Charles I's execution) was passed at all during the Restoration, indicating both its continued need and a positive public reaction to the 1649 amnesty.

At the passage of the next Act in 1678, those owing over £500 were barred from applying while creditors could, if 'his Debtor being a person formerly using any Handycraft or Day labour', rather than allow them to be released, transfer them to a workhouse, allowing them to work off the debt. Most importantly though was the Act's penultimate clause:

> That noe Prisoner shall be discharged by vertue of this Act untill he shall before the Justices of the Peace ... declare upon his Corporall Oath ... what Effects are belonging to him or what Debt or Debts are then oweing to him ... of all which a Schedule shall be made in the presence of such Justices and subscribed by the Prisoner and shall be by such Justices returned to the next Sessions there to be kept for the better Information of the Creditors of such Prisoner who ... may thereupon sue for such Debts or soe much thereof as will reasonably satisfie them ... and after the same recovered and received to render the overplus (their owne Debts and Charges first deducted) to the Prisoner.

While the need to swear to effects probably arose as a support to the general oath declaring applicants were not worth more than £10, that the specifics were recorded in a 'Schedule' which was preserved for the benefit of creditors set an important precedent. This did not constitute a form of proper creditor compensation; the ability to sue for a debtor's estate had been preserved in the previous Acts, this merely provided them with a list of what could potentially be sued for. Furthermore, creditors acted independently from one another, indicating that those who sued first might take the lion's share of the estate. However, it represented a new understanding that if such amnesties were to become regular, this being the second in less than ten years, rather than responses to particular crises (such as the Civil War or the end of the Protectorate) then the needs of creditors had to be represented. While similar legislation was not passed for twelve years suggesting seventeenth-century concern over regularity was unnecessary, it preserved the 1678 Act's structure and innovations.[15]

Insolvency Acts developed comparatively swiftly in the first two decades of the eighteenth century though they did not emerge immediately as an effective mechanism of remedying disputes. Rather than a response to general impoverishment, the 1702 Act was passed specifically due to the circumstances of national need, planning to liberate the 'very many Persons ... detained in Prison who being miserably impoverished by War Losses and other Misfortunes ... are able and willing to serve Her Majesty by Sea or Land'. The initial amnesty appears not to have led to the presumed recruitment drive as the Act was reissued in 1703 with the caveat

> that no Man shall during the present War with France and Spain be discharged from his Imprisonment ... unles such Man do and shall enter or list himself into Her Majesties Service ... and continue in such Service during the Continuance of this present War,

an innovation which appears not to have been repeated regularly though was occasionally suggested.[16] In other regards, the Act mirrored those passed in the 1690s. It did present suing out of the schedule as an inevitability though the process still required independent action by creditors.

The 1711 Act failed to build upon the developments of bankruptcy reform in 1706 (which now cleared the insolvent) by discharging debtors from their obligations. Debtors were still required to submit a schedule of their estate, now specifically including 'Lands, Tenements, Hereditaments, Goods and Chattels (... wearing Apparel, Bedding ... and Tools necessary for his or her Trade or Occupation, only Excepted)' alongside debts owed to them, from which plaintiffs could sue, which eventually ended the action. Notably, those who owed more than £50 to a single creditor were excluded from the benefit of the Act (further separating the Act from bankruptcy and leaving little remedy to those who owed between £50 1d and £99 19s 11d) and it was required for the first time that notice of a debtor's application for release 'shall be inserted in the *London Gazette* Thirty Days before such Quarter or General Sessions'.[17] By the Act of 1719, significant progress had been made in reforming the law to the benefit of both parties. Debtors no longer had to be worth less than an amount; rather their oath declared they had no worth over £10 'other than what [is] in the said Schedule contained'. The submission of a schedule for the first time constituted a discharge of their obligations as the court was 'to make an Assignment of the said Estate and Effects [detailed in the Schedule] to Such of the Creditors ... who shall apply for the same'.[18] While being required to apply still did not necessarily constitute an inherent compensation for creditors, such an application was qualitatively lesser than the need to sue, both because it did not constitute a legal submission and because the dispersal of the estate was subsequently apparently automatic. This reform was cemented in the 1724 Act, confirming the process by which an assignee sold the estate and paid each creditor a portion of so many shillings in the pound in relation to the size of the debt, the debtor also receiving a few shillings out of the proceeds from which to start afresh.[19] The Insolvency Acts subsequently represented, after seven decades of tinkering and improvement, an effective mechanism of ending disputes, both releasing debtors and compensating creditors.

Acts passed throughout the second half of the eighteenth century essentially mirrored those of the 1720s. In each Act gaolers were ordered to submit lists of those currently contained in the prison to quarter sessions, debtors were required to list their details in the *London Gazette* as well as to swear to their estate when submitting a schedule (Quakers were allowed to make a 'solemn affirmation'), and creditors were paid out of the profits following the assignee's efforts. Each Act only applied to those contained within a prison before a specific date though making provision for "fugitives" (a group including significant numbers who were merely resident overseas when writs were issued against them such as in the colonies as well as mariners alongside those who had genuinely fled their obligations) and decreed that, after being released, they could not be imprisoned for any debts contracted before this date.[20] Where creditors did not bring forward claims against imprisoned debtors and subsequently tried to arrest those cleared by an Act (having not had a remedy for their debts) they were liable to charges of false imprisonment.[21] From 1736 to 1760, Acts were passed with mechanisms which allowed for the compelling of debtors to apply for the benefit upon pain of death, though after the disastrous consequences of 1761 when removing the limits on when a debtor had been imprisoned by led to a surge in arrests, such compulsive measures were not re-introduced.[22] While minor variations were made in processing perjury or the text of the oath, the only significant variations before the 1810s were the increased upper limits placed both on the wealth that debtors were allowed to retain (reaching £20 by 1776) and on those who did not qualify. The 1719 Act excluded those who owed more than £50 to a single creditor but this doubled in 1724 before jumping to £500 in 1736, eventually rising to £1,000 in the 1770s and reaching £2,000 by 1811.[23] Such innovations reflected changing wealth and commercial growth, larger debts becoming more common and requiring remedy as well as the need to provide realistic sums to liberated debtors to prevent post-release destitution for their family. However, it also indicates a lack of desire to alter the substance of the statutes testifying both to the theoretical effectiveness of the legislation for all parties by 1724 as well as the lack of change in the wider informal credit market which created the need for such Acts.

Despite their unchanging foundations, the passage of Insolvency Acts was irregular. Between 1711 and 1801 nineteen Acts were successfully passed at intervals of five years on average. Some were passed as little as two years apart while there was a thirteen-year pause between the 1781 and 1794 Acts. Further to their irregularity, their passage arose from a variety of circumstances, not all of which accorded with immediate need. While the 1725 and 1729 Acts responded to immediate economic crisis which particularly impacted debt imprisonment, some Acts, such as that passed in 1755, appear to have been passed simply out of recognition that it had been several years since its previous iteration in 1748. These unprompted Acts reflected the issue of insolvents (trapped and unable to pay) steadily accumulating in prisons across the country rather than the gaols being suddenly flooded meaning their rate of passage is not an effective metric of economic instability in themselves. Clemency was also an expected consequence of the beginning of a new reign. Insolvency Acts followed the coronations of William and Mary, Anne, George II, and George III. While some of these Acts accorded with need (such as George II's), their inception was ceremonial as a comment on the 1760 legislation reflected:

> As this was the first session of a new reign, when acts of indemnity or mercy are usually passed, it was not to be doubted that our imprisoned debtors, whose numbers were surprisingly great, would petition for that mercy from the legislature.[24]

George I's coronation was a notable exception which did not go uncommented upon. A petition c.1715–1720 remarked that it was

> the Custome of All Christian Monarchs ascending the Throne to Grant an Act for the libertie of Insolvent Debtors to Aggrandize their Accession to their Thrones but more especially It hath been the Custome for Monarchs ascending the *British Throne* as in all late Reignes hath been practised by former Kings and Queens of Britaine to Grant such a Necessary & Charitable Act but more especially it was Expected from his Majestie King George who on his departure from his German Dominions Released not only Insolvent Debtors but also Criminals and therefore his New British Subjects did humbly hope & believe to receive the same Gratious favour from His Majestie as he hath done to his Naturall German Subjects.

The language used by the petition is striking in indicating the speed at which such legislation had come to be expected. That they were deprived an Act granted to German criminals was therefore clearly a matter of some consternation though it was not one this petition explicitly blamed upon the new King, claiming that the 'Jaile Keepers of Great Britaine opposed the Glorious intended Bill ... by Alledging that the Insolvent Debtors were Jacobites' to protect their own profit margins.[25]

It seems unlikely that claims of Jacobitism were the true reason for the failure to pass an Insolvency Act c.1715. Rather it was presumably a consequence of the 1711 Act's passage four years earlier and the assumption that similar legislation was therefore not yet warranted. Throughout the eighteenth century, while traders acknowledged the need for Acts to be passed occasionally, they resisted frequency and remained suspicious of those advocating for statutes.[26] This contrast was exemplified, like so much else concerning credit in the eighteenth century, by Daniel Defoe. Prior to 1719 only seven Insolvency Acts had been passed since their inception and yet three were passed in the subsequent decade. While the 1719 Act was essentially mundane, those passed for 1725 and 1729 reflected the economic shock of the South Sea Bubble.

Defoe in the opening of a pamphlet written to oppose the 1729 legislation acknowledged the circumstances of the day:

> the honest Debtor willing to pay, but unable, and willing to pay as far as he is able, and ready to give all reasonable Satisfaction, such as the Parliament may direct, that he is so unable, is certainly an Object recommending itself to the Charity and Compassion of the whole Nation.

Despite this recognition, Defoe found the repeated Acts and the high number of applicants to each difficult to stomach. He questioned the wisdom of regular legislation and suggested that it had opened the door to fraudulent activity, asking

> whether it is any Way probable, that there can be such a Number of miserable Insolvents in one Year ... and all actually Prisoners as have presented themselves yearly to the Magistrates, to be discharged by the Grace of Parliament, for these several Years past?

Such qualms reflected creditor responses across the period – while they acknowledged Acts had to be passed, they also could not escape the sense that they were being cheated, only acquiescing to their passage with long intermissions to prevent opportunists and ensure remaining prisoners really could not pay.[27]

The resumption of infrequency reflected both the return to economic normalcy and inherent disquiet over the Acts. Undoubtedly, the passage of only one Act in the 1730s improved their general image. Subsequently, creditor concern chiefly centred upon debtors supposedly committed on "friendly action" (being arrested by friends upon request so as to safeguard their property) who refused to take the benefit of an Act, leading to the measures of compulsion which were abandoned after 1761. However, during the period 1769–1781, Acts were passed as a matter of habit, five becoming law at two- or three-year intervals with ever-diminishing application rates. This habitual clemency contributed to renewed creditor concern and the subsequent failure to pass any legislation until 1794. Acts were called for during this intermission particularly as the prison population grew without them, one newspaper commentator suggesting in 1787 that 'there never was a period when an Act of Insolvency will be productive of so much real good and so little harm, as at the present juncture ... the human interference of the Legislature is highly necessary'.[28] While a number of Acts were introduced in the House, none successfully made it to the statute book in what Joanna Innes has described as a 'stern pro-creditor reaction'.[29]

As in Defoe's era, the repetition of Acts led to an association of those released by Insolvency Acts with fraudulent activity – commentators assuming it was improbable so many genuine debtors could be in need. Signs of strain from the repeated Insolvency Acts were evident as early as 1776. At the passage of the fourth Act in seven years, Parliament included a clause which excluded any prisoner 'who knowingly and designedly, by false pretence or pretences, shall have obtained from any person or persons, money, goods, wares, merchandises, bonds, bills of exchange, promissory notes, or other securities for money' from the benefit of the Act, building upon the exclusion of embezzlers in previous legislation.[30] Enforcement of this clause could only have been arbitrary and it represented an appeasement of the trading classes rather than a serious attempt to tackle fraud. Those actually convicted by quarter sessions were merely remanded back to debtors' prison. Newspapers reported accordingly that while 'upwards of 1,500 insolvent Debtors, Prisoners and Fugitives, belonging to the King's Bench Prison ... were discharged by Virtue of the late Act of Parliament' only 'twenty were remanded, being disqualified, or coming within the meaning of the Clause respecting Sharpers and Swindlers'.[31] It was not uncommon that debtors might be remanded back upon application particularly when they had debts contracted after the legislation's cut-off date, it being unlikely many of these twenty were proven swindlers. This did not make the new clause unpopular. The *Morning Chronicle* declared triumphantly based on just one debtor being remanded back to the King's Bench that 'the Clause ... is praise-worthy'.[32]

In June 1776, the first advertisements appeared announcing a new organisation formed earlier in the year entitled 'The Guardians, or Society for the Protection of Trade against Swindlers and Sharpers', using similar language to the legislators. 'Being desirous of promoting and extending the laudable views of the Legislature', the society announced they would hold public meetings in the Strand twice a week 'for the purpose of receiving such information from any persons' which would 'enable the Society to preclude any Swindlers of Sharpers from taking the ... Act'.[33] Their efforts were well received and the society attracted a growing membership of London's elite, though the commentator who claimed 'we want nothing but a proper Discrimination between the unfortunate Tradesman, and the wilful Defrauder, to render the Laws of England regarding Debtors as perfect as it is in the Nature of human Institutions they should be', stands somewhat alone.[34] Other writers made their view of Acts as a whole clear publishing works dedicated to the Society such as *The Swindler's Scourge*, 'a work particularly necessary at this period, as by virtue of the late Insolvent Act, these pests of society are pouring from the different jails'.[35] The Society continued to operate following the end of the 1776 statute, holding monthly meetings in taverns and acquiring a dedicated office in 1780.[36] By 1778 its membership included MPs, Aldermen, and Sheriffs (the Guardians campaigning on behalf of other members in elections), growing to over 280 prominent individuals and business partnerships by 1799 while the famous blind magistrate and police reformer Sir John Fielding was one of its earliest administrators, their activities paid for by public subscriptions.[37] From October 1776 the Society organised prosecutions of those informed against at their public meetings (usually minor frauds purchasing trifling amounts on credit under assumed identities) as well as publishing cautions to the public about reports of forged bills of exchange or the description of supposed swindlers, later launching concerted attacks on illegal lottery offices.[38]

While the Society's activity has been compared favourably to modern credit checking agencies, their behaviour should be seen more properly as little more than ideological thuggery, their self-congratulatory advertisements of their prosecutions ('Jane Cambell ... would probably have escaped unpunished if Mr Thorne had not been a member of the Society of Guardians') serving to spread fear of "the Other" and to promote disdain for the poor.[39] Their operations continued to focus on the Insolvency Acts particularly in interrupting their smooth passage. When Parliament commenced preparation of another statute in 1778, the Society announced that, 'in case the legislature should determine to pass the Insolvent Debtors Act now applied for, [the Guardians] have prepared heads of clauses to be laid before Parliament for the more effectually preventing fraudulent debtors obtaining any benefit therefrom'.[40] Their campaign was a success in the public mindset; at the passage of the 1781 Act one newspaper letter writer demonstrated the depreciated status of such legislation using language derived from the Guardians:

> Those Gentlemen, who have promoted and carryed through the Bill for the Relief of Insolvent Debtors, should have been very attentive that it should not in Effect be a Bill to encourage Frauds. ... It is well known, that most of those People who surrendered themselves ... did it with bad intentions; and to afford them Relief is directly to oppress the fair Trader. What species, Humanity or Policy, can that be which encourages Swindler to prey on industrious Tradesmen? ... The Legislature should take particular Care that their Acts, intended for humane and worthy Purposes, should not be deemed by the Publick, and with great Justice, *Acts for the Encouragement of Swindlers and Sharpers, and for rewarding the Same.*[41]

That same year an *Authentic List of Persons ... Who have Surrendered themselves ... Into the Custody of the Marshal of the King's Bench Prison* was published on behalf of the society, 'which is to much the more important to the trading part of Mankind, as the Necessity is evident in the present Cessation of the Laws for confining Debtors'.[42] While it arose as a direct response to benefits allowed under the Act relating to the Gordon Riots, this activity was an attack upon Insolvency Acts in general. The publication of the names and addresses of those who had applied to the *London Gazette* in an affordable volume constituted a direct assault upon the credit of those liberated (as was demonstrated by desperate adverts placed by those who had been falsely included) as well as representing an existential threat to those who might apply to future Acts.[43] While the *Authentic List* acknowledged that some of those included had not acted fraudulently, its author dismissed the importance of the livelihoods of these individuals as 'the *Public* Good should always precede every *private* Concern'. The general infrequency of the Insolvency Acts and their failure to comprehensively reform the system of debt imprisonment has been previously criticised as a symbol of their ineffectiveness.[44] However, in the light of the response from the Guardians and their supporters, the Acts should not be expected to have achieved this as, while not a defined element of the institution, they represented an integral part of that system rather than a response to it. Debtors unable to pay their debts between 1781 and 1794 suffered from the generosity of the legislature 1769–1781. While society remained attached to (or dependent upon) debt imprisonment, any frequency in the passage of Insolvency Acts threatened the probability of their being passed again as well as, therefore, the safety of future prisoners.

That this resource was such a necessary one which needed to be protected is demonstrated perhaps most palpably by the fact that not all prisoners who qualified actually applied for its benefit. The percentage of debtors who took advantage of an Act at the Fleet Prison (13%), Wood Street Compter (4%, rising to 6% when including those released by the Compulsive Clause in 1761), and Lancaster Castle Gaol (11%) was much lower than those simply discharged though still represented the second or third most prominent methods of release. Rates were low in part as most debtors were simply never offered the chance to apply. Due to the irregularity of legislation, debtors fortunate enough to be confined at the passage of an Insolvency Act represented a minority. Many prisoners who might have been expected to take an Act managed to achieve release after a longer than average commitment or died in gaol due to the lack of a statute during their confinement. The Fleet commitment registers record that a third of all those escaping the prison fled during the long intermission (1782–1794), suggesting an increased rate of hopelessness. Inevitably, of prisoners held at the time of an Insolvency Act, the percentage cleared was significantly greater. In the text of the Act passed for the year 1794, the legislators asked that gaolers submit a list of those 'who, upon the twelfth day of February one thousand seven hundred and ninety four, was or were … an actual prisoner or prisoners'.[45] Based on the surviving commitment registers of each prison, there were 105 debtors in Giltspur Street (as the compter had been called since 1791), 138 in Lancaster Castle, and 287 in the Fleet who had been committed prior to the 12th without having yet been released. Each prison contained an unusually high number of debtors due to an aggravated commitment rate in 1793 as well as the lack of an Insolvency Act since 1781. At the respective prisons, only 22, 57, and 173 debtors were explicitly released by the Act that year (21%, 41%, and 60%). However, by the first publication of the *London Gazette* listing applicants in June, significant numbers of prisoners had already obtained their freedom by other means. When examining only those who were present both in February and in June, the shares released rose sharply to 69%, 81%, and 79% though still representing just 11%, 20%, and 48% of all releases in 1794 each prison rapidly refilling, committing 86, 172, and 122 respectively between June and December. It is also possible that Insolvency Acts released a larger share of prisoners in 1794 than at other amnesties due to the long interval between it and the previous Act in 1781. In 1776, for example, the Wood Street share (even when excluding those released before the first *Gazette*) was only 40%, the same figure as applied for relief in 1725.[46] However, the application rate at borough prisons such as Wood Street was probably lower than at county gaols or superior court prisoners which contained greater numbers of the destitute, the insolvent, and those simply unwilling to pay.

Given that such amnesties offered freedom at a discount, it might be expected all debtors would rush to participate. However, even in high application years, the rate of those who qualified who were subsequently cleared by the Act was not total. The Insolvency Acts were not automatic and rates of those who applied to the *Gazette* were higher than the total released.[47] The extended process between submitting to the *Gazette* and the prison doors opening which included preparing a schedule, the sale of goods, and creditors being compensated, could be protracted. In 1794, at least one debtor at the Fleet died having submitted his application before the process could be completed. However, the majority of those who applied and were not released simply did not qualify or their aggrieved creditors successfully opposed release. One Giltspur Street, three Lancaster, and eighteen Fleet prisoners were listed in the *Gazette* in 1794 but were later released by other means. Two of the Lancaster prisoners were cleared by the Lord's Act later that year while the third was released by the plaintiff and the unsuccessful Giltspur Street debtor was discharged in 1795. Ten of the Fleet applicants did eventually satisfy their creditors, some as late as 1797, while the others either took later Acts, died in gaol, or were released by court process. Creditors did not normally block the release of a debtor though rejection was far from unheard of and was probably more likely for debtors owing large sums. Failure did not prevent debtors from reapplying for subsequent Acts. Thomas Trotman, a clerk owing £4,209 between his sixteen creditors, applied unsuccessfully from the Fleet in 1794 and 1797 before finally being freed by the 1801 Insolvency Act.[48] Similarly, Adam Fuller, a gentleman, banker, and debtor at the Fleet, applied for the benefit of at least six Acts between 1755 and 1778 before securing release.[49] Across the period, of those appearing in the *London Gazette* who could be traced in a surviving commitment register, 28% of Wood Street, 11% of Fleet, and 5% of Lancaster applicants were released by other means. The Wood Street share is bloated by the considerable number compelled by their creditors in 1761 whose release was blocked by the suspension of the Compulsive Clause in October. When excluding 1761, 15% of Wood Street applicants were still not fully cleared. Many of these debtors, particularly at Wood Street, probably did submit a schedule of their effects which was sold and distributed among their creditors, but their release was subsequently blocked by the court due to a portion of their debts having been contracted after the cut-off date. In 1776, James Dickson was cleared by the Act of his £20 debt but was explicitly 'remanded back again' to the compter due to a more recent £52 10s.[50] Commitment registers rarely detail remandings, presumably as the prisoner had not actually been released and re-committed, only appearing on four occasions in Wood Street as incidental notes or marginalia by prison clerks, though it seems probable that Dickson's experience was not uncommon.

The inclusion of unsuccessful applicants does not significantly increase the rate seeking the Act in 1794. Despite the benefits of being released and paying less than their obligations, debtors did not automatically feel "taking the Act" was their best exit strategy. The significant number of prisoners who qualified but secured release before June (representing the majority of those held on the 12th February at Giltspur Street and Lancaster) suggests that payment in full at the agreement of their creditors was preferable to being released at a discount. Furthermore, those who did take the Act had generally been held for longer periods indicating a probable loss of faith in their ability to secure release by their own hands. In 1794, the median Giltspur Street debtor who took advantage of the Act had been held for 391 days, the shortest commitment of 182 days being longer than 63% of the imprisonments who achieved release by other methods after the 12th February, such debtors experiencing median commitments of 183 days. Lancaster debtors who did and did not apply experienced a similar variation in commitment medians of 234 and 162 days while at the Fleet the two medians were 402 and 175 days. The average commitment length across the period of those at each prison taking an Act was longer than a year, the Fleet mean being an imprisonment of two years and two months. Insolvency Acts appear therefore to have acted as a last resort for those whose debts could never be paid by traditional means, though it was not exclusive to this group as inevitably a minority of debtors who may have been able to pay after several more months opted for early release. Long-term debtors had clearly experienced greater difficulties in procuring their release; the assistance provided by an Insolvency Act was thus of greater significance and the negatives diminished in relation. This is perhaps best shown by the debtors present both in February and June who opted not to apply. At Giltspur Street all eight were released by their creditors before the end of 1794, at Lancaster all thirteen were also released by December though four took the Lord's Act, and while at the Fleet twenty-five of the forty-two prisoners were still confined in 1795 the majority were removed by creditors before 1796. Despite not all securing release as quickly as they assumed they would, the expectation that an Insolvency Act was not their only method of avoiding dying in gaol appears to have been borne out.

These debtors did have good cause not to take the Act if they could probably pay at a later date. The schedules prisoners were required to submit were substantial in scope. The Acts typically required 'all his or her real estate, either in possession, reversion, remainder, or expectancy; and also of the whole of his or her personal estate … in trust for him or her, or for his or her use, benefit, or advantage, is or are seized of, interested in, or intitled to, or was or were in his or her possession, at any time since his or her commitment to prison, with the names of his or her several debtors … and the several sums of money from them respectively owing' be listed in the schedule. 'Wearing apparel, and bedding for myself and family, working tools, and necessary implements for my occupation and calling' were exempted as well as, by the second half of the eighteenth century, 'a sum of money not exceeding forty shillings, and these in the whole not exceeding the value of twenty pounds', having been limited to £5 or £10 in earlier Acts. However, what property belonged within the exemptions could be determined on an *ad hoc* basis by assignees when inspecting debtors' homes and deciding what to sell. Attempts to conceal anything were treated as a felony and thus punishable by death though in 1768 it was claimed there had only been one actual execution.[51] Schedules, though regularly listing debts owed to the applicant, frequently failed to list domestic property. This might suggest in some cases that applicants were greatly impoverished. However, as when goods were listed in schedules they generally were held in pawn or at second homes and no section was provided for effects on the pre-printed forms, it seems probable that – as in probate register construction – assignees were expected to use their initiative in deciding what was to be included. Debtors should have thus presumed that anything of worth could, and would, be sold. The significant psychological trauma that occurred from the loss of treasured possessions, from children's toys to family antiques, upon an individual who had already lost their solvency should not be underestimated.

The negative consequences of taking an Insolvency Act did not end at the sale of property. While the arrest of a debtor was a clear assault upon their credit standing, the satisfaction of creditors in full demonstrated trustworthiness and financial capability which while not restoring their credit, repaired it somewhat. By contrast, those who took an Act demonstrated their incapability and having been 'whitewashed' (a common term for debtors released in this manner implying, in contrast to those 'restored', that faults had merely been covered over) could struggle to procure credit, an absolute necessity for those seeking to re-enter the commercial world.[52] Johann von Archenholtz, a Prussian soldier and historian who visited England in the late eighteenth century, described debt imprisonment for a continental audience where the practice was scarcer, noting that 'the English do not think it disgraceful to be imprisoned for debt, but they think it exceedingly so to be declared *cleared by the act*'.[53] Debtors might thus perceive remaining in prison as, comparatively, worthwhile. Underneath the entry for Samuel William Carr, committed 30th December 1803 to Giltspur Street, Carr himself wrote

> I hereby require that my name may not be inserted in the Lists of Insolvent Debtors to be returned to the Sessions or Stuck up at any door or other part of this Prison – Dated this 3d day of August 1804. Sam Wm Carr.[54]

Carr, who was 'discharged' three months later, was surely not the only debtor who regarded taking an Act as the very last option and wanted to avoid even the hint of his association with such legislation.

This sense of disgrace was central to the Acts; it suggested debtors had essentially stolen what was justly owed to their creditors by their whitewashing which was worsened by regular discussions of the supposed criminality of those taking the Acts particularly during the 1770s.[55] The *Gazette* was widely read and publications of insolvency were digested as eagerly as foreign news; taking the Act was therefore, by design, always a public affair from which it was very hard to escape.[56] In the anonymous *Adventures of Mr Loveill* (1750), the author described how a debtor with the 'character of a fugitive for debt, cleared by the late act of insolvency, … found it impossible to raise money … otherwise than by an action for which he deserved something more than hanging'.[57] While his identity as a fugitive, of whom thousands applied for Acts successfully, certainly lowered his access to credit even further, that he had taken the Insolvent Act was the crux of his untrustworthiness. Similarly, an anonymous work published to raise sympathy for Rev. William Dodd shortly before his execution for forgery described the lack of subsequent commercial opportunity for those released by Acts of Insolvency:

> when the Prison Doors become open for Enlargement, the Captive in a Manner stands alone, like Adam, in a State of Nudity, but without his Innocence. Should, however, his Disposition lead him to Labour, to whom shall he apply for Employment? Friendless, forlorn, and unrecommended, the thriving World disclaim him … he has at last Recourse to illicit Practices.

Dodd had little to recommend him in 1777 and attempting to generate sympathy for his crimes by demonstrating how easily other detested debtors fell into illegal activity was a poor strategy on the part of this pamphleteer, though it does suggest a more general assumption about the post-release activities of cleared prisoners.[58] One Marshalsea debtor cleared by an Act, who had plied his trader as a cloth dealer prior to imprisonment, eventually became an officer of the prison in the 1790s. While he was not forced to turn to crime unlike the two fictional debtors, that he moved from a trade reliant upon credit to a salaried profession in an institution of the uncreditworthy is telling.[59] This does not mean that those cleared by Acts never traded on credit again, but it probably proved more difficult particularly as, by taking the Act, their untrustworthiness had been published in the official state journal. Restoring credit following an Act required time, investment, and equally public displays of honesty as businesswoman, poet, and imprisoned debtor Jane Elizabeth Moore described in 1786:

> I know a person who was cleared by an act of insolvency who [afterwards] paid to every creditor the whole of their demand, some of which were to a large amount, by which means he re-established his credit in an ample manner.[60]

It is far from inconceivable that numerous debtors similarly re-obtained credit, though the necessary exertion probably gave individuals like Carr good reason to avoid relief.

★★

These amnesties were, despite the scaremongering of men like Defoe, hardly the first choice of release for most debtors. If debtors could have repaid in full, only liquidating their estate on their own terms, they would have. As a result, the majority of those listed in the *London Gazette* were those who having chased up every lead and sold every significant item of value, were still unable to satisfy their creditors. Despite being a highly visible means of release, the Insolvency Acts therefore functioned as a pressure valve rather than a main exit flow from the prisons which prevented those who absolutely could not pay from being held indefinitely until their demise. Creditors recognised the importance of Acts for these reasons and acquiesced to their passage, but it should not be seen as surprising that they were cautious about frequency even without the associations of criminality. The failure of Parliament to pass a permanent statute or to make Acts biennial as they essentially became between 1804 and 1813, increased the probability that such amnesties could be passed and that they applied to all who needed them. In 1794, following the resumption of Insolvency Acts, John Donaldson suggested that despite it having been 'of great benefit to many', in future Acts should make 'a distinction ... betwixt natives and foreigners, and between those who were in business and those who were not'.[61] Even after the long interval there was clearly continued discomfort particularly as Donaldson suggested the benefit should only be extended to those deemed worthy and completely trustworthy by polite society – British merchants. This would have made such legislation largely indistinguishable from bankruptcy and thus essentially useless and it is difficult to see how in the eighteenth century the Acts, or even the debtors' prisons, could have functioned with this alteration. Even though they only impacted a minority of prisoners over the period, any threat to the operation of the Acts was a threat to the release valve which, in turn, threatened to explode the entire system of debt imprisonment, as unremedied overcrowding and increased rates of debtors dying in prison would have made debtors' prisons unpalatable to Regency sensibilities. The Acts therefore represent something emblematic about eighteenth-century society's attitude towards debtors' prisons and their inherent fragility. It was possible simultaneously to believe frauds and cheats should rot or that anyone who failed to repay in full should be treated with caution, and that the system as it stood ought to be protected. As most in society were vulnerable to a similar fate it was necessary that, if they themselves were one day imprisoned, there was a way out of gaol if, for unthinkable reasons, they too could not pay.[62]

Notes

1 Tawny Paul, *Poverty of Disaster – Debt and Insecurity in Eighteenth-Century Britain* (Cambridge: Cambridge University Press, 2019).

2 "Henry New, a Prisoner in Stafford Gaol. Q/SB 1789 E/85 (1789)", in *Petitions to the Staffordshire Quarter Sessions, 1589–1799*, ed. Brodie Waddell, *British History Online*.

3 Daniel Defoe, *Remarks on the Bill to Prevent Frauds Committed by Bankrupts* (London: 1706), p. 3.

4 Anon. *The Debtor and Creditor's Assistant; or, a Key to the King's Bench and Fleet Prisons* (London: 1793), p. 89.

5 Paul, *Poverty of Disaster*, pp. 105–106; Joanna Innes, "The King's Bench Prison in the Later Eighteenth Century: Law, Authority and Order in a London Debtors' Prison", in *An Ungovernable People – The English and Their Law in the Seventeenth and Eighteenth Centuries*, ed. John Brewer and John Styles (London: Hutchinson, 1980), p. 255.

6 Julian Hoppit, "The Use and Abuse of Credit in Eighteenth-Century England", in *Business Life and Public Policy – Essays in Honour of D.C. Coleman*, eds. Neil McKendrick and R. B. Outhwaite (Cambridge: Cambridge University Press, 1986), p. 71; V. Marksham Lester, *Victorian Insolvency – Bankruptcy, Imprisonment for Debt, and Company Winding-up in Nineteenth-Century England* (Oxford: Clarendon, Press, 1995), p. 103; Ian P. H. Duffy, *Bankruptcy and Insolvency in London during the Industrial Revolution* (New York: Garland Publishing Inc, 1985), p. 72; Paul Langford, *A Polite and Commercial People – England 1727–1783* (Oxford: Clarendon Press, 1998), pp. 490–491.

7 Defoe, *Remarks*, p. 15; Anon. *The Christians Gazette: Or, Nice and Curious Speculations Chiefly Respecting the Invisible World* (London: 1713), p. 39; Thomas Baston, *Observation on Trade and a Publick Spirit* (London: 1732), p. 211.

8 "Royal Bounty from George III to the City of London to Discharge Debtors from Prison and to Persons Recommended by Deputies of Wards as Destitute and Needy", 1762, City of London: Courts of Law, LMA, CLA/040/08/008.

9 Anon. *An Abstract of His Majesties Commission … for the Relief of the Poore Prisoners* (London: 1624); Craig Muldrew, *The Economy of Obligation – The Culture of Credit and Social Relations in Early Modern England* (Basingstoke: Macmillan, 1998).

10 See: Anon. *Englands Dolefull Lamentation; or, the Cry of the Oppressed and Enslaved Commons of England: Set Forth in Two Several Petitions, the One Delivered to His Majesty, the Other Presented to His Excellency Sir Thomas Fairfax* (1647), p. 3; John Musgrave, *A Fourth Word to the Wise, or A Plaine Discovery of Englands Misery … Set forth in a Letter Written by a Prisoner in the Fleete* (1647); Anon. *A Brief Dolorous Remonstrance* (1648); Anon. *A Pitiful Remonstrance, or Just Complaint* (London: 1648); Anon. *The Prisoners Remonstrance* (London: 1649).

11 "An Act for Discharging Poor Prisoners Unable to Satisfie Their Creditors", 1649, in *Acts and Ordinances of the Interregnum, 1642–1660 Vol. II*, eds. C. H. Firth and R. S. Rait (London: 1911), pp. 240–241.

12 Jay Cohen, "The History of Imprisonment for Debt and Its Relation to the Development of Discharge in Bankruptcy", *Journal of Legal History* vol. 3 (1982), p. 158.

13 "An Act for the Relief of Creditors and Poor Prisoners", October 1653, in *Acts of the Interregnum*, pp. 753–764.

14 "An Act for the Releife and Release of Poore Distressed Prisoners for Debt", 1670, in *Statutes of the Realm Vol. V, 1628–80*, ed. John Raithby (1819), pp. 734–737.

15 "An Act for the Further Reliefe and Discharge of Poore Distressed Prisoners for Debt", 1678, in *Statutes Vol. V*, pp. 887–889; "An Act for Reliefe of Poore

Prisoners for Debt or Damages", 1690, in *Statutes of the Realm Vol. VI, 1685–94*, ed. John Raithby (1819), pp. 248–250.

16 "An Act for the Relief of Poor Prisoners for Debt", 1702, 1 Anne, c.19; "An Act for the Discharge out of Prison of Such Insolvent Debtors as Shall Serve, or Procure a Person to Serve, in Her Majesty's Fleet or Army", 1703, 2&3 Anne, c.10; "An Humble Proposal to the Honble House of Commons for Raising 30 or 40 Thousand Men for His Majestys Service out of the Insolvent Debtors", no date (1714–1720), Cholmondeley Papers: Groups of Treasury Papers, Cambridge University Library: Department of Archives and Modern Manuscripts, Ch(H) Political Papers 51,70; Paul, *Poverty of Disaster*, p. 103.

17 "An Act for the Relief of Insolvent Debtors, by Obliging Their Creditors to Accept the Utmost Satisfaction They Are Capable to Make, and Restoring Them to Their Liberty", 1711, 10 Anne, c.29; Emily Kadens, "The Last Bankrupt Hanged: Balancing Incentives in the Development of Bankruptcy Law", *Duke Law Journal* vol. 59, no. 7 (April 2010), p. 1261.

18 "An Act for Relief of Insolvent Debtors, and for the More Easy Discharge of Bankrupts out of Execution, after Their Certificates Allowed", 1719, 6 George I, c.22.

19 "An Act for the Relief of Insolvent Debtors", 1724, 11 George I, c.21.

20 On fugitives see: Paul Hess Haagen, "Imprisonment for Debt in England and Wales", unpublished PhD thesis, University of Princeton (1986), pp. 312–352.

21 James Bolland, *Memoirs of James Bolland Formerly a Butcher Then Officer to the Sheriff of Surry, Afterwards Officer to the Sheriff of Middlesex, and Lately a Candidate for the Place of City Marshal; Executed at Tyburn, March 18. 1772, for Forgery* (London: 1772), p. 3.

22 "An Act for the Relief of Insolvent Debtors", 1736, 10 George II, c.26; "An Act for the Relief of Insolvent Debtors", 1742, 16 George II, c.17; "An Act for the Relief of Insolvent Debtors", 1747, 21 George II, c.31; "An Act for the Relief of Insolvent Debtors", 1755, 28 George II, c.13; "An Act for Relief of Insolvent Debtors", 1760, 1 George III, c.17.

23 6 George I, c.22; 11 George I, c.21; 10 George II, c.26; 21 George II, c.31; 28 George II, c.13; "An Act for the Relief of Insolvent Debtors; and for the Relief of Bankrupts, in certain cases", 1776, 16 George III, c.38; "Insolvent Debtors Relief Act (England)", 1811, 51 George III c.125.

24 *The London Magazine or Gentleman's Monthly Intelligencer, Vol. 31* (1762), p. 9.

25 "Humble Proposal", Ch(H)Political Papers 51,70.

26 Paul Hess Haagen, "Eighteenth Century English Society and the Debt Law", *in Social Control and the State – Historical and Comparative Essays*, eds. Stanley Cohen and Andrew Scull (Oxford: Basil Blackwell, 1986), pp. 222, 228–229; William Holdsworth, *A History of English Law Vol. VIII* (London: Methuen & co., 1925), p. 236.

27 Daniel Defoe, *Some Objections Humbly Offered to the Consideration of the Hon House of Commons, Relating to the Present Intended Relief of Prisoners* (London: 1729), pp. 4–6.

28 *World and Fashionable Advertiser*, 27th March 1787, no. 74.

29 Innes, "King's Bench Prison", p. 260; Roger Lee Brown, *A History of the Fleet Prison, London –The Anatomy of the Fleet* (Lampeter: Edwin Mellen Press, 1996), p. 145.

30 16 George III, c.38; see: "An Act for the Relief of Insolvent Debtors and for the Relief of Bankrupts in Certain Cases", 1774, 14 George III c.77.

31 *St. James's Chronicle or the British Evening Post*, 1st–3rd August 1776, no. 2403.

32 *Morning Chronicle and London Advertiser*, 3rd August 1776, no. 2248.

33 *Gazetteer and New Daily Advertiser*, 22nd June 1776, no. 14768.

34 *Public Advertiser*, 4th September 1776, no. 14640.
35 *Morning Chronicle and London Advertiser*, 27th August 1776, no. 2268.
36 *Morning Post and Daily Advertiser*, 3rd December 1776, no. 1282; *Public Advertiser*, 9th December 1780, no. 14405.
37 *Gazetteer and New Daily Advertiser*, 12th May 1777, no. 15043; *Morning Chronicle and London Advertiser*, 17th April 1778, no. 2780; *Morning Chronicle and London Advertiser*, 1st September 1781, no. 3836; Anon. *A List of the Members of the Guardians; or Society for the Protection of Trade against Swindlers and Sharpers* (London: 1799); *Daily Advertiser*, 24th October 1778, no. 14922.
38 See: *Morning Chronicle and London Advertiser*, 10th October 1776, no. 2306; *New Daily Advertiser*, no. 15043; *Gazetteer and New Daily Advertiser*, 5th December 1777, no. 15230; *Morning Post and Daily Advertiser*, 13th December 1777, no. 1606.
39 *Morning Chronicle and London Advertiser*, 13th April 1779, no. 3087. See: James Madison, "The Evolution of Commercial Credit Reporting Agencies in Nineteenth-Century America", *Business History Review* vol. 48, no. 2 (1974), p. 164; Rowena Olegario, *A Culture of Credit – Embedding Trust and Transparency in American Business* (London: Harvard University Press, 2006), p. 33.
40 *Gazetteer and New Daily Advertiser*, 23rd March 1778, no. 15321.
41 *St. James's Chronicle or the British Evening Post*, 21st–24th July 1781, no. 3183.
42 T. Brewman, *An Authentic List of Persons (Not Only in the Cities of London and Westminster, but also in the Counties in England and Scotland) Who Have Surrendered Themselves, in Consequence of the Late Act, into the Custody of the Marshal of the King's Bench Prison, between the Seventh of June, 1780, and the Thirty First of January, 1781* (London: 1781), p. 1.
43 *St. James's Chronicle or the British Evening Post*, 24th–26th July 1781, no. 3184.
44 Holdsworth, *English Law Vol. VIII*, p. 236; Tim Hitchcock and Robert Brink Shoemaker, *London Lives – Poverty, Crime and the Making of a Modern City, 1690–1800* (Cambridge: Cambridge University Press, 2015), p. 103; Jerry White, "Pain and Degradation in Georgian London: Life in the Marshalsea Prison", *History Workshop Journal* vol. 68 (Autumn 2009), p. 93; Eric Stockdale, *A Study of Bedford Prison 1660–1877* (Bedford: The Bedfordshire Historical Record Society, 1977), p. 47.
45 "An Act for the Discharge of Certain Insolvent Debtors", 1794, 34 George III c.69.
46 "List of Prisoners in the Compter Made Per out of the Ct of Ald", 15th December 1724, Wood Street Compter later Giltspur Street Compter, LMA, CLA/028/01/043.
47 Paul, *Poverty of Disaster*, p. 104.
48 *London Gazette*, 19th–22nd July 1794, no. 13686; 5th–8th August 1797, no. 14034; 14th–18th July 1801, no. 15386; "Commitment Registers", 1793–1795, Fleet Prison, TNA, PRIS 1/15.
49 *London Gazette*, 7th–10th June 1755, no. 9483, 26th–30th May 1761, no. 10108, 25th–28th April 1772, no. 11243, 26th–30th July 1774, no. 11478 ('the last Nineteen Years and Nine Months within the Walls of the Fleet Prison'), 1st–4th June 1776, no. 11671, and 2nd–6th June 1778, no. 11880.
50 "List of Prisoners Handed over by the Sheriffs to Their Successors on 28 Sept Annually, with Notes of Occurrences during the Subsequent Year", 1775, Wood Street Compter later Giltspur Street Compter, LMA, CLA/028/01/021.
51 16 George III, c.38; Anon. *The Tyburn Chronicle Vol. IV* (London: 1768), pp. 199–200; Kadens, "The Last Bankrupt Hanged".
52 Gustav Peebles, "Whitewashing and Leg-Bailing: On the Spatiality of Debt", *Social Anthropology* vol. 20, no. 4 (2012).

53 While this translation, using the term 'Acts of Grace' appears to refer to other legislative amnesties, it is clear from the context of his remarks upon King Theodore of Corsica's application in 1755, as well as other publications of his text reading 'an Insolvent Act frequently opens all the gaols ... there is a kind of infamy attached to it' that von Archenholtz was referring to Acts of Insolvency. Johann Wilhelm von Archenholtz, *A View of the British Constitution and, of the Manners and Customs of the People of England* (Edinburgh: 1794), p. 286; Johann Wilhelm von Archenholtz, *A Picture of England Vol. II* (London: 1789), p. 66.

54 "List of Prisoners Handed over by the Sheriffs to Their Successors on 28 Sept Annually, with Notes of Occurrences during the Subsequent Year", 1803, Wood Street Compter later Giltspur Street Compter, LMA, CLA/028/01/033.

55 See, for example: Jane West, *Poems and Plays Vol. II* (London: 1799), p. 176; Samuel Jackson, *Family Secrets, Literary and Domestic Vol. IV* (London: 1797), p. 324; Brewman, *Authentic List*.

56 Natasha Glaisyer, "'The Most Universal Intelligencers' – The Circulation of the *London Gazette* in the 1690s", *Media History* vol. 23, no. 2 (2017), p. 263.

57 Anon. *The Adventures of Mr Loveill Vol. II* (London: 1750), p. 64.

58 Anon. *The Life and Writings of the Rev. William Dodd* (London: 1777), pp. 23–25.

59 William Jackson, *The New and Complete Newgate Calendar Vol. V* (London: 1795), p. 116.

60 Jane Elizabeth Moore, *Genuine Memoirs of Jane Elizabeth Moore. Late of Bermondsey, in the County of Surry. Written by Herself: Containing the Singular Adventures of Herself and Family. Vol. III* (London: 1786), p. 211.

61 John Donaldson, *Sketches of a Plan for an Effectual and General Reformation of Life and Manners* (London: 1794), pp. 69–70.

62 Alex Pitofsky, "The Warden's Court Martial: James Oglethorpe and the Politics of Eighteenth-Century Prison Reform", *Eighteenth Century Life* vol. 24, no. 1 (2000), p. 89.

6 Private enterprise

Operating a debtors' prison

While the debtors' prisons hardly had a glowing reputation in print – it was far easier to take a stand against imprisonment than for the needs of commerce – the various monetary charges to which prisoners were put during their commitment provoked almost universal disdain. One of John Howard's principal recommendations in his 1777 *State of the Prisons* was that charges for debtors ought to be abolished: 'No prisoner should be subject to any demand of Fees. The Gaoler should have a salary in lieu of them; and so should the Turnkeys'.[1] He put his philosophy into practice by occasionally paying for the release of poor debtors he met in his travels who, having paid their debts, remained in gaol for their fees.[2] However, Howard's description of the gaol fees was, when placed against many contemporary discussions, relatively tame. Jacob Ilive in 1759 described gaol fees as 'cruel and barbarous' as well as 'oppressive and unreasonable' while an extract in the *Public Advertiser* in 1780 deemed charges 'an amazing Exertion of the most profligate Despotism'.[3] Another newspaper letter writer concluded the mounting of a debtor's bill represented 'torture' and 'an outrage on humanity' while the firebrand Common Councillor of London Josiah Dornford repeatedly described fees as 'evil' and a 'disgrace of our country'.[4] These sums, paid at various moments across the imprisonment experience with release usually being contingent upon their full satisfaction, enraged reformers and prisoners alike. Numerous prisoner petitions to civic courts and to benevolent societies declared that, despite the fact they were 'at last discharged by ... Creditors' they remained 'detained for Chamber Rent and Prison Fees' which they claimed to be unable to pay.[5] The frequently passed Insolvency Acts, designed to clear the prisons, generally recognised that significant numbers of prisoners unable to secure release had already satisfied their creditors but remained 'in gaols only for fees'.[6] Scholars have also seen these charges as adding insult to injury for those caught up in debt imprisonment. Tim Hitchcock and Robert Shoemaker provided a typical summary of the historical view of prison keepers when they asserted 'debtors' prisons form an extreme example of the eighteenth century's unreformed system of prison governance' as 'the position of keeper was purchased and the prison was run for profit'. Their short discussion of the prisons depicts keepers as cost cutters squeezing blood from stones – 'keepers were usually unwilling to hire the officers needed to run the prison' depending 'on the prisoners themselves' for daily management 'to save costs' while 'providing a minimum standard of care'.[7] Philip Woodfine similarly decried that 'citizens, now imprisoned through misfortune only' had 'to bribe their keepers to treat them with the ordinary respect due to those in civic life'.[8]

That fees and other charges were almost universal in the eighteenth-century debtors' prisons, that the gaols were run for profit, and that keepers cut costs where possible is abundantly clear. Beyond whether they were an unjust or cruel burden upon the already impoverished, fees and rents represented a potential weakness to the effectiveness of debt imprisonment as a means for creditors to secure speedy repayment. Even a few shillings which were extracted by bailiffs and sponging-house keepers or disappeared into the pockets of fellow prisoners through garnish might represent an impediment of repayment. However, while fees and rents could indeed be excessive on occasion, unlike at sponging houses these payments served a necessary practical purpose without which debt imprisonment would have been financially untenable. Indeed, rather than a hinderance, they represented a saving for creditors and citizens by enabling the financial self-sufficiency of prisons. Forcing debtors to pay for their own suffering was almost certainly cruel, however, focus on this inhumanity (which might be seen to be less cruel than other aspects of the contemporary or even modern justice systems) clouds the fact that someone had to pay for prisons. The cost saving advantages of these institutions for businesspeople were lost if they were required to pay for the imprisonment either directly through the groats or indirectly through increased taxation. The right to run prisons was farmed out as part of the general system of patronage and corruption which pervaded English administration in the eighteenth century, but it also reduced overall civic costs, keepers being required in most instances to pay for prison upkeep out of their income. Gaolers should not solely be depicted as greedy individuals who abused their office. Rightly, they were businesspeople (both men and occasionally women) seeking to turn a profit by minimising costs and maximising income. There were, as will be shown and allowed, some particularly bad actors who beat money out of debtors or threw them into chains and solitary confinement. Yet, rather than being a contrast between cruelty and enlightenment, such practices were the difference between poor and sensible business administration.

In this chapter, the economics of institution management are explored from the perspective of those who spent the most time in the prisons – their keepers. It discusses how prisons were managed, exploring the background of keepers, the sums involved in operating a gaol, and the ways in which revenue was generated to cover costs as well as analysing how extortionate charges actually were. By studying the surviving accounts of prisons, particularly where rents or fees were arbitrarily reduced, the necessity of these fees is demonstrated and the potential disadvantage to civic authorities of abolishing fees. Additionally, different management styles are discussed demonstrating that while fees and rents were a necessity, their scale and the tactics used to procure them were very much a business choice on the part of keepers, questioning whether a focus on short-term profits ever led to sustainable prison-keeping.

★★

Early modern debt imprisonment was a business and, if done well, a highly profitable one with an apparently inexhaustible supply of products and customers. For creditors, the prisons functioned as pawnbrokers to coerce payment, and for prison officials they represented a similarly commercial venture. The prisons had their journeymen in the form of turnkeys who curated the wares, and they had their master craftsmen – the keepers – who invested their own capital in the business. Just as all good trades did, its everyday function created a variety of other business opportunities for suppliers of necessary goods, whether they be bailiffs supplying prisoners who might take their own fees or those providing food and drink to the confined (sometimes imprisoned themselves). Competition to supply the prisons was fierce, reflecting the aura of profitability which surrounded them with various civic officers lobbying against one another for the right to arrest.[9] James Guthrie, having officiated at Newgate unofficially for eight years, was forced to seek formal appointment as Chaplain in 1734 to protect his place from rivals, pleading his poverty to stay in post despite 'that painful office' which he held certainly paying him more than a subsistence income.[10]

The mercantile aspects of prison administration were most evident in the appointment of those in charge of gaols. Unlike chaplains who at least presumably had some clerical education, few prison managers had been appointed due to their suitability for the role, many having had little experience of the prisons before taking over. Gaolers regularly came from trade backgrounds, seeking control over a particular prison as a vehicle of social advancement, the position of keeper granting them a civic importance which mere financial success could not. Thomas Griffith who began life as the lowly son of a gunner at the castle in York was a typical example. Trained as a tanner, Griffith made a healthy fortune and handed off his successful business at only fifty to his son so as to take control of the city's debtors' prison at the castle in the late 1730s. He received no salary and the benefit of this position was that it allowed him a decade later upon his retirement to be styled as 'Thomas Griffith … Gentleman'.[11] Similarly, before becoming the keeper of the Marshalsea in the 1720s William Acton had been a successful butcher though, unlike Griffith, he at least served a very brief stint as turnkey of the prison before rising to management. He spent much of his time in the gaol hobnobbing with upper-class prisoners, revelling in the elevated social status he had as the master of great men of the city. John Grano, a noted trumpeter who before his financial decline had played for the King in the Horse Guards and was part of Handel's orchestra, had frequent encounters with Acton during his imprisonment in the Marshalsea 1728–1729. While Grano was generous towards 'my Governor' and evidently proud of the favour the keeper bestowed upon him, it is clear Acton used the musician as an accessory to gain access to fashionable company. In August 1728 Grano recorded how 'Mr Acton was so good to invite me to go to a club when the Black Book was shut', the ending of the administrative day. There Grano 'play'd on my German Flute' and later 'Mr Acton sent for my Trumpet ... assoon as it came I entertain'd the Company on the Same', being required when they returned in the small hours of the morning to play 'a Tune or Two ... for ... Mrs Acton'. Being able to trot out famous prisoners like Grano for private performances allowed Acton to hob-nob with London's theatrical and civic elite, as well as to treat friends and members of his family. While Grano was happy to comply, the extent to which he had a choice was surely limited.[12]

Most keepers paid for this privilege handsomely.[13] Acton was not technically the court appointed marshal of the prison. As a committee investigating the prison reported in 1729,

> the Marshalsea doth belong to the ... King's Household ... That Sir Philip Meadows, then Knight Marshal ... did ... constitute John Darby Gent ... Keeper of the Prison ... during the term of his natural life. ... Darby, contrary

to the wishes and knowledge of the court

> hath let the Profits of the said Offices ... to William Acton Butcher ... for £140 per annum ... and did let the Benefit of Lodging of the Prisoners ... for the further Yearly Rent of £260 to be paid to him, clear of all Taxes.[14]

Acton and Darby were seen to have been acting improperly despite similar systems being ingrained into the functioning of other prisons. The multi-layered system of farming out the right to run the Fleet prison dated back to the sixteenth century and continued largely unchallenged during the 1700s.[15] Thomas Bambridge, the most infamous prison keeper of the eighteenth century whose abject cruelty led to attempted prison reform in the 1720s, paid £5,000 for the wardenship of the Fleet from John Huggins who had himself purchased it from the crown appointed Earl of Clarendon.[16] This activity was not confined to the chief prisons in London. Upon his visit to the small Liverpool Borough Gaol, John Howard was told by the gaoler, Rosendale Allen, that despite taking a £10 salary the prison was actually run by his 'Deputy who pays him £65 a year' for the privilege.[17] Even though "professional" prison keepers became more common in the late eighteenth century, it was still worthy of note that John Kirby, the keeper of the Wood Street Compter, had somehow taken over in 1766 without bribery. According to *The Annual Register*, 'although they might, as their predecessors were heretofore accustomed, have sold the same for £1,500', Kirby was given the compter by 'Sheriffs Trecothic and Kennet ... entirely gratis', a claim repeated by Josiah Dornford writing in 1786 that while 'Mr West [keeper of the Poultry Compter] purchased his place at a large expence, Mr Kirby had his given him'.[18]

"Bribery" of officials and continued payment of rent on the gaol to the city were only the beginning of costs for potential keepers. As with Acton, keepers were usually liable for all relevant taxes including at various points across the period Land, Hearth, and Window taxes as well as Church tythes. In 1726, the recently appointed Philip Jennings of the Poultry Compter wrote angrily to the Court of Alderman when the administrators of the poor rate for St Mildred's informed him that he was required to pay 2s 6d per month 'and threaten[ed] to distrain [me] in case of refusal'. While he may have felt 'oppressed and aggrieved by the said rate' the court appears not to have interceded on his behalf.[19] Furthermore, though weekly bread and meat (diversified in the later eighteenth century to include vegetables) were provided by the corporation and debtors were regularly required to purchase their own coals, keepers were responsible for maintaining the physical state of the prisons, a role which (based upon the reports of reformers) they fulfilled with varying enthusiasm.[20]

A cost which even the cheapest keepers could not avoid entirely was the payment of wages to prison staff, though some institutions (particularly those containing felons) were better staffed than others.[21] At the small gaol of Ludgate in the 1760s, the sole turnkey made £13 a year, the single largest cost the keeper was put to (though taxes combined cost him £21 6s 8d), alongside £5 4s for minor staff.[22] Where prisons maintained what might be construed a full staff, costs were significant. A week of bills survive from Newgate Prison in 1817; while by this decade its population mostly consisted of felons as well as being a period of more diligent management following administrative reform c.1805, it still provides an indicative sense of operational costs at larger gaols. The vouchers and receipts detail payment for the three Turnkeys at £2 2s each, seven Under Turnkeys at £1 10s, four Assistant Turnkeys on £1 1s, two Watchmen also on £1 1s, and a Lay Clark receiving 2s 6d for a total of £23 4s 6d per week. Additionally, four 'pumpers', four 'Wards Women', and a 'Gates man, Yards Man, & Passage Man', presumably all hired from among the prisoners, received one shilling each a week though it was only paid to them every three weeks. On this particular week, the keeper also had to pay wages relating to repair work on the prison, employing three carpenters and a painter paid 6s alongside three bricklayers and eight labourers all paid 3s 6d. Finally, listed among the incidental costs that week which included 'Gunpowder for Watchmen 2s' and '4 pr sheets washing & mending for Mens Infirmary 3s 2d', were fees paid for the work of the coroner at 4s 6d and for a 'Midwife to Sarah Hewell 10s 6d'. In payment for work alone, this week cost Mr Brown the keeper £27 10s 6d; even if only paying regular salaries Brown could expect therefore to expend around £1,200 a year.[23] Many keepers, including Brown, attempted to reduce these salary costs by combining jobs and employing prisoners in support or managerial roles. At Newgate in the 1720s, the keeper allowed the wives of his turnkeys to run the prison taproom specifically 'as Escapes are often contriving in the Goal of Newgate, the Turn Keys wives being constantly there do often prevent their villainous designs by giving timely Notice to their Husbands', these women therefore working as unpaid assistants.[24] Meanwhile, the appointment of debtors to positions usually known as stewards, as well as handling administrative matters such as the distribution of charitable gifts, helped to maintain order among the population at a discount. Stewards provoked less disconcertion than the turnkeys having been selected by the prisoners as well as usually being paid by them, contributing to a system of government by consent, a situation which was particularly necessary at prisons such as the Fleet which regularly did not maintain any staff in the gaol overnight.[25]

All costs, including start-up charges and everyday expenses, needed to be offset through direct income and at a rate which allowed for some degree of profit for the businessowner. Salaries were far from universal though were more common by the second half of the century. Of the 208 prisons for which Howard specified whether salaries were paid or not in 1777, 131 keepers received some kind of salary though the sum paid occasionally did not cover the rent they were obliged to pay sheriffs. However, seventy-three of the salaried posts were in bridewell prisons and a further eight received a salary in lieu of being able to charge fees. Only nineteen keepers of non-bridewell prisons were paid more than £20 a year while seventeen received £10 or less, the keeper of Litchfield town gaol receiving just £2 a year.[26] To provide keepers with a realistic income, they charged debtors for almost any operation requiring a prison official. While an individual gaol's charges were theoretically fixed, being displayed in tables hung in the prison, the cost of specific actions varied apparently arbitrarily between individual institutions as did what could and could not be charged for.[27]

Common to almost all prisons was the commitment fee, probably the bitterest charge as the arrestee was informed how much their own capture had just cost them. While these were usually added to the final bill due at release, those with cash on hand might be liberated of it or have coats and hats seized on the way to their cell. Reportedly, during a particularly corrupt era at the Wood Street Compter in the seventeenth century, a fresh fee was charged for the opening of each door in the winding passageways until a prisoner could pay no more and was interred in the nearest cell.[28] However, by the second half of the eighteenth century, entrance fees had frequently been reduced to under 5s and some gaols in provincial areas or those which contained poorer prisoners such as the Marshalsea, had disposed of them altogether. At the superior court prisons, fees paid for entering the prison remained relatively high, both the Fleet and King's Bench charging over a pound in the 1770s though the full sum depended on the type of accommodation sought and the nature of the action which committed them as fees were owed to the

Marshall, Deputy Marshall, Turnkey, Clerk of the Papers, and the four Tip-staffs separately.[29]

Further fees were charged upon release and, apart from at the superior court prisons, were typically higher than that paid at commitment (c.10s) presumably as it was expected a debtor who had satisfied their obligations had money on hand. These fees applied to debtors of all types and even death was not treated as reason for an exemption.[30] In 1728 at the Marshalsea, Grano was 'inform'd a Dead Carcase was stop'd for … Fees as they were carrying the same to be buried' while in 1709 Elizabeth Taylor was forced to apply for relief from the Court of Alderman as 'Mr Bigrave [the keeper of Wood Street] would not permit her Husband who dyed there on Tuesday to be Buried till Saturday Morning Because she could not pay the [5s] Fees that was due to him from her Husband'.[31] Prisons which no longer charged commitment fees in the second half of the century still regularly extracted a release fee while some even varied the release charge by the type of exit procured. When prisoners were released from York Castle gaol, 'the under-sheriff demands from each debtor five shillings and fourpence, if discharged by the plaintiff; but if by *supersedeas*, seven shillings and eightpence'.[32] Turnkeys might also informally take fresh fees to ensure debtors were squeezed as much as possible before returning to the world.[33] Having had to expend significant capital in persuading creditors to grant them a discharge, fees might therefore prolong imprisonment with debtors regularly declaring themselves imprisoned only for remaining fees.[34] Thomas Grimstead, imprisoned in the Fleet 1735–1737, was released by the Insolvency Act only for his fees two months after clearing his debts in full suggesting that charges did delay release though not indefinitely.[35] Remarkably, at superior court prisons, it may have been possible for prisoners of character to achieve release without immediate payment of fees. William Rayment, having been discharged of all the actions against him in 1780, was noted as released after 'Notes of hand given for fees & Rent £2 2s' thus acquiring a new debt the very moment he was leaving prison.[36]

A variety of other fees might be charged during the imprisonment experience including those for optional benefits. Large numbers of prisoners at the Fleet and King's Bench paid regular fees for the right to live in the semi-autonomous area around the gaols known as the *rules* or for unaccompanied day-passes as *day rulers*.[37] While such liberties did not extend to other gaols, debtors with cash could occasionally pay for the right to be taken from the prison under guard during the day to conduct business or legal meetings. During the early months of his confinement at the Marshalsea, Grano organised a concert in an attempt to raise money. While much of the preparation such as transcribing the sheet music could be conducted from his cell, he needed to be able to travel into the city to scout locations and to perform the concert itself, the costs of paying for guards eating into his minimal profits.[38]

The most regular "optional" charge, however, was that occasioned by rent. Prisoners confined on the Common Side or within Charity Wards could avoid paying rent, though many prisoners actively sought the comforts that came with paid cells. Unlike commitment fees which might be added to the final bill, rent had to be paid each week and repeated failure led to eviction. Simon Wood, confined at the Fleet in the 1730s, described how prisoners were kept in the gloomy Common Side

> till they can raise £1 8s 8d then they are dubb'd Gentlemen on the Master-Side, but often, after their Ambition, or sometimes frighten'd of Time, or their Inability and long Confinement, turn'd down again for Non-payment of Rent, and often detain'd six or eight Months, after Discharged, for Chamber-Rent.

Wood himself

> had the Misfortune to run near 40s in Debt to the Warden, for Chamber-Rent, for which Sum he was, about twelve Months ago, dismissed his Room, being forced to walk the Prison to keep Warmth within him, during the Winter-Season,

writing his account of the Fleet to raise money so 'he will be intitled to a room'.[39] Charges for access to the Master's Side were frequently worth paying for and not just for the increased comfort they provided but for the greater ability to conduct business. A cell of one's own offered the chance to cater to external clients from within the prison who would have balked at the stinking crowded wards though for some prisoners comfort and distinction alone motivated expenditure. Grano, despite residing in a shared room on the Master's Side, elected to remove to single-occupancy room charging a higher rent which he renovated extensively at his own expense. Though this offered an important psychological boost to the unlucky trumpeter, it can hardly be said to have contributed to Grano's ability to repay his debts.[40] The attractiveness of such rooms with higher rents, particularly pulling debtors to the Fleet or King's Bench, was thus a real detractor on the probability of speedy repayment for creditors in a manner that fees – deferrable until the end of confinement – were not.[41] However, debtors with as little concern as John Grano were far from the norm and such individuals, paying high rents, allowed keepers to afford avoiding charging even nominal rents to the majority on the Common Side. Thus, while individual creditors may have been irked by a profligate prisoner, such debtors were a significant contributor to the effective operation of debt imprisonment as a system.

Beyond the fact that not all prisoners paid it, rent was not necessarily financially debilitating nor were rates particularly exorbitant when placed within the context of the contemporary market. There has yet to be a study of eighteenth-century rents comprehensive enough for a full comparison between prison and non-prison expenditure, however, a survey of declarations at the Old Bailey can provide some indication of the comparative costs of residence to imprisonment.[42] In 108 trials (1740–1800), witnesses, litigants, or defendants

Table 6.1 Declarations of Rent Paid by Accommodation Type during
Old Bailey Trails in London, 1740–1800

Annual Rent	All Renters	House/Building	Room/Lodging
<£5	13	2	11
£5–10	57	13	44
£11–20	19	14	5
£21–50	14	14	0
£51–100	3	2	1
>£100	2	2	0
Total	108	47	61
Mean Yearly Rent	£18 10s	£32 10s 9d	£7 14s 9d

explicitly stated the amount of rent they paid and what type of residence they
rented in London (see Table 6.1).[43] These declarations reveal that while prison
rents were not irrelevant, they were usually below or at market rates. While
some rents were low, 80% of declarations were equivalent to more than the
2s 6d per week[44] rent of the Master's Side at prisons in the City of London
(or £6 10s per year). Furthermore, while prison rents remained largely static,
the annual average rent increased from £10 1740–1749 to over £20 by 1800,
even those only renting single rooms (47%) seeing a similar annual rent rise
from c.£4 to c.£8. Poorer prisoners therefore were likely to find prison rents
more burdensome than those used to paying £50 a year for a whole house,
but they were also less likely to seek rooms which required them. Rents such
as the 1s 9d per week (£4 11s per year) for access to the Marshalsea Master's
Side may have even provided a higher quality of accommodation per penny
than some Southwark debtors usually experienced. With the possibility that
debtors may have been paying less in rent in prison it becomes difficult to
describe the costs as particularly burdensome or cruel though it is probable
that those with families continued paying rent on external properties in addition to their cell.

How much income these charges produced was highly dependent upon the
size of the individual institution and the composition of its population. Some
gaols were never profitable from fees alone, particularly those which housed
small numbers of debtors, fees for felons and miscreants being minimal. All
but three of the bridewell keepers in Howard's survey were paid a salary
which was also frequently larger than that paid to other gaolers, eleven of
the twenty best-paid keepers being those in charge of bridewells. The keeper
of Wakefield Bridewell was paid £105 per annum (a recent raise from £80)
despite catering to just nineteen prisoners in October 1776.[45] Many bridewell
keepers still felt the need to supplement their income from the work of the
inhabitants conducted as part of their reformation. At Morpeth Bridwell,
'the Keeper, a Clothier, employs his prisoners … Men and Boys … at two
shillings a week' and the women at 1s 6d. There were no fees and though
he received a salary of £30 a year, as the three prison rooms were 'close and

dirty' compared with a 'large … warehouse and workshop … above it another workshop', their textile labour apparently constituted the bulk of the
keeper's income.[46] Newgate's manager was paid the highest salary of any
prison keeper in 1777 at £200 a year. Though he charged fees to his felons,
rent paying debtors who raised the most capital constituted less than 20% of
the inhabitants reducing his income potential and necessitating the corporation paying him such a large salary.[47] While the various keepers of Newgate
were able to make a healthy profit, the existence of salaries at more minor
gaols before the 1790s suggests that the fees of individual prisons did not produce sufficient income. Similarly, where prisons explicitly failed to provide
a keeper with a salary it can be inferred that sufficient income was extracted
from prisoners to make seeking their administration attractive.

Even where they did not require salaries, not all gaolers were wealthy.
Operators of the superior court prisons could comfortably charge high commitment fees and rents but those managing borough or provincial prisons
had much more precarious revenue streams. The variation of income due to
the nature of prison populations is demonstrated by an estimation of income
in Figure 6.1 for the Fleet Prison, the Wood Street (later Giltspur Street)
Compter, and Lancaster Castle Gaol based on the fees and rents recorded by
Howard (the reformer noting in 1777 that most gaols had not changed their
fees since the 1720s). The Fleet charged an array of gaol fees which were due
to different officials as well as for access to the *rules*; for the purpose of this
estimation only the fees paid by all prisoners (for commitment and release) to
the keeper and rents have been included. These amounted, by 1777, to £1 6s
8d for commitment to the Master's Side with 2s 6d rent or 13s 4d entrance

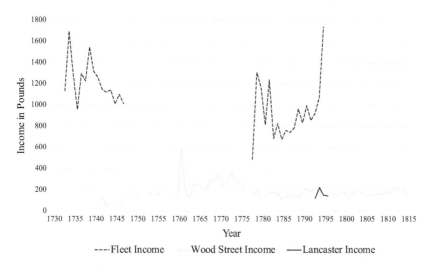

Figure 6.1 Estimated Income from Commitment Fess, Release Fees, and Rents at the
Fleet, Wood Street Compter, and Lancaster Castle 1730–1815.

to the Common Side at 1s 3d per week. The Charity Ward was free to enter and did not charge rent though prisoners from all wards paid 7s 4d at discharge. At Wood Street, those entering the Common Side paid no rent or commitment fee, only a 10s discharge fee, though 5s was charged for access to the Master's Side along with half a crown for rent and 10s 8d at release. By the 1770s, Lancaster Castle no longer charged entrance fees in any form though varied the discharge fees at 8s for *supersedeas*, 5s 8d for procuring the Insolvency Act, and 10s 6d for all others. Some prisoners were also able to access the Master's Side for 7d a week, the remainder paying no rent.[48] While it was possible to break down those released from Lancaster by their appropriate discharge fees, it is not possible to know how many or which debtors took advantage of the various wards at any of the gaols. Differentiating based on debts owed is precarious – Simon Wood, though spending much of his time in the Charity Ward, owed £300 while other debtors owing small sums might be found in the highest rent rooms or taking the *rules*.[49] However, as there is no other metric of differentiation, loose categories were constructed based upon debt. For Lancaster, as the period covered by the registers was short, it was assumed that the majority owing below £40 did not pay rent. As the recording of debts was more irregular in the other registers, and the value of a figure such as £40 changed across the period studied, rough shares of those confined per year were used to estimate rent in the London gaols. At the Fleet, 10% per year were assumed to be rent-free on the Charity Ward (reflecting the overall share owing less than £20) and 55% took the Master's Side based on those owing more than £100 while 45% of debtors committed to Wood Street, excluding those from the Court of Requests, were similarly assumed to be rent payers. At both London prisons, renters were able to pay half the rate if they agreed to share a room. To compensate, the average number of weeks debtors remained committed each year was multiplied by two-thirds of the full rent and again by the number of prisoners within each rent category. These figures are not an exact calculation of income but an indication of variation over time, the relative importance of fees or rents, and the difference between the gaols.

The separation between gaol incomes in Figure 6.1 (without the application of operational costs) is striking. Superior court prison keepers could expect comfortable accounts as, beyond the high numbers of debtors under their care, they made more money per prisoner than the other gaolers. At the Fleet, the keeper earned £3–6 a year per prisoner averaging at £4 10s while compter prisoners only brought in 13–38s per year (an average of 24s) and the gaoler of Lancaster made just 10–19s per prisoner a year. Even when annual commitment rates at Wood Street and the Fleet were relatively similar in the early 1780s, this did not translate into comparative earnings principally because the Fleet's warden only made c.29% of his income from fees for commitment and discharge which represented 42% of the Wood Street keeper's revenue due to the shorter average commitment length. Salaries were not paid to the keepers at the compter or the castle before the 1790s and their personal income was reliant upon fees. This became particularly problematic in borough gaols after 1785 when discharge fees for those committed by the Court of Requests were abolished. This was a significant threat to Wood Street's keeper John Kirby, the reformer Josiah Dornford complaining in 1786 Kirby 'has petitioned the Court, and they are going to give him a large sum of money too, by way of compensation for the loss of the Court of [Request] fees'.[50] While Dornford was outraged that the keeper was being compensated for losing what he regarded as an immoral profit, the businessowner was right to seek such a financial cushion to protect the viability of the gaol. In 1787 income per prisoner fell to its lowest ever rate of 13s 8d due to the 112 Court of Request debtors paying nothing towards their confinement. Fees constituted 56% of income in 1784 – roughly 50% of commitments coming from the Court – but by 1790 they had fallen to just 35%. Though suffering a brief drop to £121, Kirby's income ultimately did not suffer without these fees and grew steadily from £171 in 1784 to c.£200 by 1790 due entirely to the higher numbers of non-Court prisoners being committed to the gaol without whom profitability would have been questionable.

The precariousness of income was even more pronounced at Lancaster due to its lower fees. While the keeper of Lancaster Castle, John Higgin, made roughly the same as his London counterpart in the period studied, this was based on the rapid turnover and higher number of prisoners, discharge fees contributing c.60% of his income.[51] Any significant decline in commitment would have threatened income greatly. Additionally, though felons in the castle constituted a minority, the keeper drew significant income from the county related to them including £5 for each transportation. While this reflected the added expenses of administering such prisoners, it was also probably necessary to ensure that reputable individuals would want to run the gaol.[52] The lower precarious income of non-superior court debtors' prisons probably encouraged keepers to explore additional revenue streams (such as sales of ale or charging additional fees) and to attempt to increase the number of prisoners electing to become rent payers with both carrot and stick – the Common Sides need not have been the dark holes they frequently became.[53] When Kirby was eventually provided with a £30 salary, he was also granted an additional £150 a year 'in lieu of his tap' suggesting a commensurate income from alcohol on top of that received by fees and rents in previous decades.[54] Profits from taprooms could be extensive even if rented out. In 1792 the keeper of the Fleet received from the operator of the tap '15s per Butt on Porter and Amber [ale] … and 4s 6d per dozen on Wine' which prisoners drank; the c.115 prisoners residing in the Fleet that year only needed to drink 248 butts across the year (roughly five pints per person per day) to exceed his estimated existing income from fees and rents.[55] Some gaolers might credibly be described simply as innkeepers, operating a monopoly within their confined kingdom.

The charges put to debtors and the incomes they generated were smaller than the outrage they provoked, although it is unsurprising debtors complained about having to pay for almost every element of prison life even when treated well. However, while they irked debtors, if costs had been transferred to creditors, including those offset by the city such as providing food, then using imprisonment to coerce payment would have proved untenable, with charges exceeding benefits for many plaintiffs. At Lancaster Castle Gaol, just over half of prisoners who were awarded groats – maintenance payments of 4d a day – were released when their creditors refused to pay. This only represented debtors who could afford to sue for the release suggesting more creditors probably balked at any actual cost of confinement.[56] Similarly, it seems improbable that local authorities could have paid for the administration of debtors' prisons without also applying fees and rents or by imposing significant tax increases upon the wider community. If the compter figure of an income of roughly 24s per year per prisoner replicated across the capital and represented a similar amount to the cost of administering a prisoner, even exempting the Fleet the City of London would have needed to raise an extra c.£1,800 a year from taxation to avoid fees and rents alongside existing contributions for chaplains, doctors, and weekly food deliveries.

Where keepers received salaries, they were often still expected to procure the majority of their income from debtors and to be essentially self-sufficient, greatly reducing financial burdens on corporations and county governments. The cash book of Samuel Newport, the keeper of the New Prison in Clerkenwell, makes clear the benefits to the wider civic area of fees and rents. This gaol, rebuilt alongside the nearby House of Correction in the 1770s, was primarily associated with its felon population awaiting trial though regularly housed poorer debtors.[57] In his cash book, kept between April 1790 and March 1795, Newport detailed the total amount expended on salaries and 'sundries' as well as the sum in the same period raised through various unspecified fees and rents. Across the period Newport expended a total of £1,178 17s in administering the prison, raising £1,274 16s 10d for an overall profit of £95 19s 10d irregularly distributed. This profit was not for Newport's benefit as he received an unwavering salary of £300 from the city following a change of policy since 1777, presumably designed to prevent abuse or exploitation of Clerkenwell's mostly poor prisoners as the keeper had previously received only £30.[58] When the prison's accounts were positive, the city made a commensurate saving by deducting the excess revenue from the keeper's salary. In the years of the surviving cash book, the city paid out to Newport £260 4s 7d in 1791 followed by £214 15s, £264 8s 11d, £313 2s 9d, and £350 8s 11d in each year up to 1795. During the year, Newport was expected to cover any losses. Out of eighty-five recorded payment periods (each lasting roughly two to three weeks), the keeper made a loss fifty-four times, ranging from 10d in November 1792 to £13 19s 2d in June 1794. Annual costs varied little (between £224 and £249) but income was far more erratic, the loss of profitability appearing to arise from a declining prison population similar to that observed for Wood Street in this era. Twenty-nine losses occurred in the thirty-two payment periods after March 1793 and annual income fell as low as £189 by 1795. For Newport, these periods of loss were irrelevant once his salary was paid (the amount being guaranteed), though to ensure his own solvency during the year he was presumably keen to bring in rents and fees where due. For the city meanwhile, though they paid larger sums than hoped for when rents fell, the increased annual charge was still a vast saving on expenditure without fees or rents.[59]

The precariousness of profitability made prisons which relied on debtors electing to be confined there even more mercantile by their need to attract customers, advertising their gentility, quality of treatment, and reasonableness of fees. Ludgate Prison was unusual in housing only Freemen and Women of the City of London as well as their widows who, on arrest, could apply for entry through *duce facias* at a rate cheaper than *habeas corpus*. This led to almost all the prisoners being debtors alongside occasional Freemen who had committed minor offences, serious Free felons (described in 1724 as 'the blackest sort of Malefactors') being confined in Newgate.[60] The genteel nature of most of its inhabitants was revealed during the Gordon Riots of 1780 when the prisoners 'secreted themselves in the Garret in the Keeper's House', being unwilling to 'be turned [out] by the Rioters', afraid of the armed lower orders who made up the mob, a behaviour not repeated even at the superior court prisons.[61] This selecting of a higher class of prisoner than at the compters as well as the unlikelihood of being socially tarnished or physical harmed by proximity to felons created a more luxurious atmosphere which keepers did their best to promote, relying on this reputation for new customers. As early as the fifteenth century the citizens of London complained prisoners in Ludgate 'were more willing to keep abode there than to pay their debts', operating through most of its history like a club or sanctuary for unlucky but important guildsmen.[62] In 1729, one writer explicitly contrasted the 'daily Vexations' of confinement in Wood Street with the 'better usage' he experienced in Ludgate, the keeper 'being a person of humanity, who puts no hardships upon his Prisoners'.[63]

The importance of the rents paid by these willing inhabitants was demonstrated when its aura of luxury was obliterated by civic greed, emphasising that profits were earned – not just gathered – by keepers. When London's city walls which housed the gaol were demolished it became necessary to find a new location for Ludgate. At the Guildhall in November 1760 'a Scheme which will be of particular Benefit to the City' was developed to simply move the prisoners to the London Workhouse 'as it will save the Expence of a new Goal and [the City] will avail themselves of the Advantage of Letting the Ground whereon the present Goal stands for Building valuable houses'. On viewing the workhouse they concluded 'there can be no place more suitable for Reception of the Prisoners' with 'Room more than sufficient to contain them' though later directing the City Surveyor to 'prepare proper plans ... distinguishing the several rooms on each floor in order that such rooms may be fitted up for the keeper'. This committee appears to have had little conception of how Ludgate functioned, assuming that its inhabitants were indistinguishable from debtors at other gaols. Anthony Goodwin, Ludgate's keeper, appears to have barely been consulted and when Ludgate's prisoners were moved after June 1761 to the Common Side of the workhouse, repair work had not yet been completed. In a further blow to the Ludgate debtors, the workhouse residents were transferred to the Master's Side.[64] Less than three years later, the city launched an enquiry into the state of Ludgate gaol after the keeper reported that the prison's profitability had been shattered. Goodwin submitted receipts and accounts of disbursements between 1756 and 1763 revealing the significant financial shock the prison had taken as a result of the move, demonstrated in Figure 6.2. His costs, which had been static before 1761 at £56 15s 8d, had fallen on the move to £47 3s in 1762 and £43 7s in 1763, however, this saving was entirely overridden by reduced income. Profit had previously declined between 1757 and 1759 though this was the result of temporary losses at the taproom. Uncertainty 1759–1760 led to a decline in commitments while the move to the workhouse almost eradicated them. The prison still housed at least forty prisoners at the end of 1760, but by the time of the inquest in 1764 there were just fifteen resident debtors following only twenty commitments in 1763. At the previous site in 1758 Goodwin had received £92 8s 8½d in fees and rents but in the first full year at the Bishopsgate Street Workhouse in 1761 he made just £12 17s 4½d from the same source. Profitability was maintained in this first full year at the workhouse by the taproom and commitments on the Compulsive Clause[65] but, in its second year, the prison made a loss of £7 1s 6½d as the reduced number of prisoners more than halved alcohol sales. His revenue was so erratic that in 1763 Goodwin did not bother to break down his income, merely recording £59 10s 4d for all 'Receipts including Tap'. While the 1762 deficit was not

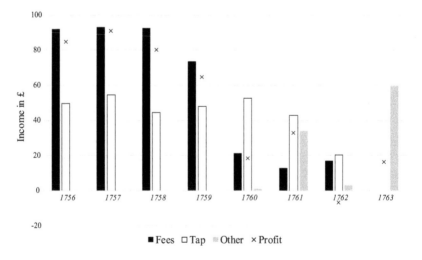

Figure 6.2 Ludgate Profits and Income from Various Sources, 1756–1763.

an unmanageable loss, this was a striking decline in profit which was personally felt by Goodwin. In 1777 the keeper received a salary of £70 which Goodwin may also have been entitled to c.1760, however, he was also liable for paying taxes for the whole workhouse and was still required to give 'Four Thousand Pounds [indemnity] to the Sheriffs to Indemnify them against any Escapes' despite the reported security of the gaol. By the time of the inquest even Goodwin was no longer residing in the prison, clearly having no desire to live alongside vagrants.[66]

Few keepers would experience such a dramatic decline in profitability and despite the lower profits on offer at prisons such as the compter, it was not necessary to squeeze blood from the stone to effectively manage a debtors' prison. By contrast, good businessmen particularly in London treated their prisoners with civility to prevent them seeking better accommodation and from complaining to civic authorities, preventing their own reputations from being publicly tarnished by a civic inquiry or pamphlet assault. John Kirby is a clear example of the growth of professional prison-keeping. Born in rural Yorkshire in 1727, Kirby was trained as a grocer before moving to Hull and launching a profitable business which traded locally and internationally with Riga and Virginia. His move to London was less successful and in 1754 Kirby was imprisoned in the Wood Street Compter. He spent nearly seven years in gaol – an unusually long commitment – before being discharged in 1761. Within two years however, and with an unrivalled knowledge of the workings of Wood Street, he returned as deputy keeper of the compter having previously worked briefly as an officer at the Poultry Compter. In 1766 he rose to keeper of Wood Street a position he held until November 1792 when his years of diligent administration were rewarded by his appointment to Newgate which he managed until his sudden death in August 1804. Kirby made prison-keeping the family business; his nephew Edward who trained under him kept the Poultry in its final years. John was well known as a compassionate and effective prison administrator being referred to publicly as 'the benevolent Mr Kirby'.[67] Beyond the fact he had not been required to pay for his position as keeper suggesting the city recognised his skills, much of his reputation originated in a small policy change he made in 1766, significantly improving standards of living at the compter. At most prisons, donations from civic organisations were given straight to prisoners. This had previously also been the policy at Wood Street and, according to Kirby, when debtors received their quarterly portion of the £54 2s 5d annual total they 'divide[d] the Money amongst them[selves] ... which they soon spent in Drunkenness, &c and were afterwards greatly distressed, and perishing through Cold and Hunger'. While most keepers had little interest in preventing prisoners wasting their money in the taproom, Kirby seized control of the annuities and instead 'advanced the Prisoners a Weekly Sum according to their Expences' which he claimed was 'chiefly laid out in Coals, Candles, Provisions for the Sick, paying for fetching in Victuals from different Taverns, Public Halls, &c. which is generally very valuable, and keep them from Want'.[68] While Kirby was always likely to tout his achievements, that this policy was continued after his departure from the compter testifies to its effectiveness.[69]

This new policy almost certainly ate into the potential profits from the prison taproom. At Newgate Kirby again eroded his income as he, 'consistent with his wonted humanity, charges none of [the debtors] anything for room rent', being able to afford the loss through the £450 salary.[70] This should not be merely seen as the actions of a generous heart. Kirby had a keen interest in the micromanagement of issues relating to his gaols (submitting an unusually detailed response to the 1792 House of Commons investigation into debt imprisonment) as well as possessing a genuine humanitarian spirit (being a subscriber to the 'School for the Indigent Blind, St George's Fields' and a collector of donations for 'The Society for Educating the Children of Debtors'), however, his behaviour also reflected good business practice.[71] While Anthony Goodwin had to encourage debtors to apply for his gaol, Kirby's revenue relied (particularly after 1786) on wealthier prisoners electing not to depart. One of the most significant potential detractors from quality of life for rent payers was the presence of those they regarded as their social inferiors, particularly if they were visibly hungry, sickly, or drunk. Some prisons "protected" genteel prisoners from the lower orders; at the Marshalsea Common Side prisoners were kept behind a high wall, preventing one even having to see the poor.[72] When the compter relocated to Giltspur Street in 1791, the two wards were positioned on opposite sides of the gaol with separate social spaces divided by administrative buildings. However, at the smaller Wood Street prison, debtors of all stripes were forced due to structural limitations to mingle in the chapel, in the taproom located beneath it, and out in the yard. While they possessed distinct sleeping quarters, the Common Side ward lay adjacent to and beneath Master's Side apartments making actual separation (particularly in terms of smell and sound) minimal.[73] Though Kirby could not rid himself of poor prisoners entirely, by minimising their presence and their suffering, wealthier prisoners were less likely to find the compter unpleasant. Preventing their drunkenness and hunger through control of the annuities inevitably had a positive impact on the bonhomie of the prison yard where prisoners ambulated, gambled, and socialised as well as in the tap where according to one visitor 'there is scarcely an evening passes but the room resounds with mirth'.[74] Additionally, Kirby claimed to have 'turned out of Prison poor persons who have been brought for small sums, by processes issuing out of the Court of [Requests], and paid the debt myself'. The shillings lost by clearing the impoverished translated into pounds retained in rent by gentleman not obtaining a *habeas corpus*.[75]

Nor was John's business strategy confined to preventative measures. The unmarried Kirby took the unusual step of allowing a small number of debtors willing to pay a commitment fee of 10s 8d to reside in his rooms alongside himself as well as to make use of his kitchen, parlour, and dining room.[76] Even those in the standard Master's Side rooms were likely to be entertained personally. Kirby frequently hosted genteel prisoners in his rooms for dinner, writing in 1784 to the *Morning Chronicle* to correct a slander that 'I never drink with any prisoner at his expense; indeed, in many instances, prisoners both eat and drink at mine, without ever my demanding of them one penny'.[77] This correction was one of several Kirby published, occasionally writing furious letters to newspapers to protect his hard won reputation as a benevolent keeper. When in 1785 the Society for the Discharge and Relief of Persons Imprisoned for Small Debts slightly misrepresented the amount he charged at release in the *Public Advertiser*, Kirby published an angry reply: 'How dare you have the effrontery … to set forth to the world so great a falsity? You know the fees as well as I do … Do you see the objects … you release? No! you do not'.[78] While the forcefulness of his reply arose from Kirby's somewhat eccentric manner, he was far from the only keeper to defend themselves against accusations by the Society or its pious allies.[79] Due to the poor reputation of gaolers it was easy to be branded as cruel and, like any other businessperson, one could not allow assaults upon reputation (and credit) to go unanswered.

While Kirby may stand out from his contemporaries both in his notability and his benevolence, he was far more representative of the silent majority of keepers than the infamous corrupt keepers of the 1720s who generally stereotype the profession. William Acton and Thomas Bambridge, though far from the only examples of brutal keepers, represent the figureheads of prison-keeping due to the high-profile House of Commons investigation into their activity headed by James Oglethorpe (1729–1730).[80] The committee's reports revealed to the public the astonishing abuses by both keepers, including locking debtors in irons, facilitating escapes for bribes, attempted or actual murder of prisoners, torture, and general extortion. The committee's work, particularly that of Oglethorpe, was held up as the activity of heroic humanitarians for decades. Hogarth's portrait depicts Oglethrope as the noble adversary of the weaselish Bambridge while Alexander Pope immortalised him in verse with 'One driv'n by strong benevolence of soul, Shall fly like Oglethorpe from pole to pole', a commendation quoted decades later by Boswell.[81] The long memory of Acton and Bambridge ensured that keepers were frequently viewed dubiously, particularly after the close of the prisons. However, while one cannot but view these two men as cruel and exhibiting a stunning lack of compassion, what emerges from a less human reading of the committee's reports is clear evidence of poor management and a lack of long-term economic thinking.

Of the two men, Thomas Bambridge appears as the most undeniably cruel, his governance of the Fleet being corrupt and arbitrary if not sociopathic, committing violent acts apparently at random for the slightest offence. It was his decision to fatally force an obstinate prisoner into a bed infected with smallpox which began the enquiry. At the very least, his willingness to endanger the lives of his charges surely impacted on the prison's reputation as well as the number willing to take a *habeas corpus* to it.[82] While William Acton was similarly depicted as cruel by the committee, when reading beyond Oglethrope's sensationalism the main impression which arises from their report is that the keeper was almost entirely inept when it came to administering the Marshalsea. More interested in socialising with wealthy prisoners, Acton had little control over his employees who abused prisoners independent of his commands. This lack of control extended to his charges, presiding over a disorderly gaol and resorting to torture to barely maintain his 'pretended authority'. One of the prisoners he was unsuccessfully charged with murdering through solitary confinement was placed there not for the purposes of extortion but because he had stabbed Acton's servant with a penknife simply for ordering him to his own room.[83] Even if he had been able to keep the peace, his attempts to raise capital were beyond short-sighted. The committee reported that the 'Goaler of the said Prison, out of a view of Gain, hath frequently refused to remove Sick Persons, upon Complaint of those who lay in the same Bed with [them]'. While he thus retained the rent of the sick on the Master's Side, the probability that this could lead to more serious outbreaks was an existential threat to income which Acton failed to consider. Furthermore, his decision to pilfer the Charity Money, even 'Defrauding the Begging-Box', may have raised short-term income but reduced the health of his prisoners to the point of starvation. Unsurprisingly considering his business decisions, during the month and a half long investigation, nine prisoners died in the gaol 'tho before, a Day seldom passed without a Death, and upon the advancing of the Spring, not less than Eight or Ten usually died every 24 Hours'. Acton's efforts ensured that his profits were 'double those of the preceding Year' but did such damage to his stock that his business was brought to a dramatic end in 1729.[84] Even without the existing parliamentary inquiry, it is difficult to conceive how such a situation could have persisted without a complete collapse in income. Trained as a butcher, Acton failed as a shepherd, being unable to look beyond the immediate profitability of his lambs.

Regardless of their cruelty, both men demonstrated their incompetence as businessmen. Nor was this merely a matter of the supposed greater brutality of the first half of the century as some have claimed.[85] The same committee which investigated the prisons of Acton and Bambridge were struck, when they turned their attention to Richard Mullens, keeper of the King's Bench, by the comparative lack of corruption. Mullens paid an eyewatering £700 annual rent for the right to run the prison which the committee surmised 'cannot be made up without great Oppression', declaring 'the Prison Fees are exorbitant' and that the 'Master's Side is in a ... Condition ... in no way adequate to the vast Rent paid for it' by prisoners. However, they also reported following interviews with prisoners on both sides

> that no Violence or Cruelty hath been used to them by the present Marshal, but, on the contrary, that he hath done many Acts of Compassion, and Charity towards those on the Common Side; by which, and by his free Confessions, and satisfactory Answers given to the Committee, upon his several Examinations before them, he hath rather intitled himself to Favour, than Blame.

Mullens principally made his income from fees for entering the *rules* and was apparently not inclined to torture his way to solvency. While the fees and rents were high and the keeper could have made a greater effort to repair the gaol, these were largely inescapable realities of the business of prison-keeping across the century that would have required public money to remedy. Oglethorpe ascribed this situation 'to the Care of the Lord Chief Justice, who ... hath kept the said Marshal strictly to the Performance of his Duty', presuming the inherent corruption of gaolers.[86] However, rather than assume every gaoler was a moment away from murdering prisoners for their last farthing unless restrained by a benevolent judge, it is more probable that Mullens, like the majority of prison keepers, observed the business challenge of having to raise a certain amount of money per annum to remain profitable and found a mechanism which would not conflict with his moral Christian character and which would – perhaps more importantly from the perspective of the smooth operation of the institution – not lead him to lose his job.

★★

'Should we see the administration of eighteenth-century jails as broadly be-nevolent, operating within a paternalist framework of gentry oversight that obviated the need for contemporaries to give serious consideration to struc-tural reform? I think not'.[87] Philip Woodfine made his view of the gaols profoundly clear in 2006, his research providing an important and neces-sary corrective to works he regarded as 'downplay[ing] the harshness of the prisoner's lot'.[88] The discussion in this chapter in which debtors are treated merely as commodities or at best as customers to be coaxed into paying for their own misery, might also be fairly aligned with those Woodfine wrote against. Debtors' prisons were highly unpleasant places and being confined within one was a cruel and punishing experience (though not in itself a pun-ishment). By tolerating debt imprisonment and failing to replace fees with state funding, society all but confirmed the body and well-being of the debtor was inferior not just to the needs of commerce but also the financial status of prison administrators.[89] Even where keepers were comparatively benevolent, it is still difficult to talk of a man like John Kirby, a trader in human flesh, in the same terms as reformers and philanthropists. During his administration, the Common Side of Wood Street was described as

> a dark hall ... The smell of the place was almost intolerable ... the beds, of such as had any, were placed in ranges, as ... shelves, over each other; and those who had none, were obliged to lie upon the boards.[90]

Kirby presumably kept the ward in a state of repair equal to the minimum required to protect his income and his place as, while Acton and Bambridge's greedy and cruel behaviour ended their business, an overly benevolent attitude could also be fatal. A visitor to the compter c.1780 recalled being told by a prisoner that they

> once had a landlord [of the prison alehouse] who ... lighted up this dismal tap-room at his own expence, made the place we sat in convenient, and furnished his guests with the best wines and other liquors; but he *trusted*, contrary to the custom of the place, by which, and other extravagances, (added he seriously) the poor man got himself into a goal.[91]

Though Kirby did not feel compelled to beat money from his debtors, he was only willing to risk so much capital on their comfort – a decision that from a business perspective appears entirely correct.

However, it is clear the bleak depiction of eighteenth-century prison-keeping has been overwrought. The supposedly tyrannous charges upon prisoners were essential in ensuring the smooth operation of their confinement and protecting the wider credit market. The institution of debt imprisonment, as this chapter shows, was always primarily a business and it is difficult to conceive of it being able to survive a reform which made it anything other than one. Fees and rents prevented costs falling upon creditors or the wider community ensuring the perseverance of the informal institution of contract enforcement. Nor were such charges necessarily extortionate in size; a Wood Street debtor having to pay 16s in fees and a rent of £3 5s (assuming the average twenty-six week commitment) represented a hardly debilitating addition to a debt likely to be at least £20. It was essential that keepers be able to earn a profit though it was up to their personal capabilities to ensure the health of their trade. Those who found it impossible to raise revenue without physical punishment were probably not suited to the profession, but paternalistic care was only a useful element of their management if it protected profits. Those housing the poorest debtors in ageing provincial gaols probably saw little benefit to alleviating suffering apart from ensuring they were healthy enough to be put to work as if they were in a bridewell. Ultimately, the system of fees and rents, while relatively secure and serving a defined purpose within the institution was, just like the Insolvency Acts, emblematic of the fragility of debt imprisonment. It was far from an ideal response to informal credit and while it worked efficiently enough for creditors, it was very much a system built upon sand which could sink if any element of it suffered from civic greed or even from the "benefits" of enlightened reform on behalf of prisoners.

Notes

1 John Howard, *The State of the Prisons in England and Wales, with Preliminary Observations, and an Account of Some Foreign Prisons* (London: 1777), p. 57.
2 *General Evening Post*, 16th–18th August 1787, no. 8383.
3 Jacob Ilive, *A Scheme for the Employment of All Persons Sent as Disorderly to the House of Correction in Clerkenwell* (London: 1759), pp. 51, 58; *Public Advertiser*, 15th February 1780, no. 14150.

4 *General Evening Post*, 24th–27th September 1774, no. 6360; Josiah Dornford, *Nine Letters to the Right Honourable Lord Mayor and Aldermen of the City of London, on the State of the City Prisons* (London: 1786), pp. 83–92.

5 See: "Petitions of Prisoners, Offices of Newgate and the Compters, and Other Persons Relating to Prison Life, Repair of Prisons, Collections, Ill Health, Abuse by Officers, for Discharge, &c", 1675–1700, Prisons and Compter – General, LMA, CLA/032/01/021.

6 "An Act for the Relief of Insolvent Debtors", 1747, 21 George II, c.31.

7 Tim Hitchcock and Robert Brink Shoemaker, *London Lives – Poverty, Crime and the Making of a Modern City, 1690–1800* (Cambridge: Cambridge University Press, 2015), pp. 102–106.

8 Philip Woodfine, "Debtors, Prisons, and Petitions in Eighteenth-Century England", *Eighteenth Century Life* vol. 30, no. 2 (Spring 2006), p. 19.

9 "Petition against Yeoman Being Allowed to Make Arrest without Serjeants", c.1710, Poultry Compter, LMA, CLA/025/PC/04/005; "Swordbearers to Enquire into Character of Yeomen or Serjeants", 1707, Poultry Compter, LMA, CLA/025/PC/04/004.

10 "Petition of James Guthrie to be Chaplain of Newgate", 1733/4, Newgate Prison – Administration, LMA, CLA/035/02/029.

11 B. R. Hartley, "Thomas Griffith of York, 'Once Governor of the Castle and Now a Debtor from the Same'", *York Historian* vol. 11 (1994), pp. 40–45.

12 Jerry White, "Pain and Degradation in Georgian London: Life in the Marshalsea Prison", *History Workshop Journal* vol. 68 (Autumn 2009), p. 79; John Grano (John Ginger ed.), *Handel's Trumpeter – The Diary of John Grano* (Stuyvesant: Pendragon Press, 1998), pp. 69–70, 93, 97.

13 Anon. *The Prisoner's Advocate, or a Caveat against under Sheriffs, and Their Officers; Jayl-Keepers, and Their Agents* (London: 1726), p. 29.

14 Anon. *A Report from the Committee Appointed to Enquire into the State of the Gaols of This Kingdom: Relating to the Marshalsea Prison* (London: 1729), pp. 1–2.

15 Walter Thornbury, *Old and New London: A Narrative of Its History, Its People, and Its Places Vol. I1* (London: Cassell, Petter, & Galpin, 1878), pp. 404; Roger Lee Brown, *A History of the Fleet Prison, London – The Anatomy of the Fleet* (Lampeter: Edwin Mellen Press, 1996), pp. 115–116.

16 Anon. *A Report from the Committee Appointed to Enquire into the State of the Gaols of This Kingdom: Relating to the Fleet Prison* (London: 1729); A. A. Hanham, "Bambridge, Thomas (d.1741)", *Oxford Dictionary of National Biography* (Oxford: Oxford University Press, 2004), online edition, https://doi.org/10.1093/ref:odnb/1255 (accessed 31st October 2019).

17 Howard, *State of the Prisons*, pp. 440–441.

18 Anon. *The Annual Register, or a View of the History, Politics, and Literature, for the Year 1766* (Dublin: 1773), p. 115; Dornford, *Nine Letters*, p. 92.

19 "Petition of Secondary of Poultry Compter against Rates", July 1726, Session Papers – Gaol Delivery and Peace, LMA, CLA/047/LJ/13/1726/003.

20 Margaret Dorey, "Reckliss Endangerment?: Feeding the Poor Prisoners of London in the Early Eighteenth Century", in *Experiences of Poverty in Late Medieval and Early Modern England and France*, ed. Anne M. Scott (Farnham: Ashgate, 2012), pp. 183–198; Howard, *State of the Prisons*, passim; James Neild, *Account of Persons Confined for Debt, in the Various Prisons of England and Wales; Together with Their Provisionary Allowance during Confinement: as Reported to the Society for the Discharge and Relief of Small Debtors, in April, May, June &c 1800* (London: 1800), passim; Journal of the House of Commons, *Report for the Committee Appointed to Enquire into the Practice and Effects of Imprisonment for Debt* (1792), passim.

21 Woodfine, "Debtors, Prisons, and Petitions", p. 10; Hitchcock and Shoemaker, *London Lives*, p. 104.

22 "Committee to Enquire into the State of the Goal of Ludgate and the Office of the Keeper Thereof", June 1764, Ludgate Prison – Administration, LMA, CLA/033/01/015.

23 "Vouchers for Wages and Petty Disbursements", 28th June 1817, Newgate Prison – Administration, LMA, CLA/035/02/055.

24 "Answer of the Keeper to the Articles Exhibited against Him ... by the Prisoners Confined for Debt", 1728/9, Newgate Prison: Administration, LMA, CLA/035/02/024; see Alexander Wakelam, "Coverture and the Debtors' Prison in the Long Eighteenth Century", *Journal of Eighteenth-Century Studies* (forthcoming, 2021).

25 Joanna Innes, "The King's Bench Prison in the Later Eighteenth Century: Law, Authority and Order in a London Debtors' Prison", in *An Ungovernable People – The English and Their Law in the Seventeenth and Eighteenth Centuries*, ed. John Brewer and John Styles (London: Hutchinson, 1980), pp. 250–298; Paul Hess Haagen, "Imprisonment for Debt in England and Wales", unpublished PhD thesis, University of Princeton (1986), pp. 209–210; Woodfine, "Debtors, Prisons, and Petitions", p. 10; "Answer of the Keeper", CLA/035/02/024; "Rules and Orders ... Debtors Side", 1808, Newgate Prison – Administration, LMA, CLA/035/02/031; Anon. *An Accurate Description of Newgate. With the Rights, Privileges, Allowances, Fees, Dues, and Customs Thereof* (London: 1724).

26 Howard, *State of the Prisons*, pp. 151–475.

27 See: William Smith, *State of the Gaols in London, Westminster, and Borough of Southwark. To Which Is Added, an Account of the Present State of Convicts Sentenced to Hard Labour on Board the Justitia upon the River Thames* (London: J. Brew, 1776); Howard, *State of the Prisons*; "Answer of the Keeper", CLA/035/02/024.

28 Walter Thornbury, *Old and New London: A Narrative of Its History, Its People, and Its Places Vol. 1* (London: Cassell, Petter, & Galpin, 1873), pp. 368–369.

29 Howard, *State of the Prisons*, pp. 156, 203–204.

30 Alex Pitofsky, "The Warden's Court Martial: James Oglethorpe and the Politics of Eighteenth-Century Prison Reform", *Eighteenth Century Life* vol. 24, no. 1 (2000), p. 90.

31 Grano *Handel's Trumpeter*, p. 64; "Proceedings of Various Courts of Aldermen and Court of Common Council Comittees", 1709, Court of Common Council – Minutes, LMA, COL/CC/MIN/01/115, p. 5; Simon Wood, *Remarks on the Fleet Prison: Or, Lumber-House for Men and Women* (London: 1733), p. 14 'dead or alive you fare alike, for, as we may say, Death, Taxes, and Goalers, spare none'.

32 Howard, *State of the Prisons*, pp. 398–400; William Hargreave, *History and Description of the Ancient City of York. Vol. II* (York: William Alexander, 1818), p. 234.

33 Anon. *Report ... Fleet*, p. 6.

34 21 George II, c.31; "Petitions of Prisoners", CLA/032/01/021 (almost all of the over hundred petitions collected in this file consist of those requesting relief frequently related to the fees).

35 "Commitment Registers", 1735–1737, Fleet Prison, TNA, PRIS 1/6.

36 "Commitment Registers", 1778–1782, Fleet Prison, TNA, PRIS 1/11.

37 Anon. *The Debtor and Creditor's Assistant; or, a Key to the King's Bench and Fleet Prisons* (London: 1793), pp. 7–11.

38 Grano, *Handel's Trumpeter*, pp. 51–83.

39 Wood, *Remarks*, pp. 8, 15–16.

40 Grano, *Handel's Trumpeter*, p. 133.

41 Anon. *Debtor and Creditor's Assistant*, p. 2.

42 George Rudé, *Hanoverian London 1714–1808* (Berkeley: University of California Press, 1971), pp. 58–59; Jeremy Boulton, "'Turned into the Street with my Children Destitute of Every Thing'; The Payment of Rent and the London Poor,

1600–1850", in *Accommodating Poverty – The Housing and Living Arrangements of the English Poor, c.1600–1850*, eds. Joanne McEwan and Pamela Sharpe (Basingstoke: Palgrave Macmillan, 2011), p. 33.

43 Results obtained from search of the phrase "rent" in all cases 1740–1800, ignoring those cases where amounts were not specified. Tim Hitchcock, Robert Shoemaker, Clive Emsely, Sharon Howard, and Jamie McLaughlin, et al., *Old Bailey Proceedings Online 1674–1913*, www.oldbaileyonline.org (accessed 14th–15th September 2017).

44 While some renters (particularly those leasing entire houses) recorded their rent *per annum*, c.60% paid rent on either a quarterly or weekly basis; for the sake of comparison all rents were calculated for the whole year though many renters may have moved regularly and most debtors were released within six months.

45 Howard, *State of the Prisons*, p. 402.

46 Howard, *State of the Prisons*, p. 428.

47 Howard, *State of the Prisons*, pp. 151–156.

48 Howard, *State of the Prisons*, pp. 156–161, 174–177, 435–437; Margaret DeLacy, *Prison Reform in Lancashire, 1700–1850 – A Study in Local Administration* (Stanford: Stanford University Press, 1986), p. 50.

49 Wood, *Remarks*, p. 13.

50 Dornford, *Nine Letters*, p. 92.

51 Neild, *Account of the Persons*, p. 25.

52 Howard, *State of the Prisons*, pp. 435–437.

53 Wood, *Remarks*, p. 9.

54 Anon. *A Brief State of the Produce of the City's Estate and How the Same Has Been Disposed of* (London: 1793), p. 30.

55 House of Commons, *Committee into Imprisonment for Debt*, p. 46.

56 "Lancaster Gaol Register of Debtors and Plaintiffs", 1793–1796, Home Office and Prison Commission Records: Prison Records Series 1, TNA, PCOM 2/440.

57 Hitchcock and Shoemaker, *London Lives*, p. 327.

58 Howard, *State of the Prisons*, p. 181.

59 "Cash Book of Samuel Newport, Keeper of the New Prison", 1790–1795, Middlesex Session of the Peace County Administration: Prisons – New Prison, Clerkenwell, LMA, MA/G/CLE/0032.

60 Jonathon Gil Harris, "Ludgate Time: Simon Eyre's Oath and the Temporal Economies of *The Shoemaker's Holiday*", *Huntington Library Quarterly* vol. 71, no. 1 (2008), pp. 22–24; Smith, *State of the Gaols*, pp. 30–31; Anon. *An Accurate Description of Newgate. With the Rights, Privileges, Allowances, Fees, Dues, and Customs Thereof* (London: 1724), p. 14.

61 House of Commons, *Committee into Imprisonment for Debt*, p. 76.

62 Richard Byrne, *Prisons and Punishments of London* (Grafton: London, 1992), p. 22.

63 Anon. *The Arbitrary Punishments and Cruel Tortures Inflicted on Prisoners for Debt* (London: 1729), p. 10.

64 "Rough Minutes and Papers of the Committee to Consider of Legal and Proper Methods for Removing the Prisoners from Ludgate to the London Workhouse", 1760–1761, Ludgate Prison – Administration, LMA, CLA/033/01/014.

65 This income classed by Goodwin separately to his normal commitment fees (here "Other) possibly to emphasise to the committee the almost instant decline in commitments.

66 "State of the Goal and the Keeper", CLA/033/01/015; Howard, *State of the Prisons*, p. 166.

67 Francis Collins (ed.), *Register of the Freemen of City of York Vol. II, 1559–1759* (Durham: Andrews & Co., 1900), pp. 228–262; "John Kirby", Debtors Schedules: Wood Street Compter, 1755, LMA, CLA/047/LJ/17/042 (unsuccessful

first application to an Insolvency Act); "John Kirby", Debtors Schedules: Wood Street Compter & Borough Compter, 1761, LMA, CLA/047/LJ/17/044; "List of Prisoners Handed over by the Sheriffs to their Successors on 28 Sept Annually, with Notes of Occurrences During the Subsequent Year", 1753–1755, Wood Street Compter later Giltspur Street Compter, LMA, CLA/028/01/005; "Trial of William Barlow and Jane Durant", 14th September 1763, *Old Bailey Proceedings Online*, t17630914-66 (Kirby called as a witness); Corporation of London, *The Names and Address of the Several Officers of the City of London* (1789), p. 64; *Lloyd's Evening Post*, 28th November 1792, no.5526; *Public Advertiser*, 5th April 1763, no.8869; *The Morning Chronicle*, 31st August 1804, no. 11009; James Peller Malcolm, *Londinium Redivivum, or an Ancient History and Modern Description of London Compiled from Parochial Records, Archives of Various Foundations, the Harleian Mss and Other Authentic Sources. Vol. IV* (London: 1807), p. 597; House of Commons, *Report from the Committee on the State of the Gaols of the City of London &c* (1814), p. 90.

68 House of Commons, *Committee into Imprisonment for Debt*, p. 79.
69 Neild, *Account of Persons Confined*, pp. 13–16.
70 Neild, *Account of Persons Confined*, p. 32; *Oracle and Daily Advertiser*, 23rd August 1800, no. 822,374.
71 House of Commons, *Committee into Imprisonment for Debt*, pp. 78–80; *True Briton*, 27th December 1796, no. 1250; *Morning Chronicle*, 29th April 1797, no. 8597; *Morning Chronicle*, 11th April 1800, no. 9637.
72 Grano, *Handel's Trumpeter*, p. 67.
73 "Plan of the Ground Floor of the Giltspur Street Compter", 1800, Surveyor's Department: Plans – Justice, LMA, COL/SVD/PL/08/0108; Anon. *The Complete Modern London Spy, for the Present Year, 1781* (London: 1781), p. 39; "Sketch plan of the ground floor showing use of rooms with dimensions, Wood Street Compter, rough Design", (no date, late 18th Century), Surveyor's Department: Plans – Justice, LMA, COL/SVD/PL/08/0088.
74 Anon. *London Spy for 1781*, pp. 39–40; Richard Maher, "Poems from the Prison Yard – A Poetic Correspondence between Charles Wogan and William Tunstall", *History Ireland* vol. 25, no. 2 (March–April 2017), pp. 20–23.
75 *Morning Chronicle and London Advertiser*, 28th May 1784, no. 4690.
76 Howard, *State of the Prisons*, pp. 174–177; "Plan of Two Pair of Stairs. Showing Use of Rooms", 1780, Surveyor's Department: Plans – Justice, LMA, COL/SVD/PL/08/0092.
77 *Morning Chronicle and London Advertiser*, 17th December 1784, no. 4865.
78 *Public Advertiser*, 5th March 1785, no. 15840.
79 See: *Morning Chronicle and London Advertiser*, 16th December 1784, no. 4864 and other responses to Dornford's campaign in Chapter 7. John Kirby was known for his rather unusual nature in the city unrelated to his role as prison keeper. He was a 'celebrated angler' (*Whitehall Evening Post*, 15th–17th June 1784, no. 5771) and spent much of his spare time promoting angling in a city with a fishless river. He patronised works on the topic such as *The Angler's Museum* lending his image to its cover (Thomas Shirley, *The Angler's Museum; or, the Whole Art of Float and Fly Fishing* (London: 1784)), though apparently doing so without discretion, *The Monthly Review* calling the work 'a paltry compilation' and remarking that 'Mr Kirby ... would have done much better, if he had kept his head within the Compter' (Anon. *The Monthly Review; or Literary Journal: From January to June, Inclusive, MDCCLXXXV. By Several Hands* vol. 72 (1785), p. 67). Furthermore, his detailed response to the House of Commons committee indicates he measured some rooms by hand, while he also answered questions not addressed to him. While one cannot diagnose Kirby from afar, other scholars have been willing to associate benevolent reformers of the prison system, extremely focussed

upon microdetail, with modern understandings of neurological conditions such as ASD. See: Philip Lucas, "John Howard and Asperger's Syndrome: Psychopathology and Philanthropy", *History of Psychiatry* vol. 12 (2001), pp. 73–101.

80 Woodfine, "Debtors, Prisons, and Petitions", pp. 1–31; White, "Pain and Degradation", pp. 69–98; Rodney M. Baine, "The Prison Death of Robert Castell and Its Effect on the Founding of Georgia", *The Georgia Historical Society* vol. 73, no. 1 (1989), p. 75; see: Hartley, "Griffith"; Philip Woodfine, "The Power and Influence of the Gaolers: Life and Death in York Castle Gaol", *Yorkshire Archaeological Journal* vol. 78 (2006), pp. 159–175.

81 William Hogarth, "The Gaols Committee of the House of Commons" (c.1729), *National Portrait Gallery*, London; Alexander Pope, *The Works of Alexander Pope Vol. IV* (London: 1751), p. 239; Edward J. Cashin, "Glimpses of Oglethorpe in Boswell's *Life of Johnson*", *The Georgia Historical Society* vol. 88, no. 3 (2004), p. 399; James Boswell, *A Letter to the People of Scotland* (Edinburgh: 1783), p. 5; Pitofsky, "Warden's Court Martial", pp. 95–96.

82 Anon. *Report ... Fleet*; see: Anon. *Mr Bambridge's Case against the Bill Now Depending, to Disable Him to Hold or Execute the Office of Warden of the Prison of the Fleet; or to Have or Exercise and Authority Relating Thereto* (London: 1729).

83 Anon. *Report ... Marshalsea*, pp. 2, 8, 10; Anon. *The Tryal of William Acton, Deputy-Keeper and Lessee of the Marshalsea Prison in Southwark, at Kingston Assizes* (London: 1729), pp. 3–9.

84 Anon. *Report ... Marshalsea*, pp. 3–5, 6–8, 10.

85 Pitofsky, "Warden's Court Martial", pp. 97–98.

86 Anon. *A Report from the Committee Appointed to Enquire into the State of the Goals of This Kingdom. Relating to the King's Bench Prison* (London: 1730), pp. 6–10.

87 Woodfine, "Debtors, Prisons, and Petitions", p. 9.

88 Woodfine, "Debtors, Prisons, and Petitions", p. 1; see Margot C. Finn, *The Character of Credit – Personal Debt in English Culture, 1740–1914* (Cambridge: Cambridge University Press, 2003).

89 See: Tawny Paul, *Poverty of Disaster – Debt and Insecurity in Eighteenth-Century Britain* (Cambridge: Cambridge University Press, 2019), pp. 214–235.

90 Anon. *London Spy for 1781*, p. 39.

91 Anon. *London Spy for 1781*, p. 39.

7   Reform and the unmaking of debtors' prisons

'The arrest of the person in the first instance for debt, has been often, and very justly complained of ... being a measure pregnant with oppression'.[1] In the opening of his *Observations on the Law of Arrest and Imprisonment for Debt* (1781), Richard Bevan entered well-trodden ground. While debt imprisonment was generally an effective means of securing repayment, this does not mean contemporaries did not find the practice distasteful or even repugnant. Across the eighteenth century, the printing presses regularly spat out tracts demanding the reform of debtors' prisons, expressing a variety of necessary alterations which were articulated in a similarly varied manner. While the call for reform was apparently uncontroversial in general terms, there was little agreement about what the reformed institution should look like or what to replace imprisonment for debt with. Figures like John Howard, with detailed practical experience of imprisonment, called for targeted limited reform such as the need for fees to be abolished and replaced with salaries for gaolers, a change which Samuel Byrom claimed in 1729 would mean 'the Gaols would not swarm as they do now'.[2] However, for many rhetorical pamphleteers, such improvement of the system was antithetical to their purpose. Declaring that the practice was abhorrent to religion and historical example (even having been abolished by the ancients), they called for more substantial reform targeted not at the day-to-day management of gaols but upon the very system of arresting. Such discussion, present across the period, began in earnest c.1770 as increased commitment rates created overcrowding within gaols designed for seventeenth-century populations, making the problem of debt imprisonment visible and urgent. While it was easy for pamphleteers to articulate what they disliked about the prisons, providing a systematic plan for how it could be changed proved more elusive. Some argued for the extension of existing practices, most notably that Insolvency Acts be made permanent or that they at least be passed at short regular intervals.[3] Occasionally reform advocates were more creative, suggesting extending bankruptcy laws to all those owing at least £20 or having all debt cases settled by Judges.[4] Typically, these plans were slim on detail as to how they could actually solve disputes though Bevan, having proposed 'that the arrest in the first instance for debt should be abolished' launched into a lengthy, complicated, almost incomprehensible, and certainly unworkable scheme by which debtors would be trusted to appear and turn over their estate voluntarily which they had not done previously.[5] Not all even provided a specified remedy, Byrom concluding 'I heartily wish, and hope, the Legislature will find out some Expedient for the satisfaction of the Creditor, and Ease of the Debtor' a later text similarly hoping that thanks to policymakers and 'their paternal tenderness for their people, we shall see a change in the present systems of legislation'.[6]

The impression in society that debtors' prisons in their current form should not be allowed to continue combined with incomprehension about how to do so, was reflected by a general absence of reform. In 1800, the system of debt imprisonment still bore most of the hallmarks of the gaols at the end of the seventeenth century. The steadfast nature of debt imprisonment in a fast changing society has accordingly led a number of scholars to describe the eighteenth-century debtors' prison simply as 'unreformed' particularly in comparison to its nineteenth-century equivalent, Paul Hess Haagen claiming that 'all of the major reforms ... were products of the nineteenth century'.[7] This categorisation is not necessarily fair and advocates for reform c.1800 would have been loath to describe their work as entirely unsuccessful. By the end of the century, reformers had been successful in limiting the fees chargeable by keepers and in closing many prison taprooms, for the latter of which debtors were presumably less grateful. The assertion that the prisons were "unreformed" emphasises that, in the scholarship as well as contemporaneously, what is meant broadly by "reform" is not action that was taken to improve the viability of the system – closing sponging houses, providing prisoners with adequate workspace, eliminating creditor costs, and abolishing *habeas corpus* for debtors – but that which led to its abolition, a moral rather than economic initiative. It was such reform of the system of arrest conducted in the nineteenth century (as celebrated by scholars) which contributed to the decline of the use of debt imprisonment, undermining its efficacy for creditors, leading to abolition by default. Notably, the Debt Act of 1869 did not even technically abolish debt imprisonment but aggressively limited arrest by abolishing *mesne* process so as to make it untenable. Court ordered debt imprisonment continued into the twentieth century; a report in 1899 found that 7,867 debtors were currently confined while Richard Ford claimed in 1926 that 11,986 people were imprisoned in 1906 though rates declined rapidly to 424 by 1921, war again reducing debt imprisonment. Practically, however, debt imprisonment had long since ceased to be a supporting mechanism for the informal credit market due to changes in the underlying economic system of contracting.[8] Some in the eighteenth century did advocate for similar reform which might be understood as abolition by proxy. The *Debtor's and Creditor's Assistant* (1793) was far from isolated by exclaiming: 'with such sad and woeful experience of the practice, it surely cannot but be truly astonishing, that it should be suffered to continue in a great and enlightened nation'.[9] However, generally this scholarly conception of "reform" does not accord with contemporary attitudes, there being little appetite for the actual end of debtors' prisons outside pamphlet literature (or the gaol taprooms), creditors making regular use of them into the nineteenth century.

Despite the lack of attempt or even desire to abolish the prisons, there was substantive reform of the system of imprisonment in the eighteenth century that has been largely overlooked and which went further than the lifestyle changes of fees and drink. This reform, like that of the nineteenth century, targeted the workability of the system of debt imprisonment by limiting those who could be pursued through it and controlled who could order confinement. Furthermore, it tarnished the truly economic nature of the prisons by, for the first time, introducing an element of punishment to the debt law when no fraud had taken place. However, this undermining of debt imprisonment appears to have been essentially accidental, reflecting a genuine desire to improve its effectiveness in accord with the generally apathetic response to abolition. This chapter explores how debtors' prisons began to be unmade through well-intentioned reform first by limiting *mesne* process to those owing more than £2 in 1725 and subsequently by limiting the prison terms of small debtors equating, for the poor, imprisonment with punishment. It discusses how an apparent decrease of the class distinctiveness of imprisoned debtors encouraged symbiotic attempts to protect the poor from confinement as well as to further discern a sense of deserving and undeserving debtors. Subsequently, it charts in detail the origins of Courts of Requests and the necessary role they played within the economy as a reaction to well-meaning reform before their own reform damaged the identity of debtors' prisons as an informal system of contract enforcement. Despite this substantial change, it is clear – as is shown in the resistance to Josiah Dornford's campaign for reform c.1786 – that civic interests and the wider public remained invested in upholding the creaking, fragile system of debt recovery upon which commercial credit was so dependent. Before credit itself changed, this institution could only be dispensed with at great risk to the trading classes.

★★

Theoretically, the debtors' prison was the great leveller, bringing low the gentleman and the carpenter in shared confinement. However, the prisons were far from commonwealths of equality.[10] Rather (as has been seen throughout this study) through their structural separation of prisoners based upon wealth, either into wards or separate prisons through *habeas corpus* and *duce facias*, they acted as a microcosm of England's hierarchical social structure at large. In 1786, Josiah Dornford described in his *Seven Letters … Upon … Arresting and Imprisoning the Bodies of Debtors* how

> debtors may be considered of three classes. The first under the description of Merchants and capital Traders. The second of Tradesmen, Mechanics, and Artificers, in the middle walk of life. The third, of the lower orders, of Journeymen, of Labourers, and Domestics.[11]

While Dornford was a passionate opponent of debt imprisonment whose views often proved too radical for the civic establishment, his tiered, class-based approach to debt imprisonment was broadly representative not only of the diversity of prisoners but also their varying experiences of confinement. It also reflected who society expected a debtor to be, generally but not exclusively those involved in commerce (an assumption borne out in the declared occupations of those applying for Insolvency Acts in Table 2.2). Notably absent from Dornford's assessment were the gentry and other "men of status". Peers of the realm and a select group of other elites were legally protected from arrest. While the needs of *land* were seen to be paramount, the wider extension of this privilege was far from popular, Edward Farley claiming in 1795 that if MPs were not protected from imprisonment while the House was in session, the King 'would be obliged to meet his parliament in the King's Bench'.[12] Protections for the establishment were eroded from the early eighteenth century as imprisonment became a more regular practice. Large numbers of social elites were confined in an array of prisons due to reduced regulation or creditors making use of loopholes; when Parliament was in recess there were no protections for members. While the stereotype of "the debtor" evidently did not keep up with practice, it appears that after the seventeenth century the class definition of prisoners became more blurred. The Financial and Consumer Revolutions disrupted the absolute economic power of land and, from the early eighteenth century, pulled the impoverished and the powerful more regularly into the realm of the unfortunate merchant. This particularly alarmed one anonymous author in 1729 writing on behalf of a 'poor Gentleman' who had lost 'an ample Fortune' both in cash and annuities through 'false Friendships … and Artifices of designing Knaves'. The pamphlet emphasised the non-merchant status of the prisoner, his fortune having 'descended to him from his worthy Ancestors … some of the noblest Families in the Kingdom – His Calamities restrain me from mentioning them, lest his unhappy Crime of being poor … should prejudice them'. Having exonerated the 'Gentleman' from fault, the advocate declared 'it is not agreeable to the Rule of Justice to thrust all Sorts of Debtors confusedly together in a Heap into a Prison, without regard to the different Qualities of Men', suggesting that greater effort was required to provide dignity to prisoners of status.[13]

Sympathy for spendthrift gentry was, unsurprisingly, not widely forthcoming. However, the greater presence of other non-appropriate debtors did inspire a targeted response. Dornford's first two categories stand apart as people of trade, wealth, and some (if minimal) status who represented the typical prisoner in contrast to the 'lower orders' against whom debt imprisonment appeared, even in the eighteenth century, to be arbitrary. This did not necessarily mean that they were to be treated with compassion; much of the literature advocating for a distinction between 'fraudulent' and 'unfortunate honest' debtors, was constructed as essentially distinguishing between the poor and the trading classes. In describing the 'fraudulent, unqualify'd, wicked, and dishonest People' who remained in prison deliberately refusing to pay, Daniel Defoe declared in 1729 that 'the Debts they lye for [are] not large, at least not to particular Men' but that for creditors 'the Injury to Trade is very considerable, nor is the Matter small among Tradesmen, tho the Debts (as above) are not singly large'.[14] Defoe was not alone in thinking the poor 'despicable' and deliberately obtuse, Robert Holloway in 1771 arguing they 'merit[ed] a more exemplary correction than the laws [currently] inflict'.[15] While this 'more exemplary correction' was not deliberately manifested, prison reform frequently focussed upon the separation of this class.

The first significant eighteenth-century reform of the operation of debt imprisonment occurred in 1725 when the 'Act to Prevent Frivolous and Vexatious Arrests' limited *mesne* process at the superior courts to £10 and to £2 in all other courts.[16] The initial Act was restricted to five years, presumably originating from a desire to quell the rate of imprisonment which had exploded following the South Sea Bubble, however, it was later extended and, in 1748, as 'great benefit hath accrued to this kingdom by' the Act, the limitation upon *mesne* process was declared 'in force ... for ever'.[17] The 1725 Act had an almost immediate impact upon imprisonment. The committee investigating the King's Bench Prison recorded that in 1729 'the Number of Prisoners, even now in the Marshal's Custody, amount to six hundred and fifty seven, which Number is much less than used to be in that Custody, before the late Acts of Parliament against frivolous Arrests, and for the relief of Insolvent Debtors'.[18] While numerous King's Bench prisoners had been released by Insolvency Acts – c.300 in 1725 and a further c.550 in 1729 – the limitation on *mesne* process kept the population at a rate the Marshal and committee regarded as low.[19] This represented a significant alteration to the system and, if this pattern was repeated nationwide, thousands of potential imprisonments were lost. The focus on 'vexatious arrests' implies a legislative belief that those owing the smallest amounts were only confined by the foolish or the cruel and so required safeguarding. While creditors would presumably disagree, this reform thus restricted the institution of debt imprisonment to the trading classes (both 'Merchants' and 'Artificers'). After 1725, the prisons cannot be regarded as "unreformed" except in the sense that they had not yet been abolished. This reform probably improved the image and healthfulness of the prisons by reducing the number of destitute prisoners as well as contributing to the lower rate of arrests exhibited in the 1730s and 1740s and the decline in mortality.

The Vexatious Arrests Act eliminated neither the desire nor the need to pursue debts under £2. While throughout the period credit might be offered in the thousands of pounds, outside of high finance or international trading, the majority of credit was for small sums, regularly under the new *mesne* limits.[20] In 1751 John Fitzsimmonds argued that a method was necessary by which the new *mesne* limits could be alleviated:

> The honest Tradesman, whose Living depends upon the Sale of his Goods to Persons in a low Way of Life, and whose Bills seldom amount to any large sum, being enabled to recover his Property with ease and

speed, would be more likely to Support himself and Family with Credit, and would perhaps be prevented from Ruin, which I know has been the Case of many, whose Debtors have refused to pay without Force.[21]

As the pace and rate of commerce accelerated, particularly in urban areas where credit might be given for almost any good or service, individual small unpaid debts accrued into mountains of fiscal risk. Myer Abraham, a butcher from London's east end, imprisoned in the Wood Street Compter in 1761 owing £60, was also well aware of this dilemma. Abraham was himself owed £110 96 8d by sixty-one customers whom he listed in detail when compelled by his creditor Henry Samuel through the Insolvency Act. Only eleven of his debtors owed enough to be imprisoned while twenty-two owed him less than £1. Apart from 'two Notes of Hand' amounting to £10 15s 4d owed by Mr Levy Saul, all his credits had been given on 'goods sold' arising directly from his business. He evidently struggled to recover even these small sums despite his debtors all being familiar members of his local Jewish community, Myer seemingly being the principal supplier of kosher meat in Aldgate. It is also probable that he felt no need to aggressively recover such small sums from his friends and neighbours before his arrest, constituting a fatal oversight of the impact of combined obligations.[22] Myer was far from unusual; of the sums owed to those compelled out of Wood Street in 1761, 74% could not have been pursued through *mesne* process.[23] William Hutton, the historian, bookseller, and magistrate, summarised the situation of countless tradespeople like Myer, writing in 1787 that 'nothing is so necessary, in the whole system of English jurisprudence, as a concise method of recovering property, and terminating disputes'.[24]

The inability to proceed at law not being to the satisfaction of creditors – a group with whom legislature usually sided – a mechanism for confining small debtors slowly developed.[25] The solution was not the removal of the common law restrictions, a cause for which apparently no one advocated publicly. Instead, a series of institutions known as the Courts of Requests or the Courts of Conscience were founded or extended.[26] The key pattern of this process was irregularity. The Courts were not established in a uniform manner as the consequence of a drive for reform; rather, they originated in a series of unique statutes driven locally by civic leaders. Nor were all Courts new to the eighteenth century. The Westminster Court of Requests, the model upon which many later Courts were based, originated as early as 1483, gaining the bulk of its significance and power under Henry VIII, where it functioned as 'a committee … for the hearing of poor men's [civil] causes'.[27] This Court's business was wide-ranging and the primary association of this institution with credit disputes only occurred during the long eighteenth century.[28] It remained the only institution of its type until the first provincial Court was created in 1689 to serve Bristol and Gloucester. A second Court for Newcastle followed later that year and in 1701 a third provincial Court was established in Norwich.[29]

Advocates, viewing them as cheaper and more effective methods of compelling repayment from the poor, called for the establishment of more Courts around the country even prior to the 1725 reform. In 1701 William Pudsey suggested 'tis some evidence of the convenience or necessity of [Courts of Requests], that Petitions come [to establish them] in almost every Session of Parliament' (though the factuality of this is certainly questionable) while in 1709 *Britannia Fortior* declared 'more of these Courts are wanting, to prevent Excessive Expences at Law'.[30] However, before the changes to *mesne* process were made permanent, the spread of the Courts was slow. While as early as 1709 the Courts had grown in notoriety enough to appear in petty literature, that they were referred to as 'either of the Courts of Conscience at Norwich or Gloucester', ignoring those in London and Newcastle, suggests there was little public knowledge of the Courts or clamour for their extension.[31] In 1750, a tract on 'the Necessity and Conveniency of Courts of Conscience, or Requests' further demonstrated their slow spread as it argued to an apparently ill-informed audience that

> when the like Acts, and (upon full Proof of their Expedience) … are granted to all the Counties and eminent Trading Cities … tis highly, and almost without Contradiction, probable, that they will be attended with a numerous Train of good Effects and happy Consequences.[32]

As this pamphlet came to print, the establishment of such Courts was, however, accelerating and would eventually spread across the Empire, being founded in Ireland, America, and India.[33] By 1846 more than 300 Courts of Requests had been established in England and Wales, the majority between 1750 and 1820. Furthermore, after the changes to *mesne* process were made permanent in 1748, the statutes founding the Courts began describing them generally as Acts 'for the more easy and speedy Recovery of Small Debts' rather than merely as 'Courts of Conscience'.[34]

While the Courts were established by Parliament, there was no coordination originating from the legislature itself. The spread of the Courts represented an almost organic reaction to mounting commercial debt and the 1748 restrictions, being founded in response to and in accordance with the wishes of specific petitions organised by prominent figures in different localities. This local challenge to centrally devised restrictions on gaols further demonstrates the essential need of debt imprisonment within the wider commercial economy as well as the ability of commercially active people to interpret existing institutions, previously rarely deployed, for new needs. Due to the lack of official legislative architecture, each individual Court varied in its composition, bench, or the breadth of its jurisdiction so that before 1786 an official of one town's Court might feel lost in a neighbouring district.[35] However, they usually shared a number of common facets, principally that they functioned as courts of equity – often subsuming the customs of the local courts they replaced – and that expediency of process was of paramount importance. By bypassing the traditionally accepted fundamentals of the operation of the law, the Courts in theory 'made access to justice more affordable and the process of law more efficient'.[36] To achieve this, as Theodore Plucknett commented, 'they embodied several legal heresies', principally the lack of a jury, the frequent barring of lawyers, summary process, no right of appeal, and a bench without trained judges.[37] Instead, local men were appointed as Commissioners, chosen, as in Derby, from 'the principal part of the town'.[38] It was only after 1786 that the system of selecting men from 'householders ... possessed of a real estate of £20 a year, or a personal one of the value of £500' was standardised across the country.[39] Previously many followed Westminster's example of appointing the equivalent of two Aldermen and twelve commoners as Commissioners, though the process for determining who qualified in some districts appeared entirely arbitrary.[40] In Tower Hamlets the parish officers were 'empowered to nominate 240 commissioners in the whole' while the 1752 Act which created the Birmingham Court required seventy-two commissioners to be appointed 'out of the body of the inhabitants', ten of which were replaced every two years. Only a fraction of the Commissioners were required at a time; in Birmingham six were 'summoned alternately by the beadle, to attend the bench every month, but their attendance is wholly optional. ... Any three form a quorum'.[41]

Proceedings might also vary between the localities, such as whether rents could be sued for, but generally the actual process of suing followed a simple pattern in all Courts.[42] Plaintiffs submitted demands to the Court, which, in turn, summoned defendants. After the demand was read aloud defendants frequently confessed. If they did not, a trial lasting hours or often just a few minutes followed, including witnesses but excluding legal professionals by design. The decision rested solely in the Commissioners who, after hearing testimony, 'as they see Cause give judgement without more ado'.[43] The bench almost always found in favour of the complainant; John Trussler recorded in 1786 that 'the plaintiff's oath is always sufficient' evidence and 'if the plaintiff swears to his debt, no oath of the defendant will avail him'.[44] The Courts were empowered to then order the sale of a debtor's goods or their imprisonment, though their most frequent order was simply that the debt under dispute be paid. While satisfaction might be ordered in full immediately, the Court was also the first empowered to order instalment payments. For example, at the Court of Requests for the small market town of Chatteris in the Isle of Ely on the 25th November 1785, Matthew Coy 'having confessed the Debt' was 'ordered' to pay Sarah Waith 'the same being 10s together with Costs 3s 2d as follows that is today 5s immediately which was paid accordingly and the remainder by Weekly payments of 1s'.[45] The payment rate, as in Coy's case, was set by the bench irregularly either per week or per month. While a rate of two shillings a month or of sixpence a week might appear indistinct, for those usually being prosecuted through the courts (the precariously employed expecting delayed delivery of their wages) the latter could be both unrealistic and cruel particularly as missing one week's payment was enough for the Court to imprison a debtor. By the nineteenth century, decisions about whether to allow instalment payments were based on individual debtor earning power, and while this probably occurred in the eighteenth century, it was only at the discretion of the famously arbitrary Commissioners as there was no legal requirement to order realistic payment schedules.[46]

The popularity of the Courts was not universal; their summary and arbitrary nature, flying in the face of centuries of socially accepted precedent on the right to trial by jury, attracted criticism even before their wide adoption, appearing to represent a greater threat to English liberty even than the debtors' prisons. A letter describing 'Reasons against the Bill for erecting Courts of Conscience' in Southwark c.1700 declared that 'this arbitrary Proceeding, contrary to the Law, and Magna Charta, (being the Subjects Birthright) will bar the Subject of the Benefit of other good Laws ... and revive old antiquated Controversies, which that Law hath buried in Oblivion'.[47] One 1730s sermon linked them to the 'arbitrary courts' erected by Charles I in which 'unspeakable Oppressions were committed ... even to Men of the first Quality'.[48] Later in the century, when almost all towns contained such Courts, detractors frequently quoted the legal theorist William Blackstone on the importance of juries: 'the liberties of England cannot but subsist, so long as this *palladium* remains sacred and inviolate'. These writers, countering assertions that Courts were more effective than traditional justice, particularly fixed upon Blackstone's comment that 'delays and little inconveniencies in the forms of Justice, are the price that all free nations must pay for their liberty'.[49] Even without recourse to Blackstone, pamphleteers expressed general discomfort about the lack of juries; in 1768 Edward Wynne compared the Court's processes to that which 'one reads of in the Turkish dominions'.[50] In Parliament in 1796 Joseph Jekyll opposed the passage of further legislation asserting that proponents 'want materially to infringe the rights of juries, and the House ought to be well assured of its necessity before they gave it their approbation'.[51] At the ground level, a short pamphlet written by a campaigner against the foundation of a Court in Staffordshire in 1794 also criticised the absence of 'the ancient and valuable privilege of trial by Jury' and claimed that 'the exercise of these extensive, not to say unlimited powers' were 'equally repugnant to the Constitution, and unknown to the common Law of England', suggesting it was not just intellectuals who found arbitrary judgement unsettling.[52]

These campaigners had little success. Hutton dismissed concerns about the integrity of the law as an exaggeration: 'That the proceedings in Courts of Conscience are entirely in derogation of common law, cannot readily be granted'.[53] Some explicitly promoted the lack of juries, prioritising efficiency for the sake of commerce.[54] George Croft, writing from Hutton's Birmingham, suggested that 'their deviation from the letter of the law enables them to do substantial justice' and dismissed the seriousness of such deviation when rated alongside the potential benefits: 'To many the practice of these Courts appears a species of legal empiricism, but it may be compared to that medical empiricism, which only undertakes slight wounds or slight bruises'.[55] The extent to which many were comfortable with the subversion of liberty rested in the inherent connection within the social consciousness of the Courts to the poor and the 'lower orders', Dornford declaring his third class of debtors were 'the subjects of the Court of Conscience'.[56] Trusler similarly noted that the 'defendants in these Courts are in general people so very low, that a gentleman would sooner lose 40s than attend them' claiming they appointed proxies to prosecute on their behalf.[57] It was regularly claimed the Courts were established 'for the Relief of Poor People' and that they prevented the 'barbarity' of their imprisonment.[58] However, this was not the sole reason they were associated with the poor as other writers advocated the Courts as a means of social control.[59] John Fitzsimmonds, for example, claimed summary prosecution limited the poor's immoral consumerism as 'the less Credit these poor People have, the less is their Consumption of Goods'.[60] Even where it was extolled as a benefit, by promoting the removal of juries in only this one legal setting, advocates implied that the restriction of common rights was acceptable in the case of the poor (this subversion being only 'slight bruises' upon the nation).

Criticism of the incompetence and partiality of the particular Commissioners administering Courts was less simple to ignore, even Croft commenting that while 'whoever resides in a large town, will be fully convinced of the usefulness of such courts, ... he may now and then have occasion to regret, that ... sufficient care is not used in selecting the commissioners'.[61] This may have been a subtle reference to Hutton who acted as a Commissioner of Birmingham's Court of Requests and was widely known in the city both for his treatises on the Courts and for his peculiar enthusiasm. The campaigner against the Staffordshire Court noted that 'every man is said to have his hobby-horse; and a Court of Requests seems to be that of the worthy Magistrate of Birmingham'.[62] While most commissioners served intermittently, Hutton served with vigour in Birmingham every Friday for nineteen years describing it in his memoirs as 'my favourite amusement'.[63] Even in his densely legalistic *Courts of Requests: Their Nature, Utility, and Powers Described* (1787) – the most detailed description of the Courts ever written – Hutton could barely restrain his enthusiasm: 'I have longed for Friday, as the school-boy for Christmas; nay, the practice of years has not worn off the keen edge of desire'.[64] Hutton's unregulated dominance of the Court and thus his significant personal role in the management of credit in Birmingham lay only in this eagerness. He exemplifies the questionable nature of the Courts, there being no better description of them than that of W.H.D. Winder, one of its few historians: 'amateur civil justice'.[65] Hutton is also emblematic of the power imbalance of this new aspect of the credit market, being, as he was, a creditor overseeing the trials of his customers. Accordingly, the Birmingham Court – its magistrates including Hutton's son and members of his tennis club – has been described accurately as 'a self-perpetuating oligarchy'.[66] This had been feared since the first inception of the Courts and, in figures like Hutton, management of the hen house had very much been turned over to the foxes.[67] More so than in any other legal institution, decisions in the Court of Requests controlled by such men depended on the whim of the bench with even Hutton admitting that sometimes his 'order was arbitrary'.[68] These decisions 'solely in them' were absolute and unappealable even in cases where there was a clear lack of diligence. While Hutton boasted that some causes could be dealt with 'in ten seconds', others complained quick trials made Commissioners 'liable to give very wrong or improper awards'.[69] Not all amateur justices were even as diligent or competent as Hutton.[70] The clerk of the Chatteris Court – which was supposed to meet at three o'clock on Friday in the George Inn – was regularly forced to record that 'There not being three Commissioners assembled for the purpose of holding the said Court the same is adjourned' sometimes, as in March and April 1789, on several consecutive occasions, undermining the supposed efficiency of justice.[71]

Despite their arbitrary and potentially incompetent nature, the Courts of Requests did, when they actually met, provide creditors with a valuable institution through which to force repayment as is testified to by the sheer number established and how busy they became. During the first eighteen months in which the Court in Tower Hamlets was in operation, 16,918 summonses were issued and 9,310 cases heard.[72] Many of the trials at these proto-small claims courts were genuine disputes between parties that, lacking the simple clarity of a bill of sale, required a formal arbiter to determine and were particularly suited to dealing with individuals who did not agree on whether debts were actually due. One contemporary legal example focussed upon a parson leasing his tithe to a vicar. The vicar after 'finding that the rent was more than the tithe was worth' concluded the deal was not fair and 'refused to hold the bargain any longer'. This dispute – the parson's contract stipulating that a debt was due but the vicar's opinion holding the contract was invalid – required a third-party judgement. It was only after the parson sued in the Court of Requests for the rent (the Commissioners finding in his favour) that the pair could move on.[73] Similarly, Hutton, in his history of Derby, was keen to emphasise the necessity of the courts for preserving neighbourly harmony: 'So long as it shall be deemed prudent to put a period to quarrels among neighbours, so long will a Court of [Requests] be useful' particularly as the 'expences of the court are exceedingly small'.[74] Plaintiffs were not 'wholly confined to publicans, petty shop-keepers, and retailers of different description' proceeding against the poor as the Staffordshire campaigner believed.[75] At Chatteris within the 265 cases described in the surviving minutes (1782–1792), unique debtors only slightly outnumbered unique creditors by 134 to 107. Furthermore, the majority of both groups only appeared in the Court once (56% of creditors and 61% of debtors) suggesting that this Court was not resorted to on a regular basis when retailers settled their books at the end of the quarter. At least nineteen creditors also appeared as debtors suggesting further that use of the Courts was not strictly hierarchical. However, some creditors in Chatteris did use the Court with enthusiasm reflecting behaviour outside of such tight-knit rural communities. Mr Richard Berridge appeared on twenty-two occasions, pursuing twenty different debtors for sums between 6s and four debts notably of £1 19s 11¾d. He sued John Hudson three times in the Court as well as Thomas and Robert Hudson who may have been relations. Berridge – perhaps unsurprisingly – was also a Commissioner. For creditors such as he, the popularity of the Courts of Requests derived principally from their representing coercive contract enforcement. They forced small debtors, untouchable by *mesne* process, into circumstances that required they focus all their efforts on satisfying their creditors, with failure to do so removing the 1725 protections by imprisoning them. In this manner, they alleviated the Vexatious Arrests Act as, before reform to the underlying system of credit, commercial actors would continue to seek and even create institutions through which they could protect their trade.

The irregular growth of the Courts of Requests, essentially subverting the *mesne* reform led almost inevitably to the period's second – and far more impactful – substantive reform of debt imprisonment. The regular imprisonment of the poor, which it was claimed had led to an increase in poverty, ran against society's recognition of a qualitative difference between petty debtors and insolvents.[76] Furthermore, the widely known inconsistencies and abuses of the Commissioners attracted the attention of the legislature and reformers in the same manner that the system of fees and rents drew their ire to prisons. As the attempted abolition of the imprisonment of the poor had been achieved essentially without controversy in the first half of the eighteenth century, it is unsurprising that its resurgence was challenged. Two statutes passed in 1785 and 1786 – the first applying to London and the second extending the changes nationwide – attempted to bring central control to the untamed Courts as well as to restore the spirit of the 1725 legislation that the poor should not be allowed to remain in prison indefinitely. It established wealth specifications for Commissioners (property being equated with honest dealing), abolished gaol fees for petty debtors (much to the chagrin of keepers), and, most importantly, placed term limits upon all prisoners committed through the Court of Requests.[77] While certain provincial prisons had previously limited imprisonment length, after 1786 all debtors committed for less than 20s could only be held for twenty days, and those owing up to 40s would be released after forty days.[78] In a stunning change of practice, as Margot Finn highlighted and commended, 'expiration of term … was now unambiguously to liquidate the debt'.[79] Hitchcock and Shoemaker similarly celebrate that 'the debtors' prison [thus] ceased to loom so large in the catalogue of misfortunes that might befall a plebeian Londoner'.[80] While clearly a moment of humanitarian reform benefiting the lives of impoverished debtors, the change had two detrimental effects upon the institution of debt imprisonment. First, it declawed imprisonment, making it ineffectual for creditors – at the end of the process of trial, arrest, and imprisonment, creditors received none of their debt and were even expected on occasion to pay 5s to the keeper of the prison at discharge.[81] Second, and while a more

theoretical effect, possibly a more important change, by the debt being liqui-
dated, in essence, Parliament criminalised, or at least deemed worthy of punishment, the state of poverty. Imprisonment as a punishment was rare in this
period and those imprisoned for debt were not being punished.[82] However,
this reform occurred in an era of growing legislative interest in imprisonment
as a corrective punishment.[83] By associating serving time with making payments, offence and correction were equated. Furthermore, the commitment
registers of the Wood Street Compter debtors' prison – Court of Requests
debtors making up 26% of its population – record that terms could be cu-
mulative, three separate actions below £1 allowing a commitment of sixty
days, for example, rather than debtors being released after the supposed forty
day maximum.[84] These term limits were thus not devised as time to prove
prisoners could not pay but as a proportional sentence. Committing debtors
who *could* be released after a term was not an explicit punishment. Court of
Request debtors could still pay and achieve their freedom early; these individuals were not punished. However, it was the end point of imprisonment
that deemed it a punishment – time served, scaled to debt size, was sufficient
penance to equal the crime of indebtedness.

William Hutton's 1787 account of the Courts, published a year after the
change in the law, exhibits a clear alignment between imprisonment and
punishment. Hutton justified the different terms for £1 and £2 debtors in
this vein: 'as the error was but half the magnitude, it was thought the punishment should be so too'. Nor was this an idle or unique use of the word "punishment" by Hutton. Completion of "punishment" explained why creditors
could be made to pay gaol fees: 'It is unjust to charge it upon the prisoner; he
has undergone a punishment equal to the fault. As he has suffered all he ought
to suffer, no farther demand can be made'. A section in his treatise was headed
'Punishment' and while it preceded that on 'Prison', it is clear Hutton linked
the two. Hutton reminded his audience that 'he who keeps near the standard of rectitude, has nothing to do with laws' for 'they were made to bind
those who go astray', again associating indebtedness with criminality. Such
criminality needed prison for 'Take away punishment, and law, like the lion
of Aesop, when deprived of his claws and his teeth, loses its terror … Punishment must follow disobedience'. If any reader still remained unclear, Hutton
specified 'the punishment consists of imprisonment'. Hutton was actually
disappointed the law went no further; while keen to stress his charitable
nature, frequently insisting punishment must equal the crime ('everything
beyond is barbarity'), he suggested that hard labour ought to be introduced as
a method both of punishment and reform.[85]

Unsurprisingly, the punitive aspect of the Courts was unpopular with the
underclasses prosecuted by them.[86] While replacing the existential institution
of private arrest and individual creditor action with a singular bench of identi-
fiable humans prosecuting all debtors was always likely to direct antipathy, in
Birmingham this smouldering resentment was enflamed by Hutton's obstinacy
and low view of the populace. He recalled being 'asked at a public meeting of

the inhabitants [of Birmingham], whether an imprisonment of forty days did not more than atone for a small debt?' Hutton, believing his behaviour just, retorted that 'one would think *that* punishment is not too great which does not cure the defect. I have known many an obstinate defendant lie the stated time in prison, merely out of revenge to the plaintiff'.[87] While the Courts were unpopular with working people across the country, the Birmingham Court and Hutton himself (well known for the weekly repetition of his favourite order to all debtors he found guilty to 'pay sixpence and come again next Friday') experienced a highly visual pushback during the Priestley Riots of 1791.[88] The rioters ostensibly attacked Dissenters and Radicals though when Hutton's home in the city was destroyed – the mob then marching three miles to his country house which 'they reduced to ashes' – the attack upon him, according to one witness, 'did not arise from his religious principles, but on account of his being a very active Commissioner of the Court of Requests'.[89] As they marched down High Street, the mob cried 'That they would be revenged of Hutton, on account of the Court'.[90] It was not just Hutton alone they raged against, also attacking the Court itself and breaking open its lock-up. Beyond physical altercation, the honour of the Court was assaulted in mockery. As Hutton's furniture was thrown into the street, the rioters held a faux auction to which each participant bid 'I'll give sixpence and come again next Friday'.[91] However, popular resentment does not mean Hutton's views regarding punishment of the poor's indebtedness were unrepresentative, certainly of the elite.[92] Direct reference to Hutton's book in the 1794 pamphlet against the Staffordshire court, suggests that it was being read by those involved in the decisions that might erect and subsequently manage such Courts even after the author himself had been forced by the mob into resentful retirement.[93]

Beyond the semantics of confinement, the legal change had a measurable impact on debt imprisonment. At Wood Street, prior to reform, commitments from the Court of Requests had steadily increased from 10–30 per year in the early 1760s to 60–120 two decades later. Growth in commitments was initially uninterrupted by the 1785 reform, either because creditors were keen to punish debtors or probably because Commissioners felt more comfortable imprisoning the impoverished with the knowledge they would not be incarcerated permanently. However, while commitments originating in the Court of Requests peaked in 1788 at 120, they subsequently declined dramatically, the rate more than halving by 1795 to 50 commitments and after 1800 commitment rates returned to the lows of the 1760s. While this was a general era of decreasing commitment due to the instability of war similarly affecting *mesne* process, creditors had apparently lost their appetite for the Courts, not wanting to risk losing their debt and instead relying on informal pressures. As the number being committed declined, the average debt owed rose from c.£1 10s at the height of use to over £2 by 1801 even before the Court's limits were raised to £5 in 1805 as those committed after 1795 were more likely to be sued by multiple creditors.[94] Twenty years after the change in the law, it seems creditors were only willing to risk their petty debtor being imprisoned for relatively significant values, with debtors owing under £1 all but disappearing by 1805. Those still being confined were also more likely to be able to pay, as only 16% of early nineteenth-century debtors were released having stayed out their time compared to 56% in 1785–1800, peaking in 1791 when 86% of those committed by the Court avoided payment. The reform therefore had a clear impact on debtors securing release, though it was not as dramatic as legislators might have expected. Prior to 1785, 54% of such debtors were released in less than six months and 98% within a year of commitment suggesting the reform was broadly unnecessary. It does seem from the registers that the letter of the law was not always being followed at the compter. In the commitment entries of 479 Court of Request debtors after 1786, both the number of days prisoners should have been held for and a final release date were recorded. On 356 occasions (74%) the actual number of days held was greater than that specified at commitment. This probably indicated that debtors entitled to their freedom on a specific day had to await the Court's order (and therefore approval) that they had served their punishment.

The 1785/1786 reform did not immediately end debt imprisonment and the majority of commercial debt could still be sued for under *mesne* process until the nineteenth century. However, it remains important to note that in attempting to make prisons less cruel, poverty was in essence criminalised, a practice which undermined the purely commercial nature of debt imprisonment. This did not lead to a rise in vengeful creditors rushing to punish their debtors, partly because it was of no financial benefit further undermining the theory that creditors only resorted to imprisonment to wound those who had betrayed them. Such prisoners were treated as qualitatively different by the system. Court of Request prisoners were regularly separated from common law debtors, either within the same prison or in different institutions, even being sent to houses of correction.[95] Reformer William Smith noted with horror in 1776 that Court of Request debtors were sent to Clerkenwell Bridewell 'where they are mixed with the felons and disorderly people' suggesting the state of poverty was being viewed as comparable to misdemeanour felonies.[96] This behaviour predated 1786 but, based on how Hutton described punishment, the new legislation emphasised, nationalised, and institutionalised it, further damaging the image of prisons as sites of neutral financial coercion. Parliament thus unintentionally enshrined distinctions between debtors based on wealth which had previously only existed conceptually: those who owed more than £10 were unfortunate and required Insolvency Acts; petty debtors were dishonest and required correction. Debtors' prisons thus became more akin to workhouses for petty debts and the establishment of such protections set a dangerous precedent which, when expanded upon by raising limits further in the nineteenth century, made the institution less and less able to contribute to commercial harmony. Creditors were through the summary nature of the Courts still able to recover money which was rightfully theirs though the choice of how to proceed and the ultimate coercive power of imprisonment were taken from them, potentially slowing recovery. Middling sort vendors, owing debts in tens or hundreds of pounds for supplies of raw materials from producers, relied upon their ability to recover sums measured in shillings for finished goods. If a vendor's only recourse was an instalment payment of sixpence a week which, upon default, could lead to the debt being lost after forty days confinement, their business was made less not more secure by the Courts of Requests.

Given this structural unpicking of debt imprisonment, it is reasonable to ask why the prisons were not abolished until 1869. While society's support for debt imprisonment had apparently softened by the late eighteenth century – the majority of works opposing arrest being published after c.1770 at a time when imprisonment rates were spiking according to the commitment register data – it had not collapsed completely. The twin reforms of 1725 and 1786 were not inspired by an attempt to significantly alter or weaken the prisons, reform with such specific motives only emerging in the nineteenth century.[97] Rather, the first reform was intended to confine arrest to those deemed appropriate "debtors" which excluded the poor arising from a moral judgement that they should not be offered sufficient credit to require their imprisonment. The later reform further attempted to remove those who were deemed not appropriate members of the debtor class, in a similar fashion as the limits upon bankruptcy theoretically barred access to those not involved in "trade". Damage was done to the institution accidentally based on a lack of knowledge of the quantitative reality. This was therefore an attempt at rectification – correcting the changes brought about by the swelling commercial economy – not reform as figures such as John Howard, James Neild, or their nineteenth century descendants would have understood it. Principally, this arose from a lack of public desire to enact actual targeted reform, those proposing it encountering visceral opposition and general apathy.

Josiah Dornford was, in the eyes of his fellow Common Councillors of London, a troublemaker. An advocate for an array of reforms including the extension of the vote and the abolition of the death penalty, Dornford regularly, as one newspaper reported of a meeting at the Guildhall in 1785, 'with his usual propensity to peace and good order, threw universal confusion into the Court'.[98] Dornford quibbled over almost any issue brought to council in his campaign against corruption in the city and reform of the prisons as well as publishing lengthy letters in the *Morning Chronicle* first under his pseudonym "Fidelio" and then under his own name which he subsequently collected and published as pamphlets.[99] Many of his complaints were quietly ignored or meetings were wrapped up before Dornford could bring forward his motions, however, his challenge to the prisons in 1784 and 1786 met with public and visceral opposition. As his attacks in 1784 included general declarations against misuse of city funds, it is unsurprising fellow councillors felt the need to refute them. However, their public removal of his "Fidelio" alias, the inquiry which entirely exonerated the Corporation and its officers, and the failed attempt to have Dornford censured represented an unusually stringent rebuke of his assertions that 'nothing but a real reform can save this sinking nation'.[100] The City paid to publish extracts from the report in the newspapers (particularly in Josiah's favourite *Morning Chronicle*) including the accounts of prison keepers asserting that Dornford's accusations amounted to lies and that no reform of the gaols was necessary.[101] This public refutation appears to have been met with agreement from the wider populous and numerous letters were published in response to the inquiry praising officers connected to gaols, even including one from Newgate's Common Side.[102] Dornford subsequently failed on several occasions to be elected an alderman, his previous advocacy for prisoners being raised by his opponents ('Rejoice, O ye thieves and be glad ye Housebreakers, the great Dornford is made an Alderman') and his defeats reported as arising from 'the inhabitants ... disapprobation of his conduct'.[103] He was even blacklisted from membership of the Society for Promoting Christian Knowledge further suggesting his advocacy for reform had made him *persona non grata* in London.[104] Apparently undeterred, in 1786 Dornford again campaigned for prison reform in the *Morning Chronicle* and then in council, raising the case of prisoners who had died in the Poultry Compter. However, advocating that the City should 'set about reforming our gaols; they are ... habitations of cruelty, abodes of misery', proved equally unsuccessful.[105] The inquiry cleared the keeper of all blame, finding the prisoners were at fault for 'bringing [themselves] into a decline' as other debtors questioned 'were well contented, and had wanted nothing'. On this occasion, Dornford was officially censured, his conduct having been found 'highly reprehensible and unbecoming a good Citizen' emphasising the sense that he had overstepped the line of acceptability by questioning the administration of specific debtors' prisons.[106] The civic establishment's efforts to protect fixed institutions such as the prisons from smears was thus conducted with a rigour and absoluteness not even matched when Dornford publicly declared the Mayor to be corrupt.[107] Josiah, however, was untroubled by his censure and in March 1787 accused the keeper of the County Gaol of Surrey of corruption, the subsequent report finding 'the Prisoners in a better State of Health than was ever before known, and ... [the gaol] in remarkable good Order'.[108]

The reaction to Josiah Dornford's campaign, particularly during the Chamberlainship of the increasingly conservative John Wilkes, reveals little new about the entrenched cronyism and self-protecting nature of the Common Council of London. However, that many in the wider civic population appear to have sided with the Council reveals the apathetic relationship most had to prison reform. Dornford's key mistake lay in singling out individual keepers; even Howard's lengthy description of the problems of every gaol he visited in his *State of the Prisons* rarely blamed or rebuked any individual keeper by name. While the populous agreed that the gaols deserved improvement in an abstract sense, particular attacks on institutions they regarded as working were unpalatable. There were numerous anonymous statements of support for Dornford published in the press, calling his 'conduct ... noble and heroic, ... he stands forth the champion of the poor and distressed', praising his 'humane exertions', and declaring 'the idea of a Dornford will ever be connected with Howard'.[109] However, many middle-class Londoners who did not make the transition from reader to contributor may have felt like "L.M." who complained to the *Morning Chronicle* in August 1786 that 'the publick has been dinned ... with the tedious and sermonizing rhapsodies of Mr Josiah Dornford'. This writer asserted that keepers were in general 'very humane' and that Dornford's proposed reforms would 'render Newgate a place of riot and bloodshed'.[110] The majority in the eighteenth century assumed that the prisons were inherently uncomfortable places – a belief fuelled by reformers. However, as there was in the writings both of Dornford and L.M. very little separation between felons and poor debtors, the public appears to have assumed both deserved their lot. Furthermore, as society already assumed the worst about prison conditions, the inquiries reformers initiated managed to undermine their case by revealing they were not necessarily bleak hell holes, weakening the argument for reform. While commercial people might concur over coffee that the state of the gaols was disgraceful, it was simply not something they felt particularly inclined to do anything about and found individuals such as Dornford who relentlessly raised the topic to be preachy. The prisons went "unreformed" (or unabolished) because most people did not care enough to advocate for it – the reform movement was a minority view and society was more likely to agree with groups such as 'The Society of Guardians' that the poor should be punished rather than potential frauds should be liberated. While keepers behaved and death rates did not spike, the wider community were content to leave prisons as they were, probably not giving debt imprisonment much thought until a friend, relative, or they themselves faced a creditor's demand.[111]

⋆⋆

Despite the view of reformers and scholars that it had not altered significantly, the debtors' prison as an institution of contract enforcement was in a poorer shape after 1800 than it had been in 1700. Aesop's lion was far from toothless but several of its talons had been pulled out by changes to the treatment of small debts and other reforms such as the increased rate of Insolvency Acts which became biennial in the early nineteenth century. However, there was also little sign at the opening in 1815 of the New Debtors' Prison for London and Westminster in Whitecross Street, built specially to house the swelling prison population in the capital, that debtors' prisons would be abolished within sixty years. In large part this is because the reforms the debtors' prisons experienced in the eighteenth century were not a response to concerted campaigns against the institution. The prisons were unmade through well-intentioned attempts to make the system more effective, but which accidentally undermined its usefulness for creditors. The organic development of the system of Courts of Requests was a direct response to the limitation of *mesne* process and, even before 1786, represented a far more arbitrary and oppressive burden on the economic lives of the working poor than debtors' prisons. However, as the experiences of traders selling on credit to those who could only afford to take-on small credit showed, there needed to be a mechanism of compelling payment. While commitment registers demonstrate that the prisons were still in regular use in the early nineteenth century, as they represented an effective and vital mechanism of securing commerce any assault upon them before the greater formalisation of credit and currency reform represented a potential weakening of the market. Creditors after 1786 were incentivised not to give credit except to other traders or those making purchases above £2. This was though largely accidental and did not utterly undermine trade as the Courts formalised many of the processes featured in the informal process of confinement – compelling the debtor to focus financial strategy upon repayment once a week, even if they were allowed to do this with their liberty intact. Furthermore, this alteration was not translated into more substantial change as it was interpreted simultaneously as making the system more effective, reducing unnecessary cruelty, and correcting the behaviour of commercially careless and mischievous working poor, not as a diminishment of imprisonment itself. Despite the high rate of publications on reform and the vocality of campaigners such as Howard (who, while he condemned the practice, stopped short of an explicit advocacy for abolition), these were not representative of common attitudes about how or even whether the prisons should be reformed.[112] In part the eighteenth-century debtors' prison went "unreformed" because practical agitation for it was so limited. By the time the Debt Act was passed in 1869, the debtors' prison was no longer a credible economic institution. This, however, arose from the fact that the pecuniary issues, commercial structure, and nature of credit were vastly altered after 1800. It was not so much that the unreformed debtors' prison ceased to be the answer to a specific problem as much as the underlying reality of the problem changed, making the unprompted reforms of 1725 and 1786 even more striking.

Notes

1 Richard Bevan, *Observations on the Law of Arrest and Imprisonment for Debt: Together with a Short Sketch of a Plan for an Amendment of that Law* (London: 1781), p. 1.

2 Samuel Byrom, *An Irrefutable Argument Fully Proving, that to Discharge Great Debts Is Less Injury, and More Reasonable than to Discharge Small Debts* (London: 1726), p. 18; John Howard, *The State of the Prisons in England and Wales, with Preliminary Observations, and an Account of Some Foreign Prisons* (London: 1777), p. 57; Josiah Dornford, *Nine Letters to the Right Honourable Lord Mayor and Aldermen of the City of London, on the State of the City Prisons* (London: 1786), pp. 83–92.

3 Anon. *Observations on Debtors and Imprisonment for Debt* (1740), p. 2; F.A.S. Murray, *Thoughts on Imprisonment for Debt Humbly Addressed to His Majesty* (London: 1788), p. 18; Anon. *An Epistolary Poem, Humbly Inscribed To the Right Honourable Frederick Lord North … On the Present Mode of Imprisonment for Debt* (London: 1773), p. 16; Anon. *Considerations on the Laws between Debtors and Creditors; and an Abstract of the Insolvent Acts. With Thoughts on a Bill to Enable Creditors to Recover the Effects of their Debtors, and to Abolish Imprisonment for Debt* (London: 1779); Bartholomew Thomas Duhigg, *Observations on the Operation of Insolvent Laws, and Imprisonment for Debt* (Dublin: 1797).

4 Anon. *An Inquiry into the Practice of Imprisonment for Debt, and a Refutation of Mr James Stephen's Doctrine. To Which Is Added, a Hint for Relief of Both Creditor and Debtor* (London: 1773) p. 46; Anon. *New, Candid, and Practical Thoughts on the Law of Imprisonment for Debt, with a View to the Regulation of it* (London: 1788), pp. 37–38.

5 Bevan, *Observations*, pp. 42–57.

6 Byrom, *Irrefutable Argument*, p. 27; Anon. *Imprisonment for Debt Considered with Respect to the Bad Policy, Inhumanity, and Evil Tendency of that Practice* (London: 1772), p. 40; Anon. *Reasons against Confining Persons in Prison for Debt, Humbly Offered to the Consideration of Parliament* (1726).

7 Margot C. Finn, *The Character of Credit – Personal Debt in English Culture, 1740–1914* (Cambridge: Cambridge University Press, 2003), Chapter 3 "Mansions of Misery": The Unreformed Debtors' Prison, pp. 109–150; Tim Hitchcock and Robert Brink Shoemaker, *London Lives – Poverty, Crime and the Making of a Modern City, 1690–1800* (Cambridge: Cambridge University Press, 2015), p. 103; Robin Evans, *The Fabrication of Virtue – English Prison Architecture, 1750–1840* (Cambridge: Cambridge University Press, 1982), p. 1; Tawny Paul, *Poverty of Disaster – Debt and Insecurity in Eighteenth-Century Britain* (Cambridge: Cambridge University Press, 2019), p. 34; Paul H. Haagen, "Eighteenth-Century English Society and the Debt Law", in *Social Control and the State – Historical and Comparative Essays*, eds. Stanley Cohen and Andrew Scull (Oxford: Basil Blackwell, 1986), pp. 228–229.

8 V. Marksham Lester, *Victorian Insolvency – Bankruptcy, Imprisonment for Debt, and Company Winding-up in Nineteenth-Century England* (Oxford: Clarendon Press, 1995), p. 120; Brianna L. Campbell, "The Economy of the Debtors' Prison Model: Why Throwing Deadbeats into Debtors' Prison Is a Good Idea", *Arizona Journal of International and Comparative Law* vol. 32, no. 3 (2015), p. 854; Richard Ford, "Imprisonment for Debt", *Michigan Law Review* vol. 25, no. 1 (November 1926), p. 31.

9 Anon. *The Debtor's and Creditor's Assistant; or, a Key to the King's Bench and Fleet prisons; Calculated for the Information and Benefit of the Injured Creditor, as well as the Unfortunate Debtor* (London: 1793), pp. 80–81; Anon. *Reasons against Confining*; James Stephen, *Considerations on Imprisonment for Debt, Fully Proving, that the Confining of the Bodies of Debtors Is Contrary to Common Law, Magna Charta, Statute Law, Justice, Humanity, and Policy* (London: 1770).

10 David Graeber, *Debt – The First 5000 Years* (New York: Melvile House, 2011), p. 7; William Fennor, *The Compters Commonwealth* (London: 1617).

11 Josiah Dornford, *Seven Letters to the Lords and Commons of Great Britain, Upon the Present Mode of Arresting and Imprisoning the Bodies of Debtors* (London: 1786), pp. 9–10. His division is not indistinct from Gregory King's 1688: those who were 'Increasing the Wealth of the Kingdom' and 'Decreasing the Wealth'. Gregory King, *Natural and Political Observations and Conclusions upon the State and Condition of England, in Two Tracts* (Baltimore: Johns Hopkins Press, 1936); For the continued relevance of King c.1780 See: John Campbell, *A Political Survey of Britain Vol. II* (London: 1774), p. 69; George Chalmers, *An Estimate of the Comparative Strength of Britain During the Current and Four Preceding Reigns* (London: 1782); Anon. *A Collection of Pamphlets Concerning the Poor* (London: 1787), pp. 103–107; Frederick Eden, *The State of the Poor; or an History of the Labouring Classes in England Vol. III* (London: 1797), p. 351.

12 Edward Farley, *Imprisonment for Debt, Unconstitutional. The Second Edition* (London: 1795), p. 28 (this second shorter edition is radically different from that of 1788); Paul Hess Haagen, "Imprisonment for Debt in England and Wales", unpublished PhD thesis, University of Princeton (1986), pp. 13–15.

13 Anon. *A Speech without Doors, in Behalf of an Insolvent Debtor in the Fleet-Prison. With Some Remarks on the Present State of Gaol-Archy* (London: 1729), pp. 2, 7.

14 Daniel Defoe, *Some Objections Humbly Offered to the Consideration of the Hon House of Commons, Relating to the Present Intended Relief of Prisoners* (London: 1729), pp. 6–7.

15 Robert Holloway, *A Letter to John Wilkes, Esq; Sheriff of London and Middlesex; In Which the Extortion and Oppression of Sheriffs Officers, with Many Other Alarming Abuses, Are Exemplified and Detected; and a Remedy Proposed* (London: 1771), p. 34.

16 Nathan Levy, "Mesne Process in Personal Actions at Common Law and the Power Doctrine", *Yale Law Journal* vol. 78 (1968), pp. 56–57.

17 "An Act to Prevent Frivolous and Vexatious Arrests", 1725, 12 George I, c.29; "An Act to Revive and make Perpetual Two Acts of Parliament, One Made in the Twelfth Year of the Reign of His Late Majesty King George I, intituled, An Act to Prevent Frivolous and Vexatious Arrests; and the Other Made in the Fifth Year of His Present Majesty's Reign, to Explain, Amend, and Render more Effectual the said Act", 1748, 21 George II, c.3.

18 Anon. *A Report from the Committee Appointed to Enquire Into the State of the Goals of this Kingdom. Relating to the King's Bench Prison* (London: 1730), p. 3.

19 *The London Gazette*, 1st–5th June, 1725, no.6378 – 15th–17th July, 1729, no.6796.

20 Craig Muldrew, *The Economy of Obligation – The Culture of Credit and Social Relations in Early Modern England* (Basingstoke: Macmillan, 1998), pp. 95, 118; Craig Muldrew, "From Credit to Savings? An Examination of Debt and Credit in Relation to Increasing Consumption in England (c.1650 to 1770)", *Quaderni Storci* vol. 137 (August 2011), pp. 402–407; Julian Hoppit, "Attitudes to Credit in Britain, 1680–1790", *The Historical Journal* vol. 33, no. 2 (June 1990), p. 313.

21 John Fitzsimmonds, *Free and Candid Disquisitions, of the Nature and Execution of the Laws of England, Both in Civil and Criminal Affairs* (London: 1751), p. 34.

22 "List of Prisoners Handed over by the Sheriffs to their Successors on 28 Sept Annually, with Notes of Occurrences During the Subsequent Year", 1760–1761, Wood Street Compter later Giltspur Street Compter, LMA, CLA/028/01/008; "Myer Abraham", Debtors Schedules: Wood Street Compter A-N, 1761, LMA, CLA/047/LJ/17/044/002; *London Gazette*, 26th–30th May, 1761, no.10108.

23 Debtors Schedules: Wood Street Compter A-N, 1761, LMA, CLA/047/LJ/17/044; Debtors Schedules: Wood Street Compter P-Y, 1761, LMA, CLA/047/LJ/17/045.

24 William Hutton, *Courts of Requests: Their Nature, Utility, and Powers Described, with A Variety of Cases, Determined in that of Birmingham* (Birmingham: 1787), p. 9.

25 Hoppit, "Attitudes", p. 313; Margot C. Finn, *The Character of Credit – Personal Debt in English Culture, 1740–1914* (Cambridge: Cambridge University Press, 2003), pp. 197–202.

26 The former name was more popular post-1750 presumably so as to separate the Courts from association with ecclesiastical justice though there was no practical difference between the two names.

27 Theodore F.T. Plucknett, *A Concise History of the Common Law* (London: Butterworth & Co., 1948), pp. 175–176.

28 A.F. Pollard, "The Growth of the Court of Requests", *The English Historical Review* vol. 56, no. 222 (April, 1941), pp. 300–303; See: Timothy Stretton, *Women Waging Law in Elizabethan England* (Cambridge: Cambridge University Press, 1998), pp. 7–9, 70–100; Timothy Stretton, *Marital Litigation in the Court of Requests: 1542–1642* (Cambridge: Cambridge University Press, 2008); On Credit: Liam J. Meyer, "Humblewise: Deference and Complaint in the Jacobean Court of Requests", *Journal of Early Modern Studies* vol. 4 (2015), pp. 261–285; Lamar M. Hill, "'Extreame Detriment': Failed Credit and the Narration of Indebtedness in the Jacobean Court of Requests," in *Law and Authority in Early Modern England – Essays Presented to Thomas Garden Barnes*, eds. Buchanan Sharp and Mark Charles Fissel (Newark: University of Delaware Press, 2007), pp. 136–156.

29 W.H.D Winder, "The Courts of Requests," *The Law Quarterly Review* vol. 52, no. 207 (1936), p. 373; Margot Finn, "Debt and Credit in Bath's Court of Requests, 1829–1839", *Urban History* vol. 21, pt. 2 (October 1994), p. 213; Michele Slatter, "The Norwich Court of Requests – A Tradition Continued", *Journal of Legal History* vol. 5, no. 3 (1984), p. 97; Ian P.H. Duffy, *Bankruptcy and Insolvency in London During the Industrial Revolution* (London: Garland Publishing, 1985), p. 112; Finn, *Character of Credit*, p. 202.

30 William Pudsey, *The Constitution and Laws of England Considered* (London: 1701), p. 208; Anon. *Britannia Fortior; or, the New State of Great Britain & Ireland, Under Our Sovereign Queen Anne* (London: 1709), p. 145.

31 William Oldisworth, *A Dialogue between Timothy and Philatheus. In Which the Principles and Projects of a Late Whimsical Book, Intituled (The Rights of the Christian Church &c) Are Fairly Stated, and Answered in their Kind Vol. I* (London: 1709), p. 114.

32 Anon. *The Junior's Precedence and the Senior's Success; or, The Younger Going before the Elder. … To Which Is Added, an Appendix Shewing the Necessity or Erecting Courts of Conscience, and of Reforming County or Sherriffs-Courts throughout the Kingdom* (London: 1750), pp. 54–60.

33 Anon. *A General History of Ireland Vol. II* (Dublin: 1781), p. 48; Anon. *A Summary Review of the Laws of the United States of North America, the British Provinces, and the West Indies* (Edinburgh: 1788), p. 54; John Bruce, *Historical View of Plans for the Government of British India, and the Regulation of Trade to the East Indies* (London: 1793), p. 104.

34 Winder, "Courts of Requests", p. 374.

35 Winder, "Courts of Requests", pp. 369, 375, 392; Duffy, *Bankruptcy and Insolvency*, p. 112.

36 Paul, *Poverty of Disaster*, p. 37.

37 Plucknett, *Concise History*, pp. 197–198.

38 William Hutton, *The History of Derby; From the Remote Ages of Antiquity, to the Year MDCCXCI* (London: 1791), p. 122.

39 John Trusler, *The London Adviser and Guide: Containing Every Instruction and Information Useful and Necessary to Persons Living in London and Coming to Reside There* (London: 1786), p. 154.

40 Winder, "Courts of Requests", p. 375.

41 John Entick, *A New and Accurate History and Survey of London, Westminster, Southwark, and Places Adjacent Vol. III* (London: 1766), p. 22; Hutton, *Courts of Requests*, pp. 72–74.

42 See: Anon. *The Citizen's Law Companion* (London: 1794), p. 142; Matthew Bacon, *A Treatise on Leases and Terms for Years* (London: 1798), p. 54.

43 Jacob Giles, *City Liberties: or, the Rights and Privileges of Freemen* (London: 1732), pp. 58–59.

44 Trusler, *London Adviser*, pp. 155–156.

45 "Isle of Ely Court of Requests … Chatteris Minute Book", September 1782 – January 1792, Dunn-Gardner Family Papers, Cambridge University Library: Department of Archives and Modern Manuscripts, MS Add.9358/7/4, p. 5.

46 Hutton, *Courts of Requests*, pp. 29–42; Duffy, *Bankruptcy and Insolvency*, p. 113; Winder, "Courts of Requests", pp. 372, 391; Finn, "Debt and Credit", pp. 218–219.

47 Anon. *A Collection of Scarce and Valuable Tracts on the Most Interesting and Entertaining Subjects Vol. I* (London: 1748), p. 373.

48 Thomas Gordon, *A Supplement to the Sermon Preached at Lincoln's Inn on January 30, 1732. By a Layman.* (London: 1733), p. 24.

49 William Blackstone, *The Commentaries of William Blackstone on the Laws and Constitution of England Carefully Abridged in a New Manner* (London: 1796), p. 530; Sir

Philip Francis, *Speech in the House of Commons on Tuesday the 7th of March 1786* (London: 1786), p. 86; Anon. *Historical Sketches of Civil Liberty* (London: 1788), p. 103; John Hawles, *Hamilton's Juryman's Guide* (London: 1794), p. 13; Henry Bynner, *The Trial of John Binns, Deputy of the London Corresponding Society for Sedition* (Birmingham: 1797), p. 42.

50 Edward Wynne, *Eunomus; or, Dialogues Concerning the Law and Constitution of England Vol. II* (London: 1768), pp. 43–44; John Rose, *A Constitutional Catechism, Adapted to All Ranks and Capacities, Illustrated with Copious Notes* (Bristol: 1795), p. 48.

51 John Debrett, *The Parliamentary Register; or History of the Proceedings and Debates of the House of Commons … During the Sixth Session of the Seventeenth Parliament of Great Britain Vol. XLIV* (London: 1796), pp. 18–19.

52 Anon. *A Letter to the Manufacturers and Inhabitants of the Parishes of Stoke, Burslem and Wolsanton, in the County of Stafford, on Courts of Request, Occasioned by the Bill Intended to be Brought into Parliament this Sessions, for the Establishment of that Jurisdiction in the Potteries; By a Manufacturer* (1794), pp. 4–5.

53 William Hutton, *A Dissertation on Juries* (Birmingham: 1789), p. 12.

54 Jean Louis de Lolme, *The Constitution of England, or an Account of the English Government; In Which it Is Compared with the Republican Form of Government, and Occasionally with the Other Monarchies in Europe* (London: 1781), p. 119.

55 George Croft, *A Short Commentary, with Strictures, On Certain Parts of the Moral Writings of Dr Paley & Mr Gisborne* (Birmingham: 1797), pp. 92–93.

56 Dornford, *Seven Letters*, p. 10.

57 Trusler, *London Adviser*, p. 155.

58 Anon. *Britannia Fortior*, p. 145; Guy Miege, *The Present State of Great Britain and Ireland* (London: 1723), p. 281; George Howard, *Queries Relative to Several Defects and Grievances in Some of the Present Laws of Ireland* (Dublin: 1763), p. 16; Pluralist, *Tithes Politically, Judicially, and Justly Considered* (London: 1794), p. 91; Gilbert Grey, *Epitome of the Annals of Great Britain* (Newcastle: 1773), p. ix; Richard Boote, *An Historical Treatise of an Action or Suit at Law* (London: 1766), p. xiii.

59 Anon. *Essays on Several Subjects* (London: 1769), p. 83.

60 Fitzsimmonds, *Free and Candid Disquisitions*, pp. 34–35.

61 Duffy, *Bankruptcy and Insolvency*, p. 115; Winder, "Courts of Requests", p. 377; Finn, *Character of Credit*, pp. 211–218, 277; Croft, *Commentary*, p. 93.

62 Anon. *A Letter to the Manufacturers*, p. 11.

63 William Hutton, *The Life of William Hutton – with Introduction by Carl Chinn* (Studley: Brewin Books, 1998), p. 57.

64 Hutton, *Courts of Requests*, pp. vii, 11.

65 Winder, "Courts of Requests", p. 369.

66 Susan E. Whyman, *The Useful Knowledge of William Hutton – Culture and Industry in Eighteenth-Century Birmingham* (Oxford: Oxford University Press, 2018), p. 102.

67 Anon. *Collection of Scarce and Valuable Tracts*, pp. 371–373.

68 Hutton, *Courts of Requests*, p. 70.

69 Hutton, *Courts of Requests*, pp. 11, 74; John Robbins, *A Bone to Pick, Recommended to the Several Water Companies of this Metropolis; or, a Check to Avarice, Tyranny and Oppression* (London: 1790), 40; Anon. *A Letter to the Manufacturers*, p. 4; Duffy, *Bankruptcy and Insolvency*, p. 112.

70 Anon. *A Letter to the Manufacturers*, pp. 10–12.

71 "Chatteris Minute Book", MS Add.9358/7/4, pp. 31, 40, 44, 48–50, 66, 80.

72 Finn, *Character of Credit*, p. 207.

73 Bacon, *A Treatise on Leases and Terms for Years*, p. 54.

74 Hutton, *History of Derby*, pp. 121–122.

75 Anon. *A Letter to the Manufacturers*, p. 4.
76 Anon. *Considerations on the Late Increase of the Poor Rate, and on Mr Gilbert's Plan for the Relief and Support of the Poor* (Norwich: 1786), pp. 1–8; David A. Kent, "Small Businessmen and their Credit Transactions in Early Nineteenth-Century Britain", *Business History* vol. 36, no. 2 (1994), 48; Finn, *Character of Credit*, pp. 211–218.
77 "An Act for Reducing the Time for the Imprisonment of Debtors Committed to Prison, Upon Prosecutions in Courts of Conscience, in London, Middlesex, and the Borough of Southwark, to the Same Periods in each Court; and for Abolishing Fees Paid by those Debtors to Gaolers, or Others, on Account of Such Imprisonment", 1785, 25 George III, c.45; "An Act for Regulating the Time for the Imprisonment of Debtors Imprisoned by Process from Courts Instituted for the Recovery of Small Debts; for Abolishing the Claim of Fees of Gaolers, and Others, in Cases of such Imprisonment; and for Ascertaining the Qualifications of the Commissioners", 1786, 26 George III, c.38.
78 John Howard, *Appendix to the State of the Prisons in England and Wales &c by John Howard* (London: 1780), pp. 170, 186; Winder, "Courts of Requests", pp. 392–393; Anon. *Debtor and Creditor's Assistant*, p. 67.
79 Finn, *Character of Credit*, pp. 218–219; Finn, "Debt and Credit", p. 214.
80 Tim Hitchcock and Robert Brink Shoemaker, *London Lives – Poverty, Crime and the Making of a Modern City, 1690–1800* (Cambridge: Cambridge University Press, 2015), p. 106.
81 Hutton, *Courts of Requests*, pp. 42–44.
82 Haagen, "English Society and the Debt Law", p. 225; Joel Mokyr, *The Enlightened Economy – An Economic History of Britain 1700–1850* (New Haven: Yale University Press, 2009), p. 379.
83 C.W. Chalklin, "The Reconstruction of London's Prisons, 1770–1799: An Aspect of the Growth of Georgian London", *The London Journal* vol. 9, no. 1 (1983), p. 22.
84 See: "List of Prisoners Handed over by the Sheriffs to their Successors on 28 Sept Annually, with Notes of Occurrences During the Subsequent Year", 1784–1810, Wood Street Compter later Giltspur Street Compter, LMA, CLA/028/01/025-038.
85 Hutton, *Courts of Requests*, pp. 43–70.
86 Mokyr, *Enlightened Economy*, p. 376.
87 Hutton, *Courts of Requests*, pp. 66–67.
88 Whyman, *Hutton*, pp. 133–149.
89 Anon. *An Authentic Account of the Riots in Birmingham, on the 14th, 15th, 16th, and 17th Days of July, 1791* (Birmingham: 1791), p. 8.
90 Anon. *A Full and Accurate Report of the Trials of the Birmingham Rioters at the Late Assizes for the County of Warwick* (London: 1791), p. 23; see: Finn, *Character of Credit*, p. 227.
91 Whyman, *Hutton*, p. 135.
92 Finn, "Debt and Credit", p. 236; Haagen, "English Society and the Debt Law", p. 225.
93 Anon. *A Letter to the Manufacturers*, pp. 10–12.
94 Winder, "Courts of Requests", p. 387.
95 Finn, *Character of Credit*, p. 208.
96 William Smith, *State of the Gaols in London, Westminster, and Borough of Southwark. To Which Is Added, an Account of the Present State of Convicts Sentenced to Hard Labour on Board the Justitia upon the River Thames* (London: J. Brew, 1776), pp. 33–34.
97 Haagen, "Debt Law", pp. 228–229.

98 *Gazetteer and New Daily Advertiser*, 12th February, 1785, no.17527; on extension of the vote see: *Morning Chronicle and London Advertiser*, 29th January, 1785, no.4902; and on the death penalty: *Morning Chronicle and London Advertiser*, 5th May, 1785, no.4984.

99 Fidelio, *Seven Letters to the Common Council of the City of London, and One to the Livery, Relative to their Committees, The Expenditure of the City Cash, Black Friars Bridge, The State of the Prisons, Court of Conscience Debtors, and the Partial Distribution of Justice to them* (London: 1784); Josiah Dornford, *Seven Letters to the Lords of the Privy Council, on the Police* (1785); Josiah Dornford, *Seven Letters to the Lords and Commons of Great Britain, Upon the Present Mode of Arresting and Imprisoning the Bodies of Debtors* (London: 1786); Josiah Dornford, *Nine Letters to the Right Honourable Lord Mayor and Aldermen of the City of London, on the State of the City Prisons* (London: 1786).

100 *Morning Chronicle and London Advertiser*, 3rd July, 1784, no.4721; *Morning Chronicle and London Advertiser*, 2nd August 1784, no.4746; *Morning Chronicle and London Advertiser*, 6th November, 1784, no.4829; *Whitehall Evening Post*, 20th–23rd November, 1784, no.5854; *General Evening Post*, 16th–18th December, 1784, no.7926.

101 *Morning Chronicle and London Advertiser*, 10th–22nd December, 1784, no.4859–4869; Anon. *The Second Report of the Committee of the Court of Common Council, of the City of London, Appointed the 1st of July 1784, To Inquire into the Assertions Lately Circulated Respecting the Affairs of the Corporation; Upon the several Charges and Insinuations of Mr Josiah Dornford* (London: 1784), pp. 7, 112–123.

102 *Morning Chronicle and London Advertiser*, 1st June, 1784, no.4693; *Public Advertiser*, 21st December 1784, no.15779.

103 *London Chronicle*, 7th–9th February, 1786, no.4560; *General Advertiser*, 10th February, 1786, no.2877; *General Advertiser*, 11th March, 1786, no.2902; *Morning Herald*, 15th June, 1786, no.1759.

104 *Public Advertiser*, 22nd June, 1786, no.16250.

105 *Morning Chronicle and London Advertiser*, 18th April, 1786, no.5280.

106 *General Evening Post*, 25th–27th April 1786, no.8188; *Public Advertiser*, 10th May, 1786, no.16214; *Gazetteer and New Daily Advertiser*, 17th May, 1786, no.17919; *Whitehall Evening Post*, 18th–20th May, 1786, no.6088; *Morning Chronicle and London Advertiser*, 17th November, 1786, no.5464.

107 *General Evening Post*, 16th–18th November, 1786, no.8264.

108 *Whitehall Evening Post*, 15th–17th March, 1787, no.6218.

109 *Morning Chronicle and London Advertiser*, 26th April, 1786, no.5287; *Gazetteer and New Daily Advertiser*, 9th September, 1786, no.18018; *Morning Chronicle and London Advertiser*, 19th August, 1786, no.5387; *Morning Chronicle and London Advertiser*, 1st September, 1786, no.5397.

110 *Morning Chronicle and London Advertiser*, 31st August, 1786, no.5396.

111 Philippa Hardman, "Fear of Fever and the Limits of the Enlightenment – Selling Prison Reform in late Eighteenth-Century Gloucestershire", *Cultural and Social History* vol. 10, no. 4 (2013), pp. 520–521.

112 Howard, *State of the Prisons*, pp. 38–40.

Conclusion

'It had stood there many years before, and it remained there some years afterwards; but it is gone now, and the world is none the worse without it'. This eulogy is Charles Dickens's introduction of the Marshalsea Prison, arguably the most important character in *Little Dorrit*, the author's great rhapsody on class and finance. The gaol impacts almost every other character in the novel and manages to stretch far out from Southwark, the prison becoming deeply intertwined with the lives of its inhabitants. When William Dorrit, 'the father of the Marshalsea', is finally released after twenty years, Dickens describes how now 'the Marshalsea was an orphan'. Perhaps more personally for the gaol it also loses "Little" Amy Dorrit who, born within the walls, is described regularly as 'the child of the Marshalsea'. However, Dickens lingers on the gaol even as the narrative follows the Dorrits out into the world, the use of the word 'orphan' signalling who has actually survived their separation. When William dies in Italy after his discharge, he is still mentally imprisoned, his mind knowing 'of nothing beyond the Marshalsea'. Even as Dickens allows Amy to leave the Marshalsea forever at the end of the novel following her beloved Arthur Clennam's own discharge from the prison, it is the human characters who disappear from view. The couple quietly dissolve into 'the roaring streets', they are 'inseparable and blessed' but indistinguishable from the 'sunshine and shade, the noisy and the eager, and the arrogant and the forward and the vain'. The Marshalsea upon which they turn their back is the only distinguishable figure of stability in the novel, all other structures being impermanent (liable to collapse) or hidden in shade. And yet, despite the Marshalsea's solid permanence, the author's first instinct when introducing the prison was to spit upon it and assure the reader that it threatened the world no more. Dickens even tried to push the gaol further into the past, describing how it 'stood a few doors short of the church' in Southwark 'thirty years ago'. While this refers to the temporal setting of his tale, it obscures the fact that, when Dickens began work on the novel, the prison had only been demolished in the previous decade. The Marshalsea of 'thirty years ago' was Charles's Marshalsea. *Little Dorrit*, for all its discussion of wider society, is a profoundly personal account of one man's inability to escape the institution of debt imprisonment. His father's imprisonment in the Marshalsea during the 1820s when Dickens was just twelve, shattering his comfortable genteel world, was evidently a spectre the novelist could never entirely shake. It was forever fixed in his imagination even if (as he seemingly assured himself) the Marshalsea was 'gone now'. Debtors' prisons appear across his work either as implied threats to characters with precarious livelihoods or as actual physical settings, protagonists frequently taking on the mantel of the young Charles or his father. The novel reveals how painfully aware Dickens was of the long-term impacts that first-hand experience of debt imprisonment wrought. His father spent only three months in gaol, but Charles was keen to reproach any reader who might consider "short" imprisonments inconsequential. In one of the most visceral moments of the novel when William Dorrit is told the release he has been dreaming of for over twenty years is to be delayed by 'but a few hours' the old man breaks into tears and, 'with a sudden passion', rebukes assertions of the insignificance of the delay: 'You talk very easily of hours, sir! How long do you suppose, sir, that an hour is to a man who is choking for want of air?'[1]

★★

What were the implications of imprisonment for debt in the eighteenth century? This book has shown that many of the easy answers to this question lack substance. The most important of these is that debt imprisonment was not inherently the end of one's life. Debtors were not cast into gaol on the assumption that they would never leave as punishment for their impoverishment. Thousands died in debtors' prisons across the period but while they are thus striking examples of the impact of debt imprisonment, they constituted a minority experience. The prisons cannot therefore simply be dismissed as places of death, not least because they were also occasionally places of new life. In October 1797, the yard of the Fleet was made raucous by the wedding ceremony and 'great feast' of the actress Mary Wells to a fellow prisoner, debtors putting aside concerns for the day to revel in celebrating this new bond.[2] Earlier that same year at the Giltspur Street Compter – which was just a five minute walk from the Fleet – Ann Richards was 'born in the lower yard of this compter' on the 12th January. The new-born remained in the compter until at least the 11th February when she was baptised by the 'Chaplain of the compter in [the] Keeper's Apartment' with a male debtor and female transport serving as godparents, Ann's entrance to the world recorded in the debtors' commitment book for want of a parish register.[3]

It was also not simply a place of commercial death as delinquency rather than disaster was characteristic of those arrested. Many individuals found their way into debtors' prison after experiencing failure and complete business collapse, their desperate creditors competing over remaining scraps. However, the fact of one's imprisonment did not confer this status of failure, arising instead from the state of one's enterprise. Any serious study of eighteenth-century business failure ought to consider debtors' prisons, having previously focussed almost entirely on bankruptcy, but a study of debt imprisonment is not necessarily a study of failure. The logic of eighteenth-century bankruptcy lay in managing the estates of those who it acknowledged were unable to pay their debts, dissolving their assets entirely and creditors receiving only a percentage of their full demand. Conversely, debt imprisonment targeted the debtor rather than their estate, suggesting implicitly that society believed they were still capable of settling their debts under their own management. Debt imprisonment signalled a failure *to* pay, not a failure of *ability* to pay. Imprisoned debtors frequently had healthy if cash-poor businesses at the moment of their arrest which could survive this credit crisis. As long as a trader had apprentices, employees, or family members to take care of the shop while confined – married male prisoners whose wives were already likely to be involved in their trade being particularly shielded – an imprisonment might represent just an interlude in trade.[4] Even those who lost their enterprise, like Richard Hogarth with whom this book opened, were able to return to entrepreneurial activity after recovering their liberty and re-establishing their trustworthiness. The fact of their imprisonment did not bar them permanently from credit, a situation emphasised by the existence of those who found themselves frequently in and out of prison.

To be imprisoned for debt in the eighteenth century was then usually a temporary condition rather than a final state. This was primarily because the debtors' prisons were a facet of market regulation not of legal justice, in the terms of which they are frequently discussed, the fulfilling of a contract rather than the person's improper behaviour being its subject.[5] This misalignment with justice arises from the apparently intrinsic relationship between the criminal law and prisons but also derives from a broader moral debate inherent to any discussion of debt in human society which questions whether to enforce debts is "just" particularly when the wealthy extract capital from the already impoverished. Throughout human history from the ancient world to the modern cultural rage following the global financial crisis in which banks were bailed out but the debts of everyday people and poorer nations were deemed to still be due, the language rejecting the compulsion to pay debts has been derived from a higher sense of right and wrong. This recourse to ill-defined morality implicitly acknowledges the undeniable economic legitimacy of debts, humans casting around for a nebulous notion of injustice to counter arguments of the necessity of standing by one's word. However, some anthropological scholarship has disputed the commercial necessity that debts be paid no matter the consequence to the borrower. Most notably David Graeber has claimed that the declaration "'one has to pay one's debts'" is itself a moral statement and that this statement isn't true 'even according to standard economic theory' as loans inherently carry the risk of default. The fault for a loan which exceeds the borrower's capacity ought, by the logic of commerce itself, to be upon the lender who foolishly gave it. However, this moral approach to credit which denies the economic necessity that debts be paid is almost always predicated upon a social structure of credit which regards all takers as in a position of weakness and all providers as elites, all debt being inherently debilitating and all credit empowering.[6] Credit was far more diverse in the early modern period and, in the context of debt imprisonment, the Graeber thesis can only be seen to apply to those processed through the Court of Requests particularly after 1786. The majority of arrested debt constituted a conflict between various members of the trading middling sorts, there being little occupational distinction between creditors and debtors. Nor was there a clear divide between creditors and debtors or the powerful and the powerless in this form of exchange. It is easy to see in this environment (in contrast to the modern era of high interest cash-lending) why the failure to pay debts was held to be more of an injustice than their enforcement.

Debtors' prisons, whenever they exist, can only be understood in regard to the context of the economy in which they are used. This context might reveal their arbitrary nature, being cruel means of class oppression, or they might reveal their commercial rationality. The eighteenth-century English institution responded directly to a world of contracting based upon personal reputation in which oral agreements were staked upon individual identity. This system of trust, built upon bravado and optimism, extended from the building labourer who was definitely sure he would be paid next week (or maybe the week after that come to think of it) asking for his daily ale to be added to his lengthening tab, through the alehousekeeper negotiating with his brewer for supplies on trust pointing to his crowded and raucous tavern for evidence of the inevitability of imminent riches, up to the barley farmer planting the new year's crop while still awaiting last year's profits from the brewer, perhaps later wandering into town to purchase a new set of clothes for his growing children on the credit of next summer's harvest. In most instances, purchasers abided by the spirit of their agreement (paying debts once they were able to as they expected their debtors would pay unto them) and informal credit was able to encourage exponential growth. By not being tied to pecuniary realities or restricted to the literate and cash-rich, personal credit facilitated the sale of the goods of the Industrial Revolution and met the demands of the Consumer Revolution. It ensured that the external forces which drove both an increased desire to consume and to commit to an increasingly industrialised form of manufacture did not encounter a glass ceiling of immature methods of exchange tied to an insufficient ore-based currency. However, this same informality was inherently precarious. The commercially active might live on extended credit for years though they were under no misconception that bills could be delayed indefinitely. While the culture of trust has been emphasised as an essential component of early modern life, reliant upon the expectation that duty would be performed appropriately, traders of the past (particularly those selling on trust to strangers without defined capital securities) were not naïve.[7] Any limited experience of trade quickly familiarised one with difficult customers who while not dishonest proved delinquent, the only offer they made being further promises of imminent satisfaction. If traders were, as a group, to continue to offer informal credit necessary for national growth they needed a reason to feel confident (even if only subconsciously) in the likelihood of payment beyond blind faith in the Christian honesty of strangers and friends, particularly as even the most honest customer might struggle to make payments due to unforeseen circumstances.

The debtors' prison had no role in creating the Industrial Revolution, but it was one of many subtle cogs in the machinery of the English economy which ensured growth was not interrupted. In theory, this institution of contract enforcement did not even have to be used. As it essentially acted as a substitute for staking defined capital, its existence prevented disincentives from trading on credit and deterred those considering willingly avoiding their obligations.[8] However, to conceive of the debtors' prison solely as a deterrent removes the profoundly human quality of the system which required users to volunteer to engage with it. Furthermore, if they served no other function than deterrence, the high commitment rates observed across the period are a testament to its ineffectiveness. Continued use necessitated effectiveness. Rather it was an active instrument of market regulation with its individual users seeking an actual means of intervening in financial quandaries and was superior to common law and bankruptcy because it could be easily and profitably made use of by a wide segment of the population. The economy of eighteenth-century capitalism was inherently insecure; many trading people lived in very real fear that they might go from *apparent* prosperity to *apparent* poverty in the course of an afternoon. They did not, however, submit to fate and took steps to prevent disaster; debt imprisonment was not merely a reaction to financial trouble or a desperate attempt to shift burdens onto others but an active mechanism of protecting profitability.[9] Debtors' prisons allowed creditors to exert actual control over the profound instability which pervaded their lives (even if at the expense of the stability of another). It was a purposeful move which reflected both emotional responses to insecurity (the act of an arrest conferring a sense of power over economic forces operating against them) and practical responses to delinquency which could not be allowed to stand for the good of one's own trade or the wider network of credit-reliant business.

What is perhaps most remarkable about debtors' prisons in the eighteenth century is that their actual use did not undermine the theory of their purpose, ensuring their long history. Debtors did – as the law implied and creditors suspected – usually have the means to make payment. It was rarely a tool of immediate redress, though a six-month delay was infinitely preferable to the indefinite obfuscation of clients who had a variety of obligations and personal objectives which minimised the importance of settling any individual debt imminently. Only two of the 18,664 debtors studied in the surviving commitment registers experienced the twenty-year commitment of William Dorrit, the overwhelming majority being released within a year of confinement and just under a third spending less than three months in gaol. The most frequent way prisoners obtained their freedom was through a creditor granting their discharge suggesting that they had been satisfied. This, in turn, meant death rates were low and reduced reliance on other mechanisms of securing liberty which frequently proved more expensive than simply paying one's debts. The amounts debtors were imprisoned to answer usually reflected more than subsistence credit but also did not constitute values any higher than they, in turn, might have on their books being sums they could reasonably be expected to pay. Reimbursement also aided prisoners as a creditor's blessing essentially confirmed the restoration of their creditability to the world. Satisfaction may not have always represented receiving full payment particularly if one was not the first creditor to bring in a demand. The prisons were evidently sites of negotiation through which parties could resolve their differences, the act of imprisonment both giving coercive power to the "wronged" and offering a clear symbol to the end of a dispute when the debtor was released. The effectiveness of debtors' prisons, once understood as responding to a particular type of exchange, should not necessarily be regarded as surprising. In a society which stored wealth in goods or other persons rather than in measurable sums of coinage, where even the wealthy might be unable to pay moderate sums when asked, it was inevitable that some debtors would need to be given an active incentive to transform their wealth into currency and stand by their word.

Prisoner strategies in correcting imbalances varied based on individual circumstance and, during their confinement, were given a significant degree of liberty to manage their own affairs. Some called in debts, others sold property (either minor or substantial), many applied for aid from friends and family, while significant numbers continued to labour at their trades from within gaol (their income being passively garnished by their creditors who visited regularly). Most combined various strategies dependent upon their abilities but also their own desires – selling goods rather than offending important clients by calling in their debts. Regardless of how they raised capital, the responsibility for resolving a creditor's need to recover was placed upon the prisoner but was not dictated to them as through court order or bankruptcy. Unlike the processes of criminal justice which were proscribed and general (even if determined individually by the bench), debt imprisonment was a highly personal experience for both the debtor and the creditor. While debt imprisonment did not differentiate between the fraudulent and the unfortunate, it was not enacted without context – not all creditors chose to imprison, nor did they arrest unilaterally under a specific set of circumstances. This personal dimension of debt imprisonment characterised the contribution of this institution to society. Frequently, institutions are discussed as being introduced or constructed to serve a purpose or that users found them not fit for purpose when they turned to them. However, particularly with debtors' prisons it is clear that people interpreted existing institutions for their individual needs. Debt imprisonment had been a facet of English law for centuries generally though not exclusively targeting struggling merchants, their imprisonment being replaced with bankruptcy from the sixteenth century. As the use of credit broadened from c.1580 and then commerce itself accelerated in the late seventeenth century, altering the economic climate, the prisons were reinvented as tools of general contractual administration. The purpose of prisons, their functioning, and even effectiveness were determined by how they were understood by those seeking them. As Douglass North suggested, institutions are essentially the rules of the economic game – actual humans (rather than fictional economic rule followers) have proved very adept at moving the goal posts when necessary without having to rebuild the arena.[10] Ultimately better institutions would be introduced but the tide of commerce could not be held back by the inefficiencies of existing structures nor could it be unleashed by them when introduced without other growth factors. Debt imprisonment was, crudely, a stop-gap solution while the new field of play was established.

Its lack of design in controlling problems of credit is evident in its inefficiencies and precariousness. The effectiveness of the institution of debt imprisonment was a miracle of accidents. It frequently relied on aspects of its administration which would never have been instituted if designed from scratch in response to a specific problem. Most notable of these was the devolved private system which placed the majority of the financial burden of facilitating imprisonment on the prisoners. If costs had been placed upon the users (creditors) or local governments, then its use would have become financially untenable and unsupportable. However, despite the impact on prisoners being low, the public ire this system drew made the institution inherently vulnerable. As each individual use of the institution was personal, little was likely to be done to improve its foundations collectively – after it had produced payment for an individual creditor they were content not to think further on the institution or were confident that it would aid them in its current form in the future. Even slight reform from a humanitarian perspective therefore threatened to undermine the institution and thus the propensity of creditors to make use of it. When *mesne* process was restricted in 1725, those in need sought out and reinterpreted a new institution, the Court of Requests, which was itself later undermined by reform. Nowhere was the institution of debt imprisonment more vulnerable due to its lack of design than in managing the minority who actually were insolvent. The lack of formal mechanisms of processing those who genuinely could not pay – their absence motivating prisoners to seek the most extreme means of raising capital – led to some highly visible debtors accumulating in gaols. They contributed to overcrowding and, without aid, were likely to die while confined. These circumstances drove the impulse to enact reform requiring external intervention in the form of the regularly passed Insolvency Acts to maintain the acceptability of the institution. Despite the fact that they aided debtors, the statutes were profoundly conservative and in the long term maintained the integrity of the institution, in essence erecting additional structural supports to the ailing construction. Though they released a smaller fraction of prisoners than might be assumed, one cannot imagine the continued existence of eighteenth-century debt imprisonment without them. However, such mechanisms could not be too frequent – let alone permanent – at the risk of limiting the coercive power creditors were granted by the institution, disrupting their approach to it. This precarious balancing act stood largely alone between the efficiency and demise of debt imprisonment.

Ultimately, the debtors' prison was the most effective tool of redress *available* to eighteenth-century creditors and was far from the ideal solution to the contemporary credit market even if both focussed on debtor personages rather than estates. This does not mean that the inherent coercive nature of debt imprisonment becomes less effective in a society with better institutions, only that when rated against more effective systems of securing credit users are economically disincentivised from using imprisonment to coerce payment. Similarly, this does not prevent those seeking to use imprisonment for less practical purposes or to extract capital which society might deem illicit (such as modern American states imprisoning the poor to raise municipal funding) from utilising the powers of debt imprisonment. This model of deliberate cruelty or theft from the powerless only applies to a minority of eighteenth-century creditors and it could potentially be said that the early modern debtors' prison was less oppressive than its modern imitators. However, this does not mean that to suffer debt imprisonment was not an oppressive experience. Its inherently personal nature meant that to experience it was to suffer harm to one's person in multifarious forms. Charles Dickens's personal Marshalsea was just one of hundreds of thousands of other Marshalseas. Even if the experience of imprisonment was less horrifying than might be assumed this did not eliminate its wounding; while John Grano had a largely pleasant time in gaol, his life was surely forever marked by his own Marshalsea. The debtors' prison was replaced by better institutions not just in terms of their direct efficiency for individual creditors but also those which minimised the damage to the individual debtor. This required formal intervention by reformers and legislators and was not dependent simply upon economic advancement. Good regulation protects the lives and prosperity of all participants, in this regard debt imprisonment can be seen as a disastrous tool of market regulation even if those suffering it were not cast out of commercial society permanently. Only by recognising the potential efficiencies of debt imprisonment for those who *seek* to use it can a society ensure the protection of those who might suffer its consequences.

The debtors' prison thrived throughout the eighteenth century and 'remained there some years afterwards' because it represented an effective tool of recovery. However, like many productive features of the early modern economy we can be confident that 'the world is none the worse without it'. Charles Dickens himself, in many ways a 'child of the Marshalsea', outlived *mesne* process by less than a year. By then, debt imprisonment as an economic institution had largely ceased to serve a useful purpose due to reform, new institutions, and improvements in the currency and means of transacting. It was by no means dead before Parliament buried it in 1869 though many of the most notable debtors' prisons had already closed. Lancaster Castle held debtors until abolition and would continue to function as a prison for felons until 2011 but the compters had been shut for decades and both the Fleet Prison and Marshalsea were closed in the 1840s. While the Fleet was methodically taken apart, the stone being 'carted away' and reincorporated into new construction projects, the latter's slow destruction in the subsequent 170 years has been far from total.[11] To this day, a short walk from bustling Borough Market in the heart of Southwark – where the only credit taken is that secured by a bank on a card which transmits the sum immediately to the seller – will take you to St George the Martyr and its unassuming churchyard fronted by a low black-brick wall and iron railing. On the opposite side to these railings of this quiet green haven is the austere brick of the south wall of the Marshalsea, the last vestige of the gaol which haunted Dickens. Hidden between shops and offices, towered over by the glass skyscrapers of modern south London finance and credit, the Marshalsea is somehow not quite 'gone now', a symbol of the slumbering institution of debt imprisonment.

Notes

1 Charles Dickens, *Little Dorrit* (London: 1857), pp. 41, 49–56, 313, 319, 489–490, 624–625; Michael Slater, "Dickens, Charles John Huffam (1812–1870)", *Oxford Dictionary of National Biography* (Oxford University Press, 2004), online edition, doi: 10.1093/ref:odnb/29016 (accessed 31st May 2018). On the role of the prison in the narrative, including alternative interpretations, see: T.N. Grove, "The Psychological Prison of Arthur Clennam in Dickens's *Little Dorrit*", *The Modern Language Review* vol. 68, no. 4 (1973), p. 755; Sean Grass, *The Self in the Cell – Narrating the Victorian Prisoner* (London: Routledge, 2003), pp. 103–150; Ben Parker, "Recognition or Reification?: Capitalist Crisis and Subjectivity in *Little Dorrit*", *New Literary History* vol. 45, no. 1 (2014), pp. 131–151.

2 Mary Wells, *Memoirs of the Life of Mrs Sumbel, Late Wells; of the Theatres-royal, Drury-lane, Covent-garden, and Haymarket. In Three Volumes. Written by Herself. Vol. I* (London: 1811), pp. 189–200; *London Evening Post*, 14th–17th October 1797, no.11585; *Craftsman or Say's Weekly Journal*, 22nd October 1797, no.1668. Unrelated to their imprisonment this marriage was a disaster and significantly complicated their debts, see: Alexander Wakelam, "Coverture and the Debtors' Prison in the Long Eighteenth Century", *Journal of Eighteenth-Century Studies* (forthcoming, 2021).

3 "List of Prisoners Handed over by the Sheriffs to their Successors on 28 Sept Annually, with Notes of Occurrences During the Subsequent Year", 1795–1800, Wood Street Compter later Giltspur Street Compter, LMA, CLA/028/01/030.

4 See: Susie Steinbach, *Women in England 1760–1914 – A Social History* (London: Weidenfeld & Nicolson, 2004), pp. 47–48; Deborah Simonton, "Claiming their Place in the Corporate Community: Women's Identity in Eighteenth-Century Towns", in *The Invisible Woman – Aspects of Women's Work in Eighteenth-Century Britain*, eds. Isabelle Baudino, Jacques Carre, and Cecile Revauger (Aldershot: Ashgate, 2005), p. 105; Alexandra Shepard, "Crediting Women in the Early Modern English Economy", *History Workshop Journal* vol. 79, no. 1 (Spring 2015), p. 16. On wives managing the trades of temporarily absent husbands (in this case mariners at sea) see: Jennine Hurl-Eamon, "The Fiction of Female Dependence and the Makeshift Economy of Soldiers, Sailors, and their Wives in Eighteenth-Century London", *Labour History* vol. 49, no. 4 (2008), pp. 491–493.

5 Joanna Innes, "The King's Bench Prison in the Later Eighteenth Century: Law, Authority and Order in a London Debtors' Prison," in *An Ungovernable People – The English and their Law in the Seventeenth and Eighteenth Centuries*, ed. John Brewer and John Styles (London: Hutchinson, 1980), p. 253; Gustav Peebles, "Washing away the Sins of Debt: The Nineteenth-Century Eradication of the Debtors' Prison", *Comparative Studies in History* vol. 55, no. 3 (2013), p. 704; Margot C. Finn, *The Character of Credit – Personal Debt in English Culture, 1740–1914* (Cambridge: Cambridge University Press, 2003), pp. 29–33; Craig Muldrew, *The Economy of Obligation – The Culture of Credit and Social Relations in Early Modern England* (Basingstoke: Macmillan, 1998), p. 262.

6 David Graeber, *Debt – The First 5000 Years* (Brooklyn: Melville House, 2011), pp. 1–18; Gustav Peebles, "The Anthropology of Credit and Debt", *Annual Review of Anthropology* (2010), pp. 225–240; Chris A. Gregory, "On Money Debt and Morality: Some Reflections on the Contribution of Economic Anthropology", *Social Anthropology* vol. 20, no. 4 (2012), pp. 380–396.

7 Lynn Johnson, "Friendship, Coercion, and Interest: Debating the Foundations of Justice in Early Modern England", *Journal of Early Modern History* vol. 8, no. 2 (2004), pp. 46–64; Carolyn Downs, "Networks, Trust, and Risk Mitigation During the American Revolutionary War: A Case Study", *Economic History Review* vol. 70, no. 2 (2017), pp. 509–528.

8 Matthew J. Baker, Metin Cosgel, and Thomas J. Miceli, "Debtors' Prisons in America: An Economic Analysis", *Journal of Economic Behaviour & Organisation* vol. 84 (2012), pp. 218–219; Brianna L. Campbell, "The Economy of the Debtors' Prison Model: Why Throwing Deadbeats into Debtors' Prison Is a Good Idea", *Arizona Journal of International and Comparative Law* vol. 32, no. 3 (2015), pp. 855–856; Julian Hoppit, "The Use and Abuse of Credit in Eighteenth-Century England", in *Business Life and Public Policy – Essays in Honour of D.C. Coleman*, eds. Neil McKendrick and R.B. Outhwaite (Cambridge: Cambridge University Press, 1986), pp. 76–77; Paul Langford, *A Polite and Commercial People – England 1727–1783* (Oxford: Clarendon Press, 1998), p. 490; Joel Mokyr, *The Enlightened Economy – An Economic History of Britain 1700–1850* (New Haven: Yale University Press, 2009), p. 379.

9 Tawny Paul, *Poverty of Disaster – Debt and Insecurity in Eighteenth-Century Britain* (Cambridge: Cambridge University Press, 2019), pp. 244–247. See: Jane Elizabeth Moore, *Genuine Memoirs of Jane Elizabeth Moore. Late of Bermondsey, in the County of Surry. Written by Herself. Vol. III* (London: 1786), pp. 197–199.

10 Douglass C. North, "The Role of Institutions in Economic Development", *United Nations Economic Commission for Europe Discussion Paper Series*, no. 2003.2 (2003), p. 3.

11 Walter Thornbury, *Old and New London: A Narrative of Its History, Its People, and Its Places Vol. II* (London: Cassell, Petter, & Galpin, 1878), p. 404.

Bibliography

Manuscripts

Cambridgeshire Archives, Cambridge

Cambridgeshire Quarter Sessions Records: Court in Session. Q/SO/4.

Cambridge University Library: Department of Archives and Modern Manuscripts, Cambridge

"An Humble Proposal to the Honble House of Commons for Raising 30 or 40 Thousand Men for His Majestys Service out of the Insolvent Debtors". (1714–20). Cholmondeley Papers: Groups of Treasury Papers, Ch(H)Political Papers 51,70.

"Isle of Ely Court of Requests … Chatteris Minute Book". 1782–92. Dunn-Gardner Family Papers. MS Add.9358/7/4.

London Metropolitan Archives, London

Sherriff's Court, City of London – Poultry Compter.
    "Swordbearers to Enquire into Character of Yeomen or Serjeants". 1707. CLA/025/PC/04/004.
    "Petition against Yeoman being Allowed to Make Arrest without Serjeants". c.1710. CLA/025/PC/04/005.

Wood Street Compter.
    "List of Prisoners Handed over by the Sheriffs to Their Successors on 28 Sept Annually, with Notes of Occurrences during the Subsequent Year". 1741–1815. CLA/028/01/001–040.
    "List of Prisoners in the Compter Made Per Out of the Ct of Ald". 15th December 1724. CLA/028/01/043.
    "Apothecary's Bill for the Prisoners in Wood Street Compter". 1675. CLA/028/03/002.

Giltspur Street Compter.
    "Papers of a Committee Concerned with the Rebuilding of the Compter". 1785–1789. CLA/029/02/001.

Poultry Compter.
    Charge and Commitment Books. 1782–1823. CLA/030/01.
    "List of Prisoners in the Poultry Compter 16 Dec 1724 with Original Causes of Detainer, None Being Detained for Fees Only". 1724. CLA/030/02/006.

Prisons and Compter – General.

"Petitions of Prisoners, Offices of Newgate and the Compters, and Other Persons Relating to Prison Life, Repair of Prisons, Collections, Ill Health, Abuse by Officers, for Discharge, &c". 1675–1700. CLA/032/01/021.

"Order of Ct. of Alderman for Payment of Apothecary's File for Medicines Delivered to a Great Number of Poor Sick Prisoners in Ludgate and the Two Compters 1770". 1748–1775. CLA/032/01/032.

"A List of Such Persons Who Appear by the Fleet Commitment Books to Have Been Removed from Other Prisons by Habeas Corpus". 1724–1729. CLA/032/04/010.

Ludgate Prison.

"Rules and Orders for the Better Government of Ludgate". 1808. CLA/033/01/001.

"Rough Minutes and Papers of the Committee to Consider of Legal and Proper Methods for Removing the Prisoners from Ludgate to the London Workhouse". 1760–1761. CLA/033/01/014.

"Committee to Enquire into the State of the Goal of Ludgate and the Office of the Keeper Thereof". June 1764. CLA/033/01/015.

Newgate Prison.

"Answer of the Keeper to the Articles Exhibited against Him … by the Prisoners Confined for Debt". 1728/9. CLA/035/02/024.

Miscellaneous Papers. 1594–1836. CLA/035/02/026.

"Petition of James Guthrie to be Chaplain of Newgate". 1733/4. CLA/035/02/029.

"Rules and Orders for the Better Government of the Debtors' Side of the Gaol of Newgate". 1808. CLA/035/02/031.

"Ventilation … Gaol Fever and Its Prevention, The Substance of Information given to a Committee". 1747–1753. CLA/035/02/049.

"Vouchers for Wages and Petty Disbursements". 28th June 1817. CLA/035/02/055.

City of London: Courts of Law – Debtors.

"Royal Bounty from George III to the City of London to Discharge Debtors from Prison and to Persons Recommended by Deputies of Wards as Destitute and Needy". 1762. CLA/040/08/008.

Debtors Petitions. 1742–1791. CLA/040/08/009.

Courts Sessions– Gaol Delivery and Peace.

"Petition of Secondary of Poultry Compter against Rates". July 1726. CLA/047/LJ/13/1726/003.

Courts Sessions – Insolvent Debtors.

Debtors Schedules. 1712–1774. CLA/047/LJ/17/018–063.

Businesses: Small Collections.

Peirce and Tait, "Bad and Doubtful Debt Book 1763–1793". 1793. CLC/B/227/MS31573.

Court of Aldermen – Prisons Committee.

"Rough Minutes of Committee to Examine the Allegations of the Petitions of the Keepers of Newgate, Ludgate, and the Two Compters as to the Act for Taking Away Liquor Taps in the Prisons". 1787. COL/CA/PCA/01/003.

Court of Common Council – Minutes.
> "Proceedings of Various Courts of Aldermen and Court of Common Council Committees". 1709. COL/CC/MIN/01/115.

Great Fire of London – Rebuilding After.
> "Wood Street Compter". 1666–76. COL/SJ/03/027.

Surveyor's Department: Plans – Justice. COL/SVD/PL/08.
New Prison, Clerkenwell.
> "Cash Book of Samuel Newport, Keeper of the New Prison". 1790–5. MA/G/CLE/0032.

Surrey History Centre, Woking

Surrey Quarter Sessions – Records Relating to the Release of Debtors, QS3/2.

The National Archives, Kew

"Lancaster Gaol Register of Debtors and Plaintiffs". 1793–6. Home Office and Prison Commission Records: Prison Records Series 1. PCOM 2/440.

Fleet Prison Commitment Books. 1686–1842. Records of the Fleet Prison. PRIS 1.

King's (Queen's) Bench Prison Commitment Books. 1719–1862. Records of the King's Bench Prison. PRIS 4.

Printed Primary

Periodicals

British Mercury.
Craftsman or Say's Weekly Journal.
Daily Advertiser.
Daily Courant.
Evening Post.
Gazetteer and New Daily Advertiser.
General Advertiser.
General Evening Post.
Lloyd's Evening Post.
London Chronicle.
London Evening Post.
London Gazette.
Morning Chronicle and London Advertiser.
Morning Herald.
Morning Post and Daily Advertiser.
New York Times.
Oracle and Daily Advertiser.
Post Boy.
Post Man and the Historical Account.
Public Advertiser.
St. James's Chronicle or the British Evening Post.

The Economist.
The Guardian.
True Briton.
Wall Street Journal.
Whitehall Evening Post.
World and Fashionable Advertiser.

Legislation

An Act Touching Orders for Bankrupts, 1571, 13 Elizabeth, c.7.
An Act for Discharging Poor Prisoners Unable to Satisfie Their Creditors, September 1649.
An Act for the Relief of Creditors and Poor Prisoners, October 1653.
An Act for the Releife and Release of Poore Distressed Prisoners for Debt, 1670, 22&23 Charles II, c.20.
An Act for the Further Releife and Discharge of Poore Distressed Prisoners for Debt, 1678, 30 Charles II, c.4.
An Act for Reliefe of Poore Prisoners for Debt or Damages, 1690, 2 William & Mary, c.15.
An Act for the Relief of Poor Prisoners for Debt, 1702, 1 Anne, c.19.
An Act for the Discharge Out of Prison of Such Insolvent Debtors as Shall Serve, or Procure a Person to Serve, in Her Majesty's Fleet or Army, 1703, 2&3 Anne, c.10.
An Act for the Relief of Insolvent Debtors, by Obliging Their Creditors to Accept the Utmost Satisfaction They Are Capable to Make, and Restoring Them to Their Liberty, 1711, 10 Anne, c.29.
An Act for Relief of Insolvent Debtors, and for the More Easy Discharge of Bankrupts out of Execution, after their Certificates Allowed, 1719, 6 George I, c.22.
An Act for the Relief of Insolvent Debtors, 1724, 11 George I, c.21.
An Act to Prevent Frivolous and Vexatious Arrests, 1725, 12 George I, c.29.
An Act for the Relief of Insolvent Debtors, 1736, 10 George II, c.26.
An Act for the Relief of Insolvent Debtors, 1742, 16 George II, c.17.
An Act for the Relief of Insolvent Debtors, 1747, 21 George II, c.31.
An Act to Revive and Make Perpetual Two Acts of Parliament, One Made in the Twelfth Year of the Reign of His Late Majesty King George I, intituled, An Act to Prevent Frivolous and Vexatious Arrests; and the Other Made in the Fifth Year of His Present Majesty's Reign, to Explain, Amend, and Render More Effectual the Said Act, 1748, 21 George II, c.3.
An Act for the Relief of Insolvent Debtors, 1755, 28 George II, c.13.
An Act for the Relief of Debtors with Respect to the Imprisonment of Their Persons, 1758, 32 George II, c.28.
An Act for Relief of Insolvent Debtors, 1760, 1 George III, c.17.
An Act for the Relief of Insolvent Debtors and for the Relief of Bankrupts in Certain Cases, 1774, 14 George III c.77.
An Act for the Relief of Insolvent Debtors; and for the Relief of Bankrupts, in Certain Cases, 1776, 16 George III, c.38.
Insolvent Debtors Relief Act, 1781, 21 George III, c.63.
An Act for Reducing the Time for the Imprisonment of Debtors Committed to Prison, Upon Prosecutions in Courts of Conscience, in London, Middlesex, and the Borough of Southwark, to the Same Periods in Each Court; and for Abolishing

Fees Paid by Those Debtors to Gaolers, or Others, on Account of Such Imprisonment, 1785, 25 George III, c.45.

An Act for Regulating the Time for the Imprisonment of Debtors Imprisoned by Process from Courts Instituted for the Recovery of Small Debts; for Abolishing the Claim of Fees of Gaolers, and Others, in Cases of such Imprisonment; and for Ascertaining the Qualifications of the Commissioners, 1786, 26 George III, c.38.

An Act for the Discharge of Certain Insolvent Debtors, 1794, 34 George III c.69.

Insolvent Debtors Relief Act (England), 1811, 51 George III c.125.

Printed Texts and Edited Source Collections

Adams, John. *A Sermon Preach'd at the Cathedral-Church of St Paul, before the Right Honourable Sir Samuel Garrard, Bar. Lord Mayor of the City of London, and the Court of Aldermen. On Tuesday, November 22 1709. Being the Day Appointed by Her Majesty's Royal Proclamation, for a Publick Thanksgiving*. London: 1709.

Allestree, Richard. *The Whole Duty of Man, Laid Down in a Plain and Familiar Way for the Use of All, but Especially the Meanest Reader*. London: 1704.

Anon. *An Abstract of His Majesties Commission … for the Relief of the Poore Prisoners*. London: 1624.

Anon. *Englands Dolefull Lamentation; or, The Cry of the Oppressed and Enslaved Commons of England: Set Forth in Two Several Petitions, the One Delivered to His Majesty, the Other Presented to His Excellency Sir Thomas Fairfax*. 1647.

Anon. *A Brief Dolorous Remonstrance*. 1648.

Anon. *A Pitiful Remonstrance, or Just Complaint*. London: 1648.

Anon. *The Prisoners Remonstrance*. London: 1649.

Anon. *The Case of the Traders and Dealers of England, Set Forth in a Dialogue between Mr Trader and Mr Cheator*. London: 1702.

Anon. *Trick Upon Trick, Being an Account of all the Cheats of Both Prisons, the Queen's Bench and Fleet … Written by one that was a Prisoner in Both Places*. London: 1703.

Anon. *The Mourning Poet; or the Unknown Comforts of Imprisonment … Written by a Poor Brother in Durance*. London: 1703.

Anon. *A Trip to a Spunging-House, or, the Spend Thrift Caught in the Powdring-tub of Affliction*. London: 1709.

Anon. *Britannia Fortior; or, the New State of Great Britain & Ireland, Under Our Sovereign Queen Anne*. London: 1709.

Anon. *A Common Law Treatise of Usury and Usurious Contracts*. London: 1710.

Anon. *The Christians Gazette: Or, Nice and Curious Speculations Chiefly Respecting the Invisible World*. London: 1713.

Anon. *The Cries of the Poor Prisoners, Humbly Offered to the Serious Consideration of the King and Parliament*. 1716.

Anon. *The Performance of Fair and Legal Contracts, the Surest Method to Support Publick and Private Credit*. 1721.

Anon. *An Accurate Description of Newgate. With the Rights, Privileges, Allowances, Fees, Dues, and Customs Thereof*. London: 1724.

Anon. *Reasons against Confining Persons in Prison for Debt, Humbly Offered to the Consideration of Parliament*. 1726.

Anon. *The Case of Richard Richards*. London: 1726.

Anon. *The Prisoner's Advocate, or a Caveat against Under Sheriffs, and Their Officers; Jayl-Keepers, and Their Agents*. London: 1726.

Anon. *A Report from the Committee Appointed to Enquire into the State of the Gaols of This Kingdom: Relating to the Fleet Prison.* London: 1729.

Anon. *A Report from the Committee Appointed to Enquire into the State of the Gaols of This Kingdom: Relating to the Marshalsea Prison.* London: 1729.

Anon. *A Speech without Doors, In Behalf of an Insolvent Debtor in the Fleet-Prison. With Some Remarks on the Present State of Gaol-Archy.* London: 1729.

Anon. *An Honest Scheme for Improving the Trade and Credit of the Nation.* London: 1729.

Anon. *Mr Bambridge's Case against the Bill Now Depending, to Disable Him to Hold or Execute the Office of Warden of the Prison of the Fleet; or to Have or Exercise and Authority Relating Thereto.* London: 1729.

Anon. *The Arbitrary Punishments and Cruel Tortures Inflicted on Prisoners for Debt.* London: 1729.

Anon. *The Tryal of William Acton, Deputy-Keeper and Lessee of the Marshalsea Prison in Southwark, at Kingston Assizes.* London: 1729.

Anon. *The Unreasonableness and Ill Consequence of Imprisoning the Body for Debt, Prov'd from the Laws of God and Nature, Human Policy and Interest.* London: 1729.

Anon. *A Report from the Committee Appointed to Enquire into the State of the Goals of This Kingdom. Relating to the King's Bench Prison.* London: 1730.

Anon. *The Kingston Atlantis: Or, Woodward's Miscellany.* London: 1731.

Anon. *The Credit and Interest of Great Britain Considered, Or the Way to Live Above Want.* London: 1735.

Anon. *The Rakes Progress; or, the Humours of Drury-Lane. A Poem.* London: 1735.

Anon. *A Compleat Collection of the Rules and Orders of the Court of Common Pleas at Westminster.* London: 1736.

Anon. *Law Quibbles: or, a Treatise of the Evasions, Tricks, Turns and Quibbles, Commonly Used in the Profession of the Law to the Prejudice of Clients.* London: 1736.

Anon. *Observations on Debtors and Imprisonment for Debt.* 1740.

Anon. *A New and Compleat Survey of London in Ten Parts. In Two Volumes. Vol. I.* London: 1742.

Anon. *The Practical Register of the Common Pleas.* London: 1743.

Anon. *A Collection of Scarce and Valuable Tracts on the Most Interesting and Entertaining Subjects Vol. I.* London: 1748.

Anon. *The Adventures of Mr Loveill Vol. II.* London: 1750.

Anon. *The Bee Reviv'd: or, The Prisoners Magazine. Containing the Greatest Curiosities in Prose and Verse, from All the Other Magazines, and the Politest Books and Papers Now in being. For the Benefit of the Compiler a Prisoner for Debt in Whitechapel Jail. ... Printed and Sold by J Lewis in Pater-Noster Row, near Cheapside.* London: 1750.

Anon. *The History of Charlotte Summers Vol. II.* London: 1750.

Anon. *The Junior's Precedence and the Senior's Success; or, The Younger Going before the Elder. ... To Which Is Added, an Appendix Shewing the Necessity or Erecting Courts of Conscience, and of Reforming County or Sherriffs-Courts throughout the Kingdom.* London: 1750.

Anon. *The Attempt: Or, an Essay towards the Retrieving Lost Liberty, Reforming the Corrupt and Pernicious Laws of This Nation, and Rendering the Recovery of Debts Easy and Effectual ... By a Prisoner in the Poultry-Compter.* London: 1751.

Anon. *The Adventures of a Valet. Vol. II.* London: 1752.

Anon. *The Life of the Famous William Stroud, Who Was Convicted at the Last Quarter Sessions for the City and Liberty of Westminster, as a Rogue and a Vagabond.* London: 1752.

Anon. *The Life and Uncommon Adventures of Capt. Dudley Bradstreet.* Dublin: 1755.

Anon. *The Irretrievable Abyss; Humbly Addressed to both Houses of Parliament.* 1757.

Anon. *The Oppressed Captive … Wrote by the Author and Sufferer in the Fleet Prison.* London: 1757.

Anon. *The Theatre of Love. A Collection of Novels.* London: 1759.

Anon. *Modern Honour: A Poem in Two Cantos.* London: 1760.

Anon. *London and Its Environs Described.* London: 1761.

Anon. *The Compulsive Clause in the Present Act of Insolvency Fully Considered. With Its Good and Bad Consequences Plainly Stated, and Clearly Answered. To Which Is Annexed, Proposals for the More Effectual Recovery of Debts, and without Arrests. With the Evils of Goals for Debtors Reasonably Exposed.* London: R. Davis & C Henderson, 1761.

Anon. *The London Magazine or Gentleman's Monthly Intelligencer, Vol. 31.* 1762.

Anon. *A Narrative of the Late Disturbances in the Marshalsea Prison.* London: 1768.

Anon. *The Tyburn Chronicle Vol. IV.* London: 1768.

Anon. *Essays on Several Subjects.* 1769.

Anon. *Imprisonment For Debt Considered with Respect to the Bad Policy, Inhumanity, and Evil Tendency of that Practice.* London: 1772.

Anon. *An Epistolary Poem, Humbly Inscribed To the Right Honourable Frederick Lord North … On the Present Mode of Imprisonment for Debt.* London: 1773.

Anon. *An Inquiry into the Practice of Imprisonment for Debt, and a Refutation of Mr James Stephen's Doctrine. To Which Is Added, a Hint for Relief of Both Creditor and Debtor.* London: 1773.

Anon. *The Annual Register, or a View of the History, Politics, and Literature, for the Year 1766.* Dublin: 1773.

Anon. *The Debtor's Pocket Guide, in Cases of Arrest.* London: 1776.

Anon. *Genuine Memoirs of Dr Dodd.* London: 1777.

Anon. *The Life and Writings of the Rev. William Dodd.* London: 1777.

Anon. *Considerations on the Laws between Debtors and Creditors; and an Abstract of the Insolvent Acts. With Thoughts on a Bill to Enable Creditors to Recover the Effects of Their Debtors, and to Abolish Imprisonment for Debt.* London: 1779.

Anon. *Observations on the Bill Now Depending in Parliament for the Relief of Debtors.* London: 1780.

Anon. *The Remembrancer; or, Impartial Repository of Public Events for the Year 1780, Part Two.* London: 1780.

Anon. *A Concise Abstract of the Most Important Clauses in the Following Interesting Acts of Parliament Passed in the Sessions of 1781.* London: 1781.

Anon. *A General History of Ireland Vol. II.* Dublin: 1781.

Anon. *The Complete Modern London Spy, for the Present Year, 1781.* London: 1781.

Anon. *The Proceedings at Large on the Trial of George Gordon, Esq.* London: 1781.

Anon. *The Ambulator; or, the Stranger's Companion in a Tour Round London.* London: 1782.

Anon. *The London Guide.* London: 1782.

Anon. *The Case of the Creditors of Joseph George Pedley, A Bankrupt of Bristol, and Now a Prisoner in that City … With Cursory Thoughts on Credit, and the Conduct of Bankers.* Bristol: 1783.

Anon. *The Second Report of the Committee of the Court of Common Council, of the City of London, Appointed the 1st of July 1784, To Inquire into the Assertions Lately Circulated Respecting the Affairs of the Corporation; upon the Several Charges and Insinuations of Mr Josiah Dornford.* London: 1784.

Anon. *The Gentleman, Merchant, Tradesman, Lawyer, and Debtor's Pocket Guide, in Cases of Arrest.* Bath: 1785.

Anon. *The Monthly Review; or Literary Journal: From January to June, Inclusive, MDC-CLXXXV. By Several Hands, Vol.72.* 1785.

Anon. *Considerations on the Late Increase of the Poor Rate, and on Mr Gilbert's Plan for the Relief and Support of the Poor.* Norwich: 1786.

Anon. *The Attorney and Agent's New and Exact Table of Costs, in the Courts of King's Bench and Common Pleas.* London: 1786.

Anon. *The Devil: Containing a Review and Investigation of All Public Subjects Whatever.* London: 1786.

Anon. *A Collection of Pamphlets Concerning the Poor.* London: 1787.

Anon. *A Summary Review of the Laws of the United States of North America, the British Provinces, and the West Indies.* Edinburgh: 1788.

Anon. *Historical Sketches of Civil Liberty.* London: 1788.

Anon. *New, Candid, and Practical Thoughts on the Law of Imprisonment for Debt, with a View to the Regulation of it.* London: 1788.

Anon. *The Monthly Mirror Vol. 81 – July to December 1789.* London: 1789.

Anon. *A Full and Accurate Report of the Trials of the Birmingham Rioters at the Late Assizes for the County of Warwick.* London: 1791.

Anon. *A Law Grammar: or, and Introduction to the Theory and Practice of English Jurisprudence.* 1791.

Anon. *An Authentic Account of the Riots in Birmingham, on the 14th, 15th, 16th, and 17th Days of July, 1791.* Birmingham: 1791.

Anon. *Copy of the Resolutions Agreed to at a Meeting of the Magistrates of the Three Divisions of the County of Lincoln.* 1791.

Anon. *A Candid Statement of the Case of the Insolvent Debtors of the Kingdom of Ireland.* Dublin: 1792.

Anon. *The London Directory for the Year 1792.* London: 1792.

Anon. *A Brief State of the Produce of the City's Estate and How the Same Has Been Disposed of.* London: 1793.

Anon. *The Debtor's and Creditor's Assistant; or, A Key to the King's Bench and Fleet Prisons; Calculated for the Information and Benefit of the Injured Creditor, as Well as the Unfortunate Debtor: Including Newgate, Ludgate, and the Three Compters. To Which Are Added, Reflections on Perpetual Imprisonment for Debt; and Outlines of a Bill for Abolishing the Same.* London: 1793.

Anon. *The Freemason's Magazine Vol. V.* London: 1793–1795.

Anon. *A Letter to the Manufacturers and Inhabitants of the Parishes of Stoke, Burslem and Wolsanton, in the County of Stafford, on Courts of Request, Occasioned by the Bill Intended to be Brought into Parliament This Sessions, for the Establishment of that Jurisdiction in the Potteries; By a Manufacturer.* 1794.

Anon. *The Citizen's Law Companion.* London: 1794.

Anon. *Rules and Orders to be Observed by the Industrious Protestant Society of Friends, United for the Mutual Support of Each Other: Instituted at the House of Mr Samuel Warren, the Three Jolly Butchers, Hoxton Market-Place, Begun April, 1784.* London: 1794.

Anon. *The Amours and Adventures of Two English Gentlemen in Italy.* Worcester: 1795.

Anon. *An Account of the Rise, Progress, and Present State of the Society for the Discharge and Relief of Persons Imprisoned for Small Debts throughout England.* London: 1796.

Anon. *A List of the Members of the Guardians; or Society for the Protection of Trade against Swindlers and Sharpers.* London: 1799.

Anon. *Anecdotes, Tales &c. Selected by a Debtor during His Confinement in Durham Jail.* Durham: 1800.

Arbuthnot, John. *Miscellanies: Containing the History of John Bull.* Dublin: 1746.

Attorney at Law. *An Attorney's Practice Common-placed.* London: 1743.

Bacon, Matthew. *A Treatise on Leases and Terms for Years.* London: 1798.

Bailey, Anne. *Memoirs of Mrs Anne Bailey.* London: 1771.

Barrell, Maria. *The Captive. By Maria Barrell, at the King's Bench.* London: 1790.

Baston, Thomas. *Observation on Trade and a Publick Spirit.* London: 1732.

Bevan, Richard. *Observations on the Law of Arrest and Imprisonment for Debt: Together with a Short Sketch of a Plan for an Amendment of That Law.* London: 1781.

Blackstone, William. *Commentaries on the Laws of England.* Oxford: 1770.

Bolland, James. *Memoirs of James Bolland Formerly a Butcher Then Officer to the Sheriff of Surry, Afterwards Officer to the Sheriff of Middlesex, and Lately a Candidate for the Place of City Marshal; Executed at Tyburn, March 18. 1772, for Forgery.* London: 1772.

Boote, Richard. *An Historical Treatise of an Action or Suit at Law.* London: 1766.

Boswell, James. *A Letter to the People of Scotland.* Edinburgh: 1783.

    The Life of Samuel Johnson Vol. I. London: 1791.

Brathwaite, Richard. *Barnaby's Journal, Under the Names of Mirtilus and Faustulus Shadowed.* London: 1774.

Brewman, T. *An Authentic List of Persons (Not Only in the Cities of London and Westminster, but Also in the Counties in England and Scotland) Who Have Surrendered Themselves, in Consequence of the Late Act, Into the Custody of the Marshal of the King's Bench Prison, between the Seventh of June, 1780, and the Thirty First of January, 1781.* London: 1781.

Brooke, Henry. *The History of Henry Earl of Moreland Vol. I.* London: 1781.

    Fool of Quality; or, the History of Henry Earl of Moreland. Vol. II. Philadelphia: 1794.

Brown, George. *The New English Letter-Writer; or, Whole Art of General Correspondence.* London: 1780.

Bruce, John. *Historical View of Plans for the Government of British India, and the Regulation of Trade to the East Indies.* London: 1793.

Burges, James. *Consideration on the Laws of Insolvency.* London: 1783.

Burn, Richard. *A New Law Dictionary: Intended for General Use, as Well as for Gentlemen of the Profession Vol. I.* London: 1792.

Burnett, Thomas. *A Second Tale of Tub.* London: 1715.

Burton, James. *The Warning: A Recourse and Divine Poem upon the Contageous Distemper amongst the Horned Cattle of This Kingdom … by James Burton, a Prisoner, in York Castle, for a Small Debt. Published for the Benefit of the Author.* York: 1752.

Burton, Philip. *Practice of the Office of Pleas in the Court of Exchequer both Antient and Modern Vol. I.* London: 1791.

Bynner, Henry. *The Trial of John Binns, Deputy of the London Corresponding Society for Sedition.* Birmingham: 1797.

Byrom, Samuel. *An Irrefutable Argument Fully Proving, that to Discharge Great Debts Is Less Injury, and More Reasonable Than to Discharge Small Debts … By Samuel Byrom … Now Confined within the Walls of the Fleet.* London: 1726.

Campbell, John. *A Political Survey of Britain Vol. II.* London: 1774.

Caraccioli, Charles. *Chiron: Or, the Mental Optician Vol. II.* London: 1758.

Cary, John. *A Discourse on Trade and Other Matters Relative to it.* London: 1745.

Chalmers, George. *An Estimate of the Comparative Strength of Britain during the Current and Four Preceding Reigns.* London: 1782.

Charke, Charlotte. *A Narrative of the Life of Mrs Charlotte Charke, (Youngest Daughter of Colley Cibber, Esq.).* London: 1755.

Choudhury, Nusrat. "Jeff Sessions Takes a Stand for Debtors' Prisons". *American Civil Liberties Union Online,* 28th December, 2017.

Coghlan, Margaret. *Memoirs of Mrs Coghlan.* Cork: 1794.

Collins, Francis (ed.) *Register of the Freemen of City of York Vol. II, 1559-1759.* Durham: Andrews & Co., 1900.

Corporation of London. *The Names and Address of the Several Officers of the City of London.* 1789.

Croft, George. *A Short Commentary, with Strictures, On Certain Parts of the Moral Writings of Dr Paley & Mr Gisborne.* Birmingham: 1797.

Croft, John. *Scrapeana: Fugitive Miscellany.* York: 1792.

Crompton, George. *Practice Common Placed: Or, the Rules and Cases of Practice in the Courts of King's Bench and Common Pleas, Methodically Arranged Vol. I.* London: 1786.

Cruttwell, Clement. *A Tour through the Whole Island of Great Britain; Divided into Journeys. Interspersed with Useful Observations, Vol. I.* London: 1801.

Dawes, Manasseh. *Commentaries on the Laws of Arrests in Civil Cases.* 1787.

de Beaumont, Jeanne-Marie. *The New Clarissa Vol. II.* London: 1768.

de Lolme, Jean Louis. *The Constitution of England, or an Account of the English Government; in Which it Is Compared with the Republican Form of Government, and Occasionally with the Other Monarchies in Europe.* London: 1781.

Debrett, John. *The Parliamentary Register; or History of the Proceedings and Debates of the House of Commons … during the Second Session of the Seventeenth Parliament of Great Britain Vol. XXXIII.* London: 1792.

   The Parliamentary Register; or History of the Proceedings and Debates of the House of Commons … during the Sixth Session of the Seventeenth Parliament of Great Britain Vol. XLIV. London: 1796.

Defoe, Daniel. *Remarks on the Bill to Prevent Frauds Committed by Bankrupts.* London: 1706.

   The Complete English Tradesman in Familiar Letters. London: 1726.

   Some Objections Humbly Offered to the Consideration of the Hon House of Commons, Relating to the Present Intended Relief of Prisoners. London: 1729.

   A Tour Thro' the Whole Island of Great Britain … Vol. III. London: 1742.

Delamayne, Thomas. *The Rise and Practice of Imprisonment in Personal Actions Examined.* London: 1772.

Department of State. *Papers Relating to the Foreign Relations of the United States Part II.* Washington: Government Printing Office, 1909.

Dickens, Charles. *Little Dorrit.* London: 1857.

Donaldson, John. *Sketches of a Plan for an Effectual and General Reformation of Life and Manners.* London: 1794.

Dorman, Joseph. *The Rake of Taste. A Poem.* London: 1735.

Dornford, Josiah (or Fidelio). *Seven Letters to the Common Council of the City of London, and One to the Livery, Relative to Their Committees, the Expenditure of the City Cash, Black Friars Bridge, The State of the Prisons, Court of Conscience Debtors, and the Partial Distribution of Justice to Them.* London: 1784.

   Seven Letters to the Lords of the Privy Council, on the Police. London: 1785.

Nine Letters to the Right Honourable Lord Mayor and Aldermen of the City of London, on the State of the City Prisons. London: 1786.

Seven Letters to the Lords and Commons of Great Britain, upon the Impolicy, Inhumanity, and Injustice of Our Present Mode of Arresting the Bodies of Debtors. London: 1786.

Duhigg, Bartholomew Thomas. *Observations on the Operation of Insolvent Laws, and Imprisonment for Debt*. Dublin: 1797.

Dunton, John. *Athenian Sport: or Two Thousand Paradoxes Merrily Argued to Amuse and Divert the Age*. London: 1707.

Durnford, Charles and Edward Hyde East. *Reports of Cases Argued and Determined in the Court of King's Bench ... Vol. V*. London: 1794.

Eden, Frederick. *The State of the Poor; or an History of the Labouring Classes in England Vol. III*. London: 1797.

Entick, John. *A New and Accurate History and Survey of London, Westminster, Southwark, and Places Adjacent; Containing Whatever Is Most Worthy of Notice in their Ancient and Present State*. London: 1766.

Everett, John. *A Genuine Narrative of the Memorable Life and Actions of John Everett*. London: 1730.

Farley, Edward. *Imprisonment for Debt Unconstitutional and Oppressive, Proved from the Fundamental Principles of the British Constitution, and the Rights of Nature*. London: 1788.

Imprisonment for Debt, Unconstitutional. The Second Edition. London: 1795.

Fennor, William. *The Compters Commonwealth*. London: 1617.

Fitzsimmonds, John. *Free and Candid Disquisitions, of the Nature and Execution of the Laws of England, Both in Civil and Criminal Affairs*. London: 1751.

Fleetwood, William. *The Justice of Paying Debts. A Sermon Preach'd in the City*. London: 1718.

Foote, Samuel. *The Genuine Memoirs of the Life of Sir John Dinely Goodere Who Was Murdered by the Contrivance of His Own Brother on Board the Ruby Man of War, in King Road Near Bristol, Jan 19 1740*. London: 1742.

Francis, Philip. *Speech in the House of Commons on Tuesday the 7th of March 1786*. London: 1786.

Gervaise, Isaac. *The System or Theory of the Trade of the World*. London: 1720.

Gildon, Charles. *The Post-Boy Robb'd of His Mail: or, The Pacquet Broke Open. Consisting of Letters of Love and Gallantry, and All Miscellaneous Subjects: In Which Are Discovered the Vertues, Vices, Follies, Humours and Intrigues of Mankind. With Remarks on Each letter*. London: 1706.

Giles, Jacob. *City Liberties: or, the Rights and Privileges of Freemen*. London: 1732.

Gooch, Elizabeth. *An Appeal to the Public, On the Conduct of Mrs Gooch, the Wife of William Gooch Esq*. London: 1788.

The Life of Mrs Gooch. Written by Herself. Dedicated to the Public. In Three Volumes. London: 1792.

Goodringe, Thomas. *The Law against Bankrupts: or a Treatise Wherein the Statutes against Bankrupts Are Explain'd, by Several Cases, Resolutions, Judgments and Decrees, Both at Common Law and in Chancery*. London: 1713.

Gordon, Thomas. *A Supplement to the Sermon Preached at Lincoln's Inn On January 30, 1732. By a Layman*. London: 1733.

Gordon, William. *The Universal Accountant and Complete Merchant Vol. II*. 1796.

Grano, John (John Ginger ed.). *Handel's Trumpeter – The Diary of John Grano*. Stuyvesant: Pendragon Press, 1998.

Grant, A. *The Progress and Practice of a Modern Attorney*. London: 1795.

Grey, Gilbert. *Epitome of the Annals of Great Britain*. Newcastle: 1773.

Grose, Francis. *A Classical Dictionary of the Vulgar Tongue*. London: 1796.

Hallifax, James. *A Sermon Preached at the Parish Church of St Paul, Covent-Garden, On Thursday, May 18, 1775, For the Benefit of Unfortunate Persons Confined for Small Debts. Published by Request of the Society*. London: 1775.

Hands, William. *A Selection of Rules Occurring in the Prosecution and Defence of Personal Actions in the Court of King's Bench*. London: 1795.

Hansard, T.C. *The Parliamentary Debates Vol. XIV.* London: 1826.

Hargreave, William. *History and Description of the Ancient City of York. Vol. II*. York: William Alexander, 1818.

Harris, Joseph. *An Essay upon Money and Coins*. Part 1. 1757.

Hawker, Peter. *The Diary of Colonel Peter Hawker 1802–1853. Vol. II*. London: Greenhill, 1988.

Hawkins, John. *The Life of Samuel Johnson*. Dublin: 1787.

Hawles, John. *Hamilton's Juryman's Guide*. London: 1794.

Hitchcock, Tim, Robert Shoemaker, Clive Emsley, Sharon Howard, and Jamie McLaughlin, et al. *Old Bailey Proceedings Online 1674–1913*. www.oldbaileyonline.org.

Hogarth, Richard. *Thesaurarium Trilingue Publicum; Being an Introduction to English, Latin, and Greek*. London: 1689.

Hogarth, William. *Anecdotes of William Hogarth*. London: 1833.

Holloway, Robert. *A Letter to John Wilkes, Esq; Sheriff of London and Middlesex; In Which the Extortion and Oppression of Sheriffs Officers, with Many Other Alarming Abuses, Are Exemplified and Detected; and a Remedy Proposed*. London: 1771.

House of Commons. *Report for the Committee Appointed to Enquire into the Practice and Effects of Imprisonment for Debt*. 1792.

> *Report from the Committee on the State of the Gaols of the City of London &c*. 1814.
> *Second Report from the Committee on the Prisons within the City of London and Borough of Southwark*. 1818.

Howard, George. *Queries Relative to Several Defects and Grievances in Some of the Present Laws of Ireland*. Dublin: 1763.

Howard, John. *The State of the Prisons in England and Wales, with Preliminary Observations, and an Account of Some Foreign Prisons*. London: 1777.

> *Appendix to the State of the Prisons in England and Wales &c by John Howard*. London: 1780.

Huntington, William. *The Modern Plasterer Detected and His Untempered Mortar Discovered*. London: 1787.

Hutton, William. *Courts of Requests: Their Nature, Utility, and Powers Described, with A Variety of Cases, Determined in that of Birmingham*. Birmingham: 1787.

> *A Dissertation on Juries*. Birmingham: 1789.
> *The History of Derby; From the Remote Ages of Antiquity, to the Year MDCCXCI*. London: 1791.
> *The Life of William Hutton – with Introduction by Carl Chinn*. Studley: Brewin Books, 1998.

Ilive, Jacob. *A Scheme for the Employment of All Persons Sent as Disorderly to the House of Correction in Clerkenwell*. London: 1759.

Ireland, John. *Hogarth Illustrated Vol. I*. London: 1793.

Jackson, Samuel. *Family Secrets, Literary and Domestic Vol. IV*. London: 1797.

Jackson, William. *The New and Complete Newgate Calendar Vol. V*. London: 1795.

Johnson, Christopher. *Considerations on the Case of the Confined Debtors in the This Kingdom*. London: 1793.

Johnson, Samuel. *The Idler in Two Volumes. Vol. I*. London: 1767.

 An Account of the Life of Mr Richard Savage. 1774.

Keimer, Samuel. *A Search after Religion, among the Many Modern Pretenders to it*. London: 1718.

Ker, Robert. *An Account of the Disorderly Way Some of the Ministers of this Present Church, and their Way of Baptizeing Children without Consent of the Father ... Robert Ker (Wright) Composed these Following Lines in the Prison House of Dalkeith*. Edinburgh: 1711.

King, Gregory. *Natural and Political Observations and Conclusions upon the State and Condition of England, in Two Tracts*. Baltimore: Johns Hopkins Press, 1936.

King, Richard. *The Frauds of London Detected; or, a Warning Piece against the Iniquitous Practices of That Metropolis*. London: 1779.

Lilly, John. *Modern Entries, being a Collection of Select Pleadings in the Courts of King's Bench, Common Pleas and Exchequer*. London: 1723.

Linley, William. *Forbidden Apartments. A Tale. Vol. II*. London: 1800.

Macdonald, Thomas. *A Treatise on Civil Imprisonment in England*. London: 1791.

Mackay, John. *A True State of the Proceedings of the Prisoners in the Fleet-Prison, in Order to The Redressing Their Grievances, before the Court of Common-Pleas*. London: 1729.

Macky, John. *A Journey through England in Familiar Letters from a Gentleman Here, to His Friend Abroad in Two Volumes, Vol. II*. London: J. Pemberton, 1722.

Malcolm, James Peller. *Londinium Redivivum, Or an Ancient History and Modern Description of London Compiled from Parochial Records, Archives of Various Foundations, the Harleian Mss and Other Authentic Sources. Vol. IV*. London: 1807.

Manley, Delarivier. *Memoirs of Europe towards the Close of the Eighth Century*. London: 1720.

Merrey, Walter. *Remarks on the Coinage of England from the Earliest Times to the Present Times, with a View to Point Out the Causes of the Present Scarcity of Silver*. Nottingham: 1789.

Miege, Guy. *The Present State of Great Britain and Ireland*. London: 1723.

Moore, Jane Elizabeth. *Genuine Memoirs of Jane Elizabeth Moore. Late of Bermondsey, in the County of Surry. Written by Herself: Containing the Singular Adventures of Herself and Family. Her Sentimental Journey through Great Britain: Specifying the Various Manufactures Carried on at Each Town. A Comprehensive Treatise on the Trade, Manufactures, Navigation, Laws and Police of this Kingdom, and the Necessity of a Country Hospital*. London: 1786.

Murray, F.A.S. *Thoughts on Imprisonment for Debt Humbly Addressed to His Majesty*. London: 1788.

Musgrave, John. *A Fourth Word to the Wise, or A Plaine Discovery of Englands Misery ... Set Forth in a Letter Written by a Prisoner in the Fleete*. 1647.

Neild, James. *Account of Persons Confined for Debt, in the Various Prisons of England and Wales; Together with their Provisionary Allowance during Confinement: As Reported to the Society for the Discharge and Relief of Small Debtors, In April, May, June &c 1800*. London: 1800.

   An Account of the Rise, Progress, and Present State, of the Society for the Discharge and Relief of Persons Imprisoned for Small Debts throughout England and Wales. London: 1802.

Nelson, Robert. *The Whole Duty of a Christian, by Way of Question and Answer.* London: 1774.

Nevil, Arthur. *Some Hints on Trade, Money, and Credit.* 1762.

Notcutt, William. *The Everlasting Love and Delights of Jesus Christ with the Sons of Men.* London: 1735.

Oldisworth, William. A *Dialogue between Timothy and Philatheus. In Which the Principles and Projects of a Late Whimsical Book, Intituled (The Rights of the Christian Church &c) Are Fairly Stated, and Answered in their Kind Vol. I.* London: 1709.

Oldys, Francis. *The Abridged Life of Thomas Pain, the Authour of the Seditious Writings, Entitled Rights of Man.* London: 1793.

P.R. *A Letter to a Friend in America.* Edinburgh: 1754.

Paget, William. *The Humours of the Fleet. A Poem.* Birmingham: T. Aris, 1749.

Paterson, Samuel. *Joineriana: or the Book of Scraps Vol. I.* London: 1772.

Paul, John. *A System of the Laws Relative to Bankruptcy. Shewing the Whole Theory and Practice of That Branch of the Law, From the Issuing the Commission to the Final Dividend and Writ of Supersedeas for Dissolving the Same.* London: 1776.

Pearce, T. *The Poor Man's Lawyer: or, Laws Relating to the Inferior Courts Laid Open.* London: 1755.

Penrice, William. *The Extraordinary Case of William Penrice, Late Deputy Marshal or Upper Turnkey of the King's Bench Prison.* London: 1768.

Pepys, Samuel (Henry B. Wheatley ed.). *The Diary of Samuel Pepys ... Transcribed from the Shorthand Manuscript ... Edited with Additions by Henry B. Wheatley. Vol. III.* London: George Bell & Sons, 1893.

Philanthropos. *Proposals for Promoting Industry and Advancing Proper Credit.* London: 1732.

Pitt, Moses. *The Cry of the Oppressed.* London: 1691.

Pluralist. *Tithes Politically, Judicially, and Justly Considered.* London: 1794.

Pope, Alexander. *The Works of Alexander Pope Vol. IV.* London: 1751.

Price. Rev. Funds. *A Just and Impartial View of the Funds of England ... First Printed in the American War: 1776.* London: 1795.

Prison Committee of Bridewell Hospital. *Propositions for Reform.* London: 1793.

Pudsey, William. *The Constitution and Laws of England Considered.* London: 1701.

Robbins, John. *A Bone to Pick, Recommended to the Several Water Companies of This Metropolis; or, a Check to Avarice, Tyranny and Oppression.* London: 1790.

Robinson, Mary (ed. M.J. Levy). *Perdita – The Memoirs of Mrs Robinson.* London: Peter Owen, 1994.

Rose, John. *A Constitutional Catechism, Adapted to All Ranks and Capacities, Illustrated with Copious Notes.* Bristol: 1795.

Scott, William. *A Sermon on Bankruptcy, Stopping Payment, and the Justice of Paying our Debts.* London: 1773.

Secker, Thomas. *Sermons on Several Subjects, by Thomas Secker, LL.D. Late Lord Archbishop of Canterbury Vol. III.* London: 1770.

Shirley, Thomas. *The Angler's Museum; or, The Whole Art of Float and Fly Fishing.* London: 1784.

Smith, Adam. *An Inquiry into the Nature and Causes of the Wealth of Nations. Volume I.* Dublin: 1776.

Smith, William. *State of the Gaols in London, Westminster, and Borough of Southwark. To Which Is Added, An Account of the Present State of Convicts Sentenced to Hard Labour on Board the Justitia upon the River Thames.* London: 1776.

Smollett, Tobias. *The Adventures of Ferdinand Count Fathom. Vol. II.* London: 1753.

Smyth, Maria. *The Woman of Letters; or, the History of Miss Fanny Belton. Vol. II.* London: 1783.

Squib, Jeremy. *The Cracker; or Flashes of Merriment: A Collection of Humorous Fire-Works Never Play'd Off Before.* London: 1770.

Stephen, James. *Considerations on Imprisonment for Debt, Fully Proving, that the Confining of the Bodies of Debtors Is Contrary to Common Law, Magna Charta, Statute Law, Justice, Humanity, and Policy.* London: 1770.

Stephens, Alexander. *Public Characters. Of 1805. Vol. VII.* London: 1805.

Stroud, William. *The Genuine Memoirs of the Life and Transactions of William Stroud.* London: 1752.

Stubbs, W. *The Crown Circuit Companion ... Vol. I.* London: 1749.

Sykes, Arthur Ashley. *The Scripture Doctrine of the Redemption of Man by Jesus Christ. In Two Parts.* London: 1755.

Thorisby, Thomas. *An Humble Proposal for Advancing the Credit of Seamens Wages, and for Preventing Their Fraudulent Selling the Same.* 1710.

Timberlake, Henry. *The Memoirs of Lieut. Henry Timberlake, Who Accompanied the Three Cherokee Indians to England in the Year 1762.* London: 1765.

Timbs, John. *Curiosities of London.* London: 1867.

Trusler, John. *The London Adviser and Guide: Containing Every Instruction and Information Useful and Necessary to Persons Living in London and Coming to Reside There.* London: 1786.

United States Bankruptcy Court, N.D. Illinois. *Matter of Morris.* 12 B.R. 321. 1981.

Vanderlint, Jacob. *Money Answers All Things: Or, An Essay to Make Money Sufficiently Plentiful amongst All Ranks of People.* London: 1734.

Vaughan, Samuel. *A Refutation of a False Aspersion.* London: 1769.

Vernon, John. *The Complete Countinghouse.* London: 1678.

von Archenholtz, Johann Wilhelm. *A Picture of England Vol. II.* London: 1789.

    A Picture of England: Containing a Description of the Laws, Customs, and Manners of England ... Translated from the French. Dublin: 1791.

    A View of the British Constitution and, of the Manners and Customs of the People of England. Edinburgh: 1794.

Waddell, Brodie (ed.). *Petitions to the Staffordshire Quarter Sessions, 1589–1799, British History Online.*

    Petitions to the Westminster Quarter Sessions, 1620–1799, British History Online.

Wagstaffe, Jeoffry. *The Batchelor: or, Speculations Vol. II.* London: 1769.

Walkingame, Francis. *The Tutor's Assistant: Being a Compendium of Arithmetic. And a Complete Question-Book.* London: 1770.

Walpole, Horace. *An Epitaph in the Churchyard of St Anne, Soho.* 1757.

Wells, Mary. *Memoirs of the Life of Mrs Sumbel, Late Wells; of the Theatres-royal, Drury-lane, Covent-garden, and Haymarket. In Three Volumes. Written by Herself.* London: 1811.

West, Jane. *Poems and Plays Vol. II.* London: 1799.

Wheelock, Mathew. *Reflections Moral and Political on Great Britain and Her Colonies.* London: 1770.

Whitmore, George. *The Duty of Not Running in Debt.* London: 1800.

Windsor, F.A. *Prosperity of England Midst the Clamours of Ruin*. 1799.

Wood, Simon. *Remarks on the Fleet Prison: Or, Lumber-House for Men and Women. Written by a Prisoner on the Common-Side, Who Hath Lain a Prisoner Near Three Years, on the Penalty of a Bond. No Debtor*. London: 1733.

Wright, William. *The Complete Tradesman: Or, a Guide in the Several Parts and Progressions of Trade*. London: 1789.

Wynne, Edward. *Eunomus; or, Dialogues Concerning the Law and Constitution of England Vol. II*. London: 1768.

Secondary

Allen, Robert C. "The High Wage Economy and the Industrial Revolution: A Restatement". *Economic History Review* vol. 68, no. 1 (2015), pp. 1–22.

Anderson, L. "Money and the Structure of Credit in the Eighteenth Century". *Business History* vol. 12, no. 2 (1970), pp. 85–101.

Ashton, T.S. *An Economic History of England – The Eighteenth Century*. London: Methuen, 1955.

    Economic Fluctuations in England 1700–1800. Oxford: Clarendon Press, 1959.

Aston, Jennifer and Paolo di Martino. "Risk, Success, and Failure: Female Entrepreneurship in Late Victorian and Edwardian England". *Economic History Review* vol. 70, no. 3 (2017), pp. 837–58.

Atkinson, Torie. "A Fine Scheme: How Municipal Fines Become Crushing Debt in the Shadow of the New Debtors' Prison". *Harvard Civil Rights-Civil Liberties Law Review* vol. 51, no. 1 (2016), pp. 189–238.

Babington Macaulay, Thomas. *The History of England from the Accession of James II – vol. III*. London: J.M. Dent & Sons, 1955.

Backscheider, Paula R. "Defoe's Lady Credit". *Huntingdon Library Quarterly* vol. 44, no. 2 (1981), pp. 89–100.

Bailey, Amanda. *Of Bondage – Debt, Property, and Personhood in Early Modern England*. Philadelphia: University of Pennsylvania Press, 2012.

Baine, Rodney M. "The Prison Death of Robert Castell and Its Effect on the Founding of Georgia". *The Georgia Historical Society* vol. 73, no. 1 (Spring 1989), pp. 67–78.

Baker, Matthew J. Metin Cosgel and Thomas J. Miceli. "Debtors' Prisons in America: An Economic Analysis". *Journal of Economic Behaviour & Organisation* vol. 84 (2012), pp. 216–228.

Baldwin, Robert, Martin Cave, and Martin Lodge. "Regulation—The Field and the Developing Agenda". In *The Oxford Handbook of Regulation*. Edited by Robert Baldwin, Martin Cave, and Martin Lodge, pp. 3–16. Oxford: Oxford University Press, 2010.

Balleisen, Edward J. *Navigating Failure – Bankruptcy and Commercial Society in Antebellum America*. Chapel Hill: University of North Carolina Press, 2001.

Baxter, William, "Observations on Money, Barter, and Bookkeeping". *The Accounting Historians Journal* vol. 31, no. 1 (2004), pp. 129–140.

Beattie, J.M. *Policing and Punishment in London, 1660–1750*. Oxford: Oxford University Press, 2001.

Bergh, Andreas and Carl Hampus Lyttkens. "Measuring Institutional Quality in Ancient Athens". *Journal of Institutional Economics* vol. 10, no. 2 (2014), pp. 279–310.

Bindman, David. "Hogarth, William (1697–1764)". *Oxford Dictionary of National Biography*. Oxford University Press, 2004. Online edition.

Boulton, Jeremy. "'Turned into the Street with My Children Destitute of Every Thing'; The Payment of Rent and the London Poor, 1600–1850". In *Accommodating Poverty – The Housing and Living Arrangements of the English Poor, c.1600–1850*. Edited by Joanne McEwan and Pamela Sharpe, pp. 25–49. Basingstoke: Palgrave Macmillan, 2011.

Breen, T.H. "The Meaning of Things: Interpreting the Consumer Economy in the Eighteenth Century". In *Consumption and the World of Goods*. Edited by John Brewer and Roy Porter, pp. 249–260. London: Routledge, 1993.

Briggs, Chris. *Credit and Village Society in Fourteenth-Century England*. Oxford: Oxford University Press, 2009.

Britnell, Richard. "Town Life". In *A Social History of England, 1200–1500*. Edited by Rosemary Horrox and Mark Ormrod, pp. 137–138. Cambridge: Cambridge University Press, 2006.

Broadberry, Stephen, Bruce M. S. Campbell, Alexander Klein, Mark Overton, and Bas van Leeuwen. "Clark's Malthus Delusion: Response to 'Farming in England 1200–1800'". *Economic History Review* vol. 71, no. 2 (2018), pp. 639–664.

Brown, Roger Lee. "The Rise and Fall of the Fleet Marriages". In *Marriage and Society – Studies in the Social History of Marriage*. Edited by R.B. Outhwaite, pp. 117–136. London: Europa Publications Ltd, 1981.

    A History of the Fleet Prison, London – The Anatomy of the Fleet. Lampeter: Edwin Mellen Press, 1996.

Burley, K.H. "An Essex Clothier of the Eighteenth Century". *The Economic History Review* vol. 11, no. 2 (1958), pp. 289–301.

Burrows, Donald. *Handel: Messiah*. Cambridge: Cambridge University Press, 1991.

Byrne, Richard. *Prisons and Punishments of London*. Grafton: London, 1992.

Calland, Gary. *A History of the Devon County Prison for Debtors in St. Thomas*. Exeter: Little History, 1999.

Campbell, Brianna L. "The Economy of the Debtors' Prison Model: Why Throwing Deadbeats into Debtors' Prison Is a Good Idea". *Arizona Journal of International and Comparative Law* vol. 32, no. 3 (2015), pp. 849–876.

Carlos, Ann M. and Larry Neal. "The Micro-Foundations of the Early London Capital Market: Bank of England Shareholders during and after the South Sea Bubble, 1720–1725". *Economic History Review* vol. 59, no. 3 (2006), pp. 498–538.

Carnegie, Garry. "Re-examining the Determinants of Barter Accounting in Isolate Communities in Colonial Societies". *Accounting History* vol. 9, no. 3 (2004), pp. 73–87.

Carruthers, Bruce G. "The Sociology of Money and Credit". In *The Handbook of Economic Sociology – Second Edition*. Edited by Neil J. Smelser and Richard Swedberg, pp. 355–378. Princeton: Princeton University Press, 2005.

Cashin, Edward J. "Glimpses of Oglethorpe in Boswell's Life of Johnson". *The Georgia Historical Society* vol. 88, no. 3 (2004), pp. 398–405.

Cervantes, Gabriel and Dahlia Porter. "Extreme Empiricism, John Howard, Poetry, and the Thermometrics of Reform". *The Eighteenth Century* vol. 57, no. 1 (Spring 2016), pp. 95–119.

Chalkin, W. "The Reconstruction of London's Prisons, 1770–1799: An Aspect of the Growth of Georgian London". *London Journal* vol. 9, no. 1 (1983), pp. 21–34.

Chatten, Elizabeth N. *Samuel Foote*. Boston: Twayne Publishers, 1980.

Clark, Gregory. *A Farewell to Alms – A Brief Economic History of the World.* Woodstock: Princeton University Press, 2007.

Cohen, Jay. "The History of Imprisonment for Debt and Its Relation to the Development of Discharge in Bankruptcy". *Journal of Legal History* vol. 3 (1982), pp. 153–171.

Coleman, Peter J. *Debtors and Creditors in America – Insolvency, Imprisonment for Debt, and Bankruptcy, 1607–1900.* Madison: The State Historical Society of Wisconsin, 1974.

Condon, Richard H. "James Neild, Forgotten Reformer". *Studies in Romanticism* vol. 4, no. 4 (Summer 1964), pp. 240–251.

Cooper, T.P. *The History of the Castle of York – From Its Foundation to the Present Day with an Account of the Building of Clifford's Tower.* London: Elliot Stock, 1911.

Dart, Gregory. *Metropolitan Art and Literature, 1810–1840 – Cockney Adventures.* Cambridge: Cambridge University Press, 2012.

deGooede, Marieke. "Mastering 'Lady Credit'". *International Feminist Journal of Politics* vol. 2, no. 1 (2000), pp. 58–81.

DeLacy, Margaret. *Prison Reform in Lancashire, 1700–1850 – A Study in Local Administration.* Stanford: Stanford University Press, 1986.

deRuysscher, Dave. "Bankruptcy, Insolvency, and Debt Collection among Merchants in Antwerp (c.1490 to c.1540)". In *The History of Bankruptcy – Economic, Social, and Cultural Implications in Early Modern Europe.* Edited by Thomas Max Safley, pp. 185–199. London: Routledge, 2013.

Devereaux, Simon. "The Making of the Penitentiary Act, 1775–1779". *The Historical Journal* vol. 42, no. 2 (1999), pp. 405–433.

Dorey, Margaret. "Reckliss Endangerment?: Feeding the Poor Prisoners of London in the Early Eighteenth Century". In *Experiences of Poverty in Late Medieval and Early Modern England and France.* Edited by Anne M. Scott, pp. 183–198. Farnham: Ashgate, 2012.

Downs, Carolyn. "Networks, Trust, and Risk Mitigation during the American Revolutionary War: A Case Study". *Economic History Review* vol. 70, no. 2 (2017), pp. 509–528.

Duffy, Ian P.H. "English Bankrupts, 1571–1861". *American Journal of Legal History* vol. 24 (1980), pp. 283–305.

    Bankruptcy and Insolvency in London during the Industrial Revolution. London: Garland Publishing, 1985.

Duncan, Cheryll. "'A Debt Contracted in Italy': Ferdinando Tenducci in a London Court and Prison". *Early Music* vol. 42, no. 2 (2014), pp. 219–229.

    "New Purcell Documents from the Court of King's Bench". *Royal Musical Association Research Chronicle* vol. 47, no. 1 (2016), pp. 1–23.

Dyson, Kenneth. *States, Debt, and Power – Saints and Sinners in European History and Integration.* Oxford: Oxford University Press, 2014.

Earle, Peter. *The Making of the English Middle Class: Business, Society and Family Life in London, 1660–1730.* London: Methuen, 1989.

Erickson, Amy Louise. "Married Women's Occupations in Eighteenth-Century London". *Continuity and Change* vol. 23, no. 2 (2008), pp. 267–307.

Evans, Robin. *The Fabrication of Virtue – English Prison Architecture, 1750–1840.* Cambridge: Cambridge University Press, 1982.

Ewen, Lorna. "Debtors, Imprisonment and the Privilege of Girth". In *Perspectives in Scottish Social History.* Edited by Leah Leneman, pp. 53–68. Aberdeen: Aberdeen University Press, 1988.

Ferdinand, C.Y. "The Economics of the Eighteenth-Century Provincial Book Trade: The Case of Ward and Chandler". In *Re-constructing the Book – Literary Texts in Transmission*. Edited by Maureen Bell, Shirley Chew, Simon Eliot, Lynette Hunter, and James L.W. West III, pp. 42–56. Aldershot: Ashgate, 2001.

Field, Jacob. "Clandestine Weddings at the Fleet Prison c.1710–1750: Who Married There?". *Continuity and Change* vol. 32, no. 3 (2017), pp. 349–377.

Finn, Margot C. "Debt and Credit in Bath's Court of Requests, 1829–1839". *Urban History* vol. 21, (October 1994), pp. 211–236.

"Being in Debt in Dickens's London: Fact, Fictional Representation and the Nineteenth-Century Debtors Prison". *Journal of Victorian Culture* vol. 1, no. 2 (1996), pp. 203–226.

The Character of Credit – Personal Debt in English Culture, 1740–1914. Cambridge: Cambridge University Press, 2003.

"Henry Hunt's *Peep into a Prison*: the Radical Discontinuities of Imprisonment for Debt". In *English Radicalism, 1550–1850*. Edited by Glen Burgess and Michael Festenstein, pp. 190–216. Cambridge: Cambridge University Oress, 2007.

Forbes, Thomas R. "Medical Supplies for Prisoners in 1675". *Bulletin of the New York Academy of Medicine* vol. 49, no. 7 (1973), pp. 592–593.

Ford, Richard. "Imprisonment for Debt". *Michigan Law Review* vol. 25, no. 1 (November 1926), pp. 24–49.

Foucault, Michel. *Discipline and Punish – The Birth of the Prison*. New York: Vintage Books, 1995.

George, Dorothy. *London Life in the Eighteenth Century*. London: Penguin, 1979 (first edition 1925).

Ginger, John. "New Light on Gawen Hamilton – Artists, Musicians, and the Debtors' Prison". *Apollo* vol. 136 (September 1992), pp. 156–160.

Glaisyer, Natasha. "A Due Circulation in the Veins of the Publick: Imagining Credit in Late Seventeenth- and Early Eighteenth-Century England". *The Eighteenth Century* vol. 46, no. 3 (2005), pp. 277–297.

The Culture of Commerce in England 1660–1720. Woodbridge: Boydell Press, 2006.

"Calculating Credibility: Print Culture, Trust and Economic Figures in Early Eighteenth-Century England". *Economic History Review*, vol. 60, no. 4 (November 2007), pp. 685–711.

"'The Most Universal Intelligencers' – The Circulation of the London Gazette in the 1690s". *Media History* vol. 23, no. 2 (2017), pp. 256–280.

Graeber, David. *Debt – The First 5000 Years*. Brooklyn: Melville House, 2011.

Graham, Aaron. "Credit, Confidence, and the Circulation of Exchequer Bills in the Early Financial Revolution". *Financial History Review* vol. 26, no. 1 (2019), pp. 63–80.

Grass, Sean. *The Self in the Cell – Narrating the Victorian Prisoner*. London: Routledge, 2003.

Grassby, Richard. *The Business Community of Seventeenth-Century England*. Cambridge: Cambridge University Press, 1995.

Gregory, Chris A. "On Money Debt and Morality: Some Reflections on the Contribution of Economic Anthropology". *Social Anthropology* vol. 20, no. 4 (2012), pp. 380–396.

Greif, Avner. "Coercion and Exchange – How Did Markets Evolve?". In *Institutions, Innovation, and Industrializations – Essays in Economic History and Development*.

Edited by Avner Greif, Lynne Kiesling, and John V.C. Nye, pp. 71–96. Woodstock: Princeton University Press, 2015.

Grief, Avner and Joel Mokyr. "Institutions and Economic History: A critique of Professor McCloskey". *Journal of Institutional Economics* vol. 12, no. 1 (2016), pp. 29–41.

Griffiths, Paul. "Contesting London Bridewell, 1576–1580". *Journal of British Studies* vol. 42, no. 3 (2003), pp. 283–315.

Grove, T.N. "The Psychological Prison of Arthur Clennam in Dickens's *Little Dorrit*". *The Modern Language Review* vol. 68, no. 4 (1973), pp. 750–755.

Haagen, Paul H. "Eighteenth-Century English Society and the Debt Law". In *Social Control and the State – Historical and Comparative Essays*. Edited by Stanley Cohen and Andrew Scull, pp. 222–247. Oxford: Basil Blackwell, 1986.

Hampson, Christopher D. "The New American Debtors' Prisons". *American Journal of Criminal Law* vol. 44, no. 1 (2016), pp. 1–48.

Hanham, A.A. "Bambridge, Thomas (d.1741)". *Oxford Dictionary of National Biography*. Oxford: Oxford University Press, 2004. Online edition.

Hardman, Philippa. "Fear of Fever and the Limits of the Enlightenment – Selling Prison Reform in Late Eighteenth-Century Gloucestershire". *Cultural and Social History* vol. 10, no. 4 (2013), pp. 511–531.

Harris, Jonathan Gil. "Ludgate Time: Simon Eyre's Oath and the Temporal Economies of the Shoemaker's Holiday". *Huntingdon Library Quarterly* vol. 71, no. 2 (March 2008), pp. 11–32.

Hartigan-O'Connor, Ellen. *The Ties that Buy – Women and Commerce in Revolutionary America*. Philadelphia: University of Pennsylvania Press, 2009.

Hartley, B. R. "Thomas Griffith of York, 'Once Governor of the Castle and Now a Debtor from the Same'". *York Historian* vol. 11 (1994), pp. 40–55.

Hill, Lamar M. "'Extreame Detriment': Failed Credit and the Narration of Indebtedness in the Jacobean Court of Requests". In *Law and Authority in Early Modern England – Essays Presented to Thomas Garden Barnes*. Edited by Buchanan Sharp and Mark Charles Fissel, pp. 136–146. Newark: University of Delaware Press, 2007.

Hitchcock, Tim and Robert Brink Shoemaker. *London Lives – Poverty, Crime and the Making of a Modern City, 1690–1800*. Cambridge: Cambridge University Press, 2015.

Hodgson, Geoffrey M. "1688 and All that: Property Rights, the Glorious Revolution, and the Rise of British Capitalism". *Journal of Institutional Economics* vol. 13, no. 1 (2017), pp. 79–107.

Holdsworth, William. *A History of English Laws Vol.VI–XIII*. London: Methuen, 1924–1952.

Hoppit, Julian. "Financial Crises in Eighteenth-Century England". *Economic History Review* vol. 39, no. 1 (February, 1986), pp. 39–58.

"The Use and Abuse of Credit in Eighteenth-Century England". In *Business Life and Public Policy – Essays in Honour of D.C. Coleman*. Edited by Neil McKendrick and R.B. Outhwaite, pp. 64–78. Cambridge: Cambridge University Press, 1986.

Risk and Failure in English Business 1700–1800. Cambridge: Cambridge University Press, 1987.

"Attitudes to Credit in Britain, 1680–1790". *The Historical Journal* vol. 33, no. 2 (1990), pp. 305–322.

"The Myths of the South Sea Bubble". *Transactions of the RHS* vol. 12 (2002), pp. 141–165.

Britain's Political Economies – Parliament and Economic Life, 1660–1800. Cambridge: Cambridge University Press, 2017.

Horby, Barbara. "The Prodigal Rector in the Fleet". *Northamptonshire Past and Present* vol. 60 (2007), pp. 72–77.

Humphries, Jane and Jacob Weisdorf. "The Wages of Women in England, 1260–1850". *Journal of Economic History* vol. 75, no. 2 (2015), pp. 405–447.

Hunt, Margaret. "Women and the Fiscal-Imperial State in Late Seventeenth- and Early Eighteenth-Century London". In *A New Imperial History: Culture, Identity and Modernity in Britain and the Empire, 1660–1840*. Edited by Kathleen Wilson, pp. 29–47. Cambridge: Cambridge University Press, 2004.

Hurl-Eamon, Jennine. "The Fiction of Female Dependence and the Makeshift Economy of Soldiers, Sailors, and their Wives in Eighteenth-Century London". *Labour History* vol. 49, no. 4 (2008), pp. 481–501.

Innes, Joanna. "The King's Bench Prison in the Later Eighteenth Century: Law, Authority and Order in a London Debtors' Prison". In *An Ungovernable People – The English and their Law in the Seventeenth and Eighteenth Centuries*. Edited by John Brewer and John Styles, pp. 250–298. London: Hutchinson, 1980.

Ishizu, Mina. "Boom and Crisis in Dinancing the British Transatlantic Trade – A Case Study of the Bankruptcy of John Leigh & Company in 1811". In *The History of Bankruptcy – Economic, Social, and Cultural Implications in Early Modern Europe*. Edited by Thomas Max Safley, pp. 141–156. London: Routledge, 2013.

John Soanes Museum. "Hogarth: 101". 20th September 2019, *The John Soane's Museum*, www.soane.org/features/hogarth-101.

Johnson, Lynn. "Friendship, Coercion, and Interest: Debating the Foundations of Justice in Early Modern England". *Journal of Early Modern History* vol. 8, no. 2 (2004), pp. 46–64.

Kadens, Emily "The Last Bankrupt Hanged: Balancing Incentives in the Development of Bankruptcy Law". *Duke Law Journal* vol. 59, no. 7 (April 2010), pp. 1229–1319.

Keibek, Sebastian and Leigh Shaw-Taylor. "Early Modern Rural by-Employments: A Re-Examination of the Probate Inventory Evidence". *Agricultural History Review* vol. 61, no. 2 (2013), pp. 244–81.

Kelly, David. "The Conditions of Debtors and Insolvents in Eighteenth-Century Dublin". In *The Gorgeous Mask: Dublin 1700–1850*. Edited by David Dickson pp. 98–120. Dublin: Trinity History Workshop, 1987.

Kent, David A. "Small Businessmen and their Credit Transactions in Early Nineteenth-Century Britain". *Business History* vol. 36, no. 2 (1994), pp. 47–64.

Lambert, Miles. "'Cast-off Wearing Apparel': The Consumption and Distribution of Second-hand Clothing in Northern England during the Long Eighteenth Century". *Textile History* vol. 35 (2004), pp. 1–26.

Langford, Paul. *A Polite and Commercial People – England 1727–1783*. Oxford: Clarendon Press, 1998.

Lannon, Colleen. "Whose Fault? The Speculator's Guilt in *Little Dorrit*". *Victorian Literature and Culture* vol. 45 (2017), pp. 413–432.

LeBaron, Genevieve and Adrienne Roberts. "Confining Social Insecurity: Neoliberalism and the Rise of the 21st Century Debtors' Prison". *Politics and Gender* vol. 8 (2012), pp. 25–49.

Leeman, Stephanie Adele. "Stone Walls do Not a Prison Make: The Debtors' Prison, York". *York Historian* vol. 11 (1994), pp. 23–39.

Lemire, Beverly. "Second-hand Beaux and "Red-armed Belles": Conflict and the Creation of Fashions in England, c.1660–1800". *Continuity and Change* vol. 15, no. 3 (2000), pp. 391–417.

Letiche, J.M. "Isaac Gervaise on the International Mechanism of Adjustment". *Journal of Political Economy* vol. 60, no. 1 (1952), pp. 34–43.

Levy, Nathan. "Mesne Process in Personal Actions at Common Law and the Power Doctrine". *Yale Law Journal* vol. 78 (1968), pp. 52–98.

Lewis, Judith S. "When a House Is Not a Home: Elite English Women and the Eighteenth-Century Country House". *Journal of British Studies* vol. 48, no. 2 (2009), pp. 336–363.

Lucas, Philip. "John Howard and Asperger's Syndrome: Psychopathology and Philanthropy". *History of Psychiatry* vol. 12 (2001), pp. 73–101.

Macfarlane, Karen A. "'Does He Know the Danger of an Oath?': Oaths, Religion, Ethnicity and the Advent of the Adversarial Criminal trial in the Eighteenth Century". *Immigrants & Minorities* vol. 31, no. 3 (2013), pp. 317–345.

Madison, James. "The Evolution of Commercial Credit Reporting Agencies in Nineteenth-Century America". *Business History Review* vol. 48, no. 2 (1974), pp. 164–186.

Maher, Richard. "Poems from the Prison Yard – A Poetic Correspondence between Charles Wogan and William Tunstall". *History Ireland* vol. 25, no. 2 (March-April 2017), pp. 20–23.

Mann, Bruce H. *Republic of Debtors – Bankruptcy in the Age of American Independence*. London: Harvard University Press, 2002.

Marksham, Lester V. *Victorian Insolvency – Bankruptcy, Imprisonment for Debt, and Company Winding-up in Nineteenth-Century England*. Oxford: Clarendon Press, 1995.

Mason, John. "Enterprise, Opportunity, and Bankruptcy in the Early Derbyshire Cotton Industry". In *King Cotton – A Tribute to Douglas A. Farnie*. Edited by John F. Wilson, pp. 133–153. Lancaster: Carnegie, 2009.

McCloskey, Deirdre. "Max U versus Humanomics: A Critique of Neo-Institutionalism". *Journal of Institutional Economics* vol. 12, no. 1 (2016), pp. 1–27.

———. "The Great Enrichment: A Humanistic and Social Scientific Account". *Scandinavian Economic History Review* vol. 64, no. 1 (2016), pp. 6–18.

McConville, Sean. *A History of English Prison Administration – Volume I 1750–1877*. London: Routledge & Kegan Paul, 1981.

McGowen, Randell. "Penal Reform and Politics in Early Nineteenth-Century England: "A Prison Must be a Prison"". In *Imagining the British Atlantic after the American Revolution*. Edited by Michael Meranze and Saree Makdisi, pp. 219–243. Toronto: University of Toronto Press, 2015.

McKendrick, Neil, John Brewer, and J.H. Plumb. *The Birth of a Consumer Society – The Commercialization of Eighteenth-Century England*. Bloomington: Indiana University Press, 1982.

McNall, Christopher "The Business of Statutory Debt Registries, 1283–1307". In *Credit and Debt in Medieval England c.1180–c.1350*. Edited by P.R. Schofield and N.J. Mayhew, pp. 68–88. Oxford: Oxbow Books, 2002.

Meyer, Liam J. "Humblewise: Deference and Complaint in the Jacobean Court of Requests". *Journal of Early Modern Studies* vol. 4 (2015), pp. 261–285.

Mokyr, Joel. "Accounting for the Industrial Revolution". In *The Cambridge Economic History of Modern Britain – Volume I: Industrialisation, 1700–1860*. Edited by

Roderick Floud and Paul Johnson, pp. 1–27. Cambridge: Cambridge University Press, 2004.

    The Enlightened Economy – An Economic History of Britain 1700–1850. New Haven: Yale University Press, 2009.

    "Bottom-Up or Top-Down? The Origins of the Industrial Revolution". *Journal of Institutional Economics* vol. 14, no. 6 (2018), pp. 1003–1024.

Muir, James. *Law, Debt, and Merchant Power – The Civil Courts of Eighteenth-Century Halifax*. Toronto: University of Toronto Press, 2016.

Muldrew, Craig. "Credit and the Courts: Debt Litigation in a Seventeenth-Century Urban Community". *Economic History Review* vol. 46, no. 1 (1993), pp. 23–38.

    "Interpreting the Market: The Ethics of Credit and Community Relations in Early Modern England". *Social History* vol. 18, no. 2 (1993), pp. 163–183.

    The Economy of Obligation – The Culture of Credit and Social Relations in Early Modern England. Basingstoke: Macmillan, 1998.

    "'Hard Food for Midas': Cash and Its Social Value in Early Modern England". *Past and Present* vol. 170 (2001), pp. 78–120.

    "Class and Credit: Social Identity, Wealth and the Life Course in Early Modern England". In *Identity and Agency in England, 1500–1800*. Edited by Henry French and Jonathan Barry, pp. 147–177. Basingstoke: Palgrave Macmillan, 2004.

    "From Credit to Savings? An Examination of Debt and Credit in Relation to Increasing Consumption in England (c.1650 to 1770)". *Quaderni Storci* vol. 137 (August 2011), pp. 391–414.

Neal, Larry and Stephen Quinn. "Networks of Information, Markets, and Institutions in the Rise of London as a Financial Centre, 1660–1720". *Financial History Review* vol. 8 (2001), pp. 7–26.

Nightingale, Pamela. "The Lay Subsidies and the Distribution of Wealth in Medieval England, 1275–1334". *Economic History Review* vol. 57, no. 1 (2004), pp. 1–32.

North, Douglas C. "Institutions". *Journal of Economic Perspectives* vol. 5, no. 1 (1995), pp. 97–112.

    "The Role of Institutions in Economic Development". *United Nations Economic Commission for Europe Discussion Paper Series*, no. 2003.2 (2003), pp. 1–10.

North, Douglas C. and Barry R. Weingast. "Constitutions and Commitment: The Evolution of Institutions Governing Public Choice in Seventeenth-Century England". *Journal of Economic History* vol. 69, no. 4 (1989), pp. 803–831.

Olegario, Rowena. *A Culture of Credit – Embedding Trust and Transparency in American Business*. London: Harvard University Press, 2006.

Palley, Thomas I. *From Financial Crisis to Stagnation – The Destruction of Shared Prosperity and the Role of Economics*. Cambridge: Cambridge University Press, 2012.

Parker, Ben. "Recognition or Reification?: Capitalist Crisis and Subjectivity in *Little Dorrit*". *New Literary History* vol. 45, no. 1 (2014), pp. 131–151.

Paul, Tawny. "Credit, Reputation, and Masculinity in British Urban Commerce: Edinburgh, c.1710–70". *Economic History Review* vol. 66, no. 1 (2013), pp. 226–248.

    "Accounting for Men's Work: Multiple Employments and Occupational Identities in Early Modern England". *History Workshop Journal* vol. 85 (2018), pp. 26–46.

    Poverty of Disaster – Debt and Insecurity in Eighteenth-Century Britain. Cambridge: Cambridge University Press, 2019.

Paulson, Ronald. *Hogarth Vol. I – The Modern Moral Subject 1697–1732*. Cambridge: Lutterworth Press, 1991.

Peebles, Gustav. "The Anthropology of Credit and Debt". *Annual Review of Anthropology* vol. 39 (2010), pp. 225–240.

   The Euro and Its Rivals: Currency and the Construction of a Transnational City. Bloomington: Indiana University Press, 2011.

   "Whitewashing and Leg-Bailing: On the Spatiality of Debt". *Social Anthropology* vol. 20, no. 4 (2012), pp. 429–435.

   "Washing away the Sins of Debt: The Nineteenth-Century Eradication of the Debtors' Prison". *Comparative Studies in History* vol. 55, no. 3 (2013), pp. 701–724.

Phillips, Nicola. *Women in Business 1700–1850*. Woodbridge: The Boydell Press, 2006.

Pitofsky, Alexander H. "The Warden's Court Martial: James Oglethorpe and the Politics of Eighteenth-Century Prison Reform". *Eighteenth Century Life* vol. 24, no. 1 (2000), pp. 88–102.

   "'What Do You Think Laws Were Made For?' – Prison Reform Discourse and the English Jacobin Novel". *Studies in Eighteenth-Century Culture* vol. 33 (2004), pp. 293–312.

Plucknett, Theodore F.T. *A Concise History of the Common Law*. London: Butterworth & Co., 1948.

Pollard, A.F. "The Growth of the Court of Requests". *The English Historical Review* vol. 56, no. 222 (April, 1941), pp. 300–303.

Qasem, A.M. "Bail and Personal Liberty". *Canadian Bar Review* vol. 30, no. 4 (1952), pp. 378–396.

Reddaway, T.F. *The Rebuilding of London after the Great Fire*. London: Jonathon Capt Ltd, 1940.

Rogers, Pat. "Defoe in the Fleet Prison". *The Review of English Studies* vol. 22, no. 88 (1971), pp. 451–455.

Rudé, George. *Hanoverian London 1714–1808*. Berkeley: University of California Press, 1971.

Rudolph, Julia. *Common Law and Enlightenment in England 1689–1750*. Woodbridge: Boydell Press, 2013.

Sahle, Esther. "Quakers, Coercion, and Pre-modern Growth: Why Friends' Formal Institutions for Contract Enforcement Did Not Matter for Early Modern Trade Expansion". *Economic History Review* vol. 71, no. 2 (2018), pp. 418–436.

Sainsbury, John. "John Wilkes, Debt, and Patriotism". *Journal of British Studies* vol. 34, no. 2 (April 1995), pp. 165–195.

   John Wilkes – The Lives of a Libertine. Aldershot: Ashgate, 2006.

Selley, Gillian. "Charles Lanyon, Merchant of Penzance: Victim of Cruelty and Corruption in the County Debtors Prison in Exeter". *The Devon Historian* vol. 83 (2014), pp. 39–48.

Sgard, Jérôme. "Bankruptcy, Fresh Start and Debt Renegotiation in England and France (17th to 18th century)". In *The History of Bankruptcy – Economic, Social, and Cultural Implications in Early Modern Europe*. Edited by Thomas Max Safley, pp. 225–235. London: Routledge, 2013.

Sharpe, James. "Civility, Civilizing Processes, and the End of Public Punishment in England". In *Civil Histories – Essays Presented to Sir Keith Thomas*. Edited by Peter Burke, Brian Harrison, and Paul Slack, pp. 215–230. Oxford: Oxford University Press, 2000.

Shepard, Alexandra. *Accounting for Oneself: Worth, Status, and the Social Order in Early Modern England*. Oxford: Oxford University Press, 2015.

"Crediting Women in the Early Modern English Economy". *History Workshop Journal* vol. 79, no. 1 (Spring 2015), pp. 1–24.

"Minding their Own Business: Married Women and Credit in Early Eighteenth-Century London". *Transactions of the Royal Historical Society* vol. 25 (2015), pp. 53–74.

Simonton, Deborah. "Claiming their Place in the Corporate Community: Women's Identity in Eighteenth-Century Towns". In *The Invisible Woman – Aspects of Women's Work in Eighteenth-Century Britain*. Edited by Isabelle Baudino, Jacques Carre, and Cecile Revauger, pp. 101–16. Aldershot: Ashgate, 2005.

Slater, Michael. "Dickens, Charles John Huffam (1812–1870)". *Oxford Dictionary of National Biography*. Oxford University Press, 2004. Online edition.

Slatter, Michele. "The Norwich Court of Requests – A Tradition Continued". *Journal of Legal History* vol. 5, no. 3 (1984), pp. 96–107.

Sobol, Neil L. "Charging the Poor: Criminal Justice Debt & Modern-Day Debtors' Prisons". *Maryland Law Review* vol. 75, no. 2 (2016), pp. 486–540.

Solar, Peter M. and John S. Lyons. "The English Cotton Spinning Industry, 1780–1840, as Revealed in the Columns of the London Gazette". *Business History* vol. 53, no. 3 (June 2011), pp. 302–323.

Spicksley, Judith M. "'Fly with a Duck in Thy Mouth': Single Women as Sources of Credit in Seventeenth-Century England". *Social History* vol. 32, no. 2 (May 2007), pp. 187–207.

Steenson, Julie. "Life Lessons: Self-Defence and Social Didacticism in Elizabeth Gooch's Life-Writing and *The Contrast*". *Women's Writing* vol. 18, no. 3 (2011), pp. 405–422.

Steinbach, Susie. *Women in England 1760–1914 – A Social History*. London: Weidenfeld & Nicolson, 2004.

Stephenson, Judy Z. "Real Wages? Contractors, Workers, and Pay in London Building Trades, 1650–1800". *Economic History Review* vol. 71, no. 1 (2018), pp. 106–132.

"Mistaken Wages: The Cost of Labour in the Early Modern English Economy, a Reply to Robert C. Allen". *Economic History Review* vol. 72, no. 2 (2019), pp. 755–769.

Stirk, Nigel. "Arresting Ambiguity: The Shifting Geographies of a London Debtors' Sanctuary in the Eighteenth Century". *Social History* vol. 25, no. 3 (October 2000), pp. 316–329.

Stockdale, Eric. *A Study of Bedford Prison 1660–1877*. Bedford: The Bedfordshire Historical Record Society, 1977.

Stratton, Arthur. "Two Forgotten Buildings by the Dances". *The Architectural Review* vol. 40 (1916), pp. 21–24.

Stretton, Timothy. *Women Waging Law in Elizabethan England*. Cambridge: Cambridge University Press, 1998.

Marital Litigation in the Court of Requests: 1542–1642. Cambridge: Cambridge University Press, 2008.

Stroud, Dorothy. "The Giltspur Street Compter". *Architectural History* vol. 27 (1984), pp. 127–134.

Styles, John. "Clothing the North: The Supply of Non-élite Clothing in the Eighteenth-Century North of England". *Textile History* vol. 25, no. 2 (1994), pp. 139–166.

Tan, Li. "Market Supporting Institutions, Guild Organisations, and the Industrial Revolution: A Comparative View". *Australian Economic History Review* vol. 53, no. 3 (2013), pp. 221–246.

Temin, Peter and Hans-Joachim Voth. *Prometheus Shackled – Goldsmith Banks and England's Financial Revolution after 1700*. Oxford: Oxford University Press, 2013.

Thaler, Richard and Cass Sunstein. *Nudge – Impowering Decisions about Health, Wealth, and Happiness*. New Haven: Yale University Press, 2008.

Thornbury, Walter. *Old and New London: A Narrative of its History, Its People, and Its Places*. London: Cassell, Petter, & Galpin, 1873–1878.

Uglow, Jenny. *Hogarth – A Life and a World*. London: Faber & Faber, 1997.

Vause, Erika. *In the Red and in the Black – Debt, Dishonour, and the Law in France between the Revolutions*. London: University of Virginia Press, 2018.

Voth, Hans-Joachim. "Living Standards and the Urban Environment". In *The Cambridge Economic History of Modern Britain – Volume I: Industrialisation, 1700–1860*. Edited by Roderick Floud and Paul Johnson, pp. 268–294. Cambridge: Cambridge University Press, 2004.

Wakelam, Alexander. "Coverture and the Debtors' Prison in the Long Eighteenth Century". *Journal of Eighteenth-Century Studies* (forthcoming, 2021).

Ware, Stephen J. "A 20th Century Debate about Imprisonment for Debt". *American Journal of Legal History* vol. 54, no. 3 (2014), pp. 351–377.

Watson, Bruce. "The Compter Prisons of London". *London Archaeologist* vol. 5, no. 5 (1993), pp. 115–121.

Weatherill, Lorna. "The Meaning of Consumer Behaviour in Late Seventeenth- and Early Eighteenth-Century England". In *Consumption and the World of Goods*. Edited by John Brewer and Roy Porter, pp. 206–227. London: Routledge, 1993.

Wennerlind, Carl. *Casualties of Credit – The English Financial Revolution, 1620–1720*. Cambridge: Harvard University Press, 2011.

White, Jerry. "Pain and Degradation in Georgian London: Life in the Marshalsea Prison". *History Workshop Journal* vol. 68 (2009), pp. 69–98.

   Mansions of Misery – A Biography of the Marshalsea Debtors' Prison. London: Bodley Head, 2016.

Whyman, Susan E. *The Useful Knowledge of William Hutton – Culture and Industry in Eighteenth-Century Birmingham*. Oxford: Oxford University Press, 2018.

Winder, W.H.D. "The Courts of Requests". *The Law Quarterly Review* vol. 52, no. 207 (1936), pp. 369–394.

Woodfine, Philip "Debtors, Prisons, and Petitions in Eighteenth-Century England". *Eighteenth Century Life* vol. 30, no. 2 (Spring 2006), pp. 1–31.

   "The Power and Influence of the Gaolers: Life and Death in York Castle Gaol". *Yorkshire Archaeological Journal* vol. 78 (2006), pp. 159–175.

Wordie, J.R. "Deflationary Factors in the Tudor Price Rise". *Past & Present* vol. 154 (1997), pp. 32–70.

Wrigley, E.A. "A Simple Model of London's Importance in Changing English Society and Economy 1650–1750". *Past & Present* vol. 37 (1967), pp. 44–70.

   The Path to Sustained Growth – England's Transition from an Organic Economy to an Industrial Revolution. Cambridge: Cambridge University Press, 2016.

Wyllie, Patricia. "Reassessing the English Financial Revolution: Credit Transferability in Probate Records of Sedbergh and Maidstone, 1610–1790". In *Faith, Place, and People in Early Modern England – Essays in Honour of Margaret Spufford*. Edited by Trevor Dean, Glyn Parry, and Edward Vallance, pp. 132–150. Woodbridge: Boydell Press, 2018.

Yaffe, Gideon. "Promises, Social Acts, and Reid's First Argument for Moral Liberty". *Journal of the History of Philosophy* vol. 45, no. 2 (April 2007), pp. 267–289.

Theses

Haagen, Paul Hess. "Imprisonment for Debt in England and Wales". Unpublished PhD thesis. University of Princeton (1986).

McNall, Christopher. "The Recognition and Enforcement of Debts under the Statutes of Acton Burnell (1283) and Merchants (1285), 1283–1307". Unpublished PhD thesis. University of Oxford (2000).

Wakelam, Alexander. "Imprisonment for Debt and Female Financial Failure in the Long Eighteenth Century". Unpublished PhD thesis. University of Cambridge (2019).

Index

Note: Page numbers followed by 'n' refer to end notes

accounting 18–19, 24–26, 172–173
Acton, William 162–163, 177–178
advice manuals 20, 26, 33, 38–39, 60, 86,
    121, 126, 195, 196
agriculture 22, 33, 73–75
alehouses *see* victuallers and vending;
    debtors' prisons–alcohol
America 3–4, 34, 51, 87, 192, 218
arrest 8, 18, 35–37, 54, 70, 72, 118–119,
    123, 125, 161, 165, 186–187, 190
attorneys 38–39, 92–94, 124, 126, 128,
    132, 193

bail 18, 39, 93–94, 119–121
bailiffs *see* arrest
bakers and bread 22, 26–27, 119, 164
bankruptcy 8, 31–34, 64, 71, 93, 106–107,
    142–144, 155, 186, 213, 216
begging 105, 133, 178
bills of exchange *see* notes of hand
Birmingham 57, 194–196, 198–199
Blackstone, William 33, 194
bridewells 51, 57, 127, 165, 168, 200

Cambridgeshire 53; *see also* Chatteris;
    debtors' prisons (institutions)–
    Cambridge City Gaol
capitalism 9, 52, 69, 70–72, 76–77, 215
castles 4, 56–57; *see also* debtors' prisons
    (institutions)
charity 39, 40, 93, 104–105, 124–125,
    131, 139, 141, 160, 176, 178; *see also*
    begging; Thatched House Society
Chatteris 193, 196
clothing 22, 24, 37, 124, 165; business
    of 33, 71–72, 74, 122, 127–128, 132,
    168–169

coercion 19, 29, 34–35, 37–38, 40, 63,
    70, 71, 72, 76, 88, 97, 100, 105, 106,
    108–109, 122, 125, 133, 140, 172,
    215–216, 218
commitment registers 10, 37–38, 53–56,
    62–63, 74, 94–95, 116, 117–120, 133,
    151, 198, 204, 212
common law 7, 21, 31, 35, 37, 191,
    194, 200
common side *see* debtors'
    prisons–accommodation
Compulsive Clause (1761) 63, 65, 92, 93,
    123, 145, 147, 174, 191
Consumer Revolution 6, 22–24, 87, 189,
    191, 214
contracting 19, 20–21, 33, 29, 35,
    117–118, 119, 123, 213–214; and
    enforcement 30–35, 41, 67, 76,
    93–108, 196; faith in debtors 23,
    27, 88, 121, 123, 127–128, 140, 214;
    informality of 25–29, 93, 108, 126,
    196; negotiation 125–126, 216; orality
    23–25, 35, 108; security of the person
    7, 24–25, 34, 119, 121, 213; *see also* bail
Court of Requests 31, 57, 71, 72, 93,
    104–106, 170–171, 176, 191–201,
    206n26, 214
credit 7, 18–30, 20–21, 40–41,
    67–68, 71–72, 88, 117–118, 140, 145,
    148–150, 153–155, 177, 187–188,
    195, 204, 213–214; book debts 26, 71;
    concerns about 22–23, 63; culture of
    21–23, 26, 41, 121, 166, 213; in prison
    (*see* debtors' prisons–use of credit
    within); sales credit 7, 21, 24–26, 72;
    subsistence 22, 72, 75, 216; trade credit
    22, 27, 67, 72, 75–76, 216

creditors 8, 25–29, 31, 37, 40, 52–53, 63, 69, 70, 76–77, 86–88, 95, 98, 100, 106, 108–109, 125–126, 140, 142–144, 146–147, 151, 161, 180, 199–200, 203–204 (*see also* debt imprisonment–arrest rate; reputation of creditors); *see also* debt imprisonment
crises and crashes 5, 23, 67, 141, 143, 145; *see also* Compulsive Clause; South Sea Bubble; war
currency, 7, 21–23, 25, 30, 120, 204, 214–216

debt enforcement 18–19, 26–30, 76, 108, 191, 193–4, 204; *see also* contracting–enforcement
debt imprisonment: abolition 52, 186–187, 201, 204; arrest rate 62–68, 76, 172, 174; commitment length 55–56, 64, 72, 89–92, 95–96, 117–120, 126, 139, 152, 170–171, 197, 199–200, 215; costs of procuring 8, 31, 37, 39, 70; as deterrent 87, 118, 215; effectiveness of 5, 88–100, 117–118, 155, 167, 212–218; history of (beyond the eighteenth century) 3–4, 7–8, 36, 86, 141–143, 173, 187, 216–219; impact on non-prisoners and local society 4–5, 86, 103, 118, 122, 123–125, 132–133, 140, 162, 211–212; opposition to 3, 7, 27–28, 77, 85–88, 140, 160, 186–188, 201–203; outside England 3–4, 6, 41, 52, 146, (*see also* America; Ireland); public opinion of 186, 189–190, 197–198, 201, 203; as punishment 9, 10, 28, 34–35, 51–53, 70, 76, 87–88, 148, 179, 188, 197–200, 212; structural weakness 35–41, 62, 140, 155, 161, 167, 180, 214, 217; term limits 106, 197–200; theory and legal basis 35, 37, 40–41, 188–190, 200, 213; *see also* mesne process
debt size 2, 24–26, 27, 31, 38, 39, 54, 55–56, 64, 70–72, 74, 100, 106, 107, 117–118, 123, 126, 139, 145, 190, 191, 193, 197–200, 216
debt trading 25, 120–121, 126; *see also* reckoning
debtor schedules 2–3, 24, 25–26, 27, 74, 122–123, 143–145, 151, 152–153, 191
debtor strategy 18–19, 24, 26–27, 29, 38, 122–132, 215–217
debtors' prisons: accommodation 56–58, 60, 65, 91, 128–129, 131–132, 165–170, 173–174, 176, 178–179, 202; alcohol 86, 115–116, 124, 131–132, 171, 174, 175 (*see also* garnish; sponging houses); birth in 164, 212; charges (*see* fees; garnish; rent; supersedeas); civic administration 53–54, 69, 116, 161, 172–177, 201–203; construction 55, 56, 58, 68, 128–129, 172–174, 176; crime committed in 92, 99, 102, 107, 116, 131–132, 178; death in 37, 46n57, 60, 86, 93, 100–104, 140, 151, 164, 166, 178, 190, 203, 212, 216; disease 53–54, 100–104, 178, 202; life and leisure in 9, 37, 58, 60, 105, 116, 124, 125–127, 129, 131–132, 176 (*see also* Grano, John); liberties of 58–60, 62, 89–91, 127, 166; non-prisoner residents 65, 86, 115, 126, 165; operational costs 53, 107, 161, 163–165, 172–175; overcrowding 65–67, 77, 103, 145–146, 186; population 65–70, 76, 174; release from 92–108; self-government of 103, 116, 161, 165; structure 56–62, 69, 76, 188–189, 200; trade and labour in 115, 122, 127–133, 164–165; upkeep 56–58, 60, 127, 161, 164, 179–180, 203; use of credit within 128, 131, 166, 180; visitors 58, 107, 116, 132, 176, 179–180; *see also* Howard, John; inquiries; Neild, James; Pringle, Dr John; Smith, Dr William
debtors' prisons (institutions): Birmingham Town Gaol 57, 199; Borough Compter (Southwark) 54, 65; Cambridge City Gaol 53, 57; Carlisle County Gaol 40; Devon County Prison for Debtors 40, 127; Fleet Prison (*see* Fleet Prison); Giltspur Street Compter 55, 79n23 (*see also* Wood Street Compter); Gloucester Castle 56; King's Bench Prison (*see* King's Bench Prison); Lancaster Castle (*see* Lancaster Castle); Leicester County Gaol 56; Litchfield Town Gaol 166; Liverpool Borough Gaol 163; Ludgate 40, 65, 98–99, 164, 173–175; Marshalsea 18, 52, 54, 55, 65, 86, 91, 154, 162–163, 165–167, 176–178, 211–212, 218–219 (*see also* Acton, William; Grano, John); New Debtors' Prison for London and Westminster 65, 107, 203; New Prison in Clerkenwell 172–173; Newgate 54, 99, 102–104,

119, 162, 164–165, 169, 175–176, 202; Poultry Compter 54, 63, 65, 69, 164, 175, 202, 219; Stafford Gaol 139; Surry County Gaol 202; Truro Gaol 124; Wood Street Compter (*see* Wood Street Compter); Whitechapel Debtors' Prison 129–130, 132; York Castle Gaol 40, 56–58, 79n26, 127–129, 130, 132, 162, 166
Defoe, Daniel 20, 22–23, 41, 71–72, 128, 132, 140, 146–147, 190
DeLacy, Margaret 57, 101
Dickens, Charles 3, 52, 86, 91, 211–212, 218–219
discharge 87–88, 93–98, 119–121, 125
dishonesty 23, 27–29, 87–88, 89–90, 147, 154, 189–190, 200; *see also* fraud
Dornford, Josiah 85, 160, 164, 188–189, 195, 201–203

economic actors 6, 8, 10, 40–41, 53, 63, 69–70; *see also* creditors
economic growth 5, 6, 52, 63–65, 67, 145, 214–217; *see also* Industrial Revolution
education 1, 75, 132, 176
employers 22, 29–30, 122, 127–128, 132–133; *see also* prison keeping
English Revolution (1640–1688) 56, 141–143
escape 59–60, 92, 93, 102, 107–108, 118–119, 165
excise 55, 92, 107, 163–164, 172
execution (death penalty) 51, 90, 107, 145, 153

failure 2–3, 5, 9–10, 34, 41, 67–68, 71, 122, 139–140, 155, 177–178, 212–213
failure to pay (deliberate) 27, 29, 31, 87–88, 89, 100, 189–190; *see also* friendly action
fear 21, 23, 26, 36, 63, 87, 91, 100–101, 103, 118, 124–125, 133
fees 35–37, 59, 160, 180, 186; commitment 165–166, 176; other 166; release 166
felony imprisonment 34, 51, 127, 146, 164, 168–169, 171, 173
female prisoners 36, 65, 69–70, 74, 89–90, 122, 124–126, 129–131, 154, 164; Charke, Charlotte 119; Gooch, Elizabeth 125; Robinson, Mary 126; Wells, Mary 60, 124, 212
Fielding, John 148

finance 5, 20–21, 25, 31, 64, 70, 92, 106, 213–214
Finn, Margot 64, 104, 197
Fleet Prison 10, 39, 40, 54–55, 58–59, 61, 63, 64, 66–67, 72–75, 87–108, 117, 120, 150–151, 165–166, 169–170, 177, 219
Foote, Samuel 124, 129–130
forced labour 116, 127, 143, 168
Foucault, Michel 51
fraud 24, 27–28, 89–91, 107, 147–149, 189
friendly action 89–91, 147
fugitives 145, 154; see also escape

gambling 29, 86, 116, 176
garnish 36–37, 161
gentry, status, and rank 23, 29, 60, 69, 74, 128, 162, 166, 173, 176, 189
Gordon Riots 54, 66, 102, 107–108, 149, 173; *see also* Priestley Riots
Graeber, David 3, 213–214
Grano, John 18–19, 37, 124–125, 127–129, 131–133, 162–163, 166–167, 218
groats 39–40, 94, 106, 161, 172
The Guardians Society for the Protection of Trade 148–150, 203

Haagen, Paul Hess 53, 61, 68, 106n74, 187
habeas corpus 58–62, 92, 99–100, 176
Hitchcock and Shoemaker 160, 197
Hogarth, William 1–2, 115, 130, 133, 177, 213
Hoppit, Julian 5, 22, 64, 140n6
Howard, John 36, 40, 54, 56, 57–58, 68, 70, 85, 100, 127, 160, 163, 165, 168, 186, 201, 202
humour 40, 126, 199
Hutton, William 25, 31, 191, 194–6, 198–199

Industrial Revolution 5–6, 8, 30, 76, 214–215
Innes, Joanna 87n12, 89, 116, 147
inquiries 53, 54, 61, 175, 201–202; House of Commons Committee (1792) 38, 40, 70, 89, 119, 128, 176; Oglethorpe Committee (1728–1730) 102, 177–179
Insolvency Acts 54, 61–64, 68–69, 73–74, 90–91, 93, 106, 123, 140–155, 159n53, 166, 186, 190–191, 217–218; application rate 150–153; history of 141–145; passage of 143, 145–149;

reception of 90, 146–150, 153–154;
　see also Compulsive Clause
instalment payments 125–126,
　193–194, 216
institutions 5–6, 25, 30, 88, 97, 118, 127,
　140, 155, 161, 214–215, 217–218;
　and interpretation, 6, 8, 30–31, 41,
　191–197, 216
Ireland 5, 59, 85, 192

Jews 75, 191
Johnson, Samuel 68, 70, 122, 125

King's Bench Prison 54, 58–59, 61, 63,
　94, 99–100, 126, 127, 129, 148, 165,
　178–179, 190
Kirby, John 102, 104, 128–129, 163–164,
　175–177, 179–180, 184n79

Lancashire 57, 72–74; *see also*
　Lancaster Castle
Lancaster Castle 10, 37–38, 40, 54–57,
　65, 72–75, 87–108, 117, 120, 150–151,
　169–171, 219
literacy 24, 25–26
literature (fiction) 85–86, 115–117, 121,
　122, 124–126, 130, 131, 154; *see also*
　Dickens, Charles
living conditions 5–6, 36, 167–168;
　see also debtors' prisons
London 1–2, 10, 24, 30, 34, 55–56,
　59–61, 63–70, 72, 74–76, 96, 98, 103,
　105, 119, 148–150, 168, 172–179,
　201–204; Great Fire of 54, 56
London Gazette 61, 69, 73, 144–145, 149,
　151, 154–155
Lord's Act 39–40, 94, 105–106

manufacturing 22, 33, 71–72, 73, 74–75,
　122, 127–129
marketplaces 4, 21, 29, 87, 132–133
market regulation, 5, 7, 213–215
master's side *see* debtors'
　prisons–accommodation
material wealth 23, 31, 89, 106, 122–124,
　152–153, 216
medicine 53, 75, 102, 104, 164; *see also*
　debtors' prisons–disease; Pringle,
　Dr John; Smith, Dr William
medieval imprisonment 7, 56; *see also*
　debt imprisonment–history of
merchants 8, 20–21, 25, 32–33, 155, 188;
　see also bankruptcy; shopkeeping and
　dealing

mesne process 37–38, 57, 95–97, 188,
　190, 197, 200
middling sort 9, 57, 70–76, 86–87, 116,
　132, 148, 167–168, 176, 189, 191,
　195–199, 201, 204, 214
Mokyr, Joel 5–6, 87
Muldrew, Craig 7, 21–23, 87–88
music 5, 18, 116, 132–133, 163, 166

Neild, James 54, 128, 201
newspapers 23, 30, 69, 147–149, 160, 177,
　201–203; *see also* London Gazette
North, Douglass 6, 217
notes of hand 18–19, 25–26, 31, 90, 96,
　126, 148–149, 166, 191

occupational structure 73–75, 131, 162

pamphlet literature 20–25, 27–29, 32–3,
　36, 38–39, 52, 77, 85–88, 89–90, 94,
　101, 115–116, 120, 130, 154, 160,
　175, 186–187, 192, 201–203; *see also*
　prison writing
parliament 63, 105, 108, 119, 140–149,
　155, 177, 187, 189, 190, 192, 194,
　197–198, 200; members of 89, 119, 148,
　177–179, 189, 194; *see also* inquiries
Paul, Tawny 9, 53, 68, 70
Peebles, Gustav 52, 76–77
petitioning 104, 106, 108, 122, 139, 146,
　151, 160, 192
the poor 21–22, 53, 72, 105, 106, 116,
　127, 149, 168, 176, 188–190, 195–199,
　201, 203; *see also* credit–subsistence
Priestley Riots 199
Pringle, Dr John 102–103
prison keeping 36, 53, 59, 104, 107, 127,
　131–132, 145, 146, 160–166, 168–180,
　188, 201–203; *see also* Kirby, John
prisoner transfer 36, 58, 93, 98, 120, 173;
　see also habeas corpus
prison writing 28, 85, 125, 129–130,
　137n68
public debt 20–21, 130

Quakers 40, 145

reckoning 29–30
recidivism 63; *see also* female prisoners–
　Wells, Mary
reform 51, 64, 103, 145, 160–161, 180,
　186–188, 190, 197–204, 217
religion 23, 26, 85, 105, 162, 164, 199; see
　also Jews; Quakers

rent 36, 163–164, 166–168, 176, 178, 183n44
reputation 7, 23–24, 27–28, 53, 87–88, 97, 118, 125, 149, 153–154, 177; of creditors 28, 32, 34, 76, 125
revenge 28, 88, 108
the rules see debtors' prison–liberties of
rural experience 7, 56–57, 69, 72, 74–75, 180

salaries 53, 160, 162–165, 168–169, 171, 175–176, 186
seasonality 61, 65–66, 99–100, 102, 167
servants or service 54, 122, 129, 131–133
sheriffs 55, 106, 148, 163–164, 175
shopkeeping and dealing 6–7, 18–19, 20–21, 24–26, 29, 33, 71–72, 73–75, 122, 127, 132, 162, 175
Smith, Adam 29–30
Smith, Dr William 101, 200
South Sea Bubble 23, 64, 69, 74, 146, 190
Southwark see London
sponging houses 18, 35–36, 60, 119, 161
spouses and relations 18, 23, 30, 74, 97, 98, 102–103, 122, 124–125, 132, 165, 166, 175, 213
suicide 102
superior courts 58–62, 74, 89, 92, 97, 99–100, 165–167, 169–170; see also Fleet Prison; King's Bench Prison
supersedeas 38–40, 92, 93, 94–95, 140, 166

Thatched House Society 36, 38, 50n126, 104–105, 177
transport and travel 58, 60, 73, 75, 99, 119
transportation (punishment) 34, 51, 171
trial 31, 37–38, 54, 96, 103, 106–107, 192–194
turnkeys 115, 154, 160–162, 164–166

Vexatious Arrests Act (1725) 57, 64, 190, 197, 201
victuallers and vending 1–2, 6–7, 21, 26–27, 29–30, 33, 59, 74, 119, 131–132, 162, 171, 174; see also sponging houses
violence 9, 37, 99, 102, 134n10, 161, 173, 177–179

wages 21, 22, 29–30, 33, 72, 74–75, 164; see also salaries
war 51, 67, 92, 107, 141, 144, 187
Wilkes, John 202
Woodfine, Philip 161, 179
Wood Street Compter 10, 36, 40, 54–55, 57, 61, 63–67, 69, 72–75, 87–108, 117, 120, 123, 150–151, 163, 165–166, 169–170, 175–177, 179–180, 191, 198–200, 212, 219; see also Kirby, John
workhouses 99, 143, 173–175

York 57–58, 162; see also debtors' prisons (institutions)–York Castle